Agency and Democracy in Development Ethics

A diverse set of expert voices from the Global North and South – philosophers, economists, policy and development scholars and practitioners – explore two themes central to development ethics: agency and democracy. Established luminaries in development ethics engage with the book's themes alongside fresh voices on the way to becoming familiar figures in the field. Their chapters work within diverse areas of development studies including human security and human rights, democratic governance in theory and practice, the capability approach, gender and development, and applied and theoretical critiques of the philosophical underpinnings of various accounts of development. The result is a varied and comprehensive discussion of current work in development ethics that significantly advances our understanding of theoretical and practical work of development. This book will interest students, scholars, and practitioners of global justice, human rights, international development, and political philosophy.

LORI KELEHER is an associate professor of Philosophy at New Mexico State University in Las Cruces, New Mexico. She is Vice President of the International Development Ethics Association (IDEA). She is also on the Executive Council and a Fellow of the Human Development Capability Association (HDCA). She is the coeditor of the *Routledge Handbook of Development Ethics* (2019).

STACY J. KOSKO is an assistant research professor at the Center for International Development and Conflict Management, University of Maryland. She has numerous articles and chapters in print on issues related to development ethics and human rights. She is on the Executive Board of the International Development Ethics Association (IDEA) and is on the Executive Council and is a Fellow of the Human Development and Capability Association (HDCA).

Agency and Democracy in Development Ethics

Edited by

LORI KELEHER
New Mexico State University

STACY J. KOSKO
University of Maryland

CAMBRIDGE
UNIVERSITY PRESS

CAMBRIDGE
UNIVERSITY PRESS

University Printing House, Cambridge CB2 8BS, United Kingdom

One Liberty Plaza, 20th Floor, New York, NY 10006, USA

477 Williamstown Road, Port Melbourne, VIC 3207, Australia

314–321, 3rd Floor, Plot 3, Splendor Forum, Jasola District Centre, New Delhi – 110025, India

79 Anson Road, #06–04/06, Singapore 079906

Cambridge University Press is part of the University of Cambridge.

It furthers the University's mission by disseminating knowledge in the pursuit of education, learning, and research at the highest international levels of excellence.

www.cambridge.org
Information on this title: www.cambridge.org/9781107195004
DOI: 10.1017/9781108163880

First published 2019

Printed and bound in Great Britain by Clays Ltd, Elcograf S.p.A.

A *catalogue record for this publication is available from the British Library.*

ISBN 978-1-107-19500-4 Hardback

For Dave

Contents

vii

Figures

Tables

Contributors

Alejandra Boni is a Professor at Polytechnic University of Valencia (Spain), and Deputy Director of the INGENIO Research Institute (CSIC-UPV). She is Extraordinary Professor of the University of the Free State, South Africa and former Vice-President of the International Development Ethics Association. Her research analyzes educational processes using the capability approach and development education. She is coauthor of *Universities and Global Human Development: Theoretical and Empirical Insights for Social Change* (with Ronald W. Walker, 2016).

Luis Camacho is Professor Emeritus at the University of Costa Rica (UCR) and President of the Costa Rica Philosophy Association. He has been a professor of logic, philosophy of science, and philosophical issues of socioeconomic development at UCR and other Latin American and American universities. Recent publications include *La ciencia en su historia* (2014), "Sustainable Development Goals: Kinds, Connections and Expectations" (*Journal of Global Ethics*, 2015), *Introducción a la lógica* (3rd ed., 2015), and "Evolución de los modelos de desarrollo: ¿necesidad o contingencia?" (*Revista de Filosofía de la Universidad de Costa Rica*, 2017), as well as articles on Leibniz's logic in *Beiträge zu Leibniz' Rezeption der aristotelischen Logik und Metaphysik* (2016) and in *Vorträge des X. Internationalen Leibniz-Kongresses, Band III* (2016).

Flavio Comim is an associate professor at Ramon Llull University in Barcelona and an affiliated lecturer in Land Economy and Development Studies at the University of Cambridge as well as a Visiting Fellow at St. Edmund's College. He has worked as Senior Economist for UNDP and as a consultant for UNEP, FAO, WHO, and UNESCO. He coordinated the 2010 Brazil Human Development Report on *Human Values* and the 2014 Panama Human Development

Report on *Children and the Youth in Panama*. He has coedited three books on the capability approach.

Adela Cortina is Professor of Ethics and Political Philosophy at the University of Valencia (Spain), where she received her doctorate in Philosophy in 1976. Soon thereafter she was awarded a grant to work at the University of Frankfurt with Karl-Otto Apel and Jürgen Habermas, the founders of discourse ethics. She was the first woman to be made a member of the Spanish Royal Academy of Moral and Political Science and holds numerous directorships and advisory positions in and out of academia. She holds five honorary doctorates and has been awarded medals from three other universities, as well as numerous international prizes. She is a member of the board of the International Development Ethics Association and of the Human Development and Capability Association, the Societas Ethica, and of the International Network of Discourse Ethics. Her most recent books include *Cordial Justice* (2010); *Neuroethics and Neuropolitics* (2012); *The Comares Guide to Practical Neurophilosophy* (2012, coord.); and *What Is Ethics really for?* (2013).

David A. Crocker is Research Professor and Director of the University of Maryland School of Public Policy's international development specialization and Founding President of the International Development Ethics Association. He specializes in international development ethics, sociopolitical philosophy, transitional justice, democracy, and democratization. A Yale graduate (M.Div., MA, PhD), Dr. Crocker taught philosophy for twenty-five years at Colorado State University, where he established one of the world's first courses in ethics and international development. His most recent publications are *Ethics of Global Development: Agency, Capability, and Deliberative Democracy*, "Development and Global Ethics: Five Foci for the Future," and "Obstáculos para la reconciliación en el Perú: un análisis ético." In 2010, Dr. Crocker received the Landmark Award "for exceptional long-term achievements in support of international life at the University of Maryland." He has directed seven UMD study-abroad trips (Morocco, Peru, and Ethiopia) and directs KEMS (Kids Excelling in Math and Science), an after-school enrichment program for middle-schoolers.

Nigel Dower is Honorary Senior Lecturer in Philosophy and Associate at the Centre for Global Development at the University of Aberdeen where he taught for thirty-seven years, with an interruption to teach for three years in Zimbabwe. His main research interests are in the ethics and philosophy of development, environment, and international relations. He is the author of *World Poverty: Challenge and Response* (1983), *World Ethics: The New Agenda* (1998, 2nd ed. 2007), *An Introduction to Global Citizenship* (2003), and *The Ethics of War and Peace* (2009) as well as coeditor of *Global Citizenship: A Critical* Reader (with John Williams, 2002). He was the second President of the International Development Ethics Association.

Jay Drydyk is Professor of Philosophy at Carleton University, Ottawa (Canada), past President of the International Development Ethics Association, and Fellow of the Human Development and Capabilities Association. His published articles and chapters concern development ethics, human rights, the capabilities approach, and social and global justice. He is coauthor of *Displacement by Development: Ethics, Rights, and Responsibilities* (2011) and coeditor of *Theorizing Justice* (with Krushil Watene, 2016) and *The Routledge Handbook of Development Ethics* (with Lori Keleher, 2019).

Alexandre Apsan Frediani is a senior lecturer in Community-Led Development in the Global South and Course Director, MSc Social Development Practice, in the Bartlett Development Planning Unit of University College London. He is a development planner specializing in squatter settlement upgrading policies and participatory approaches to development. His areas of expertise include human development, housing, urban development, participation, and Amartya Sen's capability approach. He is coeditor of *The Capability Approach, Empowerment and Participation: Concepts, Methods and Applications* (with David A. Clark and Mario Biggeri, 2017).

Des Gasper is a professor at the International Institute of Social Studies in The Hague, a graduate school of international development studies within Erasmus University Rotterdam, Netherlands. After studies in Britain in economics, international development, and policy analysis, he worked through the 1980s in Africa as a government planner and university lecturer. His recent research focuses on development ethics, ill- and well-being, and human security, with applications especially in the fields of climate change and migration. He is the author of *The Ethics of Development* (2004), and coeditor of *Development Ethics* (with Asunción Lera St. Clair, 2010), *Trans-National Migration and Human Security* (with Thanh-Dam Truong, 2011), and *Gender, Migration and Social Justice* (with Thanh-Dam Truong, Jeff Handmaker, and Sylvia I. Bergh, 2013).

Javier M. Iguíñiz Echeverría is Emeritus Professor of Economics at the Pontifical Catholic University of Perú. He holds a PhD in Economics from the New School for Social Research (USA) and a degree in Electrical Engineering from the National University of Engineering, Lima, Perú. He has been a visiting researcher or professor at the University of Ottawa (Canada), Massachusetts Institute of Technology (USA), Oxford University (UK), University of Notre Dame, Department of Economics (USA). He is the author of more than thirty books. Recent works in English include "Ethical Dilemmas of Theory or Reality? Three Approaches to the Inevitability of Sacrifices in Economic Development" (in Charles K. Wilber and Amitava Krishna Dutt, *New Directions in Development Ethics: Essays in Honor of Denis Goulet*, 2010).

Lori Keleher is an associate professor of Philosophy at New Mexico State University in Las Cruces, New Mexico. She has published essays in development ethics, ancient philosophy, and practical ethics. She is Vice President of the International Development Ethics Association and on the Executive Council and a Fellow of the Human Development Capability Association. With Jay Drydyk she is the coeditor of the *Routledge Handbook of Development Ethics* (2019).

Serene J. Khader is a moral and political philosopher working primarily on feminist issues in global justice. She is the author of *Adaptive Preferences and Women's Empowerment* (2011) and Decolonizing Universalism: A Transnational Feminist Ethic (2018). She holds the Jay Newman Chair in Philosophy of Culture at Brooklyn College, and is Associate Professor of Philosophy and Women's and Gender Studies at the CUNY Graduate Center.

Christine M. Koggel is Professor of Philosophy at Carleton University, Ottawa (Canada). Her book *Perspectives on Equality: Constructing a Relational Theory* (1998) has shaped the foundation for her research interests in the areas of moral theory, practical ethics, social and political theory, and feminism. She is the editor of *Moral Issues in Global Perspective* (1999), coeditor of *Contemporary Moral Issues* (with Wesley Cragg, 2006), *Care Ethics: New Theories and Applications* (2013), and *Gender Justice and Development: Local and Global* (with Cynthia Bisman, 2015), and author of numerous journal articles and chapters in edited collections.

Stacy J. Kosko is an assistant research professor in the Center for International Development and Conflict Management, in the Department of Government and Politics, at the University of Maryland. She holds a PhD in Public Policy and Development Studies from the University of Maryland and an MS in Foreign Service from Georgetown University. She spent the 2017–2018 academic year as a Fulbright Scholar in Moldova and has numerous articles and chapters in print on issues related to development ethics and human rights. She is on the Executive Board of the International Development Ethics Association, and is a Fellow of and on the Executive Council of the Human Development and Capability Association.

Aurora López-Fogués is a vocational education and training teacher, research fellow at INGENIO (CSIC-UPV), and a Lecturer at Polytechnic University of Valencia (Spain). She holds a PhD in Education from the University of Nottingham (UK), a Master's degree in Global Studies from the University of Leipzig (Germany), and a degree in Business Administration from the Polytechnic University of Valencia. Her interests are in the fields of education, social justice, youth, economics, transitions, policy, innovation, and the capability approach.

Colleen Murphy is Professor of Law, Philosophy, and Political Science as well as Director of the Women and Gender in Global Perspectives Program at the University of Illinois at Urbana-Champaign (USA). She is the author of *A Moral Theory of Political Reconciliation* (2010) and *The Conceptual Foundations of Transitional Justice* (2017). She is a member of the American Philosophical Association's Committee on Philosophy and Law and an Associate Editor of *The Journal of Moral Philosophy*.

Martha C. Nussbaum is Ernst Freund Distinguished Service Professor of Law and Ethics at the University of Chicago, appointed in the Law School and the Philosophy Department. Her most recent books are

Anger and Forgiveness (2016), Aging Thoughtfully (with Saul Levmore, 2017), and *The Monarchy of Fear* (2018).

Eric Palmer is Professor of Philosophy at Allegheny College (USA). He is coeditor of *Journal of Global Ethics* and President of the International Development Ethics Association. His recent research in development ethics concerns multinational corporate responsibility in developing nations, particularly in cases of resource extraction. He also focuses on vulnerability and finance, inquiring into for-profit credit schemes directed at the poor within less developed as well as more developed nations. His philosophical writing extends beyond these areas also to globalization, to business ethics, and to history and philosophy of science and culture.

Gonzalo Salas is Assistant Professor at Institute of Economics, Faculty of Science, Economics and of Administration, University of the Republic (Uruguay). His topics of interest are economic inequality, poverty, and public policy. His recent research focuses on child development and parenting, assessing the role of cognitive and noncognitive skills.

Chloe Schwenke is the Interim Executive Director of the Association of Writers & Writing Programs (AWP) in Riverdale Park, Maryland, and she is also a member of the adjunct faculty at the School of Public Policy at the University of Maryland. She formerly served as Vice-President for global programs at Freedom House and previously (as a political appointee during the Obama Administration) in the dual role of Senior Advisor on Human Rights for Africa and Senior Advisor on LGBT issues globally at the US Agency for International Development. Her publications include *Reclaiming Value in International Development: The Moral Dimensions of Development Policy and Practice in Poor Countries* (2008) and her memoir, *Self-ish: A Transgender Awakening* (2018), as well as numerous articles, reports, and chapters. She is on the Executive Board of the International Development Ethics Association, and the advisory board of World Learning.

Frances Stewart is Emeritus Professor of Development Economics, University of Oxford. She was Director of the Oxford Department of International Development (1993–2003) and the Centre for Research on Inequality, Human Security and Ethnicity (2003–2010). She has an honorary doctorate from the University of Sussex and received the

Leontief Prize for Advancing the Frontiers of Economic Thought from Tufts in 2013. Her prime recent research interests are horizontal inequalities, conflict, and human development. Among many publications, she is leading author of *Horizontal Inequalities and Conflict: Understanding Group Violence in Multiethnic Societies* (2016) and *Advancing Human Development: Theory and Practice* (with Gustav Ranis and Emma Samman, 2018).

Andrea Vigorito is Professor of Economics at Institute of Economics, Faculty of Science, Economics and of Administration, University of the Republic (Uruguay). Her research focuses on inequality, poverty, and public policy. She has coordinated research teams that collaborated in the preparation of human development reports for Uruguay and Mercosur and provided technical assistance for the design and evaluation of cash transfer programs in Uruguay.

Melanie Walker obtained her PhD from the University of Cape Town. After working in South African universities and in the UK, including as Professor of Education at the University of Nottingham, since 2012 she has been South African Research Chair in Higher Education and Human Development at the University of the Free State in South Africa. She is also Director of the Centre for Higher Education and Development where she conducts research on higher education and justice and undertakes capacity building of doctoral and early career academics, most of them from Africa.

Rachel Nussbaum Wichert is Government Affairs Associate at Friends of Animals, in the Wildlife Law Program. She holds a BA in History and German Studies from Brown University, a PhD in History from Cornell University, and a JD from the University of Washington. She is the coauthor of several articles on marine mammals. Prior to attending law school she taught at Pacific Lutheran University and The Evergreen State College.

Acknowledgments

The hardest part of any book to write.

We, the editors, owe a great debt to many colleagues, friends, and family, for making this book a reality. But, there is a real sense in which this book owes its existence to David A. Crocker. Dave is our mentor, our colleague, our friend, and our inspiration for our work together on this book. Although we were not there at the same time, Dave served as advisor for each of our PhDs at the University of Maryland (one in philosophy, the other in policy studies). We have both benefited greatly from his attention to our work, first as his students, then as his colleagues. We have also benefited from his friendship and his example. Dave takes on the world's injustices and inequalities and responds not only with knowledge and skill, but also with courage, compassion, and a genuine respect for human dignity and agency in all people. He shares this intellectually and morally virtuous approach with Eddie Crocker, his wife, who we also feel lucky to count as our friend and colleague. Together, David and Eddie have spent a lifetime promoting agency and human development in their local communities and around the world. We are so grateful for all that they have done to make our lives and the world better.

We are also deeply grateful to Eric Palmer, without whose early encouragement and detailed advice this effort would not have gotten off the ground. We owe a very special thank you to Matthew Regan who voluntarily took on the copy-editing for this entire volume. He ably and cheerfully worked up to the very last moment of this marathon process despite the many other demands on his time. We also appreciate the many talented peer reviewers who, in spite of their own busy schedules, generously provided helpful comments that resulted in improved chapters and a better book: Cory Aragon, Rutger Claassen, Séverine Deneulin, Jay Drydyk, Analia Gomez Vidal, Rebecca Gutwald, Sirkku Hellsten, David Hoekema, Yuvraj

Joshi, Christine Koggel, Will Kymlicka, Daniel Levine, Milena
Nikolova, Dick Peterson, Henry Richardson, and Areli Valencia. Our
indexer, Christu John, worked hard and long, and our team of capable
student indexers and proof readers – Katie Bemb, Christopher Duffy,
and Moshe Klein – provided invaluable support in that herculean effort.

We are fortunate to have had the privilege of working with
Cambridge University Press and especially editor Phil Good, whose
patience and guidance made completing our first book project much
smoother than it might otherwise have been, and whose wonderful
"people before books" attitude allowed us to adjust when life
circumstances demanded it.

We gratefully recognize the members of the Human Development
and Capability Association, and especially the members and Executive
Board of the International Development Ethics Association, for the
enormous amount of feedback given on presented and draft versions
of almost all of these chapters, and on the volume itself: its conception,
its purpose, its form, and its value. Thank you. We also appreciate
material and moral support from institutions and especially people at
the University of Maryland and New Mexico State University.

Finally, we thank our families: our partners, our daughters – a total
of four strong, intelligent, compassionate, justice-minded young
people – and our parents and siblings, all of whom, in different ways
and to varying degrees, bore some of the stresses of our completing this
work, and who shored us up in ways we could not have imagined and
could not have lived without.

Introduction

LORI KELEHER AND STACY J. KOSKO

Inside the Fez medina in Morocco, at the eleventh-century Chouara tannery, pictured on the cover of this book, scores of tourists on viewing balconies snap photos with their smartphones, literally looking down on tannery workers as they practice their craft, seemingly as they did a thousand years ago. Inside neighboring buildings, residents escape the overwhelming smells of urine and chromium with the help of Mexican and Turkish telenovelas beamed into homes via rooftop satellite dishes. The tannery celebrates an ancient art by affiliating with the surrounding leather shops where tourists routinely spend as much as $1,800 a day on wallets, bracelets, shoes, handbags, and jackets (Curwood 2014). The workers below, who earn between $2 and $5 a day, ignore their audience as they repeat the labor-intensive steps of their craft, first soaking cow, sheep, goat, and camel skins in open vats filled with a mixture of cow urine, pigeon feces, quicklime, salt, and water in order to soften the hides and loosen the hair and animal fat. Next, the dried hides are scraped down with double-edged knives, after which the workers plunge the skins into vats traditionally filled with plant-based dyes. Finally, the skins are dried, then hauled off in massive piles for cutting and production (Chouara Tannery 2017).

The workers, some of whom begin as apprentices at thirteen years old, put in long days outdoors, standing barefoot and bare-legged up to their thighs in the vats of liquid. On a damp January day, temperatures might not get out of the 40s Fahrenheit. In July, they can soar to 100 degrees. The stunning tourist views (and well-priced leather goods) hide the complexity of this craft, where chromium – a well-known carcinogen with other toxic health effects – has been used in the process since the 1800s and many vegetable dyes have been replaced with synthetics, sickening the workers who spend their days wading in these vats and the residents who drink the water polluted by the chemicals, bacteria, and animal by-products dumped monthly into the Sabou and Fez rivers. In Fez, fifty-five modern tanneries outside

1

the old city now use high-tech filtration to produce less pollution, and maintain high safety standards for their workers (Curwood 2014). But, when we visit as tourists, we do not want to see factories. We want to see – and buy, and take selfies with – "authentic" Moroccan crafts. Instead, we reinforce systems of exploitation and pollution that are unlikely to exist without our interest. At the same time, with so much of the Fez economy dependent on our tourist dollars, what would happen if we lost interest? Chouara alone employs two hundred men in a country with an unemployment rate of 10.4 percent (World Bank 2017).

These are some of the problems that students have wrestled with over the last decade as they stood on a leather shop balcony overlooking the colorful dye vats with University of Maryland professor David Crocker (and in one year also with then Assistant Director Stacy Kosko, one of this volume's editors). There, as elsewhere, Crocker invited us to consider the realities that outsiders often miss. We noticed the workers and also the satellite dishes that open "traditional" societies to the world. But, the world offers many visions. Limited economic agency, Crocker reminded us, requires local political agency reinforced by inclusive and deep democratic activism, sometimes with alliances of insiders and outsiders, to further the goals of worthwhile human development. In helping students of international development and public policy to come to terms with what they see – and smell – at Chouara, Crocker makes good use of the tools and insights of development ethics.

Agency and Democracy in Development Ethics

What are the justified ends and means of worthwhile human development? Whatever else the answer might entail, it is clear that agency and democracy are among the core themes of global development. They are especially important within development ethics, a field that David A. Crocker, together with many of this volume's contributors, has done much to forward. This volume brings together a diverse set of voices from scholars and practitioners with various disciplinary and geographical backgrounds to discuss these themes. The contributors use a number of techniques ranging from philosophical analysis of a priori concepts to detailed examination of empirical situations through economic, political, educational, and legal lenses. Although the volume's contributors present different ideas about how best to understand, promote, or protect agency and democracy within the many contexts of global development, development ethicists from every disciplinary background and every continent agree both that agency and democratic participation are necessary parts of ethical development and that the intellectual engagement and scrutiny of agency and democracy is a key part of development ethics.

Indeed, it is difficult to imagine serious discussions about ethical development that do not relate to the core themes of agency and democracy. Yet, there was a time, in the 1970s, when philosophical discussions about global development were limited to Peter Singer's "Famine, Affluence, and Morality" (1972), which argues along utilitarian lines that we ought to give money to aid organizations like OXFAM in order to help the poor, and Garrett Hardin's "Lifeboat Ethics" (1974), which argues against helping the world's poor through financial aid due to worries about overpopulation. (John Rawls [1971] and Robert Nozick [1974] were discussing sophisticated views of distributive justice, but these discussions were limited to distribution within the nation state.) Thus, the conversation about global development at this time was restricted to the question of should we (the rich) help them (the poor), where "help" always meant "give money" and "we" always stood in juxtaposition to "them." This was the academic landscape before philosopher David A. Crocker joined the conversation. Crocker is among the pioneers who transformed this relatively barren academic landscape populated only with narrow considerations of aid into the rich and flourishing field of development ethics, which now exists as a well-established sector of applied ethics within philosophy, and as an interdisciplinary field of study and practice within and beyond global development, throughout the world.

Since the late 1970s, Crocker's work on issues of agency and democratic participation has been linked to development, but Crocker has been concerned with these themes for more than five decades. His earliest work, including his 1970 PhD dissertation "A Whiteheadian Theory of Intentions and Actions" (Yale University), concerns authentic choice, agency, and action. After completing his dissertation, Crocker became increasingly interested in the proper relationship between individual and collective agency, and normative theory for social action. As a Fulbright scholar in Munich, Germany (1973–1974), Crocker enjoyed a deep engagement with the Frankfurt School's critical theory, especially Jürgen Habermas and his influential democratic social theory. Crocker's own notions of social action as *praxis* were also influenced by an intellectual group of Yugoslavian dissidents (Crocker 2008, p. 25 n. 9). His first book *Praxis and Democratic Socialism: The Critical Social Theory of Marković and Stojanović* (1983) reflects these interests as it critically and productively engages the Yugoslavian democratic socialist school of thought.

Crocker's knowledge of and interest in human agency and democratic participation found a new outlet in 1978 when he was asked to join two colleagues, one an animal science professor, the other a philosopher with expertise in India, in teaching a graduate seminar in "Ethics and Rural Development" at Colorado State University (Crocker 2008, p. 2). A reluctant Crocker agreed to teach the course despite his misgivings about whether his expertise in philosophical ethics, meta-ethics, and Anglo-American and European social political philosophy would prove useful to issues of rural development. Teaching this course not only drew on Crocker's expertise on agency and democracy, it challenged him to work across academic disciplines, across cultural norms, and across borders.

In preparing for this new seminar, Crocker discovered and was influenced by Denis Goulet, who is often called the "father" of development ethics (Dower 2008, p. 184; Wilber, Dutt, and Hesburgh 2010). A student of French economist Louis-Joseph Lebret, Goulet distinguished between undesirable antidevelopment and worthwhile authentic development, the kind that facilitates what Lebret called a "human accent" in which people become "more human" (Goulet 1971, pp. 189, 215). Goulet called for a human-centered development ethics that can explore and address "the ethical and value questions posed by development theory, planning and practice" (1977, p. 5). Crocker found a kindred spirit in Goulet, whose insistence that individuals be active agents in their own development resonated powerfully. In taking up questions in development theory, planning, and practice, Crocker's work on agency and democracy soon went far beyond what was expected of an academic philosopher. But, Crocker never abandoned the use of valuable philosophical insights and methods. Instead, he applied his keen mind to making useful critical distinctions and clarified concepts at work in development. In so doing, Crocker not only changed how we think about development, he also broadened the scope of practical ethics within academic philosophy and interdisciplinary ethics.

As he broadened the scope of his own research, Crocker became immersed both intellectually and personally in a deeply interdisciplinary and intercultural dialogue. During a 1986–1987 Fulbright fellowship to Costa Rica, he strengthened and began to articulate his attitudes about the kinds of relationships that are necessary for worthwhile human development to succeed. Reflections on local stakeholder "insiders" and concerned "outsiders" led to his "insider–outsider hybrid" for development practitioners and scholars and the insight that people in all of these categories have roles to play in democratic processes. This highly influential account appears in his article "Insiders and outsiders in international development ethics" (1991).

Many of Crocker's other published contributions, including his powerful 2008 book *Ethics and Global Development: Agency, Capability, and Deliberative Democracy*, further clarified and advanced the concepts of agency and democracy, especially in the Capability Approach to human development. The Capability Approach was first established by economist Amartya Sen and philosopher Martha Nussbaum in the late 1980s. Although both Nussbaum and Sen already recognized the importance of agency and democracy for ethical development, Crocker provided original, insightful, and rigorous analysis of the concepts, resulting in more refined and robust accounts of both. Crocker proposed an understanding of agency in human development (and in all human action) that gave primacy to the person, and to her exercise of critical and informed reason, including and especially through democratic deliberation, rather than only to the achievement of her preferred goal. This thinking is the basis for his influential "agency-oriented capability approach," a process-oriented view of human development that continues to evolve today, including in many of the chapters in this volume as well as in Crocker's own concluding chapter.

In the development of this agency-oriented capability approach, Crocker drew from Sen's various mentions of agency in providing a clear and complete account of the concept:

A person is an agent with respect to an action X just in case she (1) decides for herself (rather than someone or something else forcing the decision) to do X; (2) bases her decisions on reasons, such as the pursuit of goals; (3) performs or has a role in performing X; and (4) thereby brings about (or contributes to bringing about of) change in the world.

Crocker displays a characteristic wisdom in not insisting that the rigid philosophical standards for rational concepts fit the world as we find it when he writes, "[r]ather than make each one of these necessary and together sufficient for agency, let us say that the more fully an agent's action fulfills each condition, the more fully is that act one of agency" (2008, p. 157).

Crocker also developed the ideal of deliberative democracy in a way that extended work done in development ethics, including on the Capability Approach, in valuable ways. He proposed a process-focused version of deliberative democracy in which fair procedures, which allow all voices to be heard and preferences to be transformed, provide legitimacy to the democratic process. Crocker argues that democratic deliberation should be understood as an endeavor aimed at

(1) identifying specific problems and overcoming differences as to the solutions, in order to form joint intentions for action; (2) doing so in ways that further the goals of reciprocity, publicity, and accountability; (3) improving background conditions that enhance deliberation in the foregoing ways – such as equal political liberty, equality before the law, economic justice, and procedural fairness. (Drydyk 2011, pp. 222–223)

In practice, deliberative democratic participation should be open to all people (including men, women, sexual and gender minorities, religious and secular persons, insiders, outsiders, etc.) and should take place "in a variety of venues – from small villages, through development planning ministries, to the World Bank" (Crocker 2008, p. 95).

This expansive view of deliberative democracy grounds Crocker's innovative model of integrated "development theory-practice." According to Crocker, "development theory-practice is a more or less integrated totality composed of the following components: (A) ethical and normative assumptions, (B) scientific and philosophical assumptions, (C) development goals, (D) scientific or empirical understanding, (E) policy options and recommendations, (F) critique, and (G) development activities and institutions" (2008, p. 71). Crocker explains the informative relationship between the normative and nonnormative aspects and the empirical aspects of these components. Making explicit how empirical information, for example literacy rates, corresponds to normative judgments, for example that all people ought to be able to read a newspaper, allows us to see not only "value assumptions that masquerade as facts" but also "to justify beliefs about what actions we should take" (2008, p. 72). Crocker's integrated development theory-practice is not a theory, but a tool that can be used by anyone to evaluate a situation and promote a transparent dialogue about how to proceed. Taken together, Crocker's contributions offer a compelling response to Goulet's call for a human-centered development ethics that can explore and address "the ethical and value questions posed by development theory, planning and practice" (Goulet 1977, p. 5).

The Chapters

The chapters in this volume and the scholars who wrote them all share a debt to Crocker as they offer their own explorations of the ethical questions posed by development. The chapters in the first section, *Development Ethics*, are all concerned with foundational issues of the scope and nature of development ethics. Lori Keleher explicitly draws on Crocker's definition of development ethics as "the ethical reflection on the ends and means of development" in her "Why Development Needs Philosophy." Keleher explains both why development ethics is a legitimate practice for serious philosophers and why authentic development needs philosophy. She then argues that development ethics should involve not only philosophy's three established domains of ethical inquiry – meta-ethics, normative ethics, and practical (or applied) ethics, but also reflections in a new domain that she calls "personal or integral ethics."

Eric Palmer's "What Is Development?" provides a historical and conceptual analysis of how we understand "development" as a normative concept, before building on Crocker's work in participatory democracy as he argues for a dialectical process of public reason that may result in the generation of new capabilities to be promoted and protected by public institutions, including constitutions. Gasper and Comin's "Public Goods and Public Spirit: Reflections on and Beyond Nussbaum's *Political Emotions*" considers the role of public emotions and "public-spiritedness" and their influence on the democratic deliberations that determine a key part of global development: the distribution of public goods at the global level. In "The Choice of a Moral Lens: LGBTI Persons, Human Rights, and the Capabilities Approach" Chloe Schwenke considers the lenses of both global development and human rights activism as she examines the constraints that limit full human agency and diminish the well-being of people who identify as lesbian, gay, bisexual, transgender, or intersex (LGBTI). She argues that an agency-oriented capabilities approach can offer insights for critical improvements in mainstream normative lenses, improvements that ethical development requires. Finally, in "Peacebuilding, Development, Agency and Ethics," Nigel Dower highlights Crocker's ideas and thought as he argues that development ethics and peacebuilding are normatively, conceptually, and practically parallel and intimately connected. Dower argues that both agency and democracy are valuable conceptual aspects of peacebuilding and identifies both general and particular ways in which this is the case.

Although the themes of agency and democracy are woven throughout all the chapters in this volume, the second section, *Agency*, features chapters in which agency plays a prominent role as authors follow Crocker's lead in understanding agency as a necessary and important part of development. Christine M. Koggel offers a poignant critical evaluation of agency in her "Expanding Agency: Conceptual, Explanatory, and Normative Implications." She focuses on the relational capacity of people as she explains that agents are situated not only in personal relationships but that these are nested in broad and overlapping networks of relationships that create vulnerabilities and needs and shape possibilities for agency. Koggel effectively argues that focusing on relationships facilitates analyzing oppression and power at all levels from personal to global, and that the explanatory power of the relational aspect of agency makes the normative implications for enhancing agency more apparent and compelling. Serene J. Khader and Stacy J. Kosko, in "'Reason to Value': Process, Opportunity, and Perfectionism in the Capability Approach," evaluate alternative interpretations of the phrase "reason to value," which plays a key role in Amartya Sen's version of the Capability Approach. After fruitful consideration of several alternatives, the authors conclude that the idea of a capability approach whose only normative commitments are to respect for freedom and agency (at least of nonvalue-laden sorts) is untenable. Both of these chapters prove especially fruitful for Crocker's own concluding chapter of this volume. Moreover, Crocker's (re)considerations of process and perfectionism have implications for our understanding of agency in development practice, and especially in Crocker's agency-oriented version of the Capability Approach.

The remaining three chapters in the section provide powerful examples of the ways in which development ethics is truly interdisciplinary. In "The Multidimensionality of Empowerment: Conceptual and Empirical Considerations," philosopher Jay Drydyk proposes that empowerment can be conceived as a complex change in three dimensions: (1) expansion of choice; (2) shift in power relations; and (3) expansion of well-being freedom. Drydyk's understanding of empowerment is then "field tested" by participatory development specialists Alejandra Boni, Alexandre Apsan Frediani, Melanie Walker, and Aurora López-Fogués in three empowerment projects involving Spanish youth, neighborhood representatives in Kenya, and university students in South Africa. The evidence suggests that each of the three theoretical dimensions matter to real people.

Economists Gonzalo Salas and Andrea Vigorito use statistical analysis to provide an empirical illustration of agency levels and inequality in Uruguay in their chapter "Agency, Income Inequality, and Subjective Well-Being: The Case of Uruguay." The focus is on three agency domains: economic control and choice, potential for change, and impact in the community. They find that although overall agency and economic agency exhibit a progressive evolution with regards to income, increases in potential for change are higher in the middle of the distribution, and power in the community shows bigger improvements for the higher income strata. Moreover, they find a positive correlation among the overall agency index, income, and subjective well-being, which is at odds with the adaptive preferences hypothesis. Finally, in "The Legal Status of Whales and Dolphins: From Bentham to the Capabilities Approach," Rachel Nussbaum Wichert and Martha C. Nussbaum advance the discussion of agency in nonhuman animals as they address the issue of whether whales and dolphins can be accorded legal status, especially in situations such as in captivity and in scientific experiments. They then sketch an approach by which cetaceans might be understood as "nonhuman persons" who are not merely passive recipients of experience but shapers of lives, or agents.

The third section of the volume is comprised of chapters that focus on deliberative democracy and its theoretical and practical limits. In "On Some Limits and Conflicts in Deliberative and Participatory Democracy," Luis Camacho explores the ways in which participation and representation may enter into conflict. He defends the idea that limitations and conflicts are not excuses to avoid the need to improve democratic regimes by participation. However, since neither participation nor deliberation can guarantee that a decision is morally right, there will always be a role for ethical debate on normative issues. Adela Cortina directly engages with David Crocker's formulation of deliberative democracy in "An Agency-Focused Version of Capability Ethics and the Ethics of Cordial Reason: The Search for a Philosophical Foundation for Deliberative Democracy." Cortina evaluates Crocker's focus on agency in Sen's Capability Approach and deliberative democracy in development. She then seeks a normative foundation for a globalized deliberative democracy in a multicultural world, and asks if Crocker's proposal is capable of providing such a foundation, or whether this task instead requires *cordial reason*: the intersubjective recognition of dignity, or the cultivation of agency through education. In "The Double Democratic Deficit: Global Governance and Future Generations" Francis Stewart recognizes the value of deliberative democracy, before identifying and exploring the nature and agency-limiting implications of two major deficiencies in democracy as currently practiced, before proposing solutions to each. The first deficit is a lack of democratic decision-making at the global level because of deficiencies in mechanisms of global governance. The second deficit is the absence of future generations in current deliberations. Stewart suggests that new or reformed global institutions can remedy the first, while the second may require that people alive today "represent" future generations in various ways.

The final two chapters in this section apply work on deliberative democracy to two specific areas: transitional justice and national policy-making. Colleen Murphy's "Deliberative Democracy and Agency: Linking Transitional Justice and Development" directly engages Crocker's work as Murphy observes that the concepts of agency and deliberative democracy are central to his theories of both development and transitional justice. Murphy explains deeper connections among what may seem at first glance to be separate and distinct normative ideals in Crocker's theories of development and transitional justice before discussing differences and possible tensions in their joint pursuit. The final chapter in this section is Javier M. Iguíñiz Echeverría's "Consensus- Building and its Impact on Policy: the National Agreement Forum in Peru." This normatively rigorous case study explores the value of consensus-building in deliberative democracy by examining the composition, characteristics, and impact of the National

Agreement Forum in Peru over a twelve-year period. Iguíñiz Echeverría finds that this institution buttresses Crocker's claims about the power of deliberative democracy by observing that even nonbinding political decisions can have real and lasting impact on government policies when arrived at through a deliberative democratic, consensus-based process.

The final section of this book – Development Ethics, Agency, and Democracy: New Challenges and New Directions – is comprised of two separate but closely related chapters by David Crocker in which he examines the volume's twin themes and engages with a number of its contributors. He takes up several of the chapters in depth as he clarifies, defends, modifies, and deepens his own ideas about development ethics, including by responding directly to explicit challenges from Camacho, Khader and Kosko, Koggel, Murphy, and Wichert and Nussbaum. The first of these chapters, "From Agency to Perfectionist Liberalism," starts with a comprehensive analysis of several concepts of agency, and ultimately offers a liberal perfectionist argument that critical and ethically responsible agency are among the goods to be promoted in good development.

His second chapter in this section, "Perfectionist Liberalism and Democracy," is the volume's concluding chapter and takes this argument further. Here, he argues that an agency-focused Capability Approach (CA) is best understood as a form of perfectionist liberalism (in contrast to Rawls's and Nussbaum's versions of political liberalism). He reiterates the three chief human goods that have always been at the center of his agency-focused CA, and centers his refined thinking upon them, where each is intrinsically as well as instrumentally good and together form the core perfectionist substance of his version of the CA. These three goods are (1) critical and responsible agency freedom and achievement, (2) well-being freedom and achievement, and (3) moral and political equality. Or, more briefly: agency, well-being, and equality.

I am perfectionist with respect to these three goods, but I agree with Cortina and affirm that humans should be self-determining with respect to a "model of the good life" (Cortina 2002, p. 213) ... This perfectionism is *liberal* because liberty or freedom runs through all three goods: both agency and well-being have freedom, as well as achievement aspects; the answer to Sen's 1979 question "Equality of What?" is equality of (positive and negative) basic liberty. (Crocker, Chapter 17, p. 426)

Crocker continues this second concluding chapter by replying directly to criticisms by Camacho, Koggel, and Murphy, and then by arguing for liberal, deliberative, and representative democracy as both a universal value and an essential development goal, one that at once embodies, requires, and makes possible his three basic human goods. Finally, in his closing dialogue with Camacho on democracy, he arrives at a forceful agreement with his long-time colleague and friend, ending his chapter – and this volume – with Camacho's resonate claim that "there always is an important and irreplaceable role for ethics as the analysis of the difference between good and bad. The moral obligation to look for good solutions belongs to all human beings engaged in deliberation" (Camacho, Chapter 11, p. 304).

Through this critical dialog with the volume's contributors, and by revisiting his own ideas in *Ethics of Global Development* and elsewhere, Crocker aims in these final chapters to refine and improve upon the agency-focused Capability Approach to development, while guiding the current and new generations of development ethicists in promising new directions. The two-chapter final section thereby transforms the collection of chapters into a true democratic discussion about agency and democracy in global development. A note from Crocker follows this introduction. The note offers reflections on development ethics broadly, a road map for reading this book, and a preview of how he will employ some of its insights.

Crocker's Contributions

As this volume demonstrates, Crocker's contributions continue to encourage study, deliberation, and application of agency and democracy within human development. Crocker's influence on how we understand both ethical development and development ethics is so great that we now take it as an established fact that these concepts are core and necessary dimensions of ethical development. Perhaps Crocker's greatest contribution has been to give a fuller answer to that central question of development ethics: What are the justified ends and means of worthwhile human development? Worthwhile development, he tells us, should expand people's well-being freedom, and do so in ways that engage and expand their agency, especially through democratic, deliberative processes. As these chapters reflect, the influence of Crocker's thinking is felt in the work of economists, sociologists, climate scientists, political scientists, lawyers, philosophers, interdisciplinary ethicists and capability scholars, policy scientists and policy makers, and practitioners in the Global South and beyond. Crocker's work, and the work of those influenced by him, has implications for nearly every realm of human interaction. Crocker has applied his thinking directly to issues such as consumerism, hunger, transitional justice, globalization, minority rights (especially rights of minorities-within-minorities), and most recently corruption. These chapters tackle some of these and add others.

In addition to his insightful and influential published works, many of which concern the *theory* of bringing people with diverse ideas, methods, and goals together for participatory democratic processes, Crocker's career also reflects his *actual* bringing together of diverse groups of scholars and practitioners for the participatory democratic process of discussing development and the construction of the field of development ethics. In the 1980s, Crocker worked with Costa Rican philosopher Luis Camacho and others to form the International Development Ethics Association (IDEA). For more than three decades since, IDEA has brought together diverse groups of scholars and practitioners, including those in this volume, to continue to respond to Goulet's call by discussing and advancing ethical development in theory, planning, and practice. IDEA has developed into a flourishing organization whose conferences now feature a "David A. Crocker Lecture" (that is supported in part by funds generated by sales of this book).

IDEA's flourishing is in part due to Crocker's philosophical influence, but it is also a reflection of Crocker the person. David A. Crocker is a truly brilliant philosopher whose original insights, conceptual analysis, and clear expression of sophisticated concepts have forever shaped the nature and scope of development ethics and, by extension, applied philosophy. David A. Crocker is also, and even more importantly, a remarkable and good person. Blessed with charisma and a seemingly inexhaustible supply of curiosity and energy, he leads the advancement of ideas and people with integrity, kindness, and humility. He always encourages the newcomer, the student, the marginalized voice, to speak and he always listens to them with an open mind. He champions the advancement of the common good over the advancement of his own ideas. IDEA grew because people not only liked coming together and learning from one another, but also because the association continues to strive to reflect Crocker's humility in greatness.

The present collection of chapters on agency and democracy has been compiled in honor of David A. Crocker, the scholar and the person. Every contributor in the volume has been inspired not only by Crocker's brilliant mind, but also by his kind heart, his generous spirit, and his unflappable optimism in humanity. This volume is a testament to the fact that Crocker's published work and his life's example continue to shape the nature and scope of development ethics as a discipline that recognizes and seeks to promote agency and democratic participation for every person, at every level, and in every sphere of development. In Dave's own words: "If these people and groups are integrated in public discussion and democratic deliberation then we will be moving toward the right kind of development ethics and, we hope, toward a genuine development and a better world" (2008, p. 96).

References

Chouara Tannery. 2017. "Work Steps." https://chouaratannery.com/fes-tannery-process/.

Cortina, Adela. 2002. *Por una ética del consumo: la ciudadanía del consumidor en un mundo global*. Madrid: Taurus.

Crocker, David Alan. 1970. "A Whiteheadian Theory of Intentions and Actions." University of Yale dissertation.

Crocker, David A. 1983. *Praxis and Democratic Socialism: The Critical Social Theory of Marković and Stojanović*. Atlantic Highlands, NJ: Humanities Press; Brighton, Sussex: Harvester Press.

Crocker, David A. 1991. "Insiders and Outsiders in International Development Ethics." *Ethics and International Affairs*, 5: 149–173.

Crocker, David A. 2008. *Ethics of Global Development: Agency, Capability, and Deliberative Democracy*. Cambridge University Press.

Curwood, Steve. 2014. "Fascinating & Toxic – Traditional Moroccan Tanneries." *Living on Earth*. October 31, 2014. Public Media International. www.loe.org/shows/segments.html?programID=14-P13-00044&segmentID=4.

Dower, Nigel. 2008. "The Nature and Scope of Development Ethics." *Journal of Global Ethics*, 10(2): 183–193.

Drydyk, Jay. 2011. "Crocker, David." *Encyclopedia of Global Justice*. Deen K. Chatterjee (Ed.). New York: Springer Netherlands. 221–223.

Goulet, Denis. 1971. *The Cruel Choice: A New Concept in the Theory of Development*. New York: Atheneum.

Goulet, Denis. 1977. *The Uncertain Promise: Value Conflicts in Technology Transfer*. New York: IDOC/North America.

Hardin, Garrett. 1974. "Lifeboat Ethics: The Case against Helping the Poor." *Psychology Today* (September): 38–43, 124–126.

Nozick, Robert. 1974. *Anarchy, State, and Utopia*. New York: Basic Books.

Rawls, John. 1971. *A Theory of Justice*. Cambridge, MA: Harvard University Press.

Sen, Amartya. 1979. "Equality of What?" Tanner Lecture on Human Values. Stanford University, May 22.

Singer, Peter. 1972. "Famine, Affluence, and Morality." *Philosophy & Public Affairs*, 1(3): 229–243.

Wilber, Charles K., Amitava Krishna Dutt, and Theodore M. Hesburgh, Eds. 2010. *New Directions in Development Ethics: Essays in Honor of Denis Goulet*. University of Notre Dame Press.

World Bank. 2017. *World Bank Data*. https://data.worldbank.org/indicator/SL.UEM.TOTL.ZS.

A Note from David A. Crocker*

I welcome the opportunity to reply to this volume's chapters. They take up long-standing issues in international development ethics (DE), confront its new challenges, and explore novel directions. I deeply appreciate the editors' generous introduction, and the chapters, which they have invited, so insightfully analyze, probe, and evaluate my work in DE over the past four decades. I am gratified that the authors have entered into critical dialogue with my agency-focused and democratic version of the Capability Approach (CA) and, more importantly, found some of my ideas helpful in their own contributions to DE. In the process, these colleagues in DE have uncovered ambiguities, omissions, tensions, and other weaknesses in my work and have, as fellow inquirers should, exercised their own agency and proposed improvements in and alternatives to my efforts. Progress in DE, as in any inquiry, is most likely to occur in the critical dialogue and no-holds-barred deliberation – especially concerning our most cherished ideas.

New Realities and New Challenges

DE, I have argued, is moral reflection on the ends, means, and processes of beneficial social change on the local, national, and global levels. Central to that task, I argued in my 2008 book *Ethics of Global Development: Agency, Capability, and Deliberative Democracy* (hereafter *EGD*), is understanding and mitigating (if not eliminating) what I identified as five scourges that prevented people from living freely and

* I take this opportunity to thank Professors Lori Keleher and Stacy J. Kosko for conceiving and bringing about this volume and for their skillful editing of my contributions to it. I also am deeply appreciative of the team's copy editor, Matthew Regan, as well as of the support and editorial suggestions of members of my wonderful family: Edna (Eddie) Crocker, Catherine Crocker, Amanda Martocchio, David Peter Crocker, John Lawrence Crocker, and Anna Catherine Crocker Moser.

productively: (1) poverty, (2) degrading inequality, (3) violence, (4) environmental degradation, and (5) tyranny. I also argued that DE should avoid dogmatism and be open to new directions as the world changes and different and better solutions are called for. The agency-based version of the CA that I clarified and defended in that volume was an effort to provide an ethical standpoint from which those scourges might be confronted and, hopefully, overcome.

In the decade following *EGD*'s appearance, the scorecard on these five scourges is mixed. Poverty, globally and in many regions and countries, has been reduced. As Nicholas Kristof (2018) points out, "a smaller share of the world's people were hungry, impoverished or illiterate [in 2018] than at any time before [and] . . . a smaller proportion of children died than ever before." Inequalities in well-being and agency, however, have dangerously increased both within and between countries. From France and Syria to the United States and Burma, increasing ethnic hatred and religious animosity spur violence and migratory flight. Environmental degradation, including climate change, imperils the welfare of humans and animals, and threatens future earth dwellers with a broken world, one in which there are insufficient resources to sustain all the planet's inhabitants (Mulgan 2011). Finally, authoritarianism and antidemocratic populism have revived the scourge of tyranny. Although democratic experimentation continues on local, national, and global levels, the authoritarian resurgence has resulted in skepticism and cynicism about liberal – let alone participatory and deliberative – democracy.

New scourges have also emerged or are more prominent than they were a decade ago:

- Antinormative, data-driven "realism" that rejects most ethical reflection, critique, and advocacy as utopian.
- Discrimination against and repression of minorities. Not only are racial and religious minorities victimized, but also women, lesbian, gay, bisexual, transgender, or intersex (LGBTI) individuals, the disabled, the elderly, and migrants.
- Corruption as both the cause and effect of poor governance and criminal networks.
- Societal polarization due to differing ideologies, past conflicts, including human rights violations, and present animosities.

Development ethicists have tackled these old, modified, and new scourges with a variety of tools. There is a recognition that we were too optimistic that DE could bring about good and better development in the Global South and in those pockets of deprivation in the Global North. More realistic and less utopian, the development ethicists in this volume are still committed to following Denis Goulet's injunction to "keep hope alive" by criticizing unjust current practices and arguing for more humane and inclusive alternatives from the local to the global.

Luis Camacho addresses the issues of authoritarian resurgence and the ways a combination of representative, deliberative, and participatory democracy can and should respond. Nigel Dower explores the links between peacebuilding and development assistance and the role that democratic agency can and should play in both. Javier M. Iguiñiz Echeverría and Colleen Murphy argue for ways in which societies that endured conflict and suffered human rights violations can and should find ways to bring about reconciliation through deliberation for the common good. Lawyer Rachel Nussbaum Wichert and philosopher and capabilities theorist Martha C, Nussbaum extend DE and CA to the legal status and treatment of whales and dolphins. Christine M. Koggel and Chloe Schwenke argue for more capacious notions of dignity and agency, ones that are more compatible with the needs of women and LGBTI persons.

Interdisciplinary Field and Civic Engagement

A customary definition of DE is that it is moral reflection on development ends and means, where means includes not only tools, strategies, and policies but also *processes* by which development agents decide on development's benefits and burdens. Each aspect of this conception of DE calls out for much clarification and defense, but in this context I want to argue, as I have in the past, that DE is both an interdisciplinary academic field and a mode of civic engagement that advocates beneficial change and acts in various ways to bring it about. DE is interdisciplinary because there are a host of empirical, policy, and normative academic disciplines that contribute to DE in its efforts to understand and evaluate development achievements and failures and to propose worthwhile alternatives. But DE is more than a theory. It is also a practice of public discussion, advocacy, and involvement in various efforts – both individual and collective – for social change. Development ethicists not only want to devise or promote good theories about what development has been, can be, and should be, they also want to contribute directly to help prevent the world from going off a cliff, reckon with past wrongs, and make improvements in institutions, policies, everyday ethics, and, most basically, human and nonhuman lives.

This volume exhibits the conceptions of development as a theory-practice and DE as both academic field and practical engagement. Although each chapter displays its own mixture of elements, all try to take account of and address factual matters, scientific results (whether physical, biological, historical, or social), philosophical perspectives, ethical theories, and moral judgments. Most of the chapters have an explicit action-guiding and policy perspective that asks, "What should be done and who (or what) should do it?" For example, Lori Keleher argues for the conceptual, evaluative, and constructive role that philosophy can and should play in development theory-practice. Chloe Schwenke makes and defends moral judgments about defective social ethics and policies with respect to LBGTI individuals and practices in "developing" and "developed" countries, as well as international development agencies. Wichert and Nussbaum assess current laws governing treatment of whales and dolphins, and argue for the superiority of a legal and ethical approach based on a teleological concept of animal agency and a version of the CA. Des Gasper and Flavio Comim draw on social science and psychological-philosophical theories of emotions in arguing for the importance of "public spiritedness" in relation to the fair distribution of public goods.

Current development ethicists typically have been trained as philosophers, economists, sociologists, anthropologists, historians, environmentalists, educators, agriculturalists, engineers, or public health professionals. Increasingly, however, such ethicists have ventured outside their original academic formation and have become conversant – and sometimes adept – in other disciplines. Many of the new generation have obtained interdisciplinary degrees, such as those in public policy, women's studies, or sustainable development. Even more importantly, much recent work in DE has been done in interdisciplinary or multiprofessional teams. Such teams are illustrated throughout the volume.

Philosophers were central in the founding of both the International Development Ethics Association (IDEA) in 1984 and the Human Development and Capability Association (HDCA) in 2000, and, as Keleher argues, philosophy has much to contribute to development and DE. Nonphilosophers, however, are increasingly active in both groups, and they "do development ethics" in a variety of academic and development venues. In *EGD*, I described the emergence of single-authored writing, anthologies, university courses, conferences, and associations devoted to DE. I also cited some initial signs that DE, especially in relation to the capability orientation of Amartya Sen and Nussbaum, was penetrating international development institutions, popular discourse, and development policies on the ground.[1]

Yet, to be honest, DE has not had the institutional reach or, as Chloe Schwenke argues, the impact on *development* policies and practitioners that IDEA had hoped for in 1984 and that I had expected and advocated when I wrote my 2008 book. The contributors to this volume, keenly aware of DE's limited impact in both the "developing" and "developed" worlds, are exploring ways in which DE can have a salutary effect on development agendas, policies, and institutions. A good example is Wichert and Nussbaum's chapter on the impact of ethically inspired legal advocacy on the legal standing of whales and dolphins. It should be noted, however, that DE may be having a less dramatic and incremental impact than environmental or biomedical ethics. DE courses, conferences, and presentations in a variety of institutions may be nurturing "moral thinking" in a new generation of students and young professionals with respect to the ends, means, processes, and moral responsibilities of development theory and practice. For my own part, I believe that new thinking and practices concerning both agency and democracy have the promise of playing an important role in successfully combatting development scourges, both old and new.

Three Challenges to Development Ethics

Moral thinking about development theory-practices and ethically guided action to improve development requires moral judgment as well as ethical concepts and principles. Before explaining and defending a development ethic in which the ideal of agency functions as one ultimate principle, it will be helpful to very briefly identify (but not here rebut) three challenges to DE.

First, the moral skeptic rejects DE because it involves ethics, and the moral skeptic views all ethics as irrational or indefensible. The essayists in this volume assume that this skepticism is unjustified, but resist the temptation to rebut moral skepticism. There are more important things to do. However, deflating skepticism may be important in other venues.

Second, the cultural relativist or particularist rejects DE insofar as development ethicists evaluate practices in a society or culture that is not their own or employ (or assume) norms that are allegedly universal in the sense of holding for all societies at all times.[2] In her contribution to the present volume, Spanish philosopher Adela Cortina, drawing on the work of Jürgen Habermas and others, makes a promising attempt to meet the relativist challenge and offers an evaluation of my own efforts to do so. I regret not being able to address this issue in my concluding chapters.

Third, at least some types of DE have been rejected because they are too utopian or insufficiently realistic with respect to "human nature" or the "facts" about intractable social forces or structures. Even Sen (2009), as well as Christine M. Koggel in the present volume, falls victim to one form of this anti-utopianism when in his recent work he assimilates all social and development ideals to the ideal of a perfectly just society. Moreover, Sen rejects any "transcendental" kind of theory of justice in favor or a "comparative approach" that inquires how to struggle against obvious injustice and advance to a more just alternative. In my concluding chapters, I try to sort out the merits and demerits of this anti-utopianism.

Notes

1. In a lucid and systematic study, *The Capability Approach in Practice*, Morten Fibieger Byskov (2018) provides challenging answers to three questions at the core of DE: (1) Which should be the goals of development and a "development agenda"? (2) Who should decide? and (3) What methods should be employed in deciding? The "inclusive framework" for which he argues achieves a nice balance between normative and empirical aspects of development and between the rights of local stakeholders and contributions of a variety of experts.
2. For attempts to meet or circumvent the relativist/particularist challenge, see David A. Crocker (1991, 2004), Michele M. Moody – Adams (1997), and James W. Nickel (2007).

References

Byskov, Morten Fibieger. 2018. *The Capability Approach in Practice*. New York: Routledge.

Crocker, David. 1991. "Insiders and Outsiders in International Development Ethics." *Ethics and International Affairs*, 5: 149–173.

Crocker, David A. 2004. "Cross-Cultural Criticism and Development Ethics." *Philosophy & Public Policy Quarterly*, 24, 3: 2–8.

Crocker, David A. 2008. *Ethics of Global Development: Agency, Capability, and Deliberative Democracy*. Cambridge University Press.

Kristof, Nicholas. 2018. "Why 2017 Was the Best Year in Human History," *New York Times*, January 6: SR9.

Moody-Adams, Michelle. 1997. *Fieldwork in Familiar Places: Morality, Culture, & Philosophy*. Cambridge, MA and London: Harvard University Press.

Mulgan, Tim. 2011. *Ethics for a Broken World: Imagining Philosophy after Catastrophe*. Kingston, Ontario: McGill-Queens University Press.

Nickel, James W. 2007. *Making Sense of Human Rights*. Second edn. Malden, MA: Blackwell Publishing.

Sen, Amartya. 2009. *The Idea of Justice*. Cambridge, MA: Belknap Press, Harvard University Press.

PART I

Development Ethics

1 | *Why Development Needs Philosophy**

LORI KELEHER

Introduction

Philosophy is extraordinarily valuable to understanding and generating solutions to the problems of people. Yet, since the very first philosopher of the Western tradition, Thales (c. 624–546 BCE), philosophy has often been the subject of common ridicule. Legend has it that Thales tumbled down a well while looking up to study the stars. Plato tells us that a Thracian maidservant "exercised her wit" as she "scoffed at him for being so eager to know what was happening in the sky that he could not see what lay at his feet." Plato then warns that "Anyone who gives up his life to philosophy is open to such mockery" (*Theaetetus* 174). Plato's warning has proven true. Philosophers *are* subject to mockery. In Plato's fourth-century BCE Athens, Aristophanes' comedic play *The Clouds* lampooned philosophy by portraying Socrates as the head of a dysfunctional "thinkery." Today, philosophers continue to be common targets for mockery and are generally misunderstood by the public. For example, t-shirts with pithy and sarcastic slogans like "Don't worry, I have a philosophy degree" are easily found for sale. Both the fourth-century BCE playwright and the twenty-first-century CE t-shirt designer exploit for comedic gain the idea that philosophers have no relevant skills by insinuating that philosophers are merely big-talking loafers who fail to make valuable contributions to society.

Philosophers are mocked and dismissed, not only by comedians, but also by academics and professionals. Physicist Stephen Hawking declared that philosophy is dead (at Google's 2011 Zeitgeist conference in Hertfordshire, England). Fellow physicist Freeman Dyson called the

* I am grateful to David Hoekema, Matthew R. G. Regan, Nicholas Bennett, Christopher Rosales, and many members of the International Development Ethics Association and the Human Development Capability Association for insights and discussions on this theme.

field of philosophy a "toothless relic of past glories" (2012). I am not
alone in being able to tell personal anecdotes of being dismissed as
a contributor to antipoverty work *because* I am a philosopher. When
I first met one smart, experienced, and dedicated antipoverty worker in
my community, she told me, "the closer it is to philosophy, the further
it is from helpful." (Ouch.) The fact that this same person now frequently expresses gratitude for my philosophically informed participation suggests that she was simply unfamiliar with philosophy and how
very relevant and helpful it can be. Martha Nussbaum felt motivated to
remind even the relatively philosophy-friendly Human Development
and Capability Association (HDCA) of the value of philosophy in
human development during her 2013 keynote address in Managua,
Nicaragua. She lamented that many economists who "build structures
of great sophistication and precision . . . tend to regard the philosophers
as termites gnawing away at the support structure . . . And they fortify
themselves with the thought that the objections raised by philosophers
are mere trivia, not really affecting the conclusions of their science."
The idea Nussbaum is confronting is that (once again) philosophy is
not being recognized as relevant or helpful to the problems of people,
including human development. As I explain in the first section, this idea
gets further support from a surprising source: philosophers themselves.
Many philosophers are suspicious, if not outright dismissive, of the
idea that practical applications of philosophy, including human development, are a legitimate focus for serious philosophers.

My goal in this chapter is to explain and confirm the significance of
logical and practical relationships between philosophy and development and to make clear some of the important contributions philosophers make to development. To this end, I argue both (1) that human
development is a legitimate focus for philosophers, and (2) that philosophy is not merely helpful, but absolutely necessary for promoting
human development. I conclude with the pragmatic suggestion that
philosophers should have a seat at the table wherever development
issues are engaged.

The first section investigates why philosophy is often dismissed
when dealing with practical problems, including problems of human
development. I review statements from the Pre-Socratics to contemporary philosophers about the practice of philosophy. I observe that
many philosophers engage abstract puzzles and arguments that have
no obvious connection to the realities of practical problems like

hunger and poverty. I submit that this focus on abstract arguments and puzzles has led some to adopt the false understanding that philosophy consists *solely* in engaging such abstract puzzles. I argue that although logical arguments are the proper means of philosophy, the proper final end (*telos*) of philosophy is to improve human lives by actively engaging the problems of people. It follows that human development is a most legitimate focus for serious philosophers.

In the second section, I argue that the insights and methods of philosophy are not only relevant and helpful but also necessary to human development. Many chapters in the present volume demonstrate how relevant and helpful philosophy can be to human development simply by doing philosophy well (see, for example, Cortina, Crocker, Dower, Drydyk et al., Koggel, Khader and Kosko, Wichert and Nussbaum, Murphy, and Palmer). In contrast, this chapter strives to provide an explicit explanation of the relevance and value of philosophical methods and resources within development. With this goal in mind, I briefly explain some of the ways in which philosophers constructively engage in development work. Special attention is paid to the critical role that philosophers play within the relatively young field of development ethics as pioneered by philosophers, including Denis Goulet and David A. Crocker. Development ethics is defined here as ethical reflection on the ends and means of development (Crocker 2008; Dower 2008, 249). I explain how philosophical tools and insights enable us to reflect and think clearly about aspects of these ends and means on at least four levels. These levels include the three established domains of ethical inquiry – meta-ethics, normative ethics, and practical (or applied) ethics – as well as a new domain, personal integral ethics. I introduce this fourth domain with the goal of drawing the attention to the moral dimensions of the concrete and contextual or *integrated* human experience of individuals. The chapter concludes with the recommendation and the hope that once the relevance and value of philosophy is made clear, philosophers will have a permanent and protected seat at the table in policy meetings, academic programs for development studies, or think tanks–in short, wherever development issues are engaged. Philosophers should not fill all the seats of the table, but should work as allies with scholars, policy-makers, and practitioners to address the problems of people.

Why Development Is of Proper Concern for Philosophers

As noted above, philosophers have been criticized, mocked, or dismissed by comedians, physicists, economists, poverty workers, and others, but criticism of philosophy does not only come from outside the field. There has also been a recent wave of prominent philosophers publically lamenting the state of contemporary philosophy. For example, Peter Unger's book *Empty Ideas* (2014) criticizes many of the most influential philosophers and the field of philosophy of the past fifty years for being "concretely and analytically empty," in other words, utterly trivial. John Searle (2014) said that philosophy is in "terrible shape" and lacks insight. While some philosophers lament the idea that philosophy is unhelpful, others celebrate the notion; Martin Heidegger wrote, "It is entirely proper and as it should be: Philosophy is of no use" (Heidegger 1954, quoted in Pieper 1992, 9). Such lamentations and celebrations alike result in furthering the false idea that philosophy is irrelevant and unhelpful.

Those who consider philosophy to be irrelevant and unhelpful misunderstand philosophy. There are many ways to misunderstand philosophy, but here I consider only one common misunderstanding that is held not only by many working outside philosophy, but also by some philosophers. The misunderstanding is that philosophy is primarily, if not exclusively, a method of getting clear on concepts and their relationships. In what follows, I first explain the position and why some contemporary philosophers may hold it. I then argue that this position is too narrow and commits the error of mistaking one methodological part of philosophy (getting clear on concepts) for the whole of philosophy, whose proper object is the problems of people. I use historical texts to demonstrate that neither this misunderstanding of philosophy, nor the argument that the misunderstanding is too narrow, are new. I suggest that philosophers must continue to guard against the dangers of focusing entirely on the abstract arguments and puzzles generated as we search for conceptual clarity, even as we continue to cultivate these same methods for actively engaging the problems of people. Finally, I assert that the set of problems of people that concern philosophers includes the problems of human development. Thus, human development is a legitimate focus for serious philosophers.

The current dominant paradigm in Western philosophy reflects the ideas that to do philosophy is to use logic in an effort to attain conceptual clarity. William James captures this idea as he says, "Philosophy is the unusually stubborn attempt to think clearly" (quoted in Hall and Ames 1987, 29). Similarly, Ludwig Wittgenstein writes, "Philosophy aims at the logical clarification of thoughts ... Without philosophy thoughts are, as it were, cloudy and indistinct: its task is to make them clear and to give them sharp boundaries" (1922, 4.112). Thus, contemporary mainstream philosophy is primarily concerned with the sort of clarity and understanding that is gained by precise and thorough analysis of concepts and their relationships to each other. This search for sharp conceptual boundaries inspires imaginative (and fun) puzzles and paradoxes. (For example, Russell's paradox considers the set of all sets that are not members of themselves. This is a paradox, because such a set seems to be a member of itself if and only if it is not a member of itself [Irvine and Deutsch 2016].) Although many philosophers do pursue different interests within philosophy, crafting, evaluating, and responding to such paradoxes is still considered by many to be central to, if not *the* paradigmatic work of, philosophers. Engaging paradoxes is intellectually stimulating work that often generates new insights on analyticity. But, it is not difficult to see why labors on Russell's paradox might be dismissed as unhelpful and irrelevant to the vast majority of the problems that occupy people (including hunger, disease, oppression, etc.).

The idea that philosophers should be concerned with the abstract logic, conceptual boundaries, and paradoxes such work inspires, is associated with the analytic philosophy championed in the twentieth century (by Bertrand Russell, G. E. Moore, and others) but has much deeper roots within Western philosophy. Perhaps most famously Plato's character Socrates relentlessly sought definitions that identified the sharp boundaries of concepts. In the *Euthyphro* he asks: "What is piety?" and then systematically scrutinizes and rejects each of Euthyphro's attempts to provide a satisfactory definition of piety. About a hundred years before Plato wrote the *Euthyphro*, Parmenides (born 515 BCE) introduced the logical laws of bivalence (x or not x must be true) and noncontradiction (x and not x must be false). The abstract logical conclusions of Parmenides (that hold that change and motion are mere illusions) inspired Zeno's paradoxes, which attempt to demonstrate that change and motion are logically impossible (e.g., the flying arrow is always at rest). Thus, philosophers engaged abstract logical arguments and puzzles long before the analytic philosophy of the twentieth century became the dominant understanding of philosophy in the West.

To the extent that engaging such puzzles either trains our minds to better engage the problems of people, or generates insightful and new understandings of logic, language, and thought that allow us to better understand concepts, ourselves, and the world, this is valuable philosophical work. But, a misunderstanding of the nature and scope of philosophy arises when we think that simply engaging abstract logical arguments and puzzles is the whole of philosophy. In other words, Wittgenstein was wrong to claim that: "*All* philosophy is a 'critique of language'" (1922, 4.0031; emphasis mine). This important work of clarifying concepts is only an instrumentally valuable method of philosophy (even if understanding itself is intrinsically valuable). We value clarifying concepts because we value the insights and understanding such work provides. It is important *because* it is useful as we pursue the proper final end of philosophy: dealing with the problems of people. Thus, those who believe that this important methodological aspect of philosophy is *all* of philosophy have committed the error of mistaking a part of philosophy for the whole.

Failing to recognize that engaging the problems of people is the final end of philosophy leads people to dismiss philosophy as irrelevant and unhelpful. Indeed, I submit that other fields, including math and physics, are not typically mocked and dismissed despite wresting with abstract puzzles, because it is obvious that we use these findings to construct various valuable material structures like bridges and dams. It is less obvious, but no less true, that we use abstract aspects of philosophy to construct various valuable immaterial structures of society, including laws, procedural methods, protections, rights, etc. This misunderstanding about the value of philosophy is dangerous not simply because those who hold it subscribe to a false belief about philosophy, but also because they are unaware of, and often therefore fail to fully profit from, the many contributions and benefits of philosophy.

Readers may be surprised that some philosophers often regard work that uses the methods of philosophy to engage the problems of people, for example work in development ethics, medical ethics, feminist philosophy, indigenous philosophy, etc., as beyond the scope of or at best peripheral to "legitimate" philosophy. In some cases, both the problems engaged as well as the logics and methodologies used to engage them are dismissed. Consequently, such work is too often considered "not philosophy" by the gatekeepers of academic philosophy, i.e., mainstream philosophy journals, those who decide which journals are mainstream, and promotion and tenure committees. As Sally Haslanger (2017) writes:

> To many of us, mainstream philosophy journals uphold standards for the profession that are at least far too narrow and at worst, ideologically biased ... *Hypatia*, in particular, has been a site of struggle on this issue. On one hand, it has been important that the only feminist philosophy journal ... garner respect by the mainstream so that feminist scholars could be hired and promoted. (Back in the day, I had to write a letter to a Dean supporting the appeal of a departmental tenure decision that discounted articles published in *Hypatia* as "not philosophy.") At the same time, the effort to be a mainstream journal can have the effect that excellent radical or methodologically innovative work is not published.

Some may be tempted to point to published works of feminist philosophy, programs that offer specializations in medical ethics, or one of the many philosophers who recognize applied work as valuable, to suggest that I am criticizing a straw person. But, my argument is not that *all* philosophers subscribe to the error, only that a significant *some* do. In addition to the countless anecdotes of the disparagement of applied philosophical work as "weak" or "not real philosophy," some philosophers have taken up the challenge of explaining and working to repair the harm this misunderstanding does within the field of philosophy (Dotson 2013; Frodeman and Briggle 2015; Haslanger 2017). Moreover, some philosophers might not even be fully aware that they subscribe to the belief that clarifying concepts is the whole or core of philosophy. Logic is a wonderful tool for detecting bias, but we must guard against the danger of allowing our use of logic to become the bias; sometimes other tools are better suited for navigating the world and the problems of the people within it. As Bertrand Russell (2009, 56) warns:

> The distinction between words and what they designate is one which it is difficult always to remember; metaphysicians, like savages, are apt to imagine a magical connection between words and things, or at any rate between syntax and the world structure. Sentences have subjects and predicates, therefore the world consists of substances with attributes. Until very recently

this argument was accepted as valid by almost all philosophers, or rather, it controlled their opinions almost without their knowledge.

My position is that when one fails to recognize that the final end of philosophy is to engage the problems of people, she misunderstands philosophy. This is true whether she proudly declares that all (legitimate) philosophy is a "critique of language" or if she allows a bias about the legitimacy of use of philosophical methods and insights to address the problems of people to subtly control her opinions almost without her knowledge. The fact that some do proudly declare this position and that many others have expressed concern about the impact of this position should be enough to assuage concerns that I am attacking a straw person.

Moreover, this too narrow view of philosophy is not only bad for the field of philosophy and philosophers, it is also bad for those whose scholarly and practical activities could benefit from philosophy. When academic philosophy is grounded in a culture that reflects a misunderstanding of the final end of philosophy as merely clarifying concepts without any active engagement of the problems of people, it further promotes the idea that philosophy is irrelevant (and that philosophers are worthy of mockery).

I am not alone in arguing that philosophy must be about more than logic and abstract puzzles. Throughout the history of Western philosophy there is a pattern of some who identify as philosophers focusing exclusively on abstract formal systems, only to be criticized by philosophers for not doing philosophy properly, because they failed to work to understand and *actively engage* the problems of people. As early as 540 BCE Heraclitus was criticizing other ancient philosophers, including the mathematically minded Pythagoras. Heraclitus reportedly said, "Pythagoras . . . practiced inquiry more than all other men, and making a selection of these writings constructed his own wisdom, polymathy, evil trickery" and "Polymathy does not teach insight, otherwise it would have taught Hesiod and Pythagoras" (Diogenes Laertius 8.6, 9.1). The criticism seems to be that we can study abstract concepts and know formal rules (what Pythagoreans would have called the *akousmata*) but still lack genuine understanding of how the world works (an error Heraclitus would call being asleep to the *logos*).

About 150 years later, Plato argued that (highly educated) philosophers must not be allowed to act as they do in his time, as if they have already arrived at the "faraway Isles of the Blessed" where they are free to contemplate the abstract and intelligible form of the Good. Instead, philosophers must share in the labors of humankind and work to confer benefits to the community (*Republic* 519b–519e). Aristotle expresses a similar idea when he explains that action and not simply argument is required for philosophy:

The many ... take refuge in arguments, thinking that they are doing philosophy, and that this is the way to become excellent people. In this they are like a sick person who listens attentively to his doctor, but acts on none of his instructions. Such a course of treatment will not improve the state of his body; anymore than will the many's way of doing philosophy improve the state of their souls. (Nicomachean Ethics 1112b–1117b)

Likewise, Epicurus said, "Empty is that philosopher's argument by which no human suffering is therapeutically treated" (quoted in Nussbaum 2003, 102). More than 2,000 years later, John Dewey (1929) had the same message as he wrote: "philosophy recovers itself when it ceases to be a device for dealing with the problems of philosophers and becomes a method, cultivated by philosophers, for dealing with the problems of men" (8). Perhaps most widely recognized, Peter Singer (1972; 2004) continues to explicitly challenge philosophers to act in accordance with the conclusions of their arguments in order to establish a way of life in which theory and practice, "if not yet in harmony, are at least coming together" (1972, 243).

Taken together, the above passages show that for as long as people have done philosophy the proper role of philosophers has been to go beyond, but not without, arguments to actively engage with the problems of people. I adopt this slightly modified version of Dewey's "problems of men" not only because "people" is less sexist than the term "men," but also because the category of persons is not restricted to humans (see Wichert and Nussbaum in this volume). "Problems" is already a broad category, which I take to include epistemological, scientific, and metaphysical problems as well as practical problems of human suffering, distributive justice, meeting human needs, and recognizing human dignity. In any case, philosophers must not simply take refuge in arguments, but instead must use the insights generated by our "stubborn efforts to think clearly" to act in accordance with these arguments as we engage with the problems of people, including the problems of human development.

Some may argue that I am wrong to follow those who hold that the goal of philosophy is actively dealing with the problems of people. After all, as discussed above, many seem to hold that arguments and abstract analytic puzzles represent the true core of philosophy, and that so-called practical areas of philosophy, including development ethics, are at best peripheral to philosophy, if they qualify as genuine philosophy at all. This chapter is not the proper occasion to fully examine and respond to these arguments. However, I make one clarification and two observations so as not to leave this position unaddressed.

I am not arguing that contemplating the abstract and intelligible or making arguments are not appropriate philosophical tasks, nor do I read those cited above as making such an argument. On the contrary, reasoning about concepts and making arguments are critical parts of what Dewey called "the method cultivated by philosophers" for dealing with problems of people. For philosophers, logic, arguments, abstract reasoning, and reflection all play a critical role in properly understanding and taking up what Plato called the labors of humanity. Thus, some very good philosophers spend their careers cultivating the methods of philosophy in ways that generate important insights about logic, language, thought, and meaning. These insights are very useful when dealing with the problems of people, even if the logicians who develop them do not directly engage the problems. I am *not* arguing that the cultivators of methods who are dealing mainly with logic, arguments, and abstract reasoning are not true philosophers. To do so would be to misunderstand philosophy in a different way, and to keep a different, but equally harmful, set of narrow gates for the field. After all, the abstract insights and understandings generated can be both intrinsically valuable as understandings about reality, and instrumentally valuable as solutions to the practical problems that people face. For example, if we reason that all human beings are created equal and consequently have certain unalienable human rights, this understanding is intrinsically valuable–it enriches our understanding of ourselves and of reality in a most satisfying way. It is also instrumentally valuable for important philosophical work, including underpinning the Declaration of Independence of the United States of America (1776).

My position is that it is a mistake to think that the cultivators of methods are the *only legitimate* philosophers, or that they can independently achieve the final end of philosophy, or that engaging in abstract puzzles is itself the final end of philosophy. Instead, I submit that philosophers qua philosophers do engage puzzles and arguments, but they do so as a means to gain insight into dealing with the final end of philosophy, namely, the problems of people. A corollary of this position is that a person who, for example, engages paradoxes simply because she finds them amusing, or because she wants the glory of solving them, is not a philosopher, even if she accidentally generates discoveries used by others. In other words, engaging logical arguments and puzzles alone is insufficient for practicing philosophy; recognizing and striving towards a final end of actively engaging the problems of people is a necessary part of practicing philosophy. Philosophy literally means "love of wisdom." As lovers of wisdom, philosophers must not seek mere polymathy, or clever sophistry, but instead seek *wisdom*, i.e., valuable insights and understandings.[1] It is worth adding that the set of people that can do philosophy is not limited to those holding graduate degrees in philosophy or to those at work in academic philosophy departments. Economist Amartya Sen is just one example of a prominent scholar whose work qualifies as philosophy because he uses philosophical methods to the end of promoting human agency and well-being.

My first observation about why some continue to misunderstand working with arguments to be the whole of philosophy is that many others (including economists, political scientists, sociologists, physicians, engineers, biologists, etc.) work on the problems of people, for example, ending preventable human suffering, but only philosophers (or very few others, e.g., mathematicians) seem to work on abstract puzzles. Some conclude that because this latter work is unique to philosophers, it must also be the proper function of a philosopher. But, even if philosophers are the only ones who do such puzzles, it does not follow that doing such puzzles is the only or best thing philosophers do, any more than it would follow that joke-telling is the only or best thing humans do, if it happened to turn out that humans are the only species with a sense of humor.[2]

Second, as I attempt to establish above, to dismiss working on the problems of people as anything less than the central goal of philosophy is to dismiss the views of some of the most influential figures in philosophy, including Plato and Aristotle, on the nature of philosophy. In other words, to reject those who work on the problems of people as less than central or *real* philosophers is to reject Plato and Aristotle as less than central philosophers. (I personally lack both the ability and the desire to understand philosophy – the field Alfred Whitehead described as "footnotes to Plato" – without Plato as a real and central figure.) Plato understood that definitions with sharp boundaries and puzzles were important to understanding reality and training our skills of critical reasoning, but he also understood that engaging abstract problems was only part of doing philosophy. Plato and many other central figures in philosophy recognized that the true objective of the philosopher is to actively engage the problems of people. In some cases, this means using philosophical methods and insights to address the problems of human suffering, oppression, and injustice that are part of global poverty and human development. Thus, when *philosophy* is properly understood, it is obvious that human development is a legitimate concern for serious philosophers. I now turn to the second goal of this chapter, explaining why the contributions of such philosophers are not only relevant and valuable, but also logically and pragmatically necessary to development.

Why Development Needs Philosophy

In this section I argue that *philosophy* is logically and pragmatically necessary to *development*. So, we must get clear on both *philosophy* and *development*. As explained above, *philosophy* is the love of wisdom and to practice philosophy is to use philosophical methods, including, but not limited to, logic, conceptual analysis, and reflection, to generate insights and ideas that can be used to actively engage the problems of people. As Eric Palmer's chapter in this volume demonstrates, and as I have taken up elsewhere (Keleher 2014), getting clear about what we do and should mean by *development* is itself a challenging philosophical exercise. For our present purposes, it is enough to establish that at the level of conceptual understanding *authentic development* entails the use of the philosophical methods of critical thinking and ethical reflection, thus, philosophy is logically necessary to development. Moreover, we cannot practice *authentic development* without thinking critically about the ethical dimensions of the ends and means of development and trying to act in accordance with the conclusions of our arguments. Thus, philosophy is pragmatically necessary for development.

The section proceeds as follows: I first explain that much of what has gone on in the name of development is not development at all, but what Denis Goulet has called *anti-development*. I then argue that the use of critical reasoning and ethical reflection on the ends and means of development is a necessary part of what makes actions done in the name of development *authentic* development. Then, I explain some of the ways in which philosophical methods and insights contribute to the practice of authentic development. Finally, I introduce *development ethics* and discuss four levels of ethical reflection.

Since the 1950s, policies and programs have been promoted in the name of development. Unfortunately, so many of these efforts have gone so very wrong that an entire school of thought, the *Post Development School*, advocates rejecting the concept and established methods of development altogether (Escobar 1984, 1995; Esteva 1985; Sengupta 2019; Ziai 2004, 2007, 2013). Gustavo Esteva wrote, "The time has come to recognize development itself as a malignant myth … a huge, irresponsible experiment that, in the experience of a world-majority, failed miserably" (1985, 78). Although I recognize that there have been critical failures within development theory and practice, I believe it is a mistake to reject the concept of development altogether. To do so would be to throw out the proverbial baby with the bath water.

Instead, I advocate adopting Denis Goulet's distinction between undesirable anti-development and worthwhile authentic development (1977). Goulet agrees that development efforts can and do go wrong. He writes: "Upon critical reflection, much apparent development proves to be 'anti-development.'" Yet, he also recognizes that some development projects "constitute genuine progress" (215). For Goulet, such genuine progress entails more than economic growth; it requires that people become "more human." On this view, "Societies are more human, or more developed, not when men and women '*have* more' but when they are enabled to '*be* more.' The main criterion of development is not increased production or material well being but qualitative human enrichment" (1995, 6–7). I am among the many who agree with Goulet.[3] However, regardless of whether or not we agree with Goulet's understanding of what life and society should look like, it seems obviously true that: "To determine what is good and what is bad development implies *some* qualitative view of life and society" (216, emphasis mine). Thus, identifying and promoting authentic development, as opposed to anti-development, requires both (1) critical reflection about what makes for good development and (2) some qualitative view of life and society.

As discussed above, this sort of critical reflection and analysis of concepts (e.g., the concept of *development*) is the hallmark of philosophical methods, and dealing with the problems of people, including the quality of life and society, is the final objective of philosophy. Accordingly, anyone who engages in the sort of skillful reflection necessary to identify and promote authentic development engages in philosophy. In other words, philosophy is *logically* necessary for development. Moreover, without philosophical reflection and analysis of the quality of life and society as we design and implement development policies and practices, we are not accomplishing authentic development, but carrying out careless anti-development. Thus, philosophical reflection and analysis is *pragmatically* necessary. So, philosophy is absolutely necessary for authentic development.[4]

I anticipate two objections to the position that proper development requires a qualitative view of life that is best formed with ethical insight, and therefore requires critical thinking about ethics, i.e., philosophy. First, some may say that I am guilty of the logical misstep of begging the question in defining "development." They may claim that I followed Goulet in defining development as needing philosophy, then argued that it follows from the definition of development that philosophy is needed. Second, some may say that I am simply wrong about development. When writing on ethics and economics, Lionel Robbins argued that "it does not seem logically possible to associate the two studies in any form but mere juxtaposition. Economics deals with ascertainable facts; ethics with valuations and obligations. The two fields of enquiry are not on the same plane of discourse" (2007, 132). Thus, in discussing ethical dimensions of development, which is often considered to be a primarily, if not solely, economic process, one might argue that I committed the logical error of conflating the normative with the positive.

My response to both counterarguments is that the ethical dimensions of development are there whether we choose to recognize them or not. When we make decisions in development economics that result in the improvement of some lives, but not others, or at the cost of others, we are making ethical decisions. The choice not to recognize the ethical dimensions of economics *is itself a moral choice*. So, I am not begging the question in adopting Goulet's notion of authentic development. Ethics is part and parcel of development, and Goulet's definition recognizes this truth. Nor am I conflating the normative and the positive. Normative aspects of economic development and the need for ethical reflection have been there all along.[5]

Presently, I list and explain just a few examples of the philosophical methods and insights I believe are relevant and valuable to development work. Making arguments and engaging paradoxes is not the final goal of philosophy, but using logic and conceptual analysis to think clearly is still a principal method of practicing philosophy, and rightly so. Logic allows us to recognize and criticize bad arguments and to make and defend good arguments. Working with logic trains us to discover implicit biases and assumptions. For example, we might implicitly assume that because something has typically been done a certain way (e.g., making cash transfers to men, but not to women, given an assumption that men are the heads of the households) that it *should* be done that way. But, it does not follow logically from the fact that X has been done historically that X is best. Logic trains us to identify and avoid fallacious equivocations. In defining and clarifying the terms of our analysis, it becomes clear when authors use "poverty" to mean a lack of income in one sentence and a lack of valuable opportunities or diminished well-being in the next. Logical analysis also allows us to make valuable distinctions that are too often conflated in the literature. For example, high fertility rates are *correlated* with low incomes, *not caused* by low incomes. Finally, because they engage arguments, philosophers often adopt an adversarial approach to their own ideas and the ideas of others.[6] This approach trains philosophers to identify counterexamples and counterarguments in a way that render them well-suited to question thinking patterns at work in many other sciences, for example, confirmation bias, the tendency to seek and recognize the hypotheses we (prefer to) believe. These critical thinking skills are not unique to philosophers, but the work that philosophers do in logic is extremely useful in understanding and evaluating complex situations, and in turn, evaluating and informing the critical choices that must be made in development theory and practice.

As we have seen, the important methods of logic and analytic analysis are only part of doing philosophy. Philosophers from Plato to Peter Singer have called philosophers to go beyond engaging arguments. More recently, David A. Crocker has called philosophers to "go beyond Singer" as they approach problems within development. He challenges us to be less concerned with foundational issues and more committed to an ethics that is "interdisciplinary, institutionally and empirically informed, and policy-relevant" (2008, 10). Crocker is one of the architects of the field *development ethics*. Development ethics can be defined as ethical reflection on the ends and means of global development (Crocker 1991; 2008).

When we consider the ends of development, we ask: What are we ultimately trying to accomplish? In addition to Goulet's more human life and society, candidates for the ends of development include economic growth, increased GDP, higher household incomes, modernization, happiness, human well-being, freedom, and many others. There need not be one single final end. We might draw from several of the listed candidates. For example, we might strive toward *developing a more human life for each person and a more human society for all persons by expanding freedoms*. Once we identify the final goals of development we must also ask *what are the effective and ethical means for achieving these goals?* Do we invest in businesses, open markets, introduce technology, health care, education, or political/legal protections? Once we identify the means, they become lower level goals, or steps towards our final goal. So, we must then ask *what are the means to the means?* That is, *how do we achieve the lower level goals without losing sight of the final goal?* Do we offer microlending programs to women-run businesses, incentivize the development and introduction of new technology for sustainable energy, provide health-care subsidies for the least well-off, create bilingual education programs to help linguistic minorities better integrate into the economy and society, work to pass legislation that ensures the safe practice of minority religions?

Suppose we take as our final goal to *develop a more human life for each person and a more human society for all persons by expanding freedoms*. If this is our goal, then it is not good to simply strive to expand freedoms by promoting access to markets if doing so will mean violating human rights, because violating human rights will not make us more human as individuals or as a society. When considering the means we must also consider who is responsible for implementing, overseeing, and funding development interventions, and the short-term goals we hope will allow us to achieve our higher order goals.

Thus, there are countless critical choices about how to understand and implement the ends and means of development.

Philosophy can help us identify the critical choices and what follows from them. In addition to using logical analysis, philosophy can offer various insights that can help us process and understand these choices. One such insight is that there are different levels of ethical reflection and discourse that are useful in engaging the ends and means of development. Philosophers typically distinguish between three domains or levels: meta-ethics, normative ethics, and practical or applied ethics (Cavalier 2002; Fieser n.d.). In addition to these three well-established domains of ethical reflection, I submit that those working in development will find it fruitful to consider a fourth dimension: *personal or integral ethics* (Keleher 2017). I introduce each of these levels below:

- *Meta-ethics* considers higher order questions of value, the meaning of concepts, and any universal truths about ethics including: What is the Good? What is the good life or the good society? Is freedom intrinsically valuable? Are there moral duties? What does it mean to be more or less human? The question, *what is development?* And other foundational issues are discussed at this level.

- *Normative ethics* is concerned with the principles or other action guiding content or standards of moral behavior. Immanuel Kant's categorical imperative – "We ought never treat humanity whether in ourselves or another person merely as a means, but always as an end" – and Jeremy Bentham's grounding of utilitarianism – "We ought to approve or disapprove of every action according to the tendency it appears to have to augment or diminish the happiness of the party whose interest is in question" – are two prominent examples of the sort of theories found at this level.

- *Applied or practical ethics* considers more specific issues or realms of human action in a way that generates subject-specific guidelines or positions on specific questions. For example, the realm of medical ethics, or the specific question of whether or not physician-assisted suicide is morally permissible. Likewise, agricultural ethics, or the specific question of whether or not it is morally permissible to use agrochemical inputs that generate higher yields, but undermine sustainability, and may have long-term implications for human health. Note that these questions are normative questions, but that applied ethics is considered a third domain of ethics because it focuses on ethical practice or moral behavior in certain realms of life.

- *Personal or integral ethics* is the level at which we as individuals must consider the moral dimensions of our particular actions as an individual part of the various realms of life in which we participate and how we might integrate choices made in various spheres of our lives including commitments, duties, relationships, abilities, and resources. For example, consider Samantha, an agro-economist who works for a large development firm whose work undermines sustainability. Samantha personally believes that sustainability ought to be a high priority, especially in development interventions. How does she reconcile this belief with her work at the firm? She has used the established channels to suggest changes, but finds that people in authority simply dismiss her. She suspects that these dismissals are at least in part because she is a woman and the people in authority at her firm are all somewhat sexist men who tend not to listen to women. Quitting her job would mean losing the health plan that pays for her expensive medications, and would compromise her ability to provide for her three children.[7]

I explain and argue for inclusion of this fourth level below, but I first want to give an example to help readers understand how our considerations at the lower levels might be influenced by insights generated at the higher levels and vice versa. Consider Samantha the agro-economist, how does she integrate her conviction that sustainability ought to be a high priority? If her own voice is not listened to in her sexist workplace, she might try to find male and female allies who share her views and can promote the views in a way that can be heard. She might also find allies to help undermine and transform the sexist culture at work. Of course, whether or not these strategies make sense for Samantha will depend on a number of factors, but assume for our example that they do. Samantha's personal behavior will reflect her belief that unsustainable agricultural is immoral, which reflects her view in environmental ethics, which is grounded in a utilitarian notion that protecting the planet will ultimately result in the greatest happiness for the greatest number of people, which is grounded in a meta-ethical understanding of the good as happiness. Similarly, her experience of not being heard might lead her to think more about individual rights and eventually rethink her utilitarian leanings. This is just one quick and messy example, but I hope it gives readers some idea of how theory and practice can be related in context.

I propose a fourth domain of personal or integral ethics to the standard list of three domains because I think it is helpful to explicitly recognize that each of us must deliberately consider our own particular actions and how we integrate our choices made in various spheres into the personal context of our individual lives. I believe that most of us want to consider such questions so that we can live with integrity in light of our personal situations with many – often competing – demands. But, I also realize that to presuppose integrity is valuable is to beg a significant meta-ethical question, which would limit academic discussion about ethics and thereby limit philosophical inquiry. I wish to keep the gates of inquiry in this fourth domain wide open to reasonable points of view (even if I don't share them). So, this fourth domain is a space to discuss how we integrate our choices into our individual lives, and one possible (but in my view undesirable) answer is we do not integrate our choices, but instead consider each decision as it arises.[8] Like applied or practical ethics, *personal or integral ethics* is another level of normative ethics. But it too should be considered an additional domain of ethics because it focuses on the ethical practice of whole persons. Applied or practical ethics seeks to provide guidelines for operating in a specific field or realm of life. In contrast, personal or integral ethics focuses on persons as they simultaneously navigate the various realms of life.

I believe discussion at this level has been largely avoided thus far because most recognize that it would be unwise, even if it were not impossible, to try to develop an authoritative one-size-fits-all strategy for navigating the moral dimensions of our particular actions as an individual part of the various realms of life in which we participate. At the same time, to simply say "it depends on the person and her situation" is at best unhelpful, and at worst leaves the door too wide open to a dangerous moral relativism. (Of course, moral relativism would be one *academic* option at this level, no matter how undesirable.) Navigating these waters may be as difficult and dangerous as navigating Homer's Strait of Messina with Charybdis who will swallow us whole in a one-size-fits-all account on one side and the relativism of Scylla with her too many heads on the other. Nevertheless, we must risk this danger and engage in this level of ethical inquiry. Personal or integral ethics is of vital importance as it allows us to think critically about how we might integrate the abstract meta-ethical concepts and puzzles with the reality of the problems of people. For example, this fourth dimension is a space where those working within development, including academics who publish, speak publicly, and are otherwise active participants in development must ask: *On what issues do I focus my energy in publishing and teaching? Are my consumption choices in line with my views on development?* Asking these and other questions may be the best way to help us to meet Singer's challenge of establishing a way of life in which theory and practice "if not yet in harmony, are at least coming together."

I submit that within development ethics, ethical reflection on the ends and means of development should take place at each of these levels. Obviously, there is a good deal of disagreement and debate at each level of ethical reflection. It should now be abundantly clear from the discussion in this chapter that the methods and insights of philosophy, including abstract logical analysis and arguments, are valuable and relevant to fruitfully engaging these debates in a way most likely to result in authentic development. Thus, philosophers make relevant and valuable contributions to development and development ethics.

Yet, as Crocker rightly recognizes, philosophy may be necessary for development, but it is not sufficient. Philosophers are not the only ones who bring valuable skills to development, or even to development ethics. Philosophers should have a seat at the table, but the table must also have room for political scientists, agricultural specialists, lawyers, anthropologists, medical experts, religious experts, educators, engineers, and many others. We must all work together to answer Crocker's call to practice ethical development that is at once "interdisciplinary, institutionally and empirically informed, and policy-relevant."

Thales Gets the Last Laugh

This chapter began with Plato's story of Thales being mocked because he was so distracted by his distant philosophical concerns that he did not see the real and practical issues in front of him and fell into a well. Plato warns that philosophers will always be mocked by those who think philosophy is useless. In his *Politics* (1259a9–18), Aristotle tells another story about Thales to show that philosophers *choose* to do philosophy because they recognize its value.

The story goes that when they were reproaching [Thales] for his poverty, supposing that philosophy is useless, he learned from his astronomy that the olive crop would be large. Then, while it was still winter, he obtained a little money and made deposits on all the olive presses both in Miletus and in Chios, and since no one bid against him, he rented them cheaply. When the time came, suddenly many requested the presses all at once, and he rented them out on whatever terms he wished, and so he made a great deal of money. In this way he proved that philosophers can easily be wealthy if they wish, but this is not what they are interested in.

Notes

1. Here "valuable" means "can enrich people's lives" or benefit people. To determine what it means to benefit people is another philosophical exploration for another paper.
2. Aristotle's *ergon* argument holds that because reasoning about and acting in accordance with propositions is something only human beings can do, doing so is our proper function. In response, Robert Nozick asks: "If man turned out to be unique only in having a sense of humor, would it follow that he should concentrate his energies on inventing and telling jokes?" (1981, 56).
3. This way of understanding development also fits well with the human development capability approach and the Human Development Index used by the United Nations Development Programme, the integral human development introduced by Catholic Social Tradition, and several other schools of thought found in development studies.
4. For a deeper discussion of what makes for worthwhile authentic development, see Crocker 2008; Drydyk 2011, 2016; Gasper 2016; Goulet 1977, 1995; Keleher 2017; Drydyk and Keleher 2019.
5. Work in philosophy of science (Harding 1995; 2004 and Kuhn 1970; 2000) has led me to believe that given the relationship between our perceptions of reality and scientific knowledge, the vast majority of work in economics is normative whether we recognize it or not. For a good general discussion on the positive and normative aspects of development economics, see Gasper (2016).
6. This adversarial approach is a descendant of the Socratic *elenchus*, a procedure for rational scrutiny.
7. There are several situations people living in poverty regularly face in light of limited access to resources and opportunities. I choose to highlight an example of a person of privilege, who is more likely to be similar to those likely to read this chapter in the hope that the example is relatable to readers.

8. For example, some forms of the ethical theory *act-utilitarianism* might require that we evaluate each action independently of how it fits with any of our other actions.

References

Cavalier, Robert. 2002. "Meta-Ethics, Normative Ethics, and Applied Ethics." *Online Guide to Ethics and Moral Philosophy*. http://caae.phil.cmu.edu/Cavalier/80130/part2/II_preface.html.

Crocker, David A. 1991. "Toward Development Ethics." *World Development* 19(5): 457–483.

Crocker, David A. 2008. *Ethics of Global Development: Agency, Capability, and Deliberative Democracy*. Cambridge University Press.

Dewey, John. 1929. *Characters and Events: Popular Essays in Social and Political Philosophy* (Vol. I). New York: Henry Holt.

Diogenes Laertius. 1925. *Lives of Eminent Philosophers*. Translated by R. D. Hicks. Two volumes. Cambridge, MA: Harvard University Press.

Dotson, Kirstie. 2013. "How Is This Paper Philosophy?" *Comparative Philosophy* 3(1): 3–29.

Dower, Nigel 2008. "The Nature and Scope of Development Ethics." *Journal of Global Ethics* 10(2): 249–262.

Drydyk, Jay. 2011. "Development Ethics." In *Encyclopedia of Global Justice*. Deen Chatterjee (ed.). New York: Springer.

Drydyk, Jay. 2016. "Ethical Issues in Development." In *The Palgrave Handbook of International Development*. Jean Grugel and Daniel Hammett (eds.). London: Palgrave Macmillan.

Drydyk, Jay and Lori Keleher (eds.). 2018. *Routledge Handbook of Development Ethics*. New York: Taylor & Francis.

Escobar, Arturo. 1984. "Discourse and Power in Development: Michel Foucault and the Relevance of His Work to the Third World." *Alternatives* 10(3): 377–400.

Escobar, Arturo. 1995. *Encountering Development: The Making and Unmaking of the Third World*. Princeton University Press.

Esteva, Gustavo. 1985. "Development: Myth, Metaphor, Myth, Threat." *Development Seeds of Change* 3: 78–79.

Fieser, James. n.d. "Ethics." *Internet Encyclopedia of Philosophy*. www.iep.utm.edu/ethics/.

Frodeman, Robert and Adam Briggle. 2015. "Socrates Untenured." *Inside Higher Ed*. January 13, 2015. www.insidehighered.com/views/2015/01/13/essay-problems-philosophy-academe.

Gasper, Des. 2016. "Ethics of Development." In *Introduction to International Development: Approaches, Actors, Issues, and Practices.* Paul A. Haslam, Jessica Schafer, and Pierre Beaudet (eds.). Third edn. Oxford University Press.

Goulet, Denis. 1977. *The Crucial Choice: A New Concept in the Theory of Development.* New York: Atheneum.

Goulet, Denis. 1995. *Development Ethics: A Guide to Theory and Practice.* New York: Zed Books Ltd.

Hall, David L. and Roger T. Ames. 1987. *Thinking through Confucius.* New York: SUNY Press.

Harding, Sandra. 1995. "'Strong Objectivity': A Response to the New Objectivity Question." *Synthese* 104(3): 331–349.

Harding, Sandra. 2004. "Introduction: Standpoint Theory as a Site of Political, Philosophic, and Scientific Debate." In *The Feminist Standpoint Theory Reader: Intellectual and Political Controversies.* Sandra Harding (ed.). Abingdon, UK: Routledge.

Haslanger, Sally. 2017. "Focus on the Fire, Not the Spark." *Daily Nous.* May 4, 2017. http://dailynous.com/2017/05/04/focus-fire-not-spark -guest-post-sally-haslanger/.

Heidegger, Martin. 1954. *Einführung in die Metaphysik.* Berlin: De Gruyter.

Irvine, Andrew David and Harry Deutsch. 2016. "Russell's Paradox." In *The Stanford Encyclopedia of Philosophy.* Edward N. Zalta (ed.). Winter 2016 edn. https://plato.stanford.edu/archives/win2016/entries/ russell-paradox/.

Keleher, Lori. 2014. "Three and a Half Approaches to Development." A National Endowment for the Humanities Edsitement Information Page.

Keleher, Lori. 2017. "Toward an Integral Human Development Ethics." *Veritas: Revista de Filosofía y Teología* 37: 19–34.

Kuhn, Thomas S. 1970. *The Structure of Scientific Revolutions.* Second edn. University of Chicago Press.

Kuhn, Thomas S. 2000. *The Road since Structure.* James Conant and John Haugeland (eds.). The University of Chicago Press.

Nozick, Robert. 1981. *Philosophical Explanations.* Cambridge, MA: Harvard University Press.

Nussbaum, Martha C. 2003. *Upheavals of Thought: The Intelligence of Emotions.* Cambridge University Press.

Pieper, Josef. 1992. *In Defense of Philosophy: Classical Wisdom Stands Up to Modern Challenges.* San Francisco: Ignatius Press.

Robbins, Lionel. 2007. *An Essay on the Nature and Significance of Economic Science.* Auburn, AL: Ludwig von Mises Institute.

Russell, Bertrand. 2009. "Philosophy's Ulterior Motives." In *Unpopular Essays*. New York: Routledge (44–55).

Searle, John. 2014. Interview by Tim Crane ("John Searle: The Philosopher in the World"). *New York Review of Books*. June 20, 2014. www .nybooks.com/blogs/nyrblog/2014/jun/20/john-searle-philosopher-world/.

Sengupta, Mitu. 2019. "Post Development School." In *Routledge Handbook of Development Ethics*. Jay Drydyk and Lori Keleher (eds.). New York: Taylor & Francis.

Singer, Peter. 1972. "Famine, Affluence, and Morality." *Philosophy & Public Affairs* 1(3): 229–243.

Singer, Peter. 2004. *One World: The Ethics of Globalization*. New Haven, CT: Yale University Press.

Unger, Peter. 2014. *Empty Ideas: A Critique of Analytic Philosophy*. Oxford University Press.

Wittgenstein, Ludwig. 1922. *Tractatus Logico-Philosophicus*. London: Kegan Paul, Trench, Trubner & Co., Ltd.

Ziai, Aram. 2007. "Development Discourse and Its Critics: An Introduction to Post-Development." In *Exploring Post-Development: Theory and Practice, Problems and Perspectives*. Ziai Aram (ed.). Abingdon, UK: Routledge (3–17).

Ziai, Aram. 2004. "The Ambivalence of Post-Development: Between Reactionary Populism and Radical Democracy." *Third World Quarterly* 25(6): 1045–1060.

Ziai, Aram. 2013. "The Discourse of 'Development' and Why the Concept Should Be Abandoned." *Development in Practice* 23(1): 123–136.

2 | *What Is Development?* *

ERIC PALMER

We are familiar, by this point, with what development is not. It is not gross national product, not gross domestic product divided by a country's population, not gross national income per person. It is not median household income, the latest in this family of simple economic measures (Rose, Birdsall and Diofasi 2016). Philosophers still find it a standard move to point out the inadequacy of financial measures of development, well-being, and human security (e.g., Nussbaum 2011, ix); and such repudiation is also common among economists, who hedge their claims about the value of financial measures, then proceed to rely upon them anyway (e.g., Sundaram 2016). This remains the state of discussion even though nearly fifty years have passed since development economist Dudley Seers criticized his colleagues' "continued addiction" to simple econometrics and their "lip service" to philosophies of development. Seers continues: "we must ask ourselves: what are the necessary conditions for a universally accepted aim, the realisation of the potential of human personality?" (1969, 1, 3).

Seers calls for a theory of development; many have since written to present answers that reflect the concerns he articulates. His choice of expression, "the realisation of the potential of human personality," evokes the language of psychology. The current best effort at such a theory, the Capability Approach, instead incorporates language from philosophy, referring to liberal conceptions of freedom and an Aristotelian conception of flourishing. Development presents the parameters for such flourishing, characterizing the expansion of freedoms and the creation of capabilities worth having as the conditions for development of the good life.

* Very great thanks go to Lori Keleher and Stacy Kosko for their patient editorial support. Thanks go also to Keleher and Christine Koggel for substantial comment on this chapter.

49

This chapter is not focused upon capabilities, their characterization or the means to their realization, though those topics will be touched upon late in the chapter. It is primarily an inquiry into axiology – also called the study of value, or normativity.[1] Its main proposal is simple enough: value is human and social, so development is human and social. Each of these claims about value requires elaboration. First, value is human, it is characteristic of dependent, biological creatures; and second, it is social, generated by humans within social relations that involve such dependence. Because conceiving of some values involves social processes that play out over time, some revision of liberal political theory is necessary. The liberal tradition slights both relational characteristics of human life and dialectical aspects of value creation in its characterization of the autonomous individual who stands as the political subject, the subject of central concern within its theories of justice. The need for revision carries over to treatment of political process in the Capability Approach; the chapter's penultimate section will indicate that need as it pertains to Martha Nussbaum's offering of a list of central capabilities as a guide to the drafting of national constitutions.

My argument draws particularly from Carol Gould's articulation of social ontology, from Denis Goulet's account of the dialectic of recognition in underdevelopment and from David Crocker's focus upon deliberative democracy. Given Crocker's role, the argument seems especially suited to this volume. He began his path toward understanding development more than three decades ago. He was influenced particularly by Seers' question, his own early study of humanist Marxism and Goulet's action and philosophical reflection. Crocker's approach has since converged with the Capability Approach, and he endorses and articulates an "agency-focused version of capability ethics" in *Ethics of Global Development* (2008).[2] Crocker's work began especially as an intimate study of the political articulation of development; the following section will show how it continues to display that focus after he joins his thought with the Capability Approach.

David Crocker's Critical Study of Development

David Crocker's contribution to the ethics and politics of global development grew from roots in critical theory and Latin American politics. His early writing followed upon study in the mid-1970s with Belgrade social theorists Mihailo Marković and Svetozar Stojanović, who led an intellectual circle and produced a journal, *Praxis*, that aimed to create "a body of thought which is uncompromising in its rejection of all forms of human alienation, exploitation oppression and injustice, regardless of the type of society – bourgeois or socialist."[3] A visiting professorship in Costa Rica in 1986–7 allowed Crocker a perch from which to view and reflect upon policy developments, some of which reflected what John Williamson would characterize late in the decade as "the Washington Consensus." Costa Rica was turning toward international markets at the time and reducing the state's role in economic decisions. This was a shift away from social democracy and import substitution industrialization, an economic strategy intended to limit a nation's dependence on foreign markets. Crocker urged in place of both old and new trends "an ethically superior development model that gives highest priority not to economic growth but to basic human needs, democratic self-determination, environmental respect, and the real opportunity for personal development" (1989, 317). He named his view "participative eco-development"; it featured the abovementioned four "fundamental, normative principles" and allowed for the possibility of conceiving further dimensions for development theory.[4]

Crocker was one among philosophers from several traditions articulating new thinking on the relation of human concerns to older political and economic ideals of development. The "satisfaction of basic needs," which Crocker lists first among his principles, had been introduced into international development as an ideal at a 1976 International Labour Organization conference. The Basic Needs Approach also took root within the United Nations agency charged with the promotion of technical assistance, the UN Development Program. Crocker's approach, by contrast, focused upon harmony with the environment and on democratic deliberation in the context of development. Alongside humanist Marxism, Crocker would find inspiration in American pragmatism, especially due to a summer's study with Richard Rorty in 1979. These influences led him to call for a "development theory-practice" focused upon both "insiders" and development workers as "partial insiders," rather than upon the national and international institutions that promote uniform development standards (1991b, 459–61, 468–69; 1991a).

The separation from formal global institutions distinguished Crocker's approach from Amartya Sen's emerging paradigm in economics and philosophy, the Capability Approach. With Sen's support, the approach was well suited to find its place within the UN Development Program, providing the underpinnings for its first *Human Development Report* of 1990. The Capability Approach would gain Martha Nussbaum's attention and in the late 1980s she would connect it to her own thoughts on Marxian and Aristotelian conceptions of development (2000, 70; 2001, xix). Nussbaum conceived her exploration of capabilities first as the identification of "certain features of our common humanity" (1987b, 27) and later also as "the basis for fundamental political principles focused on the lives of women in developing countries," as she puts it in *Women and Human Development* (2000, xiii). This would lead her to an argument concerning constitutional principles, particularly detailed in *Frontiers of Justice* (2006) and work thereafter. Crocker's engagement, by contrast, was grounded in "the cultural identity of groups, populations, and societies," with a focus on their self-determination (1991b, 462).

The Capability Approach in its early development, then, was built from economic philosophy engaged with international institutions by Sen. Nussbaum added an Aristotelian theory married to liberalism. And Crocker's participative eco-development approach arose from social theory and engagement with peoples and development practitioners. Crocker's distinctive background emerges within a reply to Nussbaum's well-known proposal of a list of the central human capabilities and its use in politics (Crocker 2008, ch. 6). I will suggest in the next section that the developmental path that Nussbaum's theory takes, particularly over the span from 1987 to 2007, may serve to explain some characteristics that have left it subject to Crocker's criticism. Nussbaum first discusses capabilities in an Aristotelian reply to Rawls's liberalism and she settles upon the ideal of constitutional guarantees for capabilities later. As her work develops from philosophical analysis of politics to claims about the actual operations of government, and as she particularly develops an account of the function of a constitution in a just society, her proposal retains a specific role for a philosopher within a political context – and there's the rub.

The Development of Nussbaum's List and Crocker's Critical Rejoinder

Aristotle serves Nussbaum as a fruitful source for criticism of contemporary liberal thinkers and in that context his writing provides the platform for her first articulation of the Capability Approach. In "Nature, Function and Capability: Aristotle on Political Distribution," which first appeared as one of two 1987 working papers of the United Nations University World Institute for Development Economics Research (UNU-WIDER), Nussbaum brings Aristotle's thought to bear on John Rawls's account of distributive justice. Her focus is upon wealth and worth:

No item's worth can be properly assessed if we do not set it in the context of a thicker theory of good living; and when we do so, we discover that wealth has no independent worth. Rawls's theory, then, is too thin. His list ... ascribes independent significance to items whose worth can only be seen in connection with the truly primary items. (1987a, 10)

Nussbaum's analysis contrasts those truly primary items, capabilities, with Rawls's concept of primary goods. One primary good is wealth; other "social primary goods" that Rawls notes show a closer relation to the central capabilities that would appear later in Nussbaum's lists, as he includes rights, liberties, access to political institutions and access to other social institutions that support "the social bases of self respect."[5] Nussbaum characterizes the "truly primary items" that promote the "functionings of individuals" as internal capabilities ("I-capabilities"). These differ from the "external conditions for those functionings" (the "E-capabilities"), including wealth (1987a, 22, 24). Some internal capabilities may be developed through external conditions afforded by the state – through a system of public education, for example. Nussbaum argues that "Aristotle repeatedly insists that one of the legislator's first and most essential tasks is the provision of an adequate scheme for the education of the young" and she generalizes this view to indicate the role of the state in the "development of I-capabilities" (21).

"Nature, Function and Capability," then, shifts the focus in political theory from the classic foci of distributive justice to the E-capabilities. It introduces a discussion of the role of the state that develops greatly within Nussbaum's writing over the following two decades. The article lays the ground for her list of central capabilities in the claim that "we need to specify the list of things that we want people to be capable of doing and doing by their choice" (1987a, 12). Beyond supporting external conditions for I-capabilities, the role for the legislator is not further developed in the 1987 article, which, as the title indicates, is a discussion of "Aristotle on political distribution." In the early 1990s

Nussbaum develops her list of "Basic Human Functional Capabilities" and argues that ideals such as these should "be the goal of legislation and public planning" (1992, 221–22). Later, her claim is more specific: "the idea of a threshold level of capabilities, can provide a basis for central constitutional principles" (2000, 12; see also, 2002; 2003). New detail in political and legal theory arises in writing from 2006 forward, as Nussbaum articulates her account in light of Rawls's *Political Liberalism* and remarks that "One way of thinking about the capabilities list is to think of it as embodied in a list of constitutional guarantees, in something analogous to the Indian Constitution or the (shorter) Bill of Rights of the U.S. Constitution" (2006, 6, 155). Nussbaum's constitutional argument might be taken to have reached full maturity as she presents it to US jurists, highlighting an Aristotelian thread in the fabric of the modern legal tradition, in a *Harvard Law Review* article of 2007:

For several centuries, an approach to the foundation of basic political principles that draws its key insights from Aristotle and the ancient Greek and Roman Stoics has played a role in shaping European and American conceptions of the proper role of government, the purpose of constitution-making, and the nature of basic constitutional entitlements. This normative approach, the "Capability Approach" (CA), holds that a key task of a nation's constitution, and the legal tradition that interprets it, is to secure for all citizens the prerequisites of a life worthy of human dignity – a core group of "capabilities" – in areas of central importance to human life. (2007, 7; see also 56–73; fn. 15)

What was developed in 1987 as a list of characteristics of "humanness" coupled with Aristotle's views of the role of the "legislator" in their cultivation, then, has developed into normative claims about entitlements within national constitutions (1987a, 47). Nussbaum's thought evolves from political theory to claims about actual governance, yielding a list that would eventually be directed as much to practicing legislators as to academic philosophers. This political ideal provides a specific role for the philosopher in political discussion (2000, 104), presented in the "contention that the capabilities are a template for constitution-making or for constitutional entitlements in nations without a written constitution" (2014, 4).

Amartya Sen has at times greatly overstated Nussbaum's claims regarding both characteristics and uses of such a list of central capabilities. Sen worries over the possibility of its use as a piece of "pure theory" in "a cemented list of capabilities, which is absolutely complete (nothing could be added to it) and totally fixed (it could not respond to public reasoning and to the formation of social values)" (2004, 78). Some of Nussbaum's own words may point to such interpretation: the expression "template" suggests as much, as does an early article, "Human functioning and social justice: In defense of Aristotelian essentialism," which purports to characterize over five pages "the shape of the human form of life" (1992, 216–21). Even within that presentation, however, Nussbaum also presents her "essentialist proposal" as "a thick vague theory of the good" – so it is "theory" (and not "cemented") and it is vague, "deliberately so ... for ... it admits of much multiple specification in accordance with varied local and personal conceptions" (1992, 215; see also Keleher 2017, 65–68). Sen would prefer that simple openness replace such flexibility: "public discussion and reasoning can lead to a better understanding of the role, reach, and the significance of particular capabilities" (2004, 79). He also holds that "some of the basic capabilities (with which my 1979 Tanner Lecture was particularly concerned) will no doubt figure in every list of relevant capabilities in every society," so Sen also has a list – his concern lies in its proposal in the political forum (2004, 79).

David Crocker is also concerned especially with the list's influence upon the function of public reasoning. It is a philosopher's intrusion, a prior theory that encumbers the theory-practice of politics: he writes, "while philosophical dialogue aims solely at the truth or at least at reasoned agreement on beliefs and values, in democratic deliberation fellow citizens deliberate over, decide on, and bind themselves to problem-solving policies that most (all) can accept" (2008, 199). In the context of the creation of national constitutions, "people have the right and responsibility to form collective values and decide practical policies together" (208–9, and see 196ff.). These concerns continue a line of thought from much earlier in his writing, the view that we ought to elucidate "valuational dimensions ... in ways appropriate to any basic beliefs – through critical dialogue" (1991b, 467),

Crocker, then, has doubts about the philosopher's assumed role, and about the approach from a "template." His attention continues to focus on the shapes that power takes within hierarchies and groups and on the possibilities for improvement offered by individual agency, participatory democracy and development work. In such criticism, born of work spanning three decades, we find a distillation of what has made Crocker's effort distinctive and especially valuable as a contribution to the characterization of development and its ethical practice. Crocker's early focus within Marxist humanism laid the ground for his challenge to Nussbaum's approach to framing constitutions. This chapter will extend the challenge, following a foray into axiology.

Liberal Individualism, Relational Autonomy, and Dialectical Change

"Collective values" and "shared values" are expressions that are familiar enough. They are often meant to indicate that members of a group arrive at a condition that each individual agrees to or tacitly admits to, perhaps through consensus, democratic politics or continuation of a practice.[6] A group of friends agrees to watch one movie that some prefer tonight, planning to reassemble another day for the option preferred by the others; a legislator convinces her party to vote for and pass a bill; I see the point of laws that keep traffic on the right side of the road – these are cases that display the presence of values that reflect our choices for coordination and for collective decision-making.

In some cases, the values we arrive at have a distinctive property: they would not otherwise have been conceived by any of the individuals among us, but for the activity of the group, or of a group in the past. An example developed later in this chapter presents the possibility that individuals within different cultures may understand relationships to nature in very different ways that are "incompatible" (Cortez 2014, 337). Such incompatibility suggests that, to explain the difference, a story needs to be told about the way individuals in the cultures think of value, and an account explaining the fact of what they value will say too little. To explain both value and fact, the story would have to consider the history of people interacting, with different histories informing different values for various people. Such history of cultures may explain how value is conceived, as well as indicate what is valued.[7] So, there is a second sense in which these particular values are collective: they are born of collective activity that goes beyond being agreed upon by a collectivity of individuals.

I suggest that values relevant to adequate political and development theory are created as historical products of interaction that is not just agreement among individuals. To articulate this view I will draw from Carol Gould's formulation of feminist relational theory and Denis Goulet's development theory. I will invoke a familiar theory of process and say that values are dialectical products, or (better) dialectical processes, since they may continue to change. The products, but not the processes, are acknowledged within the reasoning and agreements at the focus of liberal theories, but accounting for the values of individuals in this way will not provide a sufficiently comprehensive account of the political process that allows us to discern just political arrangements or ethical development. Modern liberal theorists since Immanuel Kant, however, do generally maintain that agreement by individuals, under appropriate conditions, will suffice. I argue that such a modern conception gives too slight a regard to the social processes from which values that would not otherwise have come to be recognized are dialectically produced, and it may, as a result, yield too spare a treatment of public reasoning.

Kant presents the paradigm formulation of the modern assumption that the autonomous individual is of value, beginning the *Groundwork of the Metaphysics of Morals* with the claim, "It is impossible to think of anything at all in the world, or indeed even beyond it, that could be considered good without limitation except a good will" (4:393). The individual discerns value through practical reason, which generates a maxim that reflects Kant's opening claim (4:420–1, footnotes). The person of good will subjectively recognizes the absolute value of each will by observing rational limits upon individual activity; the modern state presents an "objective" solution to such problems of encroachment (*Metaphysics of Morals*, 6: 307–11; see also *Perpetual Peace*, 8:349). Those rational limits are the transmuted remnants of the ideal of interpersonal agreement that is found in the social contract tradition prior to Kant: his rational grounding for the state rejects both the historical fiction of the agreement that dissolves the state of nature in Hobbes and the explicit contract suggested by Rousseau. Instead, Kant holds that the "ethical law-giving" of the individual will determines "morality" and its law. The process is "internal" and subjective, and it underwrites "external lawgiving": it provides the basis of "right," which is "the external and indeed practical relation of one person to another, insofar as their actions, as deeds, can have (direct or indirect) influence on each other" (6:219, 6:230). The state is that external or objective lawgiving: "a system of laws for a people ... [who] need a rightful condition under a will uniting them, a *constitution*, so they may enjoy what is laid down as right" (6:306, 6:311). This is an atomization of the older social contract model of political relations, reducing interpersonal agreement to the pure practical reasoning of each individual. Kant also holds that the state is a "moral person." Though it is not actually composed through agreement, it is not a mere fiction; it is an entity, a "society of human beings that no-one other than itself can command or dispose of" (8:344). Kant's state is an image of the Leviathan, Hobbes' artificial person that is produced by agreement and able "to submit their wills, every one to his will." But in Kant the genuinely social remnant of the contract has disappeared: political theory and ethics become the purview of autonomous individuals as each submits to law that is the individual's own lawful willing. I need only check with myself and I need not contract with others: this is the case for each autonomous, reasoning individual who operates as legislator within "the kingdom of ends" (4:432–33).

The places Kant gives to the state and its constitution in the passages just noted indicate how liberal theories generally continue to treat the apportioning of value (to individuals), the conferral of value (by individuals) and the discernment of shared value (by individuals who generate agreements) (e.g., Korsgaard 2009, 123, 157). The political sphere is taken foremost as a space for ensuring that the individual is treated fairly, or is treated with dignity. Acting within the political sphere, we individuals agree to and commit to freedoms and entitlements for all; or, in Kant's terms, each of us legislates for himself or herself within the kingdom of ends. John Rawls carries the Kantian tradition forward by carefully disentangling political theory from Kant's metaphysics, arriving at the position of "political liberalism." For Rawls, "the constitution is seen as a just political procedure which incorporates the equal political liberties and seeks to assure their fair value so that the processes of political decision are open to all on a roughly equal basis" (1993, 99–116, 337). Nussbaum draws these threads into her own thoughts on constitutions and the Capability Approach.

Within liberal political theory, then, the focus rests upon freedoms for individuals and agreements that are attuned to reasoning by and deliberation among individuals. I think it is not misleading to rephrase this as the claim that individuals are the subjects of political theory, or are fundamental as the subjects countenanced within just politics; that is, value is conceived and understood by the individual, judged to belong to just social arrangements through employment of a capacity for practical reasoning by the individual, and evaluation occurs in reference to the good of individual humans, and perhaps also other sentient creatures.

I propose an alternative account. First, at least some value is collective in the second (dialectical) sense outlined at the start of this section. Second, an alternative account of the subject within political theory can be paired with such a theory of value: an account that takes each subject not as an autonomous will, but as an individual-in-relations. I will note two sources for such an account. Carol Gould's social ontology challenges the liberal conception of the individual, replacing it with the individual-in-relations. Denis Goulet's dialectical theory of development implicitly presents an account of the creation of value through social processes. For the purposes of political theory, these two modifications may be required to assess justice. They may similarly be required to assess development.

Carol Gould on Autonomy and Denis Goulet on Dialectical Change

Carol Gould's *Interactive Democracy* (2014) presents an account of the individual's place within just political arrangements. Gould draws upon recent work in feminist relational theory, a generalized and theoretically attuned descendant of care ethics.[8] Before approaching Gould's account, consider an explanation of the relational character of the individual and her responsibilities within care ethics, authored by Selma Sevenhuijsen:

"The ethics of care starts from the recognition that care is a moral practice, a disposition, a daily need, and a way of living. In opposition to individualism and neo-liberalism it acknowledges vulnerability, interconnectedness, dependency embodiment and finitude as basic characteristics of human life" (2013).

The individual, for the purposes of ethical theory, is understood within the context of such relations of connection to others. This is the starting assumption for an account of relational autonomy:

autonomous activity is pursued in a context, and in that context the individual's possibilities for choice are tied to embodiment and to others' choices. Sevenhuijsen continues:

[The ethics of care] develops a set of values and virtues about how to deal with this in a potentially wide range of practices, from child care and care for the elderly, to psychiatry, economy and international relations. It acknowledges the contribution of all the participants in caring practices in the deliberation about what constitutes a good life and good care and about the practical conditions of its provision.

Care ethics displays values that appear particularly in caregiving and in women's lives. Care is of political relevance: as the call of second wave feminism reminds us, the personal is political. Sevenhuijsen concludes her gloss with a call to reform politics: "Of course this implies a normative position in itself: caring about care implies democratic and inclusive forms of deliberation and a broad notion of citizenship."

Care ethics enriches liberal political theory by displaying how choices and relations are informed by values that are neglected in nonrelational framings of human well-being, goodness and justice. The social arrangements that reflect women's activities contribute to shaping the rights-holder, or the subject within liberal theories of justice. Carol Gould's introduction of relational theory in *Interactive Democracy* extends Sevenhuijsen's line of thought, providing an explicit challenge to liberal theory:

Going beyond liberal understandings of the individual (whether in terms of rational choice or utility maximization), the theory of social reality (or *social ontology*) that underlies this work takes people to be "individuals-in-relations." As subjects, they have a capacity for freedom, but also require a set of basic conditions to make this freedom effective, including equal forms of social recognition and access to the material means of life. The human rights that protect and give expression to their freedom go beyond bare legal requirements to moral desiderata; they serve as goals for developing political, economic, and social institutions that would help to fulfill them. (2014, 3)

Gould indicates in the first sentence that the liberal understanding of the individual may be an inadequate concept for politics. She situates human rights as both ends and means, since they may create some of the conditions for their own realization. She is also expressing a political approach that is familiar from Marx: the analysis of the conditions for the maintenance of political order, or the conditions for a reproduction of society over time, either as a dynamic or as a static (unchanging) social order.

Gould's reconception of individuals as individuals-in-relations presents a radical critique of the modern liberal conception of the individual as the subject of politics. Women's practices marked by caring relations are among the institutions of society that produce the conditions under which people gain their capacity for freedom. Gould also slips the expression "developing" into her explanation: though she is writing about social ontology, she may also be indicating that value is produced dialectically. The institutions we navigate may inform our understanding of freedom, since values to which individuals aspire are products of the social conditions in which the individuals find themselves. As Georg Lukács explained, "It is not men's consciousness that determines their existence, but on the contrary, their social existence that determines their consciousness" (1972, 18).

The idea that both value itself and the freedom to achieve what one values are generated through social processes has also been articulated in the context of development theory by Denis Goulet. Central to his account of development is the moment of recognition of difference and vulnerability that arises from the comparison of one's own condition with that of another. Goulet's explanation is implicitly patterned on the dialectic of master and slave; he refers to the dialectical moment of recognition as "the shock of underdevelopment," suggesting that a shock of realization that occurs when one is faced with another produces the condition within which the individual conceives of new possibilities for living (1971, 26). This leads to a collective condition that may then create political change in the process of development:

Once they become conscious of the meaning of their situation of deprivation, masses throughout the world begin thinking in explicitly political terms. This happens in all serious efforts at cultural mobilization. . . . They now begin to experience their condition as unnecessary vulnerability in the face of death, disease, hunger and the quest for dignity and freedom to control their own destinies. (1971, 42–44)

Goulet's account is implicitly patterned on Marx's idea of class consciousness, the situation of a group coming to realize that it is a "class for itself." His point, with the nineteenth-century trappings removed, is that new understanding that could not otherwise become available arises through human interaction, and political change that is development arises through such understanding.

If, as Gould argues, social and material conditions produce the subject of politics and if, as Goulet argues, the ability to conceive of new possibilities is the product of social interaction, then political approaches that neglect such interaction and such conditions will be prone to disregard aspects that are of importance to development. To close this chapter, I will try to explain these concerns in the context of Nussbaum's suggestion of a role for a list of central capabilities as a "template for constitution-making."

Central Capabilities, Important Capabilities, and Constitutional Guarantees

Nussbaum has clear and excellent reasons for demanding that central capabilities should find their image within law: she wishes to ensure "fundamental political entitlements" that reflect dignity, she wishes to ensure these through liberal democratic processes and she is aware that politics occurs in the context of struggles within which some are at a disadvantage – especially minority groups within nations and women around the globe (2011, 19, 71–73). Nussbaum finds use for the language of rights, as opposed to capabilities, in politics, since, "To say 'Here's a list of things that people ought to be able to do and to be' has only vague normative resonance. To say 'Here's a list of fundamental rights' is more rhetorically direct" (2000, 100; see also 2011, 68). And she finds merit in situating rights within slowly evolving foundational documents – state constitutions that enumerate freedoms "central for political purposes" and that provide "supramajoritarian protection" against "majority whim" (2011, 72, 73; and see 2016).

As Crocker notes, Nussbaum tends to place the responsibility for determining such protections with politicians working in consultation with philosophers. Philosophers provide "the philosophical underpinnings for an account of basic constitutional principles that should be respected and implemented by the governments of all nations, as a bare minimum of what respect for human dignity requires" (Nussbaum 2000, 5; see also Crocker 2008, 162; 197–99). Nussbaum has taken the position that "Citizens can deliberate about the fundamental political principles for which they want their nation to stand – if they are framing a new constitution, for example" (2011, 74), but she also frequently places politicians, as representatives of the people, in this role (2000, 104; 2016, 303; see also Crocker 2008, 199–200; 207–9). Here the focus will be upon possibilities that may be foregone if philosophers' lists and politicians' interpretations obviate or dominate popular voices within constitutional conversations. Public discussion might unearth ideals of "minimal social justice" (Nussbaum 2011, 73) that stand as alternatives to those noted by democratically elected politicians or listed by any philosopher. One problem, which relational theorists would affirm, is that the politicians may be insufficiently aware of all parties' concerns if they are not required to engage in ongoing consultation and, indeed, in ongoing critical dialogue with those parties. A second and more telling problem lies with essentialism: if value is a social product, the essentialist (or the "thick and vague" theorist of the good) will be unaware of possibilities that arise through dialectical processes, such as critical dialogue. The emergence of new possibilities not previously understood may even be hampered by discussion that is structured at the outset by a list of central capabilities for framing a constitution.

A new term may be useful that allows for distance from the essentialist position. I propose that some capabilities are like those Nussbaum refers to as "central": they should be recognized as of highest importance in understanding well-being once they are grasped, and many of them will deserve constitutional guarantee. These are capabilities that come into being because (1) critical dialogue will unearth some of them, (2) economic and social conditions will make others possible and (3) political contest will create others still. I will refer to these simply as "important" capabilities that are also salient to national constitutions. Such important capabilities might, following their recognition, be incorporated as new material under one of the ten central capabilities of Nussbaum's list. But some of these important capabilities, as I will argue at the end of this section, would not have appeared upon any thick and vague list that had previously been offered by a philosopher, or would not have been generated through discussion with a philosopher. Some of them might not be successfully subsumed and so may serve to destabilize a list of central capabilities. Dialectical processes may send some capabilities out of the constitutional orbit, bring new ones into being and bring them into that orbit. Important capabilities present a challenge, then, to essentialism, or to a thick vague theory of the good, because we learn what is of value, including what should be included in a political constitution, through experience of the facts and through processes of political struggle.

Thorough defense of these claims would require another paper, so, for this chapter, what must suffice is an explanation of how the link of central capabilities to constitutions might be effectively replaced with an account that refers instead to important capabilities (that is, evolving, nonessential ones). Some cases regarding the creation and alteration of constitutions are included to indicate that these concerns are not merely abstract.

I begin from the assumption that a national constitution need not enumerate all central or important capabilities that are necessary for the well-being of the people: neither all of Nussbaum's central capabilities, nor all of what I call important capabilities that are appropriate for a given time, need be treated in legal rights. Instead, as other philosophers have suggested, "specific human rights respond to familiar and recurrent threats to fundamental human interests" (Nickel 2007, 3); similarly, rights may also include commitments to accessible opportunities for advancement of human flourishing, as is the case, for example, in the right to education. What has frequently found its way into constitutions in the past and what belongs within planning for a new constitution, I suggest, is language that addresses familiar recurrent threats and accessible opportunities.

Threats are addressed through rights, but new threats arise under particular historical conditions and old ones depart. A new constitution should reflect its era and an old one should be rewritten, or should track history through amendments. For an example of a new threat, the legal right to privacy appears to be a recent and developing innovation in response to such threat (Clapham 2015, 113–20). The suggestion that a state should ensure "provisions for a zone of personal privacy" (Nussbaum 2011, 40) may be one that is appropriate in some historical conditions – from the era of ubiquity for printing presses and up to present – and not in others. This is not to say that abuse of privacy is acceptable in other circumstances; rather, there may be circumstances in which a government cannot or need not play the role of guarantor, since, once again, "specific human rights respond to familiar and recurrent threats to fundamental human interests." New important capabilities will also come into being in future. For example, no capability for access to the Internet existed before the latter half of the twentieth century, and the capability did not become an important one, in the sense intended here, before perhaps the twenty-first century. That capability may now rate as important, as emerging international and national norms suggest (UN 2003; 2015, 9.c; Ecuador 2008, Article 16.2).

Among currently accessible opportunities is "an adequate education, including, but by no means limited to, literacy and basic mathematical and scientific training" (Nussbaum 2011, 33). Education is thus incorporated under Nussbaum's fourth central capability, "Being able to use the senses, to imagine, think and reason." Education was framed as a responsibility of the state by Aristotle, as Nussbaum notes (1987a, 21), but it has only recently been treated as a guarantee for all people, since such education is made possible in certain economic and social conditions that have only recently arrived. A right to universal education probably could not have been supported as a state responsibility before the twentieth century, except in a very limited number of cases. For perspective on this choice of date, consider national and global advances in popular education. England, which was a European leader alongside the Netherlands, achieved 50 percent literacy for men about 1650, and the same for women about 1850 (Clark 2008, 179). Over the century leading up to 1900 the world literacy rate is estimated to have about doubled, reaching 21 percent. State guarantees demand particular social conditions, such as a sufficiency of literate people to both run the state and provide universal education. Though Cuba's 1961 literacy campaign provides a shining example of rapid improvement as Cuba increased its literacy to beyond 96 percent in just nine months, it began its campaign with an 85 percent literacy rate, according to one of the program's architects (Prieto 1981, 221). Consider India's case: efforts at establishing a right to education date at least from 1910, but the right to education only came to be recognized in India's courts more than eighty years later, and the clause "the State shall provide free and compulsory education" was inserted into India's Constitution as article 21a in 2002 (Selva 2009). The ideal of a right to education was expressed as Article 26 of the Universal Declaration of Human Rights (UDHR) in 1948, so it appears that it was available at the drafting of India's Constitution in 1950, but was set aside. Though capabilities refer to what people deserve, constitutions refer to what states can deliver, and they should reflect the maximum of important capabilities states can be expected deliver (see also, Crocker 2008, 205). Constitutions might sensibly be limited to justiciable guarantees, or might add directive principles for courts (McLean 2009, 7–14), or further add directive principles for policy, as India did for education in 1950, leaving further aspiration aside (India 2015, 39, 41).

The above sketch indicates how a changing set of important capabilities might take the place of central capabilities and how constitutions may be limited to contain less than a full set of important capabilities. A greater concern for approaching a constitution with a list in hand is that philosophers – and representatives, too – may not be in a position to identify rights that are important to members of groups to which they do not belong. I have in mind political struggles in which individuals come to understand their group identity through struggle. Before they have self-identified as a group, the individuals may experience their social exclusion as dysphoria, or they may adapt their preferences instead of grasping that a lack of appropriate entitlements is the source of their malaise, and they may not be capable of identifying or articulating their demands for rights until the political process is under way. A well-documented case of such dialectical development is the homophile movement of the USA, a political effort that played out from the 1940s up to the period of gay activism starting with the 1969 Stonewall riots (Faderman 2015, 53–113). In such a situation, I think, both political representatives and thoughtful philosophers may fail to identify the concern, or might identify the concern as pathological. That is to say: a list might be of no help, or might be routinely interpreted by philosophers and representatives in ways that obscure others' concerns, dissipating class consciousness.

For a constitutional case, consider Ecuador's national interpretation of the "Rights of the good way of living (*buen vivir*)" articulated within its recently adopted Constitution (Ecuador 2008, Preamble). Ecuador also frames this conception as *sumak kawsay*, a Kichwa dialect term. Eduardo Gudynas characterizes *sumak kawsay* as "fullness of life in a community together with other persons and Nature," in which "Nature becomes a subject; human beings as the only source of values are therefore displaced" (2011, 442, 445). As *sumak kawsay* is articulated in the constitution, it entails "rights of nature," including "the right to integral respect for its existence and for the maintenance and regeneration of its life cycles, structure, functions and evolutionary processes." Nature also has a "right to be restored" (Ecuador 2008, Articles 71, 72, 83). Each person has rights to live "in harmony with nature" and has attendant individual duties to "respect the rights of nature, preserve a healthy environment and use natural resources rationally, sustainably and durably ... in harmonious coexistence with nature" (Ecuador 2008, 27, 83; see also 275).

This matrix of rights and responsibilities may suggest that Ecuador's Constitution supports a central capability that Nussbaum characterizes as "being able to live with concern for and in relation to animals, plants, and the world of nature" (2011, 34). But the rights of nature and the correlate of an individual's responsibility toward nature that are called for in the constitution suggest that a very different claim is contained in this ideal of living harmoniously with nature. Indeed, this ideal may not be compatible with the liberal conception of the individual, since Kichwa political activists have explicitly identified it as a genuine departure from liberal conceptions of individual rights and of individualism (Becker 2011, 48, 51). Nussbaum may have conceptions of *buen vivir* and deep ecology in mind in *Creating Capabilities* as she notes a "basic position" concerning "animal entitlements" to which she does not subscribe, in which "Individualism [of all living organisms] is dropped [and] the capabilities of systems (ecosystems in particular, but also species) count as ends in themselves" (2011, 158). Nussbaum admits that she cannot yet make sense of the position and then she concludes "[t]hat animals can suffer not just pain but also injustice seems, however, secure" (159). This is a fallback to individualism that the Kichwa activists would appear not to find satisfactory. So, I expect *sumak kawsay* simply does not fit within Nussbaum's list. That it is not on the list and does not fit the list should not be taken to suggest that it is not a capability that is important in the sense indicated in this chapter. Indigenous activists have argued that *sumak kawsay* is central to their concept of well-being and they credit its establishment in the constitution to "decades of resistance and social movements, the indigenous movement, and diverse sectors of the Ecuadorian peoples" (Becker 2011, 59).

Debate has also arisen as to the meaning of *sumak kawsay*. Despite its presence in the constitution, the understanding of many of those engaged in drafting the document may have diverged greatly from the understanding of people who received the concept within its original cultural context. One development expert and government official, René Ramírez Gallegos, sees a close connection of *sumak kawsay* to Aristotelian thought (Ramírez Gallegos 2010, 8, 49). European academics Laura Portela and Carmen Ayerra have taken *sumak kawsay* to "very loosely" approximate the concept of capability, but find the concept of "ecodependence" a better fit (Portela and Ayerra 2013, 159). Ecuadorian philosopher David Cortez cites native Kichwa anthropologist Carlos Viteri Gualinga to argue that the constitution's treatment of *sumak kawsay* as one approach to *buen vivir* reduces the former, yielding a conflation of "being with Mother Nature" and "conditions for social welfare" (Cortez 2014, 321; see also Tibán 2000). Cortez finds improvement upon "economic liberalism" in the importance Nussbaum gives to nature (326); nevertheless, he finds that Nussbaum cleaves to "a western anthropocentric system" and he concludes:

the notion of "human development" in the approach to good living in the [Ecuador] National Development Plans and similar concepts such as "capabilities" and "quality of life" found in the readings of Amartya Sen and Martha Nussbaum reproduce an economic and political narrative that is incompatible with the perspective of *sumak kawsay*, which has lately emerged as a critique of liberal paradigms. (326, 337)

I do not wish to suggest that the introduction of a list of central capabilities such as Nussbaum's has in fact been deleterious to the drafting of Ecuador's constitution, or to the introduction of *sumak kawsay* into its text. But the turns of critical dialogue noted above suggest that a misunderstanding has arisen. The familiar language of development economics, liberalism and capabilities may obscure some perspectives when such language frames discussion. Philosophers, government officials and representatives with backgrounds dissimilar to others within the community may present a "thick, vague theory of the good" that leaves too thin a space for public reason, and so may obscure alternatives. At the least, such initial offering of language will produce much greater demands upon those who might hope to express very different views and values in diverse languages. If the public forum is not sufficiently open then there are hazards even in the proposal that we view Nussbaum's list "as a stimulus for public debate in the construction, interpretation, and application of constitutional principles" (Crocker 2008, 198).

Conclusion

I have argued that just politics and politics in the context of development diverge from liberal assumptions concerning the role that the individual takes in conceiving value. The liberal tradition slights the social, or the relational, in its characterization of the political subject within its theories of justice. Feminist relational theorists present a challenge to that tradition by introducing relational autonomy to supplant the liberal conception of individual autonomy. Goulet's theory of development also challenges individualism as it suggests the plausible hypothesis that value is produced dialectically through social interaction.

This suggests that politics and development are human and social: they involve the creation of value as a dialectical product of dependent, biological creatures. That claim is one made within axiology, theory of value or normativity; it is not a claim within ethics. Within ethics, such understanding of value underwrites further characterization of what we should value to live well. If value is produced through social processes, then those processes are also the subject matter of ethical theory. And this concern finally reaches to development ethics: if the individual as political subject is constituted in this way, and if values are created in this way, then we can find new reasons as to why democratic participation may foster development and may be the ethical choice for development as well.

Notes

1. Joseph Raz provides a contemporary account of normativity in *From Normativity to Responsibility* (2011, 1–8). This chapter is pursued especially in the spirit of Putnam's naturalist account of normativity (2002; and see De Caro, "Introduction," in Putnam 2016, 15–16). I limit discussion to "human" development in this chapter for simplicity. Like Nussbaum, I take subjects with standing for consideration in politics to include those with sentience (2011, 158). Argument in this chapter may suggest that subjects countenanced within development could include any beings with which one has relations that involve, or might in future involve, mutual value relations. Examples include humans, humans of future generations, house cats and muskrats, but not extinct dodos and not objects such as stones that we may or may not value, but that could not themselves conceive of value.
2. For an autobiographical account of Crocker's developing relation to capability theory, see the opening pages of the book.
3. Gerson Sher, "Tito Muzzles the Loyal Opposition," *The Nation* (New York, NY), March 15, 1975, 294 (quoted in Crocker 1983, 1).
4. Crocker 1989, 318, 321. This article is the third of Crocker's opening trio for *Revista de Filosofía de la Universidad de Costa Rica*, which includes

Crocker 1987 and Crocker 1988. See also the effective synthesis of these works in Crocker 1991b and its companion piece (Crocker 1991a). These writings develop ideas first presented at the 1984 Symposium focused upon development at the World Conference on Future Studies and the first International Development Ethics Association conference in 1987 and 1989 (see Crocker 1991b, 461).

5. *A Theory of Justice* [1st edition, 1971], 62; and see *Justice as Fairness, a Restatement* (2001, 58–59). In *Justice as Fairness, a Restatement*, Rawls writes of "Income and wealth, understood as all-purpose means (having an exchange value) generally needed to achieve a wide range of ends whatever they may be." The revised edition of *A Theory of Justice* (1999) almost exactly preserves the first edition's introduction of primary goods:

> For simplicity, assume that the chief primary goods at the disposition of society are rights and liberties, powers and opportunities, income and wealth. (Later on in Part Three the primary good of self-respect has a central place.) These are the social primary goods. Other primary goods such as health and vigor, intelligence and imagination, are natural goods; although their possession is influenced by the basic structure, they are not so directly under its control. (1971, 54)

6. David Gauthier's *Morals by Agreement* was a particularly clear attempt at analyzing value along these lines, with the goal of "showing why an individual, reasoning from non-moral premises, would accept the constraints of morality on his choices" (1986, 5).

7. On "fact" and "value" in this paragraph, see Putnam 2002, 96–98. On taking values as historical products, see Putnam 2016, ch. 3, especially p. 63. The "incompatibility" between two cultures I mention is not intended to imply that incompatibilities in value cannot be reconciled: if fact and value are entangled, experience and discussion might reconcile divergence.

8. For an introduction to feminist relational theory that pertains to the account in this chapter, see Gould and see especially the "Introduction" and the essay by Linda Barclay, "Autonomy and the social self," in Mackenzie and Stoljar 2000.

References

Becker, Marc. 2011. "Correa, indigenous movements, and the writing of a new constitution in Ecuador." *Latin American Perspectives*, 38(1): 47–62.

Clapham, Andrew. 2015. *Human Rights: A Very Short Introduction.* Oxford University Press.

Clark, Gregory. 2008. *A Farewell to Alms: A Brief Economic History of the World*. Princeton University Press.

Cortez, David. 2014. "Genealogía del sumak kawsay y el buen vivir en Ecuador: Un balance." In *Post-crecimiento y buen vivir*, Gustavo Endara (ed.). Friedrich Ebert Stiftung Ecuador, 315–52. http://library.fes.de/pdf -files/bueros/quito/11348.pdf.

Crocker, David. 1983. *Praxis and Democratic Socialism: The Critical Social Theory of Marković and Stojanović*. Atlantic Highlands, NJ: Humanities Press.

  1987. "Hacia una ética del desarrollo." *Revista de la Filosofía de la Universidad de Costa Rica*, XXV(62): 129–41.

  1988. "La naturaleza y la práctica de una ética del desarrollo." *Revista de la Filosofía de la Universidad de Costa Rica*, XXVI(63–64): 49–56.

  1989. "Cuatro modelos del desarrollo costarricense: análisis y evaluación ética." *Revista de Filosofía de la Universidad de Costa Rica*, XXVII(66): 317–32.

  1991a. "Insiders and outsiders in international development." *Ethics and International Affairs*, 5: 149–73.

  1991b. "Toward development ethics." *World Development*, 19(5): 457–83.

  2008. *Ethics of Global Development: Agency, Capability and Deliberative Democracy*. Cambridge University Press.

Ecuador. 2008. Asamblea Nacional de Ecuador. Political Constitution of 2008. *Political Database of the Americas*, Georgetown University. http://pdba.georgetown.edu/Constitutions/Ecuador/ecuador.html.

Faderman, Lilian. 2015. *The Gay Revolution: The Story of a Struggle*. New York: Simon & Schuster.

Gauthier, David. 1986. *Morals by Agreement*. Oxford University Press.

Gould, Carol. 2014. *Interactive Democracy: The Social Roots of Global Justice*. Cambridge University Press.

Goulet, Denis. 1971. *The Cruel Choice: A New Concept in the Theory of Development*. New York: Atheneum.

Gudynas, Eduardo. 2011. "Buen vivir: Today's tomorrow." *Development*, 54(4): 441–47.

India. 2015. Ministry of Law and Justice. The Constitution of India. November 9. http://lawmin.nic.in/olwing/coi/coi-english/coi-4March2016 .pdf.

Kant, Immanuel. 1996. *Practical Philosophy*, Mary Gregor (transl. and ed.). Cambridge University Press.

Keleher, Lori. 2017. "Sen and Nussbaum: Agency and capability-expansion." *Éthique et économique/Ethics and Economics*, 11(2): 54–70.

Korsgaard, Christine. 2009. *Self Constitution*. Oxford University Press.

Lukács, Georg. 1972. *History and Class Consciousness: Studies in Marxist Dialectics*. Rodney Livingstone (transl.) Cambridge, MA: MIT Press.

Mackenzie, Catriona and Natalie Stoljar (eds.). 2000. *Relational Autonomy: Feminist Perspectives on Autonomy, Agency and the Social Self*. New York: Oxford University Press.

McLean, Kirsty. 2009. *Constitutional Deference, Courts and Socio-economic Rights in South Africa*. Pretoria University Law Press.

Nickel, James. 2007. *Making Sense of Human Rights*. Malden, MA: Wiley-Blackwell.

Nussbaum, Martha. 1987a. "Nature, function and capability: Aristotle on political distribution." WIDER Working Paper, WP 31. Helsinki: World Institute for Development Economic Research, December 1987. www .wider.unu.edu/sites/default/files/WP31.pdf. [Published under same title in *Oxford Studies in Ancient Philosophy* Supplementary Volume 1 (1988): 145–84.]

1987b. "Non-relative virtues: An Aristotelian approach." WIDER Working Paper, WP 32. Helsinki: World Institute for Development Economic Research, December 1987. www.wider.unu.edu/sites/default/files/wp32 .pdf. [Published under same title in *Midwest Studies in Philosophy* 13 (1988): 32–53.]

1992. "Human functioning and social justice: In defense of Aristotelian essentialism." *Political Theory*, 20: 202–46.

2000. *Women and Human Development: The Capability Approach*. Cambridge University Press.

2001. *Fragility of Goodness*, 2nd edn. Cambridge University Press.

2002. "Capabilities and disabilities: Justice for mentally disabled citizens." *Philosophical Topics*, 30(2): 133–65.

2003. "Capabilities as fundamental entitlements: Sen and social justice." *Feminist Economics*, 9(2/3): 33–59

2006. *Frontiers of Justice*. Cambridge, MA: Belknap.

2007. "Foreword: Constitutions and capabilities: 'Perception' against lofty formalism." *Harvard Law Review*, 121: 4–97.

2011. *Creating Capabilities: The Human Development Approach*. Cambridge, MA: Belknap.

2014. "Introduction," in *Capabilities, Gender, Equality: Towards Fundamental Entitlements*, Flavio Comim and Martha Nussbaum (eds.). Cambridge University Press, 1–17.

2016. "Introduction: Aspiration and the capabilities list." *Journal of Human Development and Capabilities*, 17(3): 301–08.

Portela, Laura and Carmen Ayerra. 2013. "Hacia una noción post-capitalista del buen vivir: capacidades, necesidades y bienes básicos en relación con el sumak kausay/suma qamaña." *Revista del 50 Congreso de Filosofía Joven*, Hugo Aguilar *et al.* (eds.), 139–65. https://horizon tesdecompromiso.files.wordpress.com/2013/06/0141.pdf.

Prieto, Abel. 1981. "Cuba's national literacy campaign." *Journal of Reading*, 25(3): 215–21.

Putnam, Hilary. 2002. *The Collapse of the Fact/Value Dichotomy and other Essays*. Cambridge, MA: Harvard University Press.

2016. *Naturalism, Realism, and Normativity*. Cambridge, MA: Harvard University Press.

Ramírez Gallegos, René. 2010. *La felicidad como medida del buen vivir en Ecuador. Entre la materialidad y la subjetividad*. Secretaría Nacional de Planificación y Desarrollo, Quito. www.planificacion .gob.ec/wp-content/uploads/downloads/2012/08/La-Felicidad-como-Medida-del-Buen-Vivir-en-Ecuador.pdf.

Rawls, John. 1971. *A Theory of Justice*. Cambridge, MA: Belknap.

1993. *Political Liberalism*. New York: Columbia University Press.

1999. *A Theory of Justice*, revised edn. Cambridge, MA: Belknap.

2001. *Justice as Fairness: A Restatement*. Cambridge, MA: Belknap.

Raz, Joseph. 2011. *From Normativity to Responsibility*. New York: Oxford.

Rose, Sarah, Nancy Birdsall and Anna Diofasi. 2016. "Creating a better candidate pool for the Millennium Challenge Corporation." CGD Policy Paper 082. Center for Global Development, April. www.cgdev.org/sites/ default/files/CGD-Policy-Paper-82-Rose-Birdsall-Diofasi-Creating-Better-Candidate-Pool-MCC.pdf.

Seers, Dudley. 1969. "The meaning of development." IDS Communication 44. Institute for Development Studies. www.ids.ac.uk/files/dmfile/the meaningofdevelopment.pdf.

Selva, G. 2009. "Universal education in India: A century of unfulfilled dreams." *Pragoti*. http://archive.is/l9bm#selection-241.0–241.61.

Sen, Amartya. 2004. "Capabilities, lists, and public reason: Continuing the conversation." *Feminist Economics*, 10(3): 77–80.

Sevenhuijsen, Selma. 2013. "Interview in June 2013." *Ethics of Care*. http:// ethicsofcare.org/selma-sevenhuijsen/.

Sundaram, Jomo Kwame. 2016. "Poverty, vulnerability and social protection." Inter Press Service News Agency. August 4. www.ipsnews .net/2016/08/poverty-vulnerability-and-social-protection/.

Tibán, Lourdes. 2000. "El concepto del desarrollo sustentable y los pueblos indígenas." Publicación mensual del Instituto Científico de Culturas Indígenas. 2(18), September. http://icci.nativeweb.org/boletin/18/tiban .html.

United Nations. 2003. "Press Release: WSIS opening meeting discusses how digital divide is preventing equal sharing of opportunities concerning ICTS." www.un.org/press/en/2003/pi1541.doc.htm.

    2015. *Transforming our world: The 2030 Agenda for Sustainable Development.* A.RES.70.1. https://documents-dds-ny.un.org/doc/UND OC/GEN/N15/291/89/PDF/N1529189.pdf.

3 | *Public Goods and Public Spirit*

Reflections on and Beyond Nussbaum's *Political Emotions*

DES GASPER AND FLAVIO COMIM

Introduction: *Liberté, égalité – et fraternité?*

We wish to connect two fundamental topics in political and social philosophy and development ethics: the role of feelings in public life, and the nature and provision of public goods. Our chapter links philosophical discussions of publicness and of compassion in society with the policy-practice topic of public goods. Publicness is a term dating from at least the early seventeenth century, defined by the Oxford online dictionary as, '[t]he quality, condition, or fact of being public'. In recent decades public management literature has used the term in reflections on what are distinctive characteristics of a public sector and of its values and attitudes (e.g. Antonsen and Jorgensen 1997; Pesch 2008). Our chapter makes the same connection between values and activities; so we use the term to refer to both, and for thinking about the connections between public goods, public reason and people's values and cultures, including the moral sentiments that sustain the structures of cooperation and solidarity seen in a society.

Development theorists from the 1940s to the 1970s do not seem to have given much attention to the theme of publicness, except in discussions of nation-building or corruption, with reference to perceptions of what are public and private spheres (see Goulet 1971; Gasper 2006a). Some hints appeared also in the 1970s–1980s discussions of human needs, and in participatory theories of development since the 1990s. The human development work inspired by Amartya Sen has led in this direction too, including in his books with Jean Drèze; but much capability approach work has been limited by weak elaboration of social and psychological dimensions. According to the anthropologist Mary Douglas, this reflected a widespread social sciences syndrome of 'Missing Persons' (Douglas and Ney 1998): insufficient attention to the complexities of social personhood, the nature of real persons. Sen's category of commitment, meaning holding of objectives oriented to the good of others, remains a relatively empty box in his system and is not presented as foundational in the same way as the categories of freedom and equality. His work has ventured relatively little into the substantive contents and social determinants of commitment, compassion, fraternity and solidarity.[1]

Our discussion has five main elements or strands. First, we argue that public goods are essential components in human development, and that the extent of their provision is a key indication of a society's normative priorities. We will put forward a conceptualization of priority (or basic) public goods, and of public values required to induce support for provision of those goods. Public priority goods at a series of levels can be identified by a logic of derivation from normative priority principles. At a fundamental level lie values and institutions that sustain the public efforts that build and secure an equitable and decent society, and ensure that growing economic wealth is matched by broad-based human development and growing quality of life.

Correspondingly, second, public-spiritedness is essential for public goods provision, operation and maintenance. We argue that highly developed countries are countries with higher levels of publicness, in the sense both of public goods provision and the associated public spirit. Although provision of public goods is at the heart of much of human development, little attention is usually given in economic development theory and even some human development theory to how these priorities are an expression of the quality of public commitment or public spirit in a society. Instead, shrinkage of the notion of public to that in neoclassical economics matches a domination of the political community by wealth (Gasper 2002). While the importance of individualism for economic growth and development has been widely argued, and the relevance of social capital has been fashionable in social sciences since the 1990s, what of publicness? Is public spirit part of social capital? Contemporary deliberative ethics talks much more about dialogue and public reason than about public sentiments and commitment (see, e.g., Crocker 2008; Sen 2009).[2]

Comim (2015, 2019) has distinguished three levels of publicness: a Rawlsian level, concerning state support or facilitation for the provision of primary or basic goods, whether by state or other actors; a Senian level, concerning a person's degree of effective access to basic or priority functionings; but third, both those levels partly depend on a

form of public action.[9] What is chosen for actual public provision covers far less than all non-excludables, and includes some excludables. Education and health care are rivalrous and excludable services; yet both may be supported or provided by public agents to be accessible to ordinary people, often through a subsidy. They are given public priority because they are seen as merit goods, worth more socially than their market valuation, partly because their consumption brings important favourable external effects for others.[10] They are public priority goods.

The public priority goods notion itself remains insufficient, for any majority government could declare that it prioritizes in its own way, but a way that invidiously excludes some groups. The notion thus requires fuller theorization, including connection to needs theory, and institutional entrenchment of basic requirements for all, such as through a human rights formulation. One can show how a ladder of implied needs, of increasing specificity as we descend, derives from a normative priority criterion; and how this type of layered needs theory[11] matches also the structures of thinking in human rights theory and human security analysis, which use priority criteria of human dignity and vital human interests (see Gasper 2005a, 2005b).

We suggest three main points arising for the purposes of this discussion. First, one should consider not only culmination outcomes, but also many aspects of the comprehensive outcomes that are necessary to produce those achievements (Sen 2002). Thus, we need for example to consider not only actual achieved learning, but also: values that support education; economic inputs to schooling; real opportunities for schooling within a given social context; actual presence in school; and actual involvement in learning. A whole series of levels and types of corresponding public good are important. Even if capabilities are deemed the true ends in public policy deliberations, attention to them should be accompanied by attention to the motivations, processes and arrangements concerning the many prior required public goods and to their prerequisites in turn.

Second, we saw that the language of public priority goods can be used too parochially, with certain groups being downgraded as supposed reflection of a particular society's local values. In contrast the languages of human security, human development and human rights are universal, not nationally specific, and provide an essential framework for local prioritizations. They allow local variation in detailed content and emphases but not omission of fundamentals – for example, in India the exclusion of Dalits or in Europe the exclusion of Roma. Similarly, basic physical and mental health are central in any plausible theory of need (for example, as in Doyal and Gough's theory), and bring universal implications such as in regard to sanitation and reproductive health as vital for general health and dignity.[12]

Third, public spirit can be thought of as a special type of public good that is needed for the provision of most/many other public goods. It is hinted at in Doyal and Gough's preconditions level, which refers to necessary conditions for basic needs assurance, in regard to production, reproduction, cultural transmission and political authority. It becomes explicit in some human rights work, which emphasizes a human rights culture of commitment to the dignity of all persons; and in parts of the work of Rawls, Sen and Nussbaum, which similarly emphasizes sufficient social solidarity to sustain access by all to the satisfiers required for achieving basic capabilities. Many elements of culture, including a public framework for respectful and systematic deliberation, are thus priority public goods. Personal capabilities rest in important degree on concrete public goods provision; that in turn rests on appropriate institutional arrangements, that themselves rely on (and sustain) compatible public sentiments.[13]

Rawls, Sen and Nussbaum on the Public Sphere

Much of Amartya Sen's work on India has been about how to organize the provision of basic public goods. However, the stress in his theoretical work, and in the Human Development Reports that this helped to foster, has been on how provision of concrete public goods should not be taken as the true standard of achievement. In contrast to what we named the Rawlsian level of public goods – basic/primary goods – Sen focuses on the degree of effective access to valued functionings. A question then arises regarding motivational adequacy: why would or do participants give support to and/or concede duties regarding the specified concerns? We look here at this essential complementary dimension, which we have called the Nussbaumian level: the culture and attitudes – including of civility, tolerance, non-violence, mutual respect and, not least, solidarity – needed to sustain a life with dignity for all.

In *A Theory of Justice*, Rawls introduced the concept of publicity, meaning 'a knowledge of the principles that others follow' (1971, 16).

This idea of shared knowledge was expanded on in *Political Liberalism* (1993), in relation to justification for a public conception of justice that comprises a commonly shared and justified point of view. In a liberal society individuals do not need to agree with each other's comprehensive doctrines nor do they have to hide their beliefs. Rather, they adjudicate disagreements by openly arguing in favour of their convictions in terms that others could potentially agree with. This reasoning together is central to Rawls's vision of public reason, mutual respect and cooperation in a well-ordered society.

In *Justice as Fairness*, Rawls emphasized that his idea of public reason applies only to matters of 'constitutional essentials and questions of basic justice' (2001, 91), excluding issues like tax legislation, environmental legislation and laws regulating property among others. He distinguished between a 'constitutional stage' and a legislative stage. Larmore (2003, 381) notes that 'Political debate rightly shows a greater mix of voices in areas of society other than the circumscribed realm of public reason, and it would be wrong to suppose that Rawls's theory of public reason means to encompass the "public sphere" in this broader sense.' In contrast, Sen proclaims a much wider role of public reason, not restricted to specifying a constitution.

If we wish to apply Rawls's themes of publicity and public reason in the domains of human development, we need a broader understanding of mutual respect, reasonableness, reciprocity, justification and shared principles, not restricted to a constitutional stage. We need a concept such as publicness that encompasses processes in which citizens can arrive at binding decisions and also includes background cultural elements. Rawls himself frequently used the concepts of reasonableness and reciprocity as ways to circumvent the limited scope of his concept of public reason. He never sufficiently established though why participants in his system would pay serious respect to public reasoning and, fundamentally, treat each other as of equal moral worth. He argues, 'We develop a desire to apply and to act upon the principles of justice once we realize how social arrangements answering to them have promoted our good and that of those with whom we are affiliated' (Rawls 1971, 474). But acceptance of such affiliation involves more than just a cognitive recognition of interdependence or a prudentially motivated idea of not wishing to have greater advantages than others unless the arrangements also benefit them. It involves, according to

Newman (2015), several other elements of psychological preparedness which Rawls might have taken for granted.

For Sen, moral sentiments provide a starting point but need reasoned scrutiny, for us to understand and test with impartiality and objectivity the grounds for felt indignation or commitment. In *The Idea of Justice*, Sen argues (2009, viii) that 'A sense of injustice could serve as a signal that moves us, but a signal does demand critical examination, and there has to be some scrutiny of the soundness of a conclusion based mainly on signals.' Thus, public reason involves judgement, in particular through impartial reasoning that can help people handle their vested interests and preconceptions.

Sen gives emphasis to characteristics of good public reasoning such as impartiality and objectivity, more than to characterizing reasonable persons.[14] His interpretation of Rawls's notion of fairness, as being simply a demand for impartiality, frees him from examining the existence or not of reasonable behaviour as a precondition for public reason. He criticizes Rawls though for not being 'realistic' (81), in assuming that once institutions are in place individuals would behave reasonably. He warns too that: 'Demanding more from behaviour today than could be expected to be fulfilled would not be a good way of advancing the cause of justice' (81).

Sen seems more concerned with informational issues and how different arguments can survive objective reasoned scrutiny than with trying to change people's moral sentiments, at any rate directly. 'To prevent catastrophes caused by human negligence or callous obduracy, we need critical scrutiny, not just goodwill towards others' (48); and he emphasizes good public reasoning even when there is no change in individuals' emotions. He acknowledges as did Rawls the plurality of relevant values and how some irreducible conflicts between different positions can remain, and considers how we can respond. 'Judgements about justice have to take on board the task of accommodating different kinds of reasons and evaluative concerns' (395). He shows that such reasoning can make progress despite non-commensurability of values and the multiplicity of types of reason.

His arguments for using social choice theory as a framework for public reasoning do not focus then on criteria about reasonable values; instead, he studies the informational limitations that a complete theory of justice, such as Rawls's, inevitably encounters. Thus, Sen engages with Rawls's earlier concept of publicity as shared knowledge (necessary for shared communication and understanding) and Rawls's later characterization of justification in *Political Liberalism*; much more than with the psychological and moral principles that are needed to produce and give some stability to public reason itself. Yet if, as Sen argues, 'justice is partly a relation in which ideas of obligation to each other are important' (2009, 129), we should address how values of reciprocity and of recognition of each other's equal moral worth are formed. In Sen's hands this remains a cognitive challenge about 'open impartiality' and objectivity. He notes that a person's objectives can go well beyond self-interest but he prefers to focus on the plurality of possible reasons without settling for any specific motivating moral sentiment. There is nothing irrational in being concerned with others, he shows, but he does not seem to insist that there is an obligation to be concerned, including for sake of one's own psychological health (Gasper 2007a, 2007b).

Sen prefers to focus on the issue of responsibility and cooperation, leaving open the possibility of plural justifications of reasonable behaviour (either based on self-interested mutual cooperation or on feelings of responsibility and duty towards others). By using the concept of agency – which 'encompasses all the goals that a person has reasons to adopt' (2009, 287) – he builds a framework that includes a plurality of motivations (of which reasonableness or commitment can be one, but not 'the' one) rather than settling on one specific notion of reasonableness or reciprocity as the basis of individuals' sense of values. The adequacy of his approach depends on whether or not we in fact need some shared human values for achieving kinds of public reasoning that are conducive to just arrangements.

Nussbaum disputes that the ideas of agreement and justifiability are enough to sustain a notion of the good sufficient for a theory of justice. She has criticized Rawls's contractarianism for using a narrow moral psychology that excludes motivations such as compassion, sympathy, or benevolence (2006, 108, 148, 158). She advocates a shared public conception of the person,[15] and proposes to replace Rawls's idea of mutual advantage by an idea of equal human dignity within a 'richer and moralized account of the good' (163).[16] Her argument is that people's notions of the good should and do include other people, and not for the reason that a person might feel better when doing charity or would gain some advantage from caring for others. Respecting each other's dignity is a question of our 'love' of others, and our conception of ourselves as decent persons in a shared world. 'It can only be out of our attachment to justice and our love of others, our sense that our lives are intertwined with theirs and that we share ends with them' (222). In her book *Political Emotions* she lays out a moral psychology and an associated theory of the grounds for a public sphere oriented to justice.

Nussbaum's *Political Emotions*

Political Emotions asks how a liberal theory of justice can cohere; how can one, without imposing illiberal restrictions, ensure that individuals will pay attention to a common good? Nussbaum sees corresponding gaps in Rawls's *Theory of Justice*, even though 'Rawls ... knows well that human beings do not automatically pursue the common good' (2013, 9). All values require an emotional basis for them to be stable and to connect to action (127). Securing a stable basis for commitments that concern other people is especially necessary.

She rejects as illiberal, however, a family of responses that involve indoctrination plus enforcement to ensure solidarity or at least obedience to practices of solidarity. For example, Rousseau's advocacy of a civil religion that would, in his words, inculcate the 'sentiments of sociability without which it is impossible to be a good citizen or a faithful subject' (5). Implicitly she rejects the equivalents that exist in contemporary East Asia. Indeed she rejects Rousseau's General Will doctrine on grounds that it has insufficient respect for individuals (45). Further, it can accompany a type of overriding nationalism and conduce to lack of respect for other nations and individuals. We ask later whether *Political Emotions*' own nation-centred conception avoids the pitfalls of nationalism.

Nussbaum is sympathetic towards Rabindranath Tagore's appeal for a 'religion of man' and to J. S. Mill's earlier somewhat similar call, as attempts to ensure a sufficient basis of altruism. Auguste Comte's model for promotion of civic love for fostering the common good, a sort of obligatory humanistic state religion in the mould of Catholicism but intended to replace it, still leant too far in her view towards imposing feelings of obedience, hierarchy and homogeneity. While some violations of core political values, such as racial discrimination, should be coercively prevented, the main focus of her proposals is within a liberal tradition, to non-coercively educate people and their emotions. She draws inspiration from Mozart, Mill and Tagore on how moral sentiments of general sympathy, equal respect, toleration and fellow-feeling, and deeper emotions such as compassion and altruism, can be promoted: including through arts, education, urban design, and style and content of leadership. Each of these can advance sympathetic awareness in relation to other people.

Nussbaum does not agree that impartiality and objectivity in public reason suffice for appropriate behaviour. Reason and even respect are not enough to connect people, unlike emotions.[17] 'Rational deduction alone will not tell us whether women are full-fledged human beings' (261). 'If people talk without tapping into their emotions, they often don't really understand the depth of the problem, or communicate their full thinking to others' (289). Only through including emotions, she argues, can individuals adequately examine their lives and connect with each other, gaining a sense of a common fate and publicness stronger than implied by Rawls and Sen (345). Indeed, beyond what they suggested, human development needs a fuller set of ideas about what is good and bad. She holds that there is nothing illiberal about this provided that dissent is protected. Senian values of impartiality and objectivity will not be attained, maintained or adequate in the absence of empathy and sympathy with others; and Rawlsian reasonableness similarly requires specific psychological bases (Newman 2015). Nussbaum, like Newman, tries therefore to explain what shapes individuals' commitment to public reason. She looks at the 'malleability of the moral sentiments' and how we can upgrade, within the limits of liberalism, individuals' emotional life towards others.

Political Emotions is dedicated to how decent societies should cultivate appropriate public emotions. To understand limited sympathy and to counteract it we must give attention to negative emotions, including anger, shame and hatred. As discussed in her pivotal chapter 7, these emotions derive from humans' long early years of self-absorbed conscious helplessness; our greater tendency compared to other species towards self-importance, hurtful comparisons with our fellows and 'competitive self-love' (166); and our in-group socialization, which builds identity and in-group commitment partly through vilification of an out-group or groups. Ideally, the loving attention of parent-figures gradually builds a child's recognition, trust and concern for others, raises self-confidence in its ability to reciprocate and reduces its felt insecurities. However, 'the dynamics in human life that made love necessary (helplessness, fear and anger at helplessness) are not [fully or once-for-all] removed by time and growth, but persist – and thus love is an ongoing necessity for the personality in adult interactions' (190).

So, while we traditionally invoke *fraternité* as the necessary third term from the 1789 rallying cry, Nussbaum suggests this sort of masculine idiom contains a potential trap.[18] Her analysis of *The Marriage of Figaro* draws out the need and possibility for something more feminine, 'nicer', less oriented to competitive pride, status and domination. Her proposed solution inside nations, and perhaps even outside them, centres on love, by which she seems to mean empathy plus sympathy and generosity, love in a somewhat Christian sense (cf. 43).[19] This attentive generous reciprocation, explored in chapter 7, is not to be equated with 'being in love'. She proposes that 'all of the core emotions that sustain a decent society have their roots in, or are forms of, love – by which I mean intense [benevolent] attachments to things outside the control of our will' (15). For public emotions – attitudes towards other people whom one does not know personally or closely – to themselves be stable, and stable sustainers, they need to be part of a love of humanity in its finitude and particularities, that transcends any shame and disgust at being human, feelings which too often become projected onto specific others.

Here Nussbaum takes a step further, by highlighting disgust as amongst the negative emotions. Her analysis advances beyond Comte, Mill, Rawls, Sen, Habermas, or even Tagore, she suggests, for she theorizes the central 'link between overcoming disgust and broadening sympathy'" (105). Mere calls to respect the dignity of every human do not suffice to overcome inherited and newly created beliefs that some groups are disgusting (380).

Nussbaum stresses that the central importance of public emotions for solidarity does not imply that everyone should have completely the same values. 'Political emotions are the real emotions of real people; because people are heterogeneous, having different opinions, histories, and personalities, they can be expected to love, mourn, laugh, and strive for justice in specific and personal ways – particularly if their freedom of expression is protected and valued' (382–3). But one can distinguish between each individual's full set of values and the shared principles they should endorse for the political sphere in order to coexist fruitfully and avoid dictatorial regimes.

Further challenges arise beyond the local level and especially the national level. Our minds are particularistic and our emotions depend on the connections we have with people who belong to our circle of concern. The histories that partly define circles of concern are substantially shared within and partly specific to national societies: 'What moves people is a function of their sense of their nation's history, traditions and current problems' (200). She illustrates such recourse in the oratory of Lincoln and Martin Luther King.

To extend our feelings of concern beyond those to whom we are directly connected – and to include within a 'we' some others whom we do not personally know – requires, she argues, the mediation of 'symbols and poetry' (11). Art can help to convey both a necessary tragic perspective, one that 'gives insight into shared vulnerabilities', and a necessary comic perspective, one that accepts the chances and peculiarities 'of human existence with flexibility and mercy, rather than hatred' (21).[20] Vitally, all societies need formats – including the arts of tragedy and more – that channel grief 'in ways that promote reciprocity and extended, rather than narrow compassion' (201), ways that lead us to have not only self-pity but also sympathy for others; and formats – including the comic arts – that restrain disgust, 'lest it become an impediment to general concern' (201) and becomes projected onto hated out-groups, like blacks, Arabs or Untouchables.

So, Nussbaum examines the importance and substance of public emotions and proposes that they can be cultivated by societies in liberal ways. Publicness in practices can be promoted too as basis for the sustenance of these public emotions. By doing this she extends the basis of justification beyond impartiality and reason, moving the discussion towards specific contexts and active cultural and communication strategies. Her treatment, within the frame of political liberalism, is oriented to look for institutional arrangements that allow coexistence of multiple ethical doctrines and yet fulfilment of the human rights of all people.

Nussbaum is more at home discussing art than the institutionalization of empathy, sympathy and solidarity in tax systems or public sanitation. She does discuss urban planning, though mainly with reference to public monuments and parks. Still, she is well aware that 'a decent tax system, for example, could represent the insights of a duly balanced and appropriately impartial compassion' (20), and that 'tax and welfare policies ... embody sympathy, but in a way that is more stable and less prone to special pleading than is sympathy in [daily interpersonal] life' (135).

We do not look to a humanistic philosopher to go deep into the specifics of institutionalization. Let us sketch instead an initial appreciation of her analysis, with attention to two of the main building blocks: the ideas about moral sentiments, and the strong commitment to a nation-state framework.[21]

How do Nussbaum's ideas on moral sentiments relate to contemporary psychological research? Joshua Greene's survey *Moral Tribes* (2015) distinguishes two fundamental issues. The first concerns the bases for morality within a group: the issue of 'Me versus Us', as in the tragedy of the commons; members' selfishness versus concern for others. This is the problem that our moral brains evolved to solve. Greene writes that our brains contain responses to the group weakness that would be produced in relation to other groups if our group failed to cooperate internally. Various mechanisms, such as cultures of group loyalty, encourage principled cooperation.

Greene's second issue, 'Us versus Them', concerns clashes of our group's interests and values with those of another group or groups. Our established solutions for the 'Me versus Us' problem – including loyalty to our group, its declared symbols and mores – can exacerbate the 'Us versus Them' problem. He speaks therefore of the tragedy of commonsense morality. Besides mechanisms of biased perception and communication, seen in all disputes, that lead us to focus on our own grievances, here the group loyalties feed conflicts further. We internalize sheer preference for our own 'tribe' and commitment to its declared distinctive values and the icons that supposedly embody them (particular places, persons, traditions, narratives); we embrace certain beliefs and stories about the past that become badges of tribe membership and loyalty and so cannot be abandoned; and we acquire loyalties to particular doctrines about justice, which makes negotiated compromise harder for that would be to deviate from one's fundamental normative beliefs, constituent elements of one's identity.

Nussbaum illustrates this sort of trade-off from Finland, where the acceptance of high and progressive taxation reflects, she considers, the strong intra-group bonding possible in a small country (2013, 345). Finland's relative homogeneity and internal bonding contribute though to fear of immigrants and asylum-seekers. The relevant conducive factor is perhaps homogeneity more than smallness, for a large country like Japan seems to display similar intra-group bonding and wide-spread strong discomfort, even rejection, in regard to immigrants and asylum-seekers.

Next, what of Nussbaum's presumption and endorsement of a nation-state frame? Much of what *Political Emotions* proposes matches Greene's 'Commonsense Morality', notably various forms of quasi-religion concerning the nation, which can exacerbate inter-group and inter-national conflict. Some of what she proposes does not match that, and seeks to transcend such conflict.

Nussbaum adopts Mazzini's optimistic nineteenth-century claim that the nation is the necessary focus for transcending self-concern, and the unavoidable stepping-stone towards global concerns.[22] It is 'the largest unit we know until now that is decently accountable to people's voices' (2013, 17). Further, she frequently lauds patriotism, love of country and adopts the theory that 'when national love focuses on ideals of inclusion and human dignity, such love can easily lead on to a struggle for these things everywhere' (235). There is a Scandinavian grain of truth in this hypothesis, but unfortunately many counterexamples too: internally inclusive nations which remain (or even become more) resolutely self-obsessed. Further, a notion of the nation as the entity which provides a heritage to which all its members are indebted, that in fact has produced the members, and that provides a horizon of opportunity to which they all can contribute, applies more validly to the world as a whole than to the nation. The themes of heritage and indebtedness apply also for cities and localities; there is no special moral standing of the nation.

The book's dominant categories are those of the age of nations, in which in many respects the world indeed remains. In other respects, as citizens of advanced globalized capitalism in the Anthropocene era, we are long past the nation as sufficient frame for our analyses and our moral imagination. *Political Emotions* functions mainly as an American text for an intended American audience, as seen strongly in its final chapter. Even its closing paragraphs are exclusively nation-focused. Its ideas need to be deepened in dialogue with Nussbaum's more broadly conceived earlier cosmopolitan studies.

Nussbaum's analysis went deeper than Greene's by exploring emotional sources and contents, including not least the emotions of disgust. The case of India, which we look at in the following section, shows an extreme version of targeting disgust against 'outsider' groups within a country, narrowing and undermining public spirit. *Political Emotions* is relatively silent on the further challenge set by disgust targeted at other countries.[23] Our penultimate section will consider the languages of political emotion that are needed to support international fraternity and cooperation for global public goods.

India's Challenge

Political Emotions declares, 'The focus of this project will be on the role of emotions in advancing a society that is already pretty good to [move towards] fuller social justice' (Nussbaum 2013, 136). But India, the subject of much of its discussion, displays dismayingly low levels of publicness and of even minimal social justice. The message from Comim's composite index that we mentioned earlier is corroborated in surveys of Indian human development like those by Drèze and Sen and the India Exclusion Reports. Drèze and Sen focus on the levels of effective access to priority functionings and corresponding satisfiers, for example, facilities and practices for basic sanitation. Half of the households in India still practised open defecation in 2011 (Drèze and Sen 2013, 63), six or seven times the proportion in its neighbour, economically far poorer Bangladesh.

We have argued that required for sustained provision of priority public goods, for effective access and for activism that succeeds to hold the state accountable on behalf of everyone and not only mobilized privileged partisan groups, are public values of solidarity. Solidarity faces specific and extreme challenges in India. Foundational factors in Indian social organization, through the caste system, include what Nussbaum calls 'our tendency to feel disgust toward bodily fluids' (2013, 114) and towards our solid excreta. Chapter 7 in *Political Emotions* describes how we may project onto groups of other people our disgust at excreta and mortality, by associating those groups inseparably with such products and with corpses, human and/or animal. In India this tendency was built into a social system. A 'disgust-ridden way of life … is not very promising as a basis for a political community' (141), Nussbaum recognizes; notably the 'disgusted repudiation of mortality itself, and [of] the body as its seat' (160). Whether and how this set of perceptions, and their institutionalization in a system of hierarchy and discrimination, is counteracted or not is fundamental to India's trajectory.

India presents a very hard case for the approach advocated in *Political Emotions*, and indeed for the human development approach as a whole. The book gives extended attention to the thoughts of Rabindranath Tagore, Mahatma Gandhi and Jawaharlal Nehru. It extols the norms of material modesty that they bequeathed to some in India. Those norms have withered, and were never accompanied in most of the country by operational basic rights for all. Chapter 8 has a section on the Untouchables' (Dalits') great spokesman B. R. Ambedkar, and records the problems that Dalits continue to face more than any solutions via political liberalism and liberal arts. In higher education, Nussbaum thinks the legal infrastructure has been created for Dalit advancement, and attributes failures in integration to 'the [deficient] social/emotional support structure of government [education] institutions' (371). Ambedkar had presciently warned in 1949, near the outset of independence, that 'Without fraternity, equality and liberty will be no deeper than coats of paint.'

The subject of sanitation in particular needs the enlightenment of both tragic and comic arts. But neither seems yet to provide sufficient traction in the setting of India. Similarly, the question arises whether political liberalism, built in Europe and America, is enough for India. Will comprehensive public sanitation in India, for example, only be achieved when adopted by a neo-Hindu modernization agenda and set of sentiments? Each country has its peculiar path.

Wuyts (1992) summarizes how richer groups in nineteenth-century Europe's expanding cities, increasingly residentially secluded by income, paid private entrepreneurs to install water and sanitation systems for their neighbourhoods. Eventually however these public goods were extended to low-income areas by legislation and State subsidy, given the richer groups' wish to eliminate epidemics that endangered and inconvenienced them too, plus the growth of concern from increasingly organized medical and State bureaucracies and wider public opinion. The middle and upper classes in Europe evidently could imagine that misfortunes of the poor might happen to them too. In India, not all of the elements of tragic art emphasized by Nussbaum seem actively present in the public arena: that the audience should come to feel that the characters whom they watch experience misfortunes, misfortunes that are major and are largely not the characters' fault; that the misfortunes are avoidable and/or remediable; and that similar undeserved misfortunes could plausibly happen also to members of the audience. Instead, attention and sympathy in India, let alone action, are not sufficiently triggered. 'Looking Away' prevails (Mander 2015).

India, as a continental-scale country of over a billion people stretching from many of the richest in the world through to a third or more of its poorest, is in some ways a microcosm for the world as a whole. What Indian elites allow to happen is comparable to what global elites allow to happen on the global scale. India has no single 'Us', except perhaps in the contexts of its rivalries and conflicts with competitor nations. Its Dalit intellectuals reject as hypocritical the symbols of national unity provided by Indian elites. We come thus to the questions of how far the apparatus of national pride and commitment to which *Political Emotions* gives such weight can suffice, whether nationalism is a dead-end (in all senses) in a shared world, and what are the possible alternatives or supplements.

Global Challenges

Nussbaum's book proposes the elements of a national society founded in justice. She aims to complete Rawls's mid-twentieth-century intellectual project and the projects of Rousseau, Comte and others from earlier centuries. When Comte and Mill spoke of 'the religion of humanity' they meant a secular replacement for Christianity, but in a world of nation-states. Like Mazzini, they presumed that nationalism's downsides were readily tameable, in a brotherhood of democratic peoples (Mazower 2013).[24]

Is the traditional intellectual and political project to create well-ordered national societies still sufficient for the interwoven and seething globe of the twenty-first century with its swelling 'public bads' and huge global public goods deficits? Nussbaum has previously affiliated her theorizing to the human rights tradition (e.g. Nussbaum 2006), but *Political Emotions* contains little or no discussion of that global agenda; nor are sister enterprises like the Earth Charter mentioned. While she frequently quotes Walt Whitman, she here presumes that he proclaimed an ideal for America only and does not highlight his cosmopolitan declaration:

> One thought ever at the fore –
> That in the Divine Ship, the World, breasting Time and Space,
> All peoples of the globe together sail, sail the same voyage,
> Are bound to the same destination.   (Whitman 1995[1897], 497)

Instead Nussbaum repeats classic arguments that particularist loyalties – here patriotism – are inevitable and necessary in order to give our loyalties sufficient strength to motivate cooperative action. Following Aristotle, she claims cosmopolitanism offers merely 'watery motivation' (2013, 219). Following Mazzini, she says ordinary people need a local focus (209), and invokes Gandhi in this vein also (242); yet her main cases, the USA and India, are continental-scale countries that constitute microcosms of the globe. She admits that Martin Luther King himself intended the phrase 'all God's children' to mean what it says, a global scale of concern (239) but holds that few Americans accept that. She does not directly address the question whether a local loyalty needs to be exclusive; does 'love of the nation' (313) exclude love of many nations or love for them all? However, she holds that any eschewing of the heritage and symbols of patriotism would leave cosmopolitan forces hopelessly politically marginalized (256). So, in the world as it has evolved, with its long-standing nationally accepted stories of each nation's great contributions and sacrifices, we could now be stuck with nationalism.

Nussbaum frequently repeats the Mazzini argument from the mid-nineteenth century that nationalism forms a necessary and serviceable emotional bridge beyond the self and the locality, leading eventually to commitment to the world as a whole; a hypothesis much battered by the twentieth century. *Political Emotions'* longest chapter, entitled 'Compassion's Enemies: Fear, Envy, Shame', signally does not include nationalism in the list. Yet nationalism is imbricated with each of those enemies and is an additional independent underminer of compassion. It condones different standards for one's own cause; its pride suppresses many truths about oneself and others, and promotes contemptuous distortions about the others. Nussbaum recognizes this danger, and notes earlier how J. G. Herder (1744–1803) rejected the crude patriotism and masculinist blood lust that has fed into wars (47); but she holds that those problems are avoidable (212). 'Compassion's Enemies' argues that love tends to be particularistic, limited by or to person- or group-specific loyalties (318); and her subsequent discussion calls only for concern within the nation. The chapter concludes with the assertion that 'we cannot uproot particularism without uprooting love itself' (376). An earlier chapter is devoted to 'Teaching Patriotism'. But does the particularity of affect – insofar as affection is necessarily towards something particular – truly require a partisan partiality?

Some elements of the book take us further than this, through the words of two figures who in the 1940s stepped beyond the frame of the seventeenth- to nineteenth-century project that Rawls continued and that Nussbaum here largely returns to. While indeed being proud national leaders, Franklin D. Roosevelt and Jawaharlal Nehru moved to a more global frame. Nussbaum cites their words but does not seem to here follow through their full spirit. Nehru's great independence speech, 'A Tryst with Destiny', expounded commitment to not only the new India, and the tasks that awaited it, but to all humanity, in a now indivisibly interknit world:

These dreams are for India, but they are also for the world, for all the nations and peoples are too closely knit together today for any one of them to imagine that it can live apart. Peace has been said to be indivisible, so is freedom, so is prosperity now, and so also is disaster in this one world that can no longer be split into isolated fragments. (Nehru 1947; cited in Nussbaum 2013, 247)

Roosevelt, responding to the obligations on the leading power in this interknit world, adopted a firmly global language and scope. The paralysis of his legs, which had struck him in the prime of life, had empowered his compassion. He took the American language of freedoms and extended it to include positive freedoms – real capacities to achieve valued outcomes – and to apply it worldwide. Nussbaum notes how Roosevelt insisted, against his advisers, that his 1941 'Four Freedoms' State of the Union speech should extend the vision of basic human freedoms to apply to the whole globe. He paired the rethinking of freedom with a rethinking of fear and security. Security now meant the secure achievement of these four basic freedoms: freedom of speech, freedom of worship, freedom from want and freedom from fear, not only the last. Freedom from want and freedom from fear in particular were interdependent. Conflict and fear can directly undermine prosperity and undermine concern for others. Fear frequently weakens also the ability to learn about and understand others, and thus indirectly undermines societal cooperation. This perspective became foundational for the United Nations system established from 1945, incorporated in its themes of human rights and human security. Those offer a framework for mutual respectful awareness, inclusive sympathy, and prudence and compassion in action (Weiss et al. 2005; Jolly et al. 2009).

Human security thinking emphasizes the logic of (global) public goods – the logics of the public sanitation system and global environmental change – that there can be no security in one neighbourhood alone. It can also help to motivate cooperation to supply and maintain public goods, by its promotion of perception of human co-membership in a global socio-ecological system. Public goods provision cannot be reduced solely to calculations of even long-term enlightened self-interest, otherwise free-riding by selfishly calculating participants can destroy the system. As we have centrally argued, stable and sufficient provision of public goods rests also on public spiritedness: pride in and commitment to the collectivity. Authors like Joseph Stiglitz and Nicholas Stern, who helped to elaborate a reductionist economics of public goods, now fall back on the spirit of universal human rights and 'the vision, communication and organisation of Gandhi and Mandela' (Stern 2010, 183), when seeking to imbue motivation for investing in global public goods and acting against climate change (see Gasper 2013).

The public and political emotions that are needed for the twenty-first century must support global citizenship, not just the national projects of previous centuries. Greene warned us that many solutions to Problem I, the tension between public duty and self-interest within a group, exacerbate Problem II, the conflicts of interest between different groups. Solving Problem I by nationalism (solving 'Me versus Us' by emphasizing 'Us versus Them') condemns us to not solve Problem II. Harder still is what, adding to Greene, we can call Problem III, the issue of regulating and managing entry to the group. At play here are emotions of fear and disgust in relation to (potential) migrants and refugees. Rawls avoided discussing migration and refugees, including by implausibly suggesting that out-migration only arises if a state has culpably failed (1999).[25] The growth in migration that is at least partly driven by pressures deriving from global environmental change makes such a position obsolescent, even if it was not already absurd.

The metaphor of knitting, of identities and emotions, becomes central for the economically and environmentally interknit world of hypermodernity. It is an old image, which Nussbaum notes in Aristophanes' *Lysistrata* set in wartime fifth century BC Athens. The metaphor referred to linking Athens' different classes and groups, including immigrants and foreign denizens, to create a strong society. Nationalist forms of knitting ease Problem I but can do so by stoking Problems II and III. We need, therefore, Nussbaum herself suggests, cultural and organizational forms that promote 'a love of diversity in one's fellow citizens, and a sense that diversity is a source of pleasure, not of anxiety' (2013, 300). This applies not only for within national boundaries.

Conclusion and Some Lines for Further Work

This chapter reflected on public goods' provision or neglect and the connection to issues of publicness. It recognized that public attitudes involve emotions and perceptions, both crude and complex, not just arbitrary tastes and fixed selfish calculations. But while much work has tried to illuminate empathy, sympathy and their absence (see Krznaric 2015), less has connected this to public goods. Our chapter has been an exploratory reflection that can lead into various types of further work, not least the fuller investigation and delineation of concepts of publicness, and of the respective roles of cooperation and solidarity and other moral sentiments.

Two major themes, two major gaps or tensions, were confronted. We argued that public goods provision is essential for human development, and that successful public goods provision, operation and maintenance must rest on an evolved public spirit: publicness in the former dimension rests on publicness in the latter dimension. This theme receives too little attention in public and development economics and in discussions of public reason. We listed arguments of various natures in support of the links; to explore and test them requires further research.

Nussbaum's *Political Emotions* valuably addresses gaps in the work of Rawls and Sen regarding motivations and how actions against (and for) injustice arise. She presents a complex theory of emotions to help us think about the formation of public attitudes. Further work that would be useful includes to compare her arguments with those of Adam Smith ([1759] 2002) on moral sentiments and with the tradition of thinking about 'the common good'. We need to also connect more concretely, in research and practice, such work on emotions to campaigns for public goods. We may learn, for example, from the movement for the 'right to the city', including for migrants and refugees.

The central line of response in political philosophy has been, in effect, to try to build a national social contract or national political community.

The operative normative priorities in a society depend on the quality of effective concern shown by more powerful groups and majorities for their weaker fellows. Drèze and Sen, Mander and others document the enormous continuing neglect of basic public goods for the poorer half of the population in, as leading example, India, home to one-third of the world's estimated income-poor. Mander and Nussbaum address the perceptual and emotional, as well as political and institutional, forces related to this absence of public concern and public spirit. Wider work on public sentiments should be brought into fuller conversation with the work in and on India, notably on specifics of the struggles and debates around provision of particular public goods.

Political Emotions has energetically and creatively addressed the gap in regard to understanding of public spirit, exploring which factors mould divisive emotions and which mould emotions of solidarity. However, in this book Nussbaum inherits and adheres to the nation-state as the primary template for identity, loyalty and solidarity, and nation-building as the way to counteract neglect of the weak. The second major tension arises here. The nation-state form has generated and is likely to continue to generate great stresses and dangers in an intensively interconnected but competitive world of huge global public goods deficits. The defining challenges for the twenty-first century – including environmental change, and migration that is forced or induced by economic, environmental and demographic trends – involve issues of global not only national public goods (see Kaul et al. 2003; Brock 2009). Since, in Whitman's words, all peoples of the globe sail in the same boat, a relevant model for public emotions will incorporate perspectives also from Nussbaum's earlier work on cosmopolitanism and the Stoics, and connect to work on political cultures for human rights and human security. Roosevelt and Nehru, amongst others, foresaw the insufficiency of the nationally bounded imagination. The 'solution' of problems of national order via reliance on nationalism is likely to condemn us to fail on problems of global order.

Notes

1. On Sen's concept of commitment, see papers in Peter and Schmid (2007) and Gasper (2007b). Commitment can be to abstract entities too, notably the nation; those more abstract commitments can be in tension with commitment to concrete others.

2. Sen's *The Idea of Justice* contains far less on commitment than on public reasoning and dialogue; likewise the new edition of his *Collective Choice and Social Welfare* (2017). Similarly, Crocker's *Ethics of Global Development* extensively lists public reason in its index, but not public goods, public sentiments or emotions.

3. Comim (2015) discusses what indicators we can use for trends in publicness, including indicators for levels of childhood protection, other legal protections, urban planning, public spending, homicides, etc.

4. The composite index considered: for the Rawlsian level, public expenditure on health as per cent of GDP; for the Senian level, a blend of the under-five mortality rate and expected years of schooling; and for the Nussbaumian level of how people deal with each other, the homicide rate. Despite India's relatively low homicide rate, it comes bottom on the resulting composite index ratings, using the latest data available as of mid-2015: at 0.3 on a zero-to-1 scale, whereas China, Russia and Brazil all appear as in a different universe of publicness, around 0.7; only South Africa, at around 0.4, is close to India.

5. Exclusivism is the practice of excluding a person or group from a privilege (online dictionary definition). We employ the phrase 'possessive exclusivism' as a counterpart to C. B. MacPherson's 'possessive individualism' (1962).

6. Nussbaum's terminology oscillates between 'political emotions', the title of the book, and 'public emotions', the title of its second half. The former category seems broader, encompassing also for example concerns for heritage and legacy, but the book does not discuss the distinction. Chapter 1 rapidly adopts 'public emotions' (2, 3) and leaves the meaning of 'political' somewhat hazy: 'all those institutions that influence people's life chances pervasively and over the entire course of their lives (John Rawls's notion of "the basic structure")' (16).

7. See also Gasper (2002, 2007a), Deneulin and Townsend (2007), Geaves and Penning-Rowsell (2016). Parts of this section build on ideas in Gasper (2002).

8. Rivalrousness: my consumption of a good means that you cannot consume it. Excludability: exclusion of others from access to a good can be implemented at an affordable cost.

9. Thus for Drèze and Sen (1989), 'public action' is action for public benefit, which can be done by various agents, including private agents too.

10. Musgrave's term 'merit goods' is not sufficient though. Acknowledging greater merit in something than the valuation awarded to it in markets is considerably less than deciding to give it priority in public action.

11. See, e.g., Doyal and Gough's influential *Theory of Human Need* (1991).

12. See, e.g., the *India Exclusion Report 2013–2014* (CES 2014) on the frequent absence of separate girls' toilets in schools in India, and its implications.

13. A separate paper is needed to explore the relationship of our stance here to the philosophical tradition of moral sentimentalism. We do not adopt a Humean assertion of the priority of feelings, and instead seek to elaborate a more Smithian, Senian and Nussbaumian approach in which, as we discuss later, moral sentiments provide a starting point but need reasoned scrutiny, but where in addition, as stressed by Nussbaum, effective moral views are those adopted as sentiments.

14. For example, Sen holds that 'all of us are capable of being reasonable through being open-minded about welcoming information and through reflecting on arguments coming from different quarters, along with undertaking interactive deliberations and debates on how the underlying issues should be seen' (2009, 43).

15. For Nussbaum:

    The person leaves the state of nature not because it is more mutually advantageous to make a deal with others, but because she cannot imagine living well without shared ends and a shared life. Living with and toward others, with both benevolence and justice, is part of the shared public conception of the person that all affirm for political purposes. (2006, 158)

16. In her words (2006, 295), 'For the capabilities approach, at any rate, equality is important at the very base of the theory; for it is not just human dignity that must be respected, it is equal human dignity.'

17. 'Respect on its own is cold and inert, insufficient to overcome the bad tendencies that lead human beings to tyrannize over one another' (Nussbaum 2013, 380).

18. She often still uses though the term 'fraternity' for fellow-feeling and solidarity (2013, 37).

19. For example, St Paul in 1 Corinthians 13:4–7 and 13:13.

20. To illustrate communication of a tragic perspective she discusses the 1930s US Government use of photographs of victims of the Great Depression.

21. Her system includes also of course a strong, and reasoned, commitment to liberalism. Sometimes Nussbaum uses liberal as a normative praise term or ideal, not as a descriptor of actual societies: 'A liberal society asks people to be ashamed of excessive greed and selfishness' (2013, 23); but which liberal society really does that? Nussbaum's left-liberalism (cf. Fawcett 2015) elsewhere acknowledges that really-existing liberalism typically becomes illiberal in regard to weaker groups and persons, and needs to be bounded.

22. Page 121 claims that her *Frontiers of Justice* provided a full defence of this presumption. See commentaries though in Gasper (2006b).
23. The phrase 'shithole countries', adopted by one American statesman, provides a noxious illustration.
24. Mill was cosmopolitan in his declared long-term aims, but *much* less so in his stances during a thirty-five-year career as a senior British East India Company colonial administrator (Lal 1998).
25. The index of Greene's *Moral Tribes* too has no mention of the basic issue of migration/immigration.

References

Ambedkar, B. R., 1949. Speech to Indian Constituent Assembly, 25 November 1949.

Antonsen, M., and Jorgensen, T. B., 1997. The 'Publicness' of Public Organizations. *Public Administration* 75(2): 337–57.

Brock, G., 2009. *Global Justice: A Cosmopolitan Account*. New York: Oxford University Press.

CES, 2014. *India Exclusion Report, 2013–2014*. New Delhi: Centre for Equity Studies. www.indianet.nl/pdf/IndiaExclusionReport2013-2014 .pdf (accessed 21 August 2018).

CES, 2016. *India Exclusion Report, 2015*. New Delhi: Centre for Equity Studies. www.im4change.org/docs/91763text-final_India-Exclusion-R eport-round2Final.pdf (accessed 21 August 2018).

CES, 2017. *India Exclusion Report, 2016*. New Delhi: Centre for Equity Studies. www.defindia.org/wp-content/uploads/.../India%20Exclusion %20Report%202016_low.pdf (accessed 21 August 2018).

Comim, F., 2015. Development and Publicness: Rawls, Sen and Nussbaum. Paper presented at the HDCA conference, September 2015, Georgetown University, Washington, DC.

Comim, F., 2019. Publicness and Human Development: an illustration from BRICS. In *Handbook of BRICS and Emerging Economies*, P.B. Anand, S. Fennell, and F. Comim (eds.), Oxford: Oxford University Press.

Crocker, D., 2008. *Ethics of Global Development: Agency, Capability, and Deliberative Democracy*. New York: Cambridge University Press.

Deneulin, S., and Townsend, N., 2007. Public Goods, Global Public Goods and the Common Good. *International Journal of Social Economics* 34 (1/2): 19–36.

De Swaan, A., 1988. *In Care of the State: Health Care, Education and Welfare in Europe and the USA in the Modern Era*. Cambridge: Polity.

Douglas, M., and Ney, S., 1998. *Missing Persons: A Critique of the Social Sciences*. Berkeley, CA: University of California Press.

Doyal, L., and Gough, I., 1991. *A Theory of Human Need*. Basingstoke: Macmillan.

Drèze, J., and Sen., A., 1989. *Hunger and Public Action*. Oxford: Clarendon Press.

Drèze, J., and Sen., A., 2013. *An Uncertain Glory: India and its Contradictions*. London: Allen Lane.

Fawcett, E., 2015. *Liberalism: The Life of an Idea*. Expanded edn. Princeton University Press.

Frederickson, H. G., 1996. Principles for South African Public Administration in the Transformation Decades: An American Perspective. In *Challenges in Change*, A. P. J. Burger, F. Theron and A. van Rooyen (eds.), Bellville, South Africa: Stellenbosch University, 298–323.

Gasper, D., 2002. Fashion, Learning and Values in Public Management. *Africa Development* 27(3): 17–47.

Gasper, D., 2005a. Needs and Human Rights. In *The Essentials of Human Rights*, R. Smith and C. van den Anker (eds.), London: Hodder & Stoughton, 269–72.

Gasper, D., 2005b. Securing Humanity: Situating 'Human Security' as Concept and Discourse. *Journal of Human Development* 6(2): 221–45.

Gasper, D., 2006a. Working in Development Ethics: A Tribute to Denis Goulet. *Ethics and Economics / La revue Éthique et Économique* 4(2): 1–24.

Gasper, D. (ed.), 2006b. Cosmopolitanisms and the Frontiers of Justice. *Development and Change* 37(6): 1227–334.

Gasper, D., 2007a. Goods and Persons, Reasons and Responsibilities. *International Journal of Social Economics* 34 (1/2): 6–18.

Gasper, D., 2007b. Adding Links, Adding People, Adding Structures: Using Sen's Frameworks. *Feminist Economics* 13(1): 67–85.

Gasper, D., 2013. Climate Change and the Language of Human Security. *Ethics, Policy and Environment* 16(1): 56–78.

Geaves, L., and Penning-Rowsell, E., 2016. Flood Risk Management as a Public or a Private Good, and the Implications for Stakeholder Engagement. *Environmental Science & Policy* 55: 281–91.

Goulet, D., 1971. *The Cruel Choice*. New York: Atheneum.

Gray, J., 1993. *Beyond the New Right: Markets, Government and the Common Environment*. London: Routledge.

Greene, J., 2015. *Moral Tribes: Emotion, Reason, and the Gap between Us and Them*. London: Atlantic Books.

Jolly, R., Emmerij, L. and Weiss, T. G., 2009. *UN Ideas That Changed the World*. Bloomington, IN: Indiana University Press.

Kaul, I., Conceição, P., Le Goulven, K. and Mendoza, R. U. (eds.), 2003. *Providing Global Public Goods: Managing Globalization*. New York: Oxford University Press.

Krznaric, R., 2015. *Empathy*. London: Rider Books/Random House.

Lal, V., 1998. *John Stuart Mill and India*, a Review-Article. *New Quest* 54: 54–64.

Larmore, C., 2003. Public Reason. In *The Cambridge Companion to Rawls*, S. Freeman (ed.), Cambridge University Press, 368–93.

MacPherson, C. B., 1962. *The Political Theory of Possessive Individualism: From Hobbes to Locke*. Oxford University Press.

Mander, H., 2015. *Looking Away: Inequality, Prejudice and Indifference in New India*. Delhi: Speaking Tiger.

Mazower, M., 2013. *Governing the World: The History of an Idea*. London: Penguin.

Nehru, J., 1947. Speech on the Granting of Indian Independence, 14 August 1947, https://sourcebooks.fordham.edu/mod/1947nehru1.asp?Speech (accessed 21 August 2018).

Newman, O., 2015. *Liberalism in Practice: The Psychology and Pedagogy of Public Reason*. Cambridge, MA: MIT Press.

Nussbaum, M., 1995. Emotions and Women's Capabilities. In *Women, Culture and Development*, M. Nussbaum and J. Glover (eds.), Oxford: Clarendon Press, 360–95.

Nussbaum, M., 2001. *Upheavals of Thought*. Cambridge University Press.

Nussbaum, M., 2006. *Frontiers of Justice*. Cambridge, MA: Harvard University Press.

Nussbaum, M. 2013. *Political Emotions: Why Love Matters for Justice*. Cambridge, MA: Harvard University Press.

Oxford English Reference Dictionary. 1996. Oxford University Press.

Pattanaik, P., 2014. Introduction. In *The Arrow Impossibility Theorem*, E. Maskin and A. Sen, New York: Columbia University Press.

Pesch, U., 2008. The Publicness of Public Administration. *Administration and Society* 40(2): 170–93.

Peter, F., and Schmid, H. B. (eds.), 2007. *Rationality and Commitment*. Oxford University Press.

Rawls, J., 1971. *A Theory of Justice*. Cambridge, MA: Harvard University Press.

Rawls, J., 1993. *Political Liberalism*. New York: Columbia University Press.

Rawls, J., 1999. *The Law of Peoples*. Cambridge, MA: Harvard University Press.

Rawls, J., 2001. *Justice as Fairness*. Cambridge, MA: Harvard University Press.

Raz, J., 1986. *The Morality of Freedom*. Oxford: Clarendon Press.

Sen, A., 2002. *Rationality and Freedom*. Cambridge, MA: Harvard University Press.

Sen, A., 2009. *The Idea of Justice*. London: Allen Lane.

Sen, A., 2017. *Collective Choice and Social Welfare*. Expanded edn. London: Penguin.

Sennett, R., 1977. *The Fall of Public Man*. New York: Knopf.

Sennett, R., 2012. *Together: The Rituals, Pleasures and Politics of Cooperation*. London: Penguin.

Smith, A., [1759] 2002. *Theory of Moral Sentiments*. K. Haakonssen (ed.), Cambridge University Press.

Stern, N., 2010. *A Blueprint for a Safer Planet*. London: Vintage Books.

Weiss, T. G., Carayannis, T., Emmerij, L. and Jolly, R., 2005. *UN Voices: The Struggle for Development and Social Justice*. Bloomington, IN: Indiana University Press.

Whitman, W., 1995 [1897]. One Thought Ever at the Fore. In *The Works of Walt Whitman*. Ware, Herts: Wordsworth Editions, 497.

Wuyts, M., 1992. Deprivation and Public Need. In *Development Policy and Public Action*, M. Mackintosh, T. Hewitt and M. Wuyts (eds.), Oxford University Press, 13–37.

4 The Choice of a Moral Lens

LGBTI Persons, Human Rights, and the Capabilities Approach

CHLOE SCHWENKE

The lived realities of lesbian, gay, bisexual, transgender, and intersex (LGBTI) persons are complicated and extremely diverse across generations, cultures, genders, and economies. With respect to all marginalized populations everywhere, including those LGBTI persons who live in the less developed countries of the world (the Global South), the challenge for all those with a concern for furthering sustainable, equitable, and effective international development for this marginalized population begins with resolving how best to understand, evaluate, respond to, and support their development aspirations and needs. As argued so eloquently by David Crocker throughout his book *Ethics of Global Development: Agency, Capability, and Deliberation* (2008), progress in human development is only achieved and sustained when agency demands are respected, capabilities are expanded, and when deliberative participation excludes no one – provisions which no doubt David Crocker would certainly agree also apply to LGBTI persons.

This is no trivial undertaking; the plight of LGBTI persons is complicated by vastly differing social and legal contexts, by the pervasive influence of religious values that are often intolerant of sexual and gender minorities, by the larger society's general lack of concern for the extreme persecution and violence that is routinely visited upon members of the LGBTI community in many countries, by a near total lack of reliable empirical data on the daily lives of LGBTI persons, and by a profoundly detrimental and disempowering legacy of comprehensive exclusion of LGBTI persons from social services (education, health, social services, employment, rule of law, etc.) and from democratic participation. In addition, the deep economic insecurity and unemployment, the extreme vulnerability to certain sexually transmitted diseases, and the general marginalization experienced by LGBTI persons around the world has historically rendered them unable to advocate effectively for their own dignity. The voice of LGBTI persons is only now beginning to be heard within an increasingly globalized world, as their agency begins to grow.

Marginalized communities (including but not limited to persons with disabilities, ethnic minorities, certain indigenous populations, and sexual and gender minorities) have a long history of exclusion, stigmatization, persecution, injustice, and sometimes even violent victimization. Humanity has been slow to embrace the universal arguments that underlie the concepts of human dignity and human rights, even if progress is discernible. The global ethical challenge confronting humanity's moral evolution now is to make the claim of universal, equal human dignity genuine in practice, not merely in theory. Two moral lenses – the capabilities approach[1] and human rights frameworks – each make significant contributions toward this end, but as demonstrated by the plight of LGBTI persons and other very marginalized populations around the world, the path ahead will be long and difficult. In addressing these difficulties, is one of these two lenses more efficacious?

Global progress has been made in the pursuit of a "truly human"[2] quality of life for all persons everywhere, and the now mature field of international development ethics has played an important role in such progress. Still, development ethics remains characterized by a yawning chasm between academics and practitioners. That isn't to imply that the separation is absolute; many practitioners exercise the scholarly discipline of keeping abreast of the most notable contributions to the literature associated with the norms of international development emanating from the academy and the think tanks. Still, personal anecdotal experience from those few individuals like me with a foot in each camp would suggest that a relatively paltry number of practitioners are able, motivated, or even invited to participate in the theoretical and evaluative discourse that university programs in international development and the think tanks engender in the context of ethics and values. This separation between town and gown may account for an interesting phenomenon: while universities with international development programs now regularly feature courses and events on what is arguably the most sophisticated ethical framing of quality of life and international development – the capability approach – the practitioner, donor, philanthropist, and diplomatic world associated with international development remains largely detached from any form of structured ethical reflection on the means and ends of international development, with the important exception being the occasional reference (if often only rhetorical) to traditional human rights frameworks (political, legal, and moral).

Institutionally, the major multilateral and bilateral institutions of international development share a common absence of any robust institutional mechanisms, resources, spaces, processes, or practices directly linked to normative reflection, analysis, explication, justification, or criticism of international development policies, programs, opportunities, constraints, or priorities. This wasn't always the case. For close to twenty-five years there was an informal World Bank discussion group on the ethics of development that met at the Bank in Washington every Friday morning at 8 a.m., which David Crocker and I frequently attended. This remarkable group was founded by David Beckmann, Ramgopal Agarwala, Sven Burmester, and Ismail Serageldin, and embraced discussions on an extensive range of ethical, spiritual, religious, and moral aspects of international development. There was also the World Bank's Development Dialogue on Values and Ethics which sponsored several very engaging events, but which ceased operation in 2010. From 2002 to 2007 the Inter-American Development Bank, with funding from the Norwegian government and other donors, established a short-lived Initiative for Social Capital and the Ethics of Development (ISED) where both David Crocker and I served as consultants. Unfortunately, after the resignation of Enrique Iglesias as that Bank's president, no subsequent leader stepped forward as an institutional champion for this agenda within that Bank.

In contrast, beginning with its unequivocal advocacy of universal human dignity and human rights in the Universal Declaration of Human Rights in December of 1948, and more recently through the United Nations Development Program (UNDP)'s annual Human Development Reports, the UN has established a critically important leadership role in introducing the principles of the capability approach to a very wide audience and by providing a solid resource on the moral dimensions of human rights approaches. In the latter context, the Human Development Report edition from 2000 (UNDP 2000, for which Amartya Sen provided many sections) has come to be regarded by many in the practitioner community as the primary resource for human rights theory and practice. The UNDP, along with many other United Nations institutions, continues to provide thought leadership in normative concepts such as human development, social inclusion, non-discrimination, and human rights.

In 2005–6, David Crocker and I were able to attract a joint commission to coauthor a short publication for the US Agency for International Development (USAID), *The Relevance of Development Ethics for USAID*, but this received little feedback from that Agency and none of the short list of recommendations that we put forward were acted upon (Crocker and Schwenke 2006).[3] Undaunted, my efforts to proselytize to USAID about the importance of the moral lens continued. In 2011, while I was a political appointee under the Obama Administration assigned to USAID, I proposed to the agency's Bureau for Policy, Planning, and Learning a policy "white paper" on development ethics. In the preparation of this concept paper, I attempted to identify practical ways in which USAID might reduce the gap between its publicly stated broad moral and ethical principles that occasionally appear in its publications and in official speeches, and the work that USAID actually does – its "practice." By bridging that gap, I argued that USAID might be empowered to know how to apply these moral principles in practical ways to guide the quality, scope, and direction of its policies and programs, to justify how USAID officials make critical trade-offs (e.g., in deciding priorities in the context of scarce resources and urgent development needs), and to assist them as they explain USAID's mission to their stakeholders and to the American public in cohesive, ethically justifiable, and accountable ways. While many individual USAID staff responded very warmly and energetically to this initiative, it too failed to attract any institutional support from the Agency's leadership. To this day, USAID at best makes only passing references to the capability approach, and does not incorporate this lens in any robust sense in its policies, operations, and overall decision-making.

USAID is not unique in this sense. None of the leading donor institutions have positions on their salaried or consulting staffs for development ethicists, and none have any regular institutionalized processes in place to routinely evaluate their operations from moral and ethical perspectives (outside of the legal and regulatory compliance-focused dimension of codes of conduct and disclosure). This pervasive absence of structured methods or institutional mechanisms for ethical reflection among the workplaces and institutions of development practitioners is perhaps indicative of larger societal priorities, but the failure of this community to embrace the capability approach as a regular design and evaluative tool in international development is more than unfortunate. In many ways, the capability approach is uniquely positioned to expand and refine the way that international development is conceptualized, and to guide the evaluation of the significance of the results achieved. For example, among the many proponents of the capability approach two central questions are frequently posed and assessed with respect to international development. First, what is important to the good life, to human well-being? And second, how should this good and important thing be distributed? In responding, the capability approach asserts that the emphasis ought to be people-focused, recognizing that people can differ greatly in their needs, diversity, cultures, and values. While human rights frameworks impose normative thresholds and empower people to demand government compliance in meeting their rights-based claims, the capability approach challenges people to delineate their own ideals of the good life, to contemplate those freedoms and opportunities that are and are not available to them, and to demand that essential gaps in their well-being be remedied. To date, LGBTI persons and their civil society organizations in the Global South have largely advocated for their development priorities on the basis of universal human rights principles and laws, and more recently using narratives to emphasize principles of social inclusion, yet the dialogue on quality of life and human well-being is certainly not absent. The still-prevailing choice by this community of the human rights lens is largely a function of the existence of an international infrastructure of human rights treaties and laws, clearly stated in several key treaty instruments and declarations, through which focused advocacy is deemed to have more traction. That is a presumption that may not be correct; arguably the capability approach lens offers the greater potential to engage the public of the Global South in a deeper discourse on core values of human well-being and agency, leading in time to a softening of homophobic and transphobic attitudes.

In the context of international development, Amartya Sen originated the capability approach in the early 1980s and has since continued to elaborate it in the context of a variety of development issues. Other philosophers, economists, and scholars such as Martha Nussbaum,

David Crocker, Sabina Alkire, Severine Deneulin, Mozaffar Qizilbash, Des Gasper, Stacy Kosko, Jay Drydyk, Elizabeth Anderson, and Lori Keleher have articulated variations and applied them to particular development challenges such as the meaning of dignity (Nussbaum) or justice (Drydyk), consumption practices (Crocker), the measurement of multidimensional poverty (Alkire), democratic citizenship and deliberative participation (Anderson, Crocker), children's rights (Kosko), displaced peoples (Drydyk), gender equity (Nussbaum, Gasper, Keleher), indigenous peoples (Kosko), and the concept of well-being (Qizilbash, Crocker). Given the profusion of excellent publications on the capability approach, it is not surprising that many international development practitioners have heard of this moral theory, yet the core concepts upon which this theory (in its many variations) is structured remain less well understood. Simply put, the capability approach identifies valuable human functionings that correlate with central human capabilities. Beyond the basic physical human functionings (such as digestion, longevity, health, sleep, recreation, and procreation), there are other activities individuals have reason to value, although they may specify and weigh them in different ways.

Academics and theorists have been laboring over the past two decades and longer to generate one or more effective normative frameworks that can be applied by analysts, practitioners, and scholars as lenses to illuminate, measure, and explicate the many complex dimensions of international development. And while some of the leading capability approach thinkers such as Nussbaum have created their own lists of central human capabilities, none of these lists is accepted (or were ever proposed) as being definitive. Even the one normative framework that is relatively well known in the practitioner community, as featured in Nussbaum's *Women and Human Development* (2000, 78–80) is rarely found to be applied by practitioners in development programming, policies, or evaluation techniques. This particular iteration by Nussbaum included, in summary form, the following elements:

(1) Being able to live a normal life span;
(2) Being able to enjoy bodily and reproductive health and shelter;
(3) Being able to enjoy freedom of movement and respect for bodily integrity against security threats and violence;
(4) Being able to use and enjoy the senses, imagination, and thought in a "truly human way";

(5) Being able to have emotional attachments to places, things and people, and to live without emotional abuse;
(6) Being able to use practical reason to form a conception of one's life plan;
(7) Being able to affiliate – to live with, for and "toward" others, to have self-respect, and to exercise compassion;
(8) Being able to live in a concerned and respectful relationship to other species;
(9) Being able to play; and
(10) Being able to enjoy freedom to participate in government and in the control over one's environment.

(2000, 78–81)

It's a robust framework, and its near-absence in pragmatic practitioner application is curious. Perhaps practitioners find it to be politically naïve, as according to most capability approach thinkers each of these central human capabilities must be satisfied at least to its threshold level before any discussion of trade-offs can be entertained, if they can be considered at all. The satisfaction of each human capability does not require direct government intervention, but instead demands that government delivers the enabling environment – Nussbaum calls it the "social basis" – for all of these capabilities: "In order to be doing what they should for their citizens, states must be concerned with all the capabilities, even when these seem not so useful for economic growth, or even for political functioning" (90).

Fortunately for the field of international development, Amartya Sen won the 1998 Nobel Prize in Economics. Being thus recognized both as a leading philosopher and economist, Sen's influence has been and continues to be immense, including among many in the practitioner community. In advocating for the capability approach, Sen exposed practitioners and their institutions to numerous writings by him and by many authors on the applicability of the capability approach to international development means and goals. Institutions such as the World Bank, UNDP, the regional development banks, most of the European bilateral foreign aid agencies, and to a lesser extent USAID, now have on their staff development practitioners who are at least familiar with the capability approach. Yet, despite this, when it comes time to design, implement, measure, or evaluate foreign assistance interventions, policies, or programs, the preeminence of approaches based primarily on political economy principles, economics, or technical criteria dominate. The only normative influence of any substance on such institutions are human rights approaches, but even here the focus is more closely directed to concerns about the prevention, mitigation, or prosecution of human rights abuses than on the impacts of the promotion of human rights principles or values.

While moral frameworks are relatively rare in the practitioner world of international development, human rights-based approaches remain the best entrenched. There are very good reasons for this. Human rights precepts exist not only as very comprehensive – if regularly debated – moral assertions, but they also constitute a very extensive body of international human rights laws, treaties, protocols, agreements, and measurement systems based on such legal concepts. In practical terms, when development practitioners discuss human rights, the default assumption is that they are referring to the legal frameworks and not the moral approaches that underpin legal constructs. The unit of normative analysis largely remains the nation-state, which aligns well with such legal concepts, instead of the individual, which is more attuned to individual (or at least "household") quality of life moral considerations.

Within the narrow space allocated to normative considerations, the marked preference for reliance on a human rights lens within the practitioner community doesn't entirely displace consideration of the capability approach, with the latter's more comprehensive focus on human dignity, freedoms, agency, and opportunities, and its direct relevance to democratic principles. After all, capability approach thinking does share a close relationship with human rights approaches, in particular those capability approach frameworks that make some reference to certain identified rights as "human rights" and which call out valuable functions that are to be protected and promoted by rights – as goals or as tools. Nussbaum emphasizes that political liberties have a central importance in establishing the human quality of well-being, and – referring to Sen's writings – in characterizing the mutual respect that people owe each other. Yet, Nussbaum's view is that the capabilities approach[4] does more than complement human rights approaches, arguing that the best way to think about rights is to see them as combined capabilities:[5]

The right to political participation, the right to religious free exercise, the right of free speech – these and others are all best thought of as capacities to

function. In other words, to secure rights to citizens in these areas is to put
them in a position of combined capability to function in that area. (2000,
96–98)

Human rights depend on two foundational concepts. First, an identifi-
able subject who has entitlements exists. Second, a duty-bearer who is
obliged to respond to claims of such entitlements also exists (Dunne and
Wheeler 1999, 3). Jack Donnelly also differentiates the duty-bearer's
distinct obligations to accept that the *possession* of a human right is
innately a function of being human and is not bestowed by the state; that
the state and all citizens share a mutual and reciprocal duty to *respect*
a person's human rights, and that the measure of such respect is to be
seen and measured in the *enforceability* of that right (1989, 11–12).
Another central claim about human rights is that they are universal –
a contention that is grounded in several moral theories including that
known as natural law. This universalist premise is not without controversy, but it does not depend for its defense on natural law. However, the
moral debate between the implications of adopting universalist or relativist (e.g., traditional cultural) assumptions – or something bridging
these two – characterizes many heated debates on human rights, particularly in the context of sexual and gender minorities (LGBTI persons).

All 192 member countries of the United Nations are signatories to
the Universal Declaration of Human Rights (UDHR), and most have
signed similar international agreements.[6] By signing, these countries
formally acknowledge that all persons possess certain human rights,
beginning with those described in the UDHR's thirty articles.
In practice, however, a significant number of these human rights are
not respected, and may not be influential in the establishment of public
policy or legislation. Furthermore, where public policy and/or legislation is derived from human rights principles there is often a failure of
political will or capability, so that the human right remains merely an
unenforced right or a symbolic but toothless instrument of government
rhetoric. The failure of a government to legislate or enforce human
rights does not necessarily mean that the government concerned actually rejects the existence of that human right, but they clearly do not
respect that right. The negative impacts of the failure to enforce such
disrespected rights are considerable.

Human rights provide a basis for assessing (negatively or positively)
legal rights and protections. Human rights however are not just linked

to what might be viewed as abstract values; the concept of human rights also embraces those social practices by which these values are realized, and makes explicit those social practices that stand in the way of the full recognition of universal human dignity. Certain social practices, such as the persecution, exclusion, and abuse of those within marginalized communities, are themselves violations of universal human rights, and frequently lead to further disrespect for dignity and additional gross and pervasive violations of such rights.

Defining and building a consensus on the "list" of human rights is challenging – engaging both political and philosophical minds. Because human rights are norms or prescriptions, no scientific means will yield a list of human rights. Instead, formulating a list and subsequently codifying this into law in large measure relies on a process of political dialogue, or more accurately perhaps, political struggle. Moral considerations inform this struggle, as human rights advocates invoke principles of social justice, social inclusion, nondiscrimination, intersectionality, care and compassion, and human dignity to expand human rights concepts and human rights-based laws to cover persons without regard to ethnic origins, gender, religion, age, physical ability, nationality, sexual orientation, gender identity, or other such characteristics. The arduous, knotty process by which the UDHR was formulated in the mid-1940s is an excellent example of the intensity and valuable results of this struggle, yet even this document makes no claims to be a definitive list of all human rights. Clearly, not all rights are human rights. Both human rights-based moral theories and legal rights focus on claims to various entitlements and freedoms, such as claims of ownership, property rights, and claims for decent working conditions. The role of rights in moral theories and law also varies. Some view rights as desirable ends in themselves (e.g., Ronald Dworkin), others (e.g., Charles Beitz, John Rawls, David Hume) conceive of rights as the means to achieve certain desirable ends,[7] while yet other moral theories and legal conceptions of rights understand rights as both means and ends (e.g., Immanuel Kant). In the choice to apply human rights as a lens to guide international development, it is therefore important to be specific in defining what is intended by the term "human rights."

LGBTI persons may wish to be cautious in opting for the human rights lens. Recently, there have been concerns expressed among some international development practitioners and theorists about what they consider to be the unbridled proliferation of human rights categories and claims (Mchangama and Verdirame 2013). Such critics argue that "new" human rights are being advocated all the time, which makes the overall application of human rights to development means and ends less well defined, less defensible, and hence more problematic. It is therefore helpful to look back at two earlier and more parsimonious approaches to how human rights were conceived. Four decades ago, Henry Shue based his conceptual framework on what would now be considered a very narrow premise, arguing for the moral priority of what he terms "basic human rights" associated with the enjoyment of such essential "substances" as subsistence, security, and certain human liberties. Shue asserted that if human rights do not protect these three valuable features of a person's life, there's little purpose in seeking rights-based protections for the enjoyment of other valuable features (due legal process, freedom to marry and found a family, education, and so forth). Shue defined "subsistence" as minimum economic security – unpolluted air/water, adequate food/clothing/shelter, and minimum preventative public health care; "security" as full physical security – not to be subjected to murder, mayhem, torture, assault, or rape; and "liberty" as a right to both mobility and to participation in the control of the political and economic policies and institutions that determine the fulfillment of security, subsistence, and other rights (1996, 8–9, 18–23, 67, 78).

Peter Brown also proposed a parsimonious human rights structure based on just three unranked rights: bodily integrity; moral, political, and religious choice; and subsistence. He asserted that government ought to be held to be the ultimate guarantor of these rights. To this structure, Brown adds the following nested set of three duties: (1) all persons have obligations to respect the basic rights of all other persons, (2) governments have backup obligations to enforce and/or execute themselves the obligations of individuals when individuals fail to discharge them, (3) the international community has the backup obligations to enforce and/or execute these obligations when nations fail to discharge them (2000, 20–21).

Satisfying even these relatively modest sets of human rights obligations would represent a radical improvement in the lived realities of LGBTI persons in much of the Global South, where such factors as constant physical insecurity and victimization, lack of respect for their basic rights made manifest through pervasive social norms of exclusion and humiliation, and the denial of access to licit forms of livelihood are now commonplace – and debilitating – for this community.

While both Shue's and Brown's approaches, along with several other "basic rights" framings, remain influential in moral deliberations on the essential nature and foundations of human rights, the current international human rights regime is not based directly on concepts arising out of philosophical basic rights thinking as applied to international development. Instead, the international human rights regime effectively began as a political process with the 1944 United Nations Charter and with the 1948 Universal Declaration of Human Rights. Neither definitively establishes the existence of human rights, and neither sets limits on what constitutes human rights in ethical terms. In the Preamble to the Universal Declaration, the principal actors are conceived to be nation-states, and the principal actions called for are "progressive measures, national and international" (United Nations 1948). Only much later did UNDP redirect some of the discussion toward the role of human rights in international development, offering its own comprehensive statement in its *Human Development Report 2000*.

According to the UNDP's conception, development and human rights need each other. Human development[8] has many valuable features that human rights are intended to protect and promote. Yet, human rights themselves also are among the list of valuable features, capturing the sense of the implicit value of human rights as an objective that is worth securing and as an expression of our essential humanity and shared dignity. While acknowledging that human rights and human development have overlapping motivations and aims, UNDP does recognize that each is substantially different from the other. The basis of human rights – the insistence on a claim on others – is a larger ambition than that of most human development thinking. Human development thinking typically is more focused on what development ought to *be* and *how* it ought to be achieved than (if at all) on *who or what* has the duty to achieve it. It is even less demanding on *when* development ought to be achieved. Instead, the human development dialogue concentrates on the characteristics of human flourishing, by what means this flourishing can be promoted and protected, and on a diverse and comprehensive range of empirical indicators to monitor progress in many aspects of human development. Human development theories rarely impose specific moral duties upon others to bring about human development, although human rights proponents are inclined to ask *when* and *by whom* questions, and to demand specific answers.

The way ahead, as asserted by the UNDP in 2000, is to concentrate efforts in the realization and securing of a distillation of the UDHR's thirty articles into seven essential freedoms, both positive (freedom for/ of) and negative (freedom from), into a more parsimonious lens as follows:

(1) Freedom from discrimination – for equality.
(2) Freedom from want – for a decent standard of living.
(3) Freedom from being thwarted in self-realization – for the realization of one's human potential.
(4) Freedom from fear – with no threats to personal security.
(5) Freedom from injustice.
(6) Freedom from repression – for participation, expression and association.
(7) Freedom from exploitation – for decent work.

(UNDP 2000, 31)

This was a very ambitious and comprehensive agenda for 2000, and remains so to this day. If truly acted upon by governments, with deep popular commitment and political will, the international changes to the economic, political, and social environment at all levels – global to local – would be profound. The marginalization and exclusion of sexual and gender minorities in the Global South would no longer be tolerated, and the efforts made toward poverty alleviation and eradication would be exponentially larger and more intense. Representative and participatory democracy would flourish, and a morally rich process of deliberative dialogue would characterize development planning and governance at all levels. Social and political institutions would not be exclusively characterized as mechanisms for bargaining between competing interests, but more as the internalization of agreed upon and shared moral values and as a basis for expanded collaboration. Perhaps above all, the enabling environment would change so that a human rights culture based on a broad consensus on the significance and universality of human dignity would find fertile ground to flourish and take root – both within government and civil society. Such outcomes would be transformative for the LGBTI peoples of the Global South.

To achieve a world characterized by a pervasive human rights culture would require significant changes in how governments conceive of their own role (morally, politically, and practically), a genuine change of ethos toward public service, and the consistent public manifestation of values that are not currently associated with most elite groups who control governments. Given a long legacy of poor human rights performance (and in some cases flagrant human rights abuses) by governments, the citizens who assert their human rights claims (often in adversarial mode) seldom actually expect that their governments will respond in a morally defensible and satisfactory manner, which again begs the question of whether holding the unit of analysis at the nation-state level is persuasive. Perhaps an approach to human flourishing such as the capability approach that is more focused on building common ground among empowered persons each exercising her or his moral agency in harmony with their peers, ideally within a democratic framework, would achieve better results?

To explore this, consider the plight of LGBTI persons in the Global South in one of the eighty-five countries where same-sex sexual orientation is criminalized, and where the legal status of transgender and intersex persons is either unrecognized, conflated with gays and lesbians, or mired in confusion.[9] In these countries, the prevailing social values (often explicitly reinforced by their governments) assert that traditional cultural values that stridently reject homosexuality and nonconforming gender identity ought to take precedence over human rights principles, effectively rejecting the universalist premise shared by both human rights moral theories and by the capability approach. This leaves those who are worst affected by such homophobic and transphobic values little option but to make their choice for the human rights lens, to appeal to the international community for the protection of their human rights, effectively exacerbating the adversarial positioning that is so common to human rights advocacy. The alternative choice that is the underlying premise of the capability approach as a lens – that individuals within a social unit would gather to deliberate and seek agreement upon a shared "list" of the attributes of a truly human life – remains untested and is probably overly optimistic. In the best case, the prospect of people gathered to agree upon common development means and goals might well allow for personal narratives to surface that would dispel the deep stigma that is attached to individuals within the LGBTI community, but this would assume a tolerance currently not present in many societies in the Global South to allow that degree of diversity to characterize the deliberative assembly. The challenge of empowering sexual and gender minorities so that they can achieve full democratic participation and have their human dignity respected is complicated by their relatively small numbers, and by the pervasiveness of toxic social attitudes against them in so many societies. Unless people outside the LGBTI community yet within the same society begin to genuinely care about the plight of sexual and gender minorities and seek their inclusion, the prospect of any development intervention aimed at capability expansion and based upon the principles of the capability approach is questionable. As noted by Clare Poolman (2012), the capability approach is self-focused with respect to the expansion of freedoms and human agency, and the status quo of socio-economic power structures that are comprised of people who do not care for certain others is unlikely to be shifted by any arguments derived from capability approach thinking.

The practical challenges of applying the capability approach at the individual level to build social solidarity across deep fault lines of exclusion and stigma are hardly insignificant, but deliberative, democratic, and participatory processes have been demonstrated to overcome socioeconomic and ethnic differences.[10] In the context of LGBTI concerns, the initial hurdle would be to establish this deliberation on the basis of agency, opportunities, and freedoms, and not on sexual behavior or on the presumption on gender immutability or a fixed gender binary. Misinformation and ignorance about the nature of homosexuality and about nonconforming gender identities are widespread, and the limited population with experiential reality of same-sex-oriented sexual behavior combined with the absence of any settled consensus regarding the scope and meaning of the transgender and intersex phenomena all serve to threaten the stability of the established binary gendered division of societal roles. Such conversations would be considered to be very edgy and many straight (heterosexual) and nontransgender (cisgender) people are loathe to even approach such a deliberation. Human rights frameworks could play a powerful intermediate role when the majority population initially balks at engaging with people who are identified as members of sexual and gender minorities, by challenging the intolerant majority to justify the basis upon which they would deny the fundamental human rights of individual LGBTI persons – human rights that the heterosexual and cisgender majority may take for granted. Only when it is made clear to all prospective participants that the sexual behavior of consenting adults is a matter of privacy and not public discourse, and that the gender identity claims of transgender and intersex persons are neither arbitrary nor inauthentic, is there a plausible (if still remote) prospect that the participatory and democratic deliberations might instead be focused exclusively on the shared quest for the identification and prioritization of a list of shared attributes of a "truly human" life. Until such a level of shared and reciprocally respectful discourse is achieved, LGBTI persons may have no other recourse but to rely on existing human rights frameworks as their lens of choice, even though this places them in an isolated and adversarial position, and leads many outside their community to misrepresent their human rights claims as being directed at some subset of "special" human rights.[11] In fact, the human rights claims of LGBTI persons around the world are simply that they be afforded the same human rights respect and protections enjoyed by all persons outside of their community.

Human rights approaches do help to clarify the lived realities of LGBTI persons, and concerns about the treatment experienced by LGBTI persons in developing countries are relevant across all seven categories of the UNDP's "Seven Freedoms" human rights lens described earlier. LGBTI persons are subject to severe and extensive forms of discrimination, often sanctioned within a country's legal code. They are frequently subject to loss of employment, housing, and insecurity due to their sexual orientation or gender identity, and until the recent yet still largely nascent mobilization of LGBTI civil society movements they have been denied democratic participation in shaping decisions that most directly affect their well-being. Clearly, there are also many justice and social inclusion issues affecting LGBTI persons that remain unresolved throughout the world, including in countries with more advanced economies such as the United States. Yet, human rights frameworks go only so far. Missing from the UNDP's "Seven Freedoms" lens, and from any other international human rights standards, is any direct reference to "freedom of identity" or a human right simply to be oneself. Is there a human right or other persuasive moral basis upon which transgender or intersex persons can be justified in claiming a gender identity contrary to that which was assigned to them at birth?

Any moral consideration of gender identity must first begin with an assessment of whether "gender identity" is a moral category. Clearly, there exists a long historical legacy of multiple and often conflicting relativistic moral values that are linked with societal perceptions of masculine and feminine. Disagreements now emerge when we consider whether certain universal moral values ought to be assigned to or associated only with the standard gender binary categories, and instrumentally even the act of assignment of gender arguably gives rise to certain moral concerns: "Gender is a key dimension of personal life, social relations and culture. It is an arena in which we face difficult practical issues about justice, identity and even survival" (Connell 2009, ix).

As challenging as gender categories and assignments may be in moral terms, the situation gets exponentially more complicated when the basis for gender assignment itself is open to moral questions. Moral disputes start from the question of who has the moral right to assign a person's gender identity and on what basis, to what constitutes "authentic" gender, and includes whether gender categories are framed by a binary structure or lie upon a gender continuum. There are some people who reject the notion of gender categories altogether, and seek to be respected as dignified but *ungendered* human beings. Others would make the moral case for a "third gender" that may or may not be defined to include transgender or intersex persons. Still others question whether "transgender" constitutes a rational identity, worthy of respect.

What choice of lens ought LGBTI persons to make? As described above, the human rights lens aligns more closely with the global structures of international law and the role of nation-states as moral agents. The capability approach however offers a more nuanced conversation about the characteristics of a truly human life and the capacities needed to achieve and sustain such a threshold, which is highly relevant given the current inaccessibility of such ambitions for most members of any marginalized minority including LGBTI persons. By choosing the capability approach lens, LGBTI activists and their allies would be able to shift away from the largely adversarial type of politicized advocacy approach on human rights now in common application, to instead move the discussion to foster a consensus on identifying and pursuing a more comprehensive list of development goals and aspirations that can be articulated within a more localized context. Arising out of such an articulation would be a more explicit understanding that the aspirations for a truly human life and the recognition of universal human dignity sought by marginalized LGBTI persons aligns remarkably well with the aspirations of the larger public. That realization alone would go a great distance in ending the stigmatization of LGBTI persons, and to fostering far greater social inclusion.

The practical obstacle inherent in selecting the capability approach lens has to do with the process of forming such a consensus, and with the nature of democratic deliberation more generally. Unfortunately, LGBTI individuals do not always cohere well within umbrella organizations, and the emerging global trend within civil society is to fragment into groups that align more directly with each "letter" (i.e., a separate group for gay men, for lesbians, etc.). This fragmentation makes the small demographic of sexual and gender minorities even smaller, further diminishing their effectiveness in forging cross-cutting consensus positions within society. Yet, relying on the assertive claims-based (and generally adversarial) mechanisms such as the human rights lens offers has its own drawbacks for such a small and marginalized population, unless adequate allies can be enlisted from those who are identified as being outside these sexual and gender minorities but who are (as allies) in close alignment with their universal claims for human dignity and rights. Such allies are often rare in the Global South given the pervasive stigma attached to LGBTI persons, and government initiatives directed against the "promotion" of homosexuality.[12] Sadly, it is probably unrealistic in the short term to expect to find an adequate level of willingness among non-LGBTI persons within their societies to join with LGBTI persons either to demand human rights performance (the human rights lens), or to deliberate on the establishment of a capability approach list of "truly human life" elements (the capability approach lens). LGBTI persons and their capacity to exercise agency remain deeply diminished by their marginalization.

Arguably, this current impasse is one instance where international development practitioners from the Global North together with practitioners from other countries in the Global South, all with their extensive field experience and deep knowledge of the local cultures and norms in the countries in which they have worked on development projects, might be uniquely well placed to objectively facilitate processes intended to foster greater social inclusion and tolerance for diversity within societies in the Global South. Such pragmatic "outsider"[13] involvement by practitioners, coupled with the persuasive intellectual approaches of academics and theorists, potentially offer some traction for both lenses: human rights approaches and the capability approach. Over time and incrementally, each lens has the potential to expand the circle of development beneficiaries and participants to include those within the LGBTI community in the Global South.

Notes

1. The capabilities approach was pioneered by Amartya Sen and Martha Nussbaum, and has been expanded and further developed by both of these philosophers as well as by other leading thinkers, including David A. Crocker who has formulated and forwarded an explicitly "agency-oriented" version of the capabilities approach. In this chapter, the version of the capabilities approach that the author relies on is primarily the capabilities approach of Martha Nussbaum.
2. Martha Nussbaum used the term "truly human" (and, interchangeably, "fully human") to call attention to the centrality of reason and affiliation within her list of ten essential capabilities, as reason and affiliation enable a person to "organize and suffuse all other capabilities, making their pursuit truly human" (Nussbaum 1997, 286, 288).
3. This publication bears my prior name, before my gender transition.
4. Nussbaum prefers the term "capabilities approach" over "capability approach," although the latter is now generally deemed to refer to both Sen's and Nussbaum's approaches, as well as later variations.
5. For Nussbaum, "combined capabilities" are conceived as the dynamic outcome of "internal capabilities" and specific external economic, social, and personal circumstances. Nussbaum thinks of internal capabilities as a person's unique personality traits, physical and health attributes, emotional and intellectual and emotional capacities, etc. (Garrett 2008).
6. The International Bill of Human Rights consists of the Universal Declaration of Human Rights, the International Covenant on Economic, Social and Cultural Rights, and the International Covenant on Civil and Political Rights and its two Optional Protocols.
7. Such "desirable ends" can vary considerably, from asserting notions of gender equity, offering protections against political malfeasance and authoritarian impunities, or creating a comparative evaluative framework for assessing the performance of one or more governments in how they treat their people and who they hold themselves accountable to.

8. "Human development" is well defined by John Hammock: "Human development is about the flourishing of *each* person in society" (2012, 1).
9. The meaning of the terms *lesbian, bisexual,* and *gay* are now widely understood. Julia Serano unpacks *transgender* and *intersex* when she says that transgender is

> used primarily as an umbrella term to describe those who defy societal expectations and assumptions regarding femaleness and maleness; this includes people who are transsexual (those who live as members of the sex other than the one they were assigned at birth), intersex (those who are born with a reproductive or sexual anatomy that does not fit the typical definitions of female or male), and genderqueer (those who identify outside of the male/female binary), as well as those whose gender expression differs from their anatomical or perceived sex (including cross-dressers, drag performers, masculine women, feminine men, and so on). (2007, 25)

10. Deliberative democracy has been employed, for example, to allocate local budgets on a participatory basis in several cities such as in Porto Alegre, Brazil, and to undertake major public projects, such as the rebuilding of New Orleans, Louisiana after Hurricane Katrina.
11. Addressing the human rights of LGBTI persons in the Global South fits seamlessly into the international human rights regime – from the 1948 Universal Declaration of Human Rights to the more recent civil society generated Yogyakarta Principles on the Application of International Human Rights Law in relation to Sexual Orientation and Gender Identity (International Commission of Jurists 2006).
12. The "promotion" of homosexuality is explicitly illegal in countries such as Gambia, Russia, Tunisia, and Uganda (Human Rights First 2013; Law Library of Congress 2014).
13. David Crocker's pioneering work on the optimal role of outsiders and insiders in international development processes is highly relevant in this instance (1991).

References

Brown, P. G. 2000. *Ethics, Economics and International Relations: Transparent Sovereignty in the Commonwealth of Life.* Edinburgh University Press Ltd.

Connell, R. 2009. *Gender in World Perspective.* 2nd edition. Cambridge: Polity.

Crocker, D. 1991. "Insiders and Outsiders in International Development Ethics." *Ethics & International Affairs* 5: 149–173.

Crocker, D. 2008. *Ethics of Global Development: Agency, Capability, and Deliberation.* Cambridge University Press.

Crocker, D. and Schwenke, C. 2006. *The Relevance of Development Ethics for USAID.* http://pdf.usaid.gov/pdf_docs/Pnadd048.pdf.

Donnelly, J. 1989. *Universal Human Rights in Theory and Practice.* Ithaca, NY: Cornell University Press.

Dunne, T. and Wheeler, N. J. (eds.). 1999. *Human Rights in Global Politics.* Cambridge University Press.

Garrett, J. 2008. *Martha Nussbaum on Capabilities and Human Rights.* http://people.wku.edu/jan.garrett/ethics/nussbaum.htm#icap.

Hammock, J., with de Alba, A.; Barham, A.; and Rounseville, M. 2012. *Desk Study on the Human Development Approach, and its Potential Applicability to USAID.* Washington, DC: Management Systems International. www.msiworldwide.com/wp-content/uploads/Human-Development-Approach.pdf.

Human Rights First. 2013. *Convenient Targets: The Anti-"Propaganda" Law and the Threat to LGBT Rights in Russia.* www.humanrightsfirst.org/uploads/pdfs/HRF-russias-anti-gay-ban-SG.pdf.

International Commission of Jurists. 2006. *Yogyakarta Principles on the Application of International Human Rights Law in Relation to Sexual Orientation and Gender Identity.* www.yogyakartaprinciples.org/.

Law Library of Congress. 2014. Global Legal Research Center, United States. *Criminal Laws on Homosexuality in African Nations.* www.loc.gov/law/help/criminal-laws-on-homosexuality/african-nations-laws.php.

Mchangama, J. and Verdirame, G. 2013. "The Danger of Human Rights Proliferation: When Defending Liberty, Less Is More." *Foreign Affairs,* July 24.

Nussbaum, M. C. 1997. "Capabilities and Human Rights." 66 *Fordham Law Review* 273 http://ir.lawnet.fordham.edu/flr/vol66/iss2/2.

Nussbaum, M. C. 2000. *Women and Human Development: The Capabilities Approach.* Cambridge University Press.

Poolman, C. 2012. "Humanity in the Capabilities Approach to Development." *POLIS Journal* 7: 366–408.

Serano, J. 2007. *Whipping Girl: A Transsexual Woman on Sexism and the Scapegoating of Femininity.* 2nd edition. Berkeley, CA: Seal Press.

Shue, H. 1996. *Basic Rights: Subsistence, Affluence, and U.S. Foreign Policy.* Princeton University Press.

United Nations. 1948. *Universal Declaration of Human Rights.* www.un.org/en/universal-declaration-human-rights/.

United Nations Development Programme. 2000. *Human Development Report 2000.* Oxford University Press.

5 | Peacebuilding, Development, Agency and Ethics

NIGEL DOWER

1 Introduction

The main themes and theses of this chapter are as follows: There are parallels and overlaps between peacebuilding and development, both at the level of general concepts and at the level of particular conceptions of each. This chapter explores both levels. It offers some considerations in favour of conceptions of both development and peacebuilding which emphasise (a) that key normative elements such as justice, respect for rights and democratic voice plus sensitivity to cultural variations are properly embedded in them, and (b) that, whilst there are vital roles for external international actors and indeed for country-level governmental agencies, a key to successful development and peacebuilding is the active role of people at grass-roots levels acting both as agents and as definers of what is good for them, not merely as recipients of solutions externally and often uniformly provided. In so doing the chapter highlights various ideas in the thought of David Crocker about development which can in fact be applied to peacebuilding as well and illustrate well the parallels and overlaps between them. Some of these relate more to the general concepts of development and peacebuilding (Section 3) and some more to particular conceptions of them (Section 5).

To anticipate later discussion of the last theme several points may be briefly mentioned here. Crocker characterizes development as 'beneficial societal change'; this description fits remarkably what peacebuilding might be seen to be too. Crocker emphasises the centrality of agency in his account of development along with deliberation and democratic participation – both arguably important elements in any transition to more peaceful relations. A theme in his account of development is the need for justice as a key element. Likewise, peacebuilding needs to have justice built into it and clearly Crocker's work on rectifying past wrongs has a bearing on this. Crocker makes much of the importance of having both insiders and outsiders in development, and this turns out to be an important element in peacebuilding too.

This is not to claim that Crocker sees himself doing peacebuilding theorising, let alone more generally that we should see peacebuilding studies subsumed under development studies or vice versa. But it is helpful to consider the parallels and overlaps, since each sphere of enquiry may benefit from insights from the other. For instance, if peacebuilding includes concern for transitional justice, then we can see that development in an imperfect world is really about this too. Before I turn to these connections, I give an account of the general idea of peacebuilding. Although there is already much recognition of the empirical connections, there is less discussion of the various ways in which the ideas of development and peace/peacebuilding are conceptually entwined. This chapter seeks to tease out some of these complex connections. (See Dower 1999 for a different conceptual exploration of violence and development.)

Here is a representative sample of what has been said in recent years about the relationship between peacebuilding and development. Peter Uvin remarks: 'The development enterprise spent the first three decades of its charmed life in total agnosticism towards conflict and security. When violent conflict occurred, it was treated as an unfortunate occurrence, forcing development workers out and humanitarians in – an order to be reversed when the conflict was over and conditions were safe for normal development work to resume' (2002, 6).

Likewise, Wisler says, 'Peacebuilding and international development historically have functioned as discrete sectors of practice.' But she goes on to say, 'More recently scholars and practitioners have recognised that there exists an undeniable correlation between the two sectors that necessitates collaboration. Nearly two thirds of development programming now operates within conflict-affected countries' (2013, 57). Once we see this, it is easy to see that aid is not neutral in respect to war and peace. As Anderson notes, 'when international assistance is given in the context of violent conflict it becomes part of that context and also part of the conflict'. She also notes that when given in conflict settings 'aid can reinforce, exacerbate, and prolong the conflict' (1999, 1). For Anderson the challenge is to find ways to act so as to 'do no harm'. O'Gorman recognises that violent conflict has proved a hindrance to achieving the Millennium Development Goals (MDGs) and conversely how development is contestably 'well-placed to respond to a number of the root causes of violent conflict, such as poverty, social injustice, and ethnic tensions, through structural interventions with the state and economy' (2011).

This recognition of the empirical or causal connections is well illustrated by what Craig Zelizer, editor of *Integrated Peacebuilding*, says in the preface, 'over the last fifteen years it has become abundantly clear that development work cannot advance without addressing the underlying dynamics of violence, whilst peacebuilding is not effective without addressing the basic needs of people through economic opportunity, basic health services, and a functioning legal system' (Zelizer and Oliphant 2013, xii).

The idea that there may also be conceptual connections is illustrated by Kristoffer Liden, writing about the same time at Zelizer, who says: 'With the global prevalence of political and economic liberalism since the end of the Cold War, the overarching framework of peacebuilding has been defined by an ideal of "liberal peace": a world order consisting of sovereign liberal states with a democratic political system, free market economy, legal protection of human rights and extensive international collaboration' (Liden 2014, 1). In other words, an understanding of peace and peacebuilding is assumed which is a liberal conception with the same elements that a liberal conception of development has. Liden himself is highly critical of this conception, and as we will see later, there are various alternative ways of looking at both peacebuilding and development.[1]

The chapter falls into two main parts: first a general exploration of conceptions of peace and how peacebuilding fits into these; second a general comparison of peacebuilding discourse and development discourse both in terms of conceptual connections between them and in terms of causal connections between development and peace, using at various stages points drawn from Crocker's work on authentic development.

2 What Is Peacebuilding?

Peacemaking, Peacekeeping and Peacebuilding

Peacebuilding is generally contrasted with peacemaking and peacekeeping in several respects. This followed distinctions drawn by Galtung in 1975 and largely adopted by Boutros-Ghali in *An Agenda for Peace* in 1992 in the wake of the peace dividend at the end of the cold war and of the new possibilities of engagement by the international community in re-enforcing peace. To some extent the distinctions are stipulative (these words do not have to mean these things or make these contrasts and in any case the boundaries between them are contestable), but they do pick out some real differences between different kinds of activity done 'for the sake of' peace.

Peacemaking is generally an event, often involving the intervention of outside actors, to terminate a period of war/violence/hostilities. Peacekeeping is an ongoing activity, often involving outside agencies such as United Nations (UN) peacekeeping forces, of maintaining peace as the absence of war and overt violence. Peacebuilding is a dynamic process of establishing peace as a set of relations between parties which is both durable/sustainable (i.e. has within it the tendency to continue) because peace is more secure in that the parties are *less* likely to resort (or resort again after conflict) to violence, that is, more likely to *maintain* 'negative peace', and deeper in the sense of being more than merely negative peace.

Negative and Positive Peace

It is commonly recognised then that we need to distinguish between negative peace and positive peace (or minimalist peace and maximalist peace as Sandole calls them (2010, 10). Whilst negative peace is relatively straightforward in meaning (though there are of course grey areas), what really constitutes the alternative of positive peace is open to much greater differences in interpretation. Peacebuilding is about building positive peace, so there will be corresponding differences of interpretation of peacebuilding, about its levels and dimensions and so on. Clearly whichever account is favoured, there can be degrees of it.

Calling 'negative peace' negative however is not because it is a bad thing, but because it is the 'absence' of something. Indeed, peace as a continued period of absence of war and overt violence along with the expectation of its continuation is immensely valuable. Whatever extra benefits come from successful peacebuilding in terms of greater trust, social harmony, sense of justice and so on, it is the making of the period of basic absence of war and overt violence more likely to continue that remains the most valuable consequence.

Towards a Definition of Peacebuilding

As Boutros-Ghali puts it in *An Agenda for Peace* (1992), peacebuilding was defined as 'action to identify and support structures which will tend to strengthen and solidify peace in order to avoid a relapse into conflict' (para 21). Peacebuilding can however be usefully defined in a slightly broader way to include in fact two phases to it – proactive and reactive. Boutros-Ghali focused on post-conflict peacebuilding only. Following Lederach, we need to include pre-conflict peacebuilding, i.e. making peace more robust so that overt violence is prevented or made less likely. As the United Nation's (2005) much later doctrine *Responsibility to Protect* (R2P) recognised, measures can and should be taken to build the conditions of peace so that it is less likely that war will break out.[2] However, after an armed conflict much urgently needs to be done to rebuild the conditions of peace, and most of the peace-building operations since the end of the cold war have been of the reactive kind. Whilst the details may be different concerning what needs to be done, the fundamental nature of peacebuilding in both phases is broadly the same. Whilst pre-conflict (i.e. armed conflict) peacebuilding may have to attend to tensions, conflicts and injustices, real and perceived, post-conflict peacebuilding may have to attend to reconciliation and rectification in the face of fractured relations and even war crimes in a way and to an extent that proactive peacebuilding generally does not. Lederach offers the following definition: 'Here peacebuilding is understood as a comprehensive concept that encompasses, generates, and sustains the full array of processes, approaches, and stages needed to transform conflict towards more sustainable, peaceful relationships' (1997, 20).[3]

Another common assumption, at least in the domain of peacebuilding *within* countries, is that peace as the absence of overt conflict should not be thought of being maintained mainly by fear or deterrence (the Hobbesian model; see Hobbes 1651). Much more is needed if peace is to become durable, and indeed more valuable, since living a life dominated by fear is, by that fact alone, less satisfactory than it would be otherwise.[4] Indeed we can reinforce the distinction between peace maintained by the threat of violence and peace maintained in other ways as in genuine peacebuilding in the following way. If peace between parties is achieved by the credible threat of violence against one or some parties (or both or all in the case of mutual deterrence) if they were to step out of line, then the maintenance of peace (albeit with different degrees of threat) is a matter of a *tendency/inclination* to resort to violence being *checked* – this is a form of 'peacekeeping', albeit not by external agents like UN peacekeeping forces. By contrast peacebuilding is a positive process and is a matter of *strengthening* the tendency/inclination not to resort to violence because the motives and impulses of parties to resort to violence against other parties are either reduced and counterbalanced by other stronger motives or disappear. Jenkins for instance argued that peace becomes more stable once the *habits* of peace are established and also once people develop a wide range of relationships with others in other groups such that they are less likely to fight with any one other group because of their overlapping relationships in other groups, certainly within a country and also between countries (Jenkins 1973). (Sen, responding to the rise of extremism after 9/11, pursued a point related to Jenkins' second point, in arguing that if we have multiple significant identities we are less likely to want to go to war in the name of just one identity (see Sen 2006).)

Various Approaches to Peacebuilding

What things more generally need to be done to strengthen peace? Various more detailed accounts are given about how to make peace sustainable, or about what actions, practices, institutions, guiding values/norms and so on are seen as key elements in or means to building peace. Models of peacebuilding may vary considerably in terms of different dimensions regarded as important, different levels as important, and different core values as stressed. That peacebuilding has a number of dimensions is recognised by the Geneva Peacebuilding Platform (GPP). It says that 'socio-economic recovery is central to peacebuilding is well attested' (2009, 12) but there are also three other areas, namely 'security, governance, and justice' (13). Lederach identifies three different levels which he represents as a pyramid: namely top-level/middle-range/grass-roots leadership (1997, 39). Top leaders include military/political/religious leaders focusing on high-level negotiations, middle-range leaders including ethnic leaders, academics and humanitarian leaders (non-governmental organizations, or NGOs) involving things like training in conflict resolution and peace commissions and grass-roots leaders like leaders of indigenous NGOs, local health officials, refugee camp leaders focusing on things like local peace commissions, prejudice reduction and psychological work in post-war trauma.

Many thinkers see a core element to peacebuilding to lie in certain moral values that should inform practices, institutions and general culture. Primarily amongst them is justice. Many thinkers link peacebuilding with creating a 'just peace' or a peace based on 'justice post bellum', and we shall see later there are various dimensions to justice and ways of interpreting it. Developing a culture of peace and the internalisation of certain moral norms may also seem to be important. For instance, the idealist account of Macquarrie of peace as 'shalom' or harmonious social relationships is interesting because it illustrates the importance some thinkers attach to basic moral attitudes for peacebuilding (1973). Likewise, a core moral value like respect for diversity of belief and practice, going beyond any legal rights framework, may be seen as significant.

Much peacebuilding involves attention being paid to explicitly developing peaceful relations, attending to past wrongs, work on reconciliation, empowering women's voices in peace processes, training in non-violent ways of addressing social wrongs often on a very small local scale. For example, there is Quaker work in developing the Alternatives to Violence Project (AVP) in Kenya and Rwanda (see Quakers in the World 2016), and in Kenya, in conjunction with Change Agents for Peace International (CAPI), the Turning the Tide (TTT) training which helps people oppose injustice in non-violent ways (see Turning the Tide 2016). As Lederach says, 'Building peace in today's conflicts calls for long-term commitment to establishing an infrastructure across the levels of a society, an infrastructure that empowers the resources for reconciliation from within that society and maximizes the contribution from outside' (1997, xvi; see also Murithi 2009 for an exploration of various forms of peacebuilding).

3 Peacebuilding and Development: Conceptual Parallels and Links

Parallels

There are distinct parallels between peacebuilding and development. Peacebuilding as a dynamic process is structurally similar to the progressive process of active development in which government agents and/or other agents build the conditions in which people's lives generally go better, expressed in phrases like the progressive realisation of socio-economic rights. Lederach sees a parallel between the move from aid as emergency or humanitarian assistance to longer-term development assistance and from peacemaking to peacebuilding, both involving longer time frames (1997, 74). The parallel is however not merely between peacebuilding and development assistance but also with development itself since much of peacebuilding is, as Lederach himself argues, internal to a country and not centred on external assistance.

Complexity

Peacebuilding processes are not merely progressive, they are also complex. In addition to various specific elements of Crocker's thought that bear interesting parallels to ways of thinking about peacebuilding to be noted later, we should note that his whole general approach to authentic development has a complexity to it which complements an appropriate conception of peacebuilding. There is a consonance between Crocker's model of 'development theory-practice' (2008, 71–3) and the model of multi-layered peacebuilding proposed by Lederach and noted earlier, in respect to the various stages, elements and iterations involved. Lederach has been very much engaged in practical peacebuilding (as Crocker has been engaged with development projects), and out of this comes a richness born of the interaction of theory and practice. This is a salutary reminder that, whether in the field of development or in the field of peacebuilding, there are dangers in too much theorising without engagement with practice and too much practice without being deepened by exposure to theorising. There is also the danger of focusing on one element involved in peacebuilding or development and regarding that as *the* key element. Development like peacebuilding is not merely the progressive realisation of human rights or greater achieving of human well-being by (or for) people, it involves complex structures and relationships, like building a house. Both involve building and developing *other* things – laws, customs, socio-economic improvement, channels of communication – many of which are common to both.

More Than Close Parallels?

Crocker's characterisation of development as 'beneficial societal change' (2008, 1) suggests something more than a mere parallel.

Peacebuilding is clearly also beneficial social or societal change albeit under certain conditions. Perhaps then development should be seen as one dimension of beneficial societal change and peacebuilding as another. But they may be more closely linked than this. First, if successful peacebuilding is undertaken *before* a conflict occurs, it makes resort to violence less likely to occur, but does so by enabling changes to occur such as addressing injustices (perceived or real), increasing respect between different groups, greater dialogue/participation, increasing people's sense of security, etc. That is, it both maintains something (peace as lack of overt conflict) and involves positive, i.e. beneficial social changes. These changes may also feature in an account of development as beneficial social change; indeed, development is both about maintaining what is good or already achieved as well as involving positive change. Second, if peacebuilding occurs *after* a conflict, it likewise makes the return to violence less likely to occur by enabling changes of various kinds as indicated above, but including a more explicit focus on repairing fractured relationships.

This process is often called post-conflict reconstruction, but reconstruction is really a special case of development under certain conditions – namely a form of beneficial social change from a really bad state to a less bad state. But then often development even when there has not been a war is just that or partly that. That is, development is not merely or even primarily a process in which people who are already in a good state are moving to an even better state in ways which are largely harmonious and cooperative; it is a process very often in which certain groups who are disadvantaged have to struggle in the face of entrenched inequality, injustice, oppression, discrimination and so on. So, Crocker's definition is very amenable to making the case for linking peacebuilding with development *conceptually*.

Security

Conceptually development and peacebuilding are also linked via the concept of security. Human beings wish to be secure in a range of goods – for instance, economic well-being, health, a safe and clean environment, the safety of their persons and possessions and having civil and political liberties. That is, they wish to have these goods on a sustained basis into the future, with these neither being taken away nor threatened. One way of understanding beneficial societal change is to say that such change occurs when there is the progressive securing on a sustainable basis of socio-economic goods, personal integrity, possessions and freedoms (including freedom from external oppression or attack). One could say the first covers development, the others peacebuilding, but the distinction is too sharp: for instance, the progressive securing of freedom is also part of development (see, e.g., Sen 1999), and more economic security is part of what makes a society more peaceful.

Furthermore, if development is the securing of socio-economic goods in ways that express *justice* (understood as realising socio-economic rights, distributional fairness or lack of discrimination), and peacebuilding is about strengthening peace in the sense of a *just* peace, then there is no sharp distinction between the two.

Common Concern for Justice

Indeed, the idea of justice links the two very well. Peacebuilding is generally assumed to be, whatever else, about establishing a just peace, hence promoting justice. But so is development. There are, in fact, a number of different aspects to justice that are relevant here. At least four primary dimensions in respect to what make a society just are identified (not necessarily all by the same thinker). The basic social structure is one of social relationships backed by the rule of appropriate laws which are not oppressive (that is, they are not ones of domination) or discriminatory (that is, they do not discriminate against groups in virtue of arbitrary characteristics like race, religion or gender). There is respect for civil rights in terms of basic freedoms or liberties (including due process of law). There is political participation (that is, rights to have one's voice heard and to participate in democratic processes). There is a fair distribution of income and wealth, understood in terms of everyone having basic socio-economic rights progressively realised, if not some more in terms of more radical ideas of distributive fairness (see, e.g., Rawls 1971).

There are also two aspects of corrective justice generally assumed: bringing to justice and punishing those who violate the laws (in acts of private wrong-doing), and bringing to account those who, generally for political, religious or other ideological reasons, deliberately flout principles of primary justice as indicated above in one or more respects, whether or not it was at the time covered by law or according to law, e.g. in ethnic discrimination or oppression and war crimes in times of war. There is finally what I shall call promotional justice: the acceptance of an obligation of justice to promote justice – as Rawls argued, but adding 'without too much cost' (1971, 115) – by working to create or strengthen the institutions and practices of justice, where they do not already exist or exist adequately, to express, or express more fully, one or other of the primary areas of justice.

This outline is not intended to be definitive. What is important to, or included in, the list may be disputed, and different interpretations given. My point is merely to illustrate how any one of these elements are equally relevant, or at least could be, given certain interpretations, to a full account of development and a full account of peace/peacebuilding. Arguably a just peace is one in which discrimination and oppression are checked, distributional inequalities at least to some extent reduced, arbitrary restrictions on freedoms are removed and people have a proper voice in decision-making. Furthermore, addressing past wrongs is a significant part of moving forward after conflict. But so too all these elements relate to authentic development. Finally, promoting justice may not seem a particularly important aspect of justice but it is significant because it maps onto the motivation of those who wish to promote peace, that is peacebuilding and also those involved in promoting development, for instance through development assistance.

Crocker on Rectifying Past Wrongs

As aspect of justice that is particularly pertinent to peacebuilding after war is, as just noted, rectifying past wrongs, and this is an area where Crocker has made a significant contribution (see, e.g., Crocker 1999; 2000), though of course it is not the only aspect of justice in relation to development in his writings – there are certainly frequent references to ideas of distributive justice, non-discrimination and human rights including the right to democratic engagement.

As Crocker says, there may be many goals for trying to rectify past wrongs. These may include 'truth, a public platform for victims, accountability and punishment, the rule of law, compensation to victims, institutional reform and long-term development, reconciliation, and public deliberation' (1999, 43). But they are all aspects of transitional justice. And Crocker indicates a new aspect to development ethics in order to enable a society to move forward into a more stable and positive future:

Often a group, nation, or region cannot advance to a better future of genuine development until it reckons ethically and effectively with a terrible past. Failure to hold past rights-abusers accountable for their crimes contributes to a 'culture of impunity' and disregard for the rule of law, both obstacles to good development. Reckoning appropriately with past wrongs, in contrast, may contribute to (as well as benefit from) equitable and democratic development. (2008, 52–3)

Crocker speaks of these as relevant to development, but of course they are all equally relevant to peacebuilding. Whilst reconciliation may seem to be the only activity listed above that is directly linked to peace, they all contribute towards ways of creating the right framework for making peace more durable and just, because it is based on justice or at least less injustice, as perceived by the various parties.

Parallels in Failures

A way of bringing out the parallels and interconnections, particularly conceptual interconnections, between development and peacebuilding is to look at how we might assess failures in peacebuilding (or more generally peace-directed endeavour) and failures in development. At a very basic level the two may seem to be somewhat separate. If peace is simply lack of overt violent conflict, then those committed to maintaining it, insofar as they could have or should have done things to prevent it from ceasing, fail, if it ceases. Those committed to pursuing development as poverty reduction fail, insofar as they could have or should have done things to improve things, if the evil of extreme poverty continues or gets worse. Conceptually they are very different things (though the imperatives to tackle both are equally serious and have a common moral source) – violence and extreme poverty.

But if peacebuilding and development are concerned with creating or strengthening conditions of more than merely absence of overt conflict or conditions of human flourishing well beyond the mere absence of extreme poverty respectively, more conceptually complex (and contestable) accounts may be given of what a richer peace would be like and what human flourishing actually consists of, then the two accounts are likely to converge. For instance, if peace is about reducing or removing tensions, a sense of impotence, a sense of injustice and a lack of recognition or voice, are these not the very same things as or at least cognate to the things that development involves beyond removal of extreme poverty – empowerment, recognition, justice and so on? One might say that the very same conceptions of justice and human flourishing are at work, maybe below the surface, of what a really satisfactory peace or really satisfactory state of development for people consists of.

Means and Ends

Whilst this is not the most prominent part of Crocker's thinking about development ethics, there is a theme running through his writings about the relations between means and ends which have a bearing on peacebuilding too. This is reflected in the following passage: 'We want an ethics of the means as well as an ethics of principle and vision. We want an ethics of social change in an unjust world, where we want to avoid being either moral fools or amoral operators. We want good outcomes but we want to achieve them by just and fair means' (2008, 89). Another prominent development ethicist Denis Goulet made much of this is his ideas of the 'means of the means' (see Dower 2010). Whilst emphasising that development ethics is about the ethical ways in which development is pursued does not settle the question of what makes the means ethical, it does indicate an important locus of ethical reflection. There is a *presumption* I would suggest that if we are for instance trying to promote development in which justice is established or human rights generally respected and promoted, then the promotion of it should ideally be by just means and not violating the rights of others in the process. (Here I am reminded of Gandhi's meta-principle 'the means are the ends in the making'; see, e.g., Gruzalski 2001). This does not mean that hard choices do not have to be made sometimes in which the end justifies the means.

Exactly the same issues arise in connection with peacebuilding, since clearly the way peace is built or promoted is important ethically, not merely because unethical means may be counterproductive, but because generally the right thing to do is to promote peace by peaceful, just, rights-respecting ways. Not all would agree with the Quaker claim that 'peace is a way' (see Bailey 1993), but the presumption that peace should be pursued by peaceful means unless there are very strong countervailing considerations might be more widely accepted. No doubt there are circumstances in which peacekeeping forces are very important, and some would argue, as Collier does, that sometimes outside military intervention may be necessary to help countries escape from the trap of civil war (Collier 2007, ch. 8). Adam Curle, himself an effective Quaker peacemaker, argued that liberation struggle might be needed in order to achieve a 'just peace' (Curle 2007). The main point here is that peacebuilding is concerned with the ethics of the building of peace not merely with the ethical values of the peace built, and this provides a useful parallel with a strand in Crocker's thought. Different thinkers will have different views about the ethics of the means, but those differences are likely to be the same in respect to peacebuilding and development.

4 Causal Connections

This chapter is mainly concerned with broad conceptual issues rather than empirical analysis, but a brief summary of types of causal relation may be given. There is indeed plenty of recognition that there are causal connections between the two, as evidenced in the quotations at the beginning. The connections are in both directions and at two levels. Peace positively enables development to occur but at the same time, negatively, violence or the absence of peace undermines development. We can also see that development – at least appropriate forms of it that are not premised on highly competitive material acquisition but rather focus on greater access to the conditions of flourishing for the poor – makes peace more likely within and between societies (where there is economic exchange), and at the same time lack of development in the form of extreme poverty can be one of the causes of or fuel violent conflict – as illustrated by some support that is given to the Islamic State, and noted by Collier (2007, 20).

That is, there are extensive though not universal positive patterns of mutual support for the progressive realisation of these. It is not merely that where there is peace (as absence of war/violent conflict) development can take place, that war, particularly civil war, undermines development and that development as economic activity motivates people to want peace with those with whom they have economic transactions. It is not an 'all or nothing' matter. Beyond peace as merely absence of war, there are degrees of peace and different qualities in the kinds of peaceful relations, and these correlate with the manner and extent of progress in development. Greater peace makes it generally more possible for appropriate development to occur, and appropriate development reinforces the patterns of peaceful relations. The positive links are not however universal, but nor are there, for that matter, universal positive reinforcings between different strands within development or different aspects within peacebuilding.

A couple of examples illustrate this. Much attention in development may be paid to providing education, health clinics and opportunities for gainful and meaningful work (all clearly part of development) but be partly rationalised as contributing to the conditions of peace. On a grander scale, whilst there may have been many different motives for the Marshall Plan for the reconstruction of Europe after the Second World War, certainly one of them was to help all of Europe, vanquished as well as victors, achieve economic prosperity in order to make war less likely in Europe: similarly this was a main motive behind the setting up of the European Steel and Coal Community which became the EEC – the European Economic Community (see Sandole 2010, 92–102).

The recognition of causal connections has an important normative or prescriptive consequence. Causal understanding is not *merely* causal understanding: cause and effect become means and ends because we have reason to do or promote something – here peace or development. So, if you have ethical reason to build peace and believe meeting basic needs will help do this, then you have ethical reason to do the latter (apart from any other reasons for so doing).[5]

5 Comparisons of Liberal Peacebuilding/Development and Other Approaches

Liberal Peace

Granted the earlier account of peacebuilding as complex and multidimensional, what alternative models are possible? Let us start with the so-called liberal paradigm. This 'liberal peace' has many dimensions to it and even amongst its advocates it is contested. Nevertheless, there had been what Richmond calls a 'peacebuilding consensus' that has emerged since the end of the cold war (given the impetus by *Agenda for Peace* in 1992 and developed in the UN through the Resolution in 2005

Responsibility to Protect and the establishment of the Commission on Peacebuilding in 2006) (Richmond 2005). This consensus centred on the ideas of democracy, human rights, liberal markets, state-building (in the face of so many 'failed' states), which critics see as hegemonic and as ways of making the world order in the image of the dominant powers. Thus, in the last thirty years efforts by the international community to pursue what has been called the liberal peacebuilding paradigm show striking similarities to the attempts to spread a liberal conception of development in the name of democracy, human rights and free markets.

Liden remarks in assessing the 'liberal peace' record:

critics contend that even if operations have often had a positive effect on the reduction of war and violence, they have had negative effects on the broader social and political fabric of the affected societies, effects that ought to be recognised and dealt with ... A normative verdict on the *legitimacy* of liberal peacebuilding can therefore not be reached on the basis of its statistical effects on the reduction of war and suffering alone. Further consideration of its social and political character and effects is required. (Liden 2014, 8)

Indeed, there is a widespread recognition that although there have been a lot of peacebuilding missions in the last twenty-five years, many under the auspices of the UN, some large, some small, these generally have not been very successful (see Liden 2014 for a useful survey). Prominent examples might be Libya, Afghanistan or Iraq. Overt conflicts remain or re-emerge, quite apart from the question about whether the peace that is being aided is right or appropriate for the countries anyway. However, there are some successes: Collier argues that the UK's limited and brief intervention in Sierra Leone in 2000 helped prevent a very bad situation from emerging (2007, 127–9).

Alternatives

So, given dissatisfactions, alternatives emerge centring on developing better social relationships and being deeply embedded in culturally sensitive local tradition, which are relevant to both peacebuilding and development. Liden indicates three types of response: 'Three "ideal types" of prescriptive alternatives that revisionists cultivate and combine can be derived: "re-liberal", "social" and "multicultural" peacebuilding' (2009, 620). Paris for instance has argued for a re-liberal conception involving a more coercive state approach in order to establishing liberal norms (Paris 2004, ch. 1), whereas Richmond, for instance, argues for a 'social model which emphasises social and economic rights, a locally based bottom-up approach which he calls "emancipatory liberal peace"' (Richmond 2005, quoted in Liden 2009, 622). This is, it should be noted, a modification to rather than a rejection of the liberal peace model, in line with a more 'social liberalism' understanding of liberalism as opposed to the neoliberal (or libertarian) conception.

The multicultural approach advocated for instance by MacGinty emphasises a multicultural approach opposed to the liberal 'one solution fits all' approach. For instance, he says 'many traditional societies developed and maintained sophisticated mechanisms for non-violent dispute resolution and constructed complex conceptions of peace' (MacGinty 2008, 149), far removed from colonial or western ideas. Likewise, Iyer regrets the fact that the liberal peacebuilding model parallels the neoliberal economic models of development, which creates a formulaic peace that ignores many locally driven visions for peace (Iyer 2011, as represented by Wisler 2013, 60).

Lederach also stresses the importance of activities at the grassroots level in what he calls capacity-building. Empowerment is about *inter alia* 'how to create and sustain within individuals and communities the movement from "I/we cannot effect desired change" to "I/we can"' (1997, 109). He combines this with the importance of the cultural/cultural diversity, since both socio-economic resources and socio-cultural resources are needed. By the latter he means 'people and their various cultural traditions' (87). It is interesting to note that the Geneva Peacebuilding Platform actually concluded inter alia that 'peacebuilding directed by external interveners is no longer a politically and practically viable approach' (2015, 3) and that the key is 'strengthening peacebuilding as prevention of violent conflict by building on local expertise' (4).

What is striking is that the three approaches identified by Liden are not merely approaches to peacebuilding or merely approaches to development, but to both. They go hand-in-hand. Without trying to assess the relative merits of these various approaches, I follow the general approach of Lederach who certainly sees merit both in the importance of local initiatives, socio-cultural resources, recognition of cultural diversity, as well as the international framework. I conclude with three elements of Cocker's thought that provide useful insights too for successful peacebuilding.

Agency

Crocker, developing the theme of agency in the works of Amartya Sen (see, e.g., Sen 1999), says this generally of agency: 'One is an agent when one deliberates and decides for oneself, acts to realise one's aim, and, thereby, makes an intentional difference to the world' (Crocker 2008, 298). Specifically in regard to the importance of agency of the poor he quotes with approval Kuper: 'poor people are neither powerless nor ignorant in respect of important problems and opportunities for action; they need to be addressed as agents, capable independent action as well as cooperative assistance' (Crocker 2008, 9; see Kuper 2002, 16). But Crocker stresses that, depending on various factors, people have different degrees of agency (Crocker 2008, 298) – a point made by Onora O'Neill (1989) that one of the most morally troubling aspects of extreme poverty is that the very poor are disempowered. This does not mean that they are not agents at all but that appropriate development is about enabling them to build up their agency, often by removing external obstacles that limit their agency. Beyond the basic idea of people being in control of their lives, there are two aspects of agency which I want to focus on which turn out to be crucial to peacebuilding – the idea of a full life and, second, deliberative democracy.

First, is the idea of an agent being able, in conditions of freedom, to exercise a full range of capabilities, developed in the first place through proper education and nurture, as one chooses in a full life. That is, another important aspect of agency is shown in the possession and exercise of, in a broad sense of autonomy, a person's capacity to have a rounded and full understanding of his or her life in its many dimensions. Now, this aspect of agency is clearly central to development. Arguably real or genuine development occurs when people as agents do not merely have economic powers but are also able through the combination of their own inner developed capability and suitable social, legal and political conditions, to take part in the life of their community, and are able to lead full lives they have 'reason to value' (to use the phrase much used by Sen; see, e.g., Sen 1999, 86).

How is this relevant of peacebuilding? Insofar as people can exercise their agency in a fulfilling way within their socio-political-legal-economic framework, they have less reason to resort to violence than if they feel impotent. Perhaps the resort to violence by people who feel helpless is precisely the sense that the resort to violence is a dramatic exercise of agency in making a difference, as Collier notes (2007, 20). Indeed, it would be a mistake more generally to suppose that the more agency people have, the more they prefer to avoid violence. It cannot be denied that some people may see their agency as making a difference to the world in terms of exercising *power over others* and using violence or military methods to that end. But still, generally, one can say that if people are not and do not feel victims of circumstance and powerless in the social and political order they are in, that is they live in an ordered and peaceful environment which enables them to make the choices essential to their leading a fulfilling life, they are less likely to have reason to change that order through violence or revolution.

Deliberative Democracy

Second, Crocker links the role of agency with a person's capacity to engage in public life, which he characterises as engaging in deliberative democracy (see Crocker 2008, chs 9, 10). As Crocker says, we need to give proper weight to citizen participation and democratic decision-making (2008, 19). He welcomes Sen's move from a 'notion of agency from a theory of motivation which makes room for altruistic action, to a normative ideal that affirms the importance of the individual and group freedom to deliberate, be architects of their own lives' (2008, 19). What is important for our current purpose is the point about *group* decision-making. Deliberation does not occur here in isolation but involves people interacting in a public space according to norms with a view to reaching collective decisions. An important aspect of agency then is the kind of deliberative agency shown in participation in decisions with other people on matters that affect how life goes for a person. What Crocker then calls the 'deliberative version of the agency and capability approach' (2008, 297) is one in which there is engagement in deliberative democracy – not the democracy of taking part (or having the right, often not exercised, to take part) every few years in elections but ongoing democratic engagement at all levels from the local to the national (and indeed participation in global civil society). This is akin to what Miller (1999) called the republican conception of citizenship (as opposed to what he calls the liberal conception of the enjoyment of rights), where citizens are engaged in *res publica* ('public things'). Crocker spells this out thus: 'if countries are to progress towards the goal of authentic development, it will be largely because of critical discussion among and collective participation by citizens themselves, especially those worst off' (2008, 90).

How does this relate to peacebuilding? Even if we think of an established peace as an ongoing period of absence of war/violence, that period is maintained or constituted by a large network of relationships – personal, social, legal, political, economic – which because of their structure and underlying motivations make it likely to continue. Peacebuilding is about making these relationships more likely to sustain peace, where robust peace is not in place particularly after conflict. Positive peace-enhancing relationships require *active* building. Built by whom? Clearly in some situations, intervention by outside agents (e.g. international peacekeeping forces) or through central government support or improved legislative frameworks may be important. But for peaceful *relationships* to be strengthened, it requires the active engagement of individuals and groups who have these relationships. One cannot build peaceful relationships without engagement with other people and groups. Whatever else is needed, this engagement, as much at local level as at any other, is needed, as Lederach notes and as Crocker, in the case of development, stresses (Crocker 2008, ch. 10). This involves discussion, dialogue, negotiation or, in short, meaningful communication. If this happens, either interactions between individuals and groups who have been in conflictual relations continue to reflect existing inequalities of power and so on – in which case unpeaceful relations are likely to be replicated – or they reflect an attempt to listen (more) to other voices and to reach decisions in a genuinely democratic way through public deliberation. This is easier said than done, because it is precisely in situations of conflict – whether before a possible war or post-conflict – that parties are less likely to listen to each other. But the point is that the model of deliberative democracy Crocker is advancing provides a model/ideal for what is really needed if both peace and development are to be properly advanced.

I have stressed two elements in Crocker's account of agency as having a relevance for understanding peacebuilding: a rich account of agency along the lines of the capability orientation (as Crocker calls the cluster of views often referred to as the capability (or capabilities) approach) and the specific account of deliberative democracy. It is worth noting that this account is considerably richer than what is often presented as a liberal (or neoliberal) account of agency and hence development as focused on free markets. Liberalism can of course mean many things,[6] but insofar as it stresses the importance of agency as economic agency, then it provides a less rich account of development because economic agency can be exercised by people whose lives are otherwise impoverished and who may not engage with *res publica* through any exercise of democratic agency. Likewise, a liberal model of peacebuilding which puts stress on economic liberty is inadequate for catching the dynamics of building peace. (I do not pursue this; but see Liden (2014) for an interesting analysis of the weaknesses of the approach.)

No doubt all the various accounts of development/peacebuilding will have some account of agency within them. We need one that is grounded in social relations richer than market relations and sensitive to local traditions, but at the same time allows the agent the full potential to develop his or her powers or capabilities, and to exercise deliberative agency in collective decision-making. An appropriate account of agency holds the key to successful peacekeeping as well as successful development. Crocker's account is important in this respect.

Insider/Outsider

One of the themes in Crocker's writing has been that of the roles of the outsiders and insiders in development (see, e.g., Crocker 1991). Authentic development requires a central role of agents of change *within* society, from planning in central government to grass-roots agents of change, but the outsider's expertise and perspective can be useful too. But the outsider's role should not be dominant, or insensitive to the needs and conditions of those whose development they are assisting. (Consider the image of the international expert arriving with one-size-fits-all solutions expecting them to be imposed.) He uses the interesting idea of an 'insider-outsider hybrid' (see Crocker 2008, 19). Development ethics may be premised for many on a kind of universalism, but it has to be one that is seriously sensitive to cultural variation and local knowledge and values.

This is consonant with what Lederach argues. He also stresses the role of international actors, and gives the example of 'strategic resource groups' which are both international and multidisciplinary: 'people working in relief, development, conflict resolution, diplomacy and peacekeeping' (Lederach 1997, 101). What is important about this approach is that it acknowledges the relevance of actors at all levels. Collier (2007) for instance recognizes that countries that make up the 'bottom billion' and are caught in one or more of four 'traps' (conflict, natural resources, being landlocked and poor governance) may need external interventions to help escape, as we noted earlier in regard to peacebuilding. Real peacebuilding requires grass-roots agency, local perspectives and deliberative discussion. But it also needs a framework set by governments, along with appropriate inputs from international peacebuilding experts and advisers.

I would add that there is an aspect of the outsider impact on both development and peacebuilding connected with what may be called the international political, legal and institutional environment which, if it is right, helps and does not impede development. However, this environment often does not favour genuine peacebuilding or genuine development because it impedes them. Some examples would be the way tax havens deprive poor countries of much potential tax revenue and international trade rules, e.g. rules concerned with intellectual property rights create avoidable costs to poorer countries (see Pogge 2003 for a general critique of the international regime). Likewise sometimes poorer countries recovering from conflict are seen as theatres for proxy wars (see, e.g., Collier 2007, ch. 2), and generally the international arms trade is a contributing factor in the incidence of war and violence in the world. These are of course controversial examples, but they illustrate a general point that one of the most significant ways in which outsiders can play a part in creating the conditions in which genuine development and genuine peacebuilding can occur, is actually removing the obstacles. The outsider here is not the international expert present in a country that needs help with peacebuilding or development. He or she is in the background. But it is an important background which affects us all as global citizens.

Concluding Note

What has implicitly underlain the position of those who think of development and peacebuilding is a cosmopolitan perspective. A cosmopolitan or global ethics assumption, certainly shared by Crocker and myself, is that the international community (and indeed global citizens generally) have an obligation to promote both peacebuilding and development. That is, the ethical basis is the same, namely promoting conditions in which (more) human beings can flourish (better) anywhere, since both war and lack of development undermines these conditions. The relevance of the 'outsider' perspective is premised on the validity of a global ethics approach, albeit one sensitive to cultural differences: otherwise outsiders would be at best a mere irrelevance, and, if they intervened, they would be unwelcome imperialists. However, this does not mean that these ethical bases are actually examined very much, particularly in terms of how the two concerns might be considered together as arising from a common ethical source. This chapter has, hopefully, been a small contribution to that examination.

Notes

1. This chapter owes a debt to Kristoffer Liden, whose PhD thesis on liberal peacebuilding, for which I was an opponent in December 2014, inspired me to explore the possible parallels between peacebuilding and development. I became aware in preparing for it how much more had been written than I had anticipated or could fully cover. So, this set of reflections is by no means authoritative, but intended to stimulate some development ethicists into thinking about the links between peacebuilding and development.
2. An example of a relatively successful proactive peacebuilding operation was that of Macedonia through the UN's programme called United Nations Preventive Deployment Force (UNPREDEP) (see Sandole 2010, 83–93).
3. Perhaps my sympathy for his approach is not surprising given he is a Mennonite and I am a Quaker.
4. There is less agreement over this however in respect to international relations, since it is often assumed, partly on 'realist' grounds, that the only way to maintain peace between countries is through deterrence. This is not the concern of this chapter.
5. Furthermore assuming that peace (negative or positive for that matter) is a goal and assuming that development, especially poverty-reduction oriented development, is a goal, then practical reasoning requires us to think of what mix of actions will best achieve these goals. Indeed if extreme poverty undermines human well-being and violence undermines human well-being, albeit sometimes in different and

sometimes in linked ways, then the global moral obligation to support peacebuilding is at root similar to the global imperative of development assistance. See my account of cosmopolitan pacifism (Dower 2009).

6. Crocker and I are broadly liberal ourselves. See Dower 2014 for a sympathetic account of social liberalism.

References

Anderson, M. 1999. *Do No Harm: How Aid Can Support Peace – or War.* Boulder, CO: Lynne Rienner.

Bailey, S. 1993. *Peace Is a Process.* London: Quaker Books.

Boutros-Ghali, B. 1992. *An Agenda for Peace.* New York: UN Department of Information.

Collier, P. 2007. *The Bottom Billion.* Oxford University Press.

Crocker, D. A. 1991. 'Insiders and Outsiders in International Development Ethics'. *Ethics & International Affairs* 5: 149–73.

Crocker, D. A. 1999. 'Reckoning with Past Wrongs: A Normative Framework'. *Ethics & International Affairs* 13: 43–64.

Crocker, D. A. 2000. 'Truth Commissions and Transitional Justice'. *Philosophy and Public Affairs Quarterly* 20(4): 23–31.

Crocker, D. A. 2008. *Ethics of Global Development: Agency, Capability, and Deliberative Democracy.* Cambridge University Press.

Curle, A. 2007. *True Justice: Quaker Peace Makers and Peace Making.* London: Quaker Books.

Dower, N. 1999. 'Development, Violence, and Peace: A Conceptual Exploration'. *The European Journal of Development Research* 11(2): 44–64.

Dower, N. 2009. *The Ethics of War and Peace: Cosmopolitan and other Perspectives.* Cambridge: Polity Press.

Dower, N. 2010. 'Development and the Ethics of the Means', in *New Directions in Development Ethics: Essays in Honor of Denis Goulet*, C. K. Wilber and A. K. Dutt (eds.). University of Notre Dame Press, 29–37.

Dower, N. 2014. 'Liberalism', in *Unlocking Liberalism: Life after the Coalition*, R. Brown, G. Gloyer and N. Lindsay (eds.). Peterborough: Fastprint Publishing.

Galtung, J. 1975. 'Three Approaches to Peace: Peacekeeping, Peacemaking, and Peacebuilding', in *Peace, War, and Defence: Essays in Peace Research*, Vol. II. Copenhagen: Christian Ejlers.

Geneva Peacebuilding Platform. 2009. *Peacebuilding in Geneva: Mapping the Landscape.* Geneva Peacebuilding Paper 1, Geneva Peacebuilding Platform.

Geneva Peacebuilding Platform. 2015. *White Paper on Peacebuilding*. Geneva Peacebuilding Platform.

Gruzalski, B. 2001. *Gandhi*. Belmont, CA: Wadsworth.

Hobbes, T. 1651. *Leviathan*. Reprinted, R. Tuck (ed.). 1991. Cambridge University Press.

Iyer, P. 2011. 'Development versus Peacebuilding: Overcoming Jargon in Post-War Sierra Leone'. *Africa Peace and Conflict Journal* 4(1): 15–33.

Jenkins, I. 1973. 'The Conditions of Peace'. *The Monist* 57(4): 507–26.

Kuper, A. 2002. 'More Than Charity: Cosmopolitan Alternatives to the "Singer Solution"'. *Ethics and International Relations* 16(2): 107–28.

Lederach, J. P. 1997. *Building Peace*. Washington, DC: United States Institute of Peace.

Liden, K. 2009. 'Building Peace between Global and Local Politics: The Cosmopolitan Ethics of Liberal Peacebuilding'. *International Peacekeeping* 16(5): 616–34.

Liden, K. 2014. Between Intervention and Sovereignty – Ethics of Liberal Peacebuilding and the Philosophy of Global Governance. PhD thesis, University of Oslo.

MacGinty, R. 2008. 'Indigenous Peace-Making versus the Liberal Peace'. *Cooperation and Conflict* 43(2): 139–64.

Macquarrie, J. 1973. *The Concept of Peace*. New York: Harper & Row.

Miller, D. 1999. 'Bounder Citizenship', in *Cosmopolitan Citizenship*, K. Hutchings and R. Dannreuther (eds.). Basingstoke: Macmillan.

Murithi, T. 2009. *The Ethics of Peacebuilding*. Edinburgh University Press.

O'Gorman, E. 2011. *Conflict and Development: Development Matters*. New York: Zed Books.

O'Neill, O. 1989. Faces of Hunger: An Essay on Poverty, Justice and Development. London: Allen & Unwin.

Paris, R. 2004. *At War's End: Building Peace after Civil Conflict*. Cambridge University Press.

Pogge, T. 2003. *World Poverty and Human Rights*. Cambridge University Press.

Quakers in the World. 2016. www.quakersintheworld.org/quakers-in-action/128, accessed 20 April 2016.

Rawls, J. 1971. *A Theory of Justice*. Oxford University Press.

Richmond, O. P. 2005. *The Transformation of Peace*. Basingstoke: Palgrave Macmillan.

Sandole, D. J. D. 2010. *Peacebuilding: Preventing Violent Conflict in a Complex World*. Cambridge: Polity Press.

Sen, A. 1999. *Development as Freedom*. Oxford University Press.

Sen, A. 2006. *Identity and Violence: The Illusion of Destiny*. London: Allen Lane.

Turning the Tide. 2016. http://turning-the-tide.org/node/588, accessed 20
    April 2016.
Uvin, P. 2002. 'The Development/Peacebuilding Nexus: A Typology and
    History of Changing Paradigms'. *Journal of Peacebuilding and
    Development* 1(1): 5–24.
Wisler, A. 2013. 'International Development and Peacebuilding', in
    *Integrated Peacebuilding: Innovative Approaches to Transforming
    Conflicts*, C. Zelizer (ed.). Boulder, CO: Westview Press, 57–75.
Zelizer, C. and Oliphant, V. (2013). 'Introduction to Integrated
    Peacebuilding', in *Integrated Peacebuilding: Innovative Approaches to
    Transforming Conflicts*, C. Zelizer (ed.). Boulder, CO: Westview Press,
    3–30.

PART II

Agency

6 | Expanding Agency

Conceptual, Explanatory, and Normative Implications

CHRISTINE M. KOGGEL

Introduction

David Crocker opens *Ethics of Global Development* by telling us that his aim "is to move development ethics and the capability approach forward by working out and defending an *agency-focused* version of capability ethics" (2008, 1, his emphasis). He also tells us that "his agency-oriented perspective is an effort to build on, make explicit, and strengthen Sen's recent turn to the ideals of public discussion and democratic participation as integral to freedom-enhancing development" (2). Crocker then provides a brief description of Sen's account of agency as "a normative ideal that affirms the importance of the individual and group freedom to deliberate, be architects of their own lives, and act to make a difference in the world" (19). Finally, Crocker links this ideal of agency to empowerment, which addresses "those conditions and processes that enable individuals and groups to strengthen and exercise their agency" (19). I will begin where Crocker begins: with the capabilities approach and Sen's agency-oriented perspective. As with Crocker and Sen, I am interested in exploring agency and the role that public discussion plays in accounts of agency. Before turning to Crocker's expansion of Sen on agency and the role of public discussion, however, I will set the stage by evaluating Sen's version of the capabilities approach and his account of *women's* agency and what can enhance it (1999, chapter 8).

In this chapter, I argue that what Sen and others in the liberal tradition take as important for removing inequalities for women and for enhancing their agency falls short of addressing the following: (1) possibilities for enhancing women's agency cannot be *fully realized* in and through a justice approach or standard market-oriented policies for removing gender inequalities; (2) entrenched gender norms

155

shape roles and practices that can impede participation in economic, social, and political institutions even when these institutions are designed to allow equal participation in the shaping of public policy; and (3) explicit attention to the full effect of gender norms entrenched in networks of relationships at familial, institutional, national, and global levels can challenge and expand our understanding of agency itself as integrally connected with enhancing the agency of others. My main argument is that although theorists are aware of the detrimental influences of gender norms on women's agency, how this plays out in development theory and the policies endorsed in a global context reflects assumptions about who agents are and what agency involves.

To carry out the argument in this chapter, I explore the first shortcoming listed above by discussing the objection that Sen's focus on individual freedoms to the exclusion of social values such as care assumes a particular sort of rational and market-maximizing agent. This objection, however, does not go far enough in challenging assumptions about agents, what they value, or their ability to be full participants in public discussion and the shaping of policy. This leads to a discussion of point (2) above, for which I turn to Crocker's account of deliberative participation. I argue that Crocker takes us partway in addressing issues of unequal participation, but he does not go far enough in uncovering gender norms that shape agency in ways that determine who is heard in public discussion and what is valued in people's lives.

I then turn to Nancy Fraser, who exposes the two models of agents and agency on offer in the liberal tradition, both of which assume the male as norm. Uncovering the norms that are in place shows why they are hard to dislodge and result in limited options for addressing gender inequalities. However, while Fraser endorses a third model, that of the "Universal Caregiver," her account also falls short in assuming a norm that fits the lives of women in the North American context. To develop this critique of Fraser and to begin to unpack point (3) above, I examine Alison Weir's model of the "Universal Global Caregiver" because it draws attention to the exploitation and marginalization of caregivers in a global context in which rich countries depend on poor countries to have caregiving needs met. What emerges is the need to pay attention to the full and thoroughgoing relationality of agents and agency in a global context.

Developing a richer and fuller relational account of agents and agency lays bare what is at stake in the liberal account of individual agents as needing to be free to deliberate, make choices, and plan a life they have reason to value. I borrow from Sarah Clark Miller's account of agency as including and needing emotional, relational, *and* rational capacities to point to what agency is or should be for *all* human beings. A thoroughgoing relational account of agents interacting with and responding to others by making use of agential skills of relationality, emotionality, and rationality can best explain the importance of our obligations for meeting the needs of others. This account of agential skills can also reveal how agency for self and others is enhanced in and through networks of relationships at all levels of the personal, local, national, and global.

This chapter, then, explores answers to several sorts of questions about those whose lives and experiences tend to be most visible and valued in the mainstream literature on agency. How do entrenched gender norms that exist in relationships at all levels from the personal to the global shape debates on structures and policies and one's ability to challenge or change these? Is the very account of agency adopted by Sen and those who follow him itself fraught with assumptions about what it means to live a life one has reason to value? What might attending to these norms and the lives and choices shaped by them tell us about agency and about the role of public discussion?

The Capabilities Approach and Agency

In general terms "capability ethics," as Crocker calls it, focuses on what people are able to be and to do. Sen's version of the capabilities approach on which Crocker builds provides a powerful challenge to dominant views of development and theories of justice. The gist of Sen's critique of mainstream theories of justice, such as those advanced by utilitarians, libertarians, and Rawlsians, is that they fail to capture the diversity of human beings and the heterogeneity of contexts and conditions needed for an account of what justice demands: "The respective roles of personal heterogeneities, environmental diversities, variations in social climate, differences in relational perspectives and distributions within the family have to receive the serious attention they deserve for the making of public policy" (1999, 109). For Sen, facts of diversity mean that no simple descriptions of agents and no definitive list of measures that can enhance agency can be had. Context and conditions matter to the description and analysis. Sen provides examples of

capabilities like being able to avoid such deprivations as starvation, under-nourishment, escapable morbidity and premature mortality, as well as the freedoms that are associated with being literate and numerate, enjoying political participation and uncensored speech and so on. In this constitutive perspective, development involves expansion of these and other basic free-doms. Development, in this view, is the process of expanding human free-doms, and the assessment of development has to be informed by this consideration. (36)

Sen's account, thus, allows an examination into whether individuals in specific contexts and under certain conditions have the freedom to function in ways that matter to themselves (their subjective assessment of what matters to them) and to their well-being (an objective account of capabilities that allow one to live well). Sen's account is, therefore, important for providing a context-sensitive approach that makes the interconnectedness of kinds of unfreedoms clear and convincing.

For Sen, development as freedom gives a central role to agency; individuals ought to be able to act for themselves and control the course of their own life. As against previous accounts of development, Sen argues that people "need not be seen primarily as passive recipients of the benefits of cunning development programs" and that they should be treated as agents who "can effectively shape their own destiny and help each other" (11). Two aspects of freedom are also relevant to an account of agency. Enhancing agency can mean removing barriers and thus opening up a broader range of options from which people can choose. What one chooses is then up to the person's subjective assessment of what matters to them. This aspect of agency is captured by the notion of agency freedom. However, agency is also about being able to make one's life better – by accessing and making use of primary goods such as health care, education, and work; using the abilities one has to make substantive use of opportunities; and being free to parti-cipate in, deliberate about, and have a say in the shaping of economic, social, and political institutions. This aspect of agency is captured by the notion of well-being freedom. With respect to the second aspect, removing unfreedoms such as premature mortality, undernourishment, and ill-health as well as lack of access to education, work, and political participation can, then, expand an individual's capacity to pursue goals and objectives he or she values and has "reason to value" (56, 63). What one values is both differentiated from and connected with what one has "reason to value." For Sen, the subjective elements of agency freedom are integrally connected with the objective elements of well-being freedom.

In Sen's view, judgments about what is of value and about what policies will remove unfreedoms and enhance agency should be made in and through democratic processes that emphasize the importance of the exercise of public reasoning; that focus on implementing policies applicable to specific contexts and conditions; and that can provide justifications for why some processes or policies are better than others for addressing injustices or for achieving better or more justice in specific contexts. Sen frequently turns to examples to capture the complexity of his account. He tells us that African Americans have higher incomes than people in other parts of the world, but "an absolutely lower chance of reaching mature ages than do people of many third world societies" (6). Sen's point is that deprivations can come about even when one has income to meet basic needs and when legal and formal barriers to voting and participation are removed. The disenfranchisement and alienation of African Americans from democratic processes of voting and participating in debates as well as their overrepresentation in prison populations and the ranks of the poor distort and have deleterious effects on policies for removing these injustices.

As mentioned earlier, Sen emphasizes the importance of public discussion and deliberation to the making of public policy (2009, 392). The discussion of African Americans alerts us to the fact that Sen is aware of the ways in which some people are barred from entering public discussion or having an influence on public policy. These constitute injustices that emerge from racism in the USA. Direct attention, then, needs to be paid to background conditions of oppression that determine who gets to engage in the public discussion that then shapes public policy. Yet, I will argue that Sen's failure to fully account for the detrimental effects of oppressive norms is reflected in the agency-enhancing policies that he ends up endorsing. These policies already reveal norms that escape the scrutiny and challenge required for the kind of public discussion that can lead to real change. We need to attend to broader framework issues that reflect and manifest social and political structures and conditions of oppression. Once the pieces of my argument are in place, I will circle back to the example of African Americans and have much more to say about agency and the role of public discussion than is possible on Sen's account or in standard liberal theory more generally. But, before I get there, I need to discuss Sen's account of women's agency.

Sen on Women's Inequalities and Policies for Enhancing Women's Agency

Sen is rightly credited for paying attention to women's agency: "[t]he extensive reach of women's agency is one of the more neglected areas of development studies, and most urgently in need of correction. Nothing, arguably, is as important today in the political economy of development as an adequate recognition of political, economic and social participation and leadership of women. This is indeed a crucial aspect of 'development as freedom'" (1999, 109). For Sen, women's agency can be effectively enhanced when their lack of freedom in specific areas such as access to health care, education, economic and work opportunities, and political participation is removed. When women's agency is expanded in these ways, women are better able to live lives they have "reason to value" (56, 63).

Let me clarify that it is not that Sen fails to recognize that entrenched gender norms act as barriers to women being able to exercise agency and well-being freedoms. Rather, it is that Sen assumes and attends to freedoms valued by a particular kind of person, one who works outside the home and has influence in economic, social, and political spheres. The thrust of this criticism can be captured by returning to an item on Sen's list of diversities and heterogeneities quoted earlier; that of unequal "distributions within the family" that affect what women can be and do. It is certainly true that inequalities in the family hinder possibilities for enhancing women's agency and well-being freedoms. However, on my critique, diminishing the impact of these entrenched gender norms through the removal of the kinds of unfreedoms that Sen identifies will not be enough. When it comes to promoting women's agency and well-being freedoms, Sen turns to the usual set of liberal strategies and policies:

empirical work in recent years has brought out very clearly how the relative respect and regard for women's well-being is strongly influenced by such variables as women's ability to earn an independent income, to find employment outside the home, to have ownership rights and to have literacy and be educated participants in decisions within and outside the family. Indeed, even the survival disadvantage of women compared with men in developing countries seems to go down sharply – and may even get eliminated – as progress is made in these agency aspects. (191)

Elsewhere I have argued that by explicitly promoting freedoms such as being educated, being able to work outside the home, owning property, and having access to health care, Sen at least *implies* that women's agency is best expanded when they *reject* the work and values associated with caring for others (Koggel 2003, 2009). One observation would have us say that Sen is certainly right to suggest that when women refuse to limit themselves to care work, they expand their agency and well-being freedoms. Another observation would have us say that he is right to suggest that the best strategy is for women to insist that they have the full range of options (agency freedom) open to them and that they avail themselves of these options to improve their lives (well-being freedom). However, both observations mean that Sen leaves an unexamined assumption in place: the home is mainly a domain of unfreedoms for women. Under these conditions of unfreedoms (that certainly persist for many women around the world), it is not perceived as "rational" for women to "choose" to limit their agency and well-being freedoms by having their life plans and goals wrapped up in caring for others.

To be clear about the argument I am advancing, I am *not* claiming that these policies do not enhance women's agency and well-being freedoms. Removing unfreedoms in areas such as work opportunities and political participation can enhance women's agency. My questions are about what gets assumed and what gets left out when these sorts of policies are endorsed. To show this, I argue, we need to engage in a closer examination of the role of gender norms in the shaping and reshaping of women's lives and their possibilities for agency. Background conditions of oppression and entrenched gender norms shape perceptions of what women can do and be in ways that are hard to recognize let alone dislodge. It will take more than endorsing the importance of the "political, economic, and social participation and leadership" of women. Care, whether of children, the elderly, or the disabled, tends to be what women do but it is devalued in political, economic, and social spheres. In other words, Sen's account falls short of being able to capture the full scope of conceptual, explanatory, and normative implications for agency as displayed in values and activities assumed in and relegated to the private sphere. Women's lives continue to be subject to gender norms that affect their ability to enhance their agency and well-being freedoms as well as their ability to enhance the agency and well-being freedoms of *others*.

The underlying issue is Sen's problematic focus on individuals and on the goal of enhancing their agency so that they can live lives they value or have reason to value: "individual agency is, ultimately, central to addressing these deprivations" (1999, xi). Unsurprisingly, Sen's individuals tend to be people who are rational choosers, eager participants in market structures, and central actors in public and political spheres. Many women throughout the world, who take on the responsibilities of or are assumed to be responsible for meeting the needs of others, tend not to be eager participants in market structures or political actors. Yet, on Sen's account, this kind of nonpolitical or nonmarket person is merely encouraged to engage in public discussions that shape public policy: "there is a real need – for social justice – for people to be able to take part in these social decisions, if they so choose" (242). Nevertheless, members of oppressed groups tend to be subject to norms that stereotype who they are and what they can be and do. This makes it difficult for them to engage in public discussion that can lead to devising policies that speak to who they are and what they do that is of value to themselves and to families and communities.

I already mentioned that Sen cannot be faulted for failing to recognize the role of gender norms in shaping women's inequalities and limiting their agency. My argument against Sen is two-pronged: (1) the strategies and policies that he ends up endorsing make large parts of women's lives invisible or unimportant in what counts and is valued in social, economic, and political participation; and (2) making the invisible visible not only challenges standard liberal policies that tend to get endorsed by capability theorists and justice theory more generally, but allows us to sketch an enriched account of agents themselves. Before I turn to unpacking these criticisms of Sen, and of liberal theory more generally, it will be useful to repeat that mainstream liberal theorists recognize the impact of gender norms at the same time as they advocate particular sorts of agency-enhancing measures that assume the male norm of the economic, political, and social actor. In other words, the default is to endorse liberal strategies of greater access to jobs, education, and representation in political structures as ways to increase women's agency and well-being. Exploring these accounts of women's agency will allow me to highlight what goes wrong with conceptions of agency and policies for enhancing agency when oppressive social norms limit or thwart possibilities for participating in public discussion that can challenge or change those norms.

Crocker on Expanding Agency through Deliberation and Participation

Capability ethics is clear that agency freedom (the negative freedom to do what one chooses without barriers or interference from others) should be viewed as integrally connected with well-being freedom (the positive freedom to avoid deprivations and develop capabilities one has and has reason to value). In *Ethics of Global Development*, Crocker defends Sen on issues of underspecifying freedoms and refusing to prioritize kinds of freedoms because, like Sen, he wants to leave room for interpretation, decision-making, and policy implementation in specific contexts – in other words, to leave room for people to exercise their political agency. For Sen, political agency, as exemplified by participation in public discussion and debate, is crucial to the making of public policy (2009, 392). These are aspects of Sen to which Crocker is drawn in using Sen to frame and develop his own account of deliberative democracy and participation.

Crocker recognizes the role that deliberation can play in settling disagreements and shaping public policy, but he also recognizes that some people can be excluded or marginalized in these processes designed to formulate policy through the deliberation of participants. It can be said, then, that Crocker is more detailed and specific than is Sen on the issue of people being "able to take part in these social decisions, if they so choose" (Sen 1999, 242). This is why Crocker sets out to delineate principles that are meant to regulate and enable deliberative participation. These principles are: *reciprocity* ("each member can make proposals and offer justification in terms others can understand and could accept"); *publicity* ("each member be free to engage [directly or by representation] in the deliberative process, that the process be transparent to all ... and that each know that to which she is agreeing or disagreeing"); and *accountability* ("each group member is accountable to all [and not to himself or herself alone] in the sense of giving acceptable reasons to the others") (2008, 312–313). Crocker also argues, in the end, that the effectiveness of these principles for addressing existing inequalities or for including those who are marginalized require background conditions of equal political liberty, equality before the law, economic justice, and procedural fairness (317–318). In other words, as I have argued elsewhere (Koggel 2015), Crocker can be said to privilege constitutional guarantees of particular kinds of freedoms. These elements that structure deliberative participation may put Crocker in the uneasy position of being closer to Nussbaum than to Sen on the issue of underspecification that he endorses in Sen. Yet, Crocker is explicit in his turn to Sen and against Nussbaum on the issue of having a list (2008, 19). Crocker also reports that in his earlier work he merely noted that Nussbaum "lacked Sen's notion of agency" and that he now understands agency as necessary to an account of "citizen participation and democratic decision-making" (19). *Ethics of Global Development* is, therefore, Crocker's reflections on the evolution of Sen's notion of agency and his own attempt to give substance to the connection between economic, social, and political agency and the deliberative participation that can shape public policy.

That said, I still want to ask whether Crocker is closer to Nussbaum than Sen in his overspecification of conditions or foundations for deliberative participation. Is the kind of deliberation Crocker endorses possible in nonliberal societies or between nonliberal and liberal societies? In other words, the conditions that can enable deliberative participation and enhance political agency are those that Rawls defends as the institutional framework that structures liberal democracies. Sen also defends democratic freedoms when he delineates the intrinsic, instrumental, and constructive roles that democracy can play, all of which rest on something like the enabling conditions Crocker defends (Sen 1999, chapter 6). Yet, these do not play a foundational role for Sen whose context-sensitive account leaves the deliberation to those in particular societies who need to make policies that are effective for their societies. These are large foundational issues that deserve treatment in a separate paper. My concern in this chapter is with whether Crocker's explicit attention to formulating principles and conditions to address inequalities that result in marginalization and exclusion in deliberative participation can succeed in giving voice to the agents

I have identified as either invisible or excluded from exercising political agency. I will show in the section that follows that attending to the liberal assumptions about economic, social, and political actors and institutions is no accident or a mere tangent. These assumptions undergird each of the accounts by Sen, Nussbaum, and Crocker. They are assumptions that are difficult to identify and dislodge – even by those theorists critical of the "independent and rational market actor" so central to mainstream theories of justice and to development theory and policy.

Exposing the Rational and Individualist Agent and Expanding an Account of Agency

In a much-misunderstood paper published in the special issue on Sen in *Feminist Economics*, Des Gasper and Irene van Staveren side with Nussbaum against Sen on the issue of what they take to be Sen's problematic turn to the language of freedom. They challenge Sen's use of freedom as the overarching value to the exclusion of specifying other important values. They argue that Sen's account "implicitly idealizes *Man* as independent, already autonomous, rather than a social being, someone socialized into the norms and values of a community, cared for by parents, and having personal bonds as well as rights and duties towards society" (Gasper and van Staveren 2003, 140, their emphasis). Their critique may seem to offer little more than the standard one against many liberal theorists: Sen falls into the trap of having the individualist, autonomous, and independent self as a stand-in for all human beings. Gasper and van Staveren insist that care be specified as a unique and important social value and set of activities that cannot be subsumed under freedom. In other words, they charge Sen with taking his main actor to be the sort of individual whose identity and life plans are not shaped by the values and practices of caring and meeting the needs of others. Individuals are not only or mainly "choosers who reason" about their own lives (149). For them, Sen's account of freedom and agency is not helpful for thinking about care as a value in and of itself, for understanding the content of care as a value distinct from freedom, or for promoting care as a value that defies being subsumed under freedom.

Gasper and van Staveren's point is not that freedom can't be *made* to cover or explain values and practices associated with care, but that how freedom can do this and at the same time capture the range and diversity of agents needs to be specified, articulated, and defended. Otherwise, assumptions will be made about how agents are best able to enhance agency and well-being freedoms; that is, assumptions will be made that they can best do this through venues that enhance "political, economic and social participation and leadership." However, if this participation already embeds gender norms about caregiving and about who cares, it will not result in the sort of public discussion that can challenge the detrimental influence of these norms or change policies for enhancing women's agency. Their critique is important, but I want to argue that Gasper and van Staveren do not go far enough either in challenging Sen or raising questions about Nussbaum's project of using a list of capabilities (one that includes social values of care) to generate a theory of justice. While Nussbaum's account may be better able to incorporate the importance of care in women's lives, it is still from the perspective of expanding an individual woman's set of options so she can *choose* to take up caring for others as the kind of life she has reason to value. Moreover, the person who cares for others can choose this freely when the standard set of options of being able to work outside the home, have access to education and political participation, and so on are available and then rejected by her. In other words, the most that Nussbaum's theory of justice can do is to make it easier for women to choose to care for others – against a background that keeps oppressive gender norms in place.

Of course, feminists who want to acknowledge the importance of care in many women's lives and to their identities and yet do not want to limit an account of women's agency to merely embracing these values, identities, and practices to the exclusion of the self face a difficult task. Perhaps the problem of over- or undervalorizing care can be best handled if we focus on how gender norms are shaped in and through relationships of power – in various domains and at a variety of levels. Entrenched gender norms prescribe *who* should take responsibility for meeting the needs of others. Care roles and practices are necessary for the survival and the thriving of children, families, and communities, but they usually impede political, social, or economic participation. Thus, both the standard moves of either questioning or finding value in gender norms tend to keep institutional structures of what counts as contributing to economic, social, or political spheres in place. This makes it difficult to understand how these institutional structures often work to diminish women's agency (in both senses of agency freedom and well-being freedom) and their ability to enhance the agency and well-being freedoms of others.

Sen broadens the informational base for assessing inequalities and thereby captures the many, varied, and interconnected features of agents and possibilities for enhancing agency. However, his account does not capture how particular sorts of agents have lives shaped by norms and institutional structures that often leave them powerless to remove, challenge, or change them. These agents may have all the enabling conditions that Crocker defends – equal political liberty, equality before the law, economic justice, and procedural fairness – yet they may be marginalized or silenced when it comes to the effective realization of the principles of reciprocity, publicity, and accountability. To understand how caring for others tends to limit one's agency means understanding how assumptions about the value and practices of care shape institutions, structures, and world views so that they are taken for granted and perceived as not needing to be challenged or changed. These assumptions reach to the very notion of who an agent is understood to be and what decisions and choices an agent makes or should make.

There is another point to be made about Sen's account that is not properly addressed in the Gasper and van Staveren critique. Sen does not ignore the importance of social relations and values to agents: "Expanding the freedoms that we have reason to value not only makes our lives richer and more unfettered, but also allows us to be fuller social persons, exercising our own volitions and interacting with – and influencing – the world in which we live" (1999, 14–15). We may say, instead, that Sen assumes that lives that are *very* social in the sense that they are integrally connected with promoting the agency and well-being of others do not fit the norm of lives "we have reason to value." Such an agent might be perceived as "influencing the world in which we live," but such an agent may be limiting, or at least be perceived as limiting, rather than exercising their "own volitions." Sen may be best understood, then, as recognizing that care as it is currently perceived and practiced (devalued) creates gender inequalities in homes and families, restricts opportunities, and limits women's economic, social, and political freedoms. The point that needs to be made, however, is that he says little to address or change the institutions and structures that assume and embed norms that devalue caring practices – for various women in multiple ways in different contexts. These are norms that tend to make it incoherent to say that caring for others can be integral to enhancing agency and well-being freedoms for oneself or others. Moreover, possibilities for engaging in public discussions about the effect of these norms on people's lives are not likely to be present or be able to influence the debate that leads to public policies that challenge and change these.

To sum up thus far, we seem to be trapped in a conceptual framework that assumes and keeps in place the norm of the economic, social, and political actor as independent and best viewed as needing to identify and pursue their rational plan of life. This means that public discussion and participation will not be about the very structures that frame who gets to live a life "one" has reason to value. While Crocker escapes some of this critique by zeroing in on principles and enabling conditions for effective deliberative participation, his account still falls prey to these conditions not being accessible or effective for challenging gender norms that shape assumptions about who gets to engage as political actors and who can shape public policy. In the end, then, none of the accounts we have examined thus far, whether by Sen, Crocker, or Gasper and van Staveren and their defense of Nussbaum, succeeds in moving us out of the liberal framework that assumes and embeds norms about what individuals tend to or should pursue as lives they have reason to value. Because this critique questions the very frameworks themselves and how they structure the debates, it will be useful to examine the frameworks more closely.

Models of Agents and Agency in Liberal Theory

Nancy Fraser's discussion of the two models of agents and policies that dominate liberal theory is useful for illuminating how both fail to address or remove unfreedoms emerging from structures and institutions that embed gender norms. "The Universal Breadwinner Model" aims to foster gender equality by promoting women's employment and supporting employment-enabling services such as day care. The assumption is that everyone should work for wages and that women's agency is enhanced when their freedom to work outside the home is the same as men's. I have shown how these assumptions are evident in and emerge from Sen's account. "The Caregiver Parity Model" aims to foster gender equality by supporting informal care work through state provision of caregiver allowances. With this model the goal is not to make women's lives the same as men's but to "make their difference costless" by elevating informal domestic and reproductive labour "to parity with formal paid labour" (Fraser 1997, 55). This could be said to be the model that Gasper and van Staveren defend in their critique of Sen. And it seems to fit with Nussbaum acknowledging the importance of care by making it possible for women to *choose* this kind of life by making "their difference costless."

Fraser argues that both models are supported by liberals and many feminists, but that neither succeeds in uncovering or questioning the implicit "male as norm" and neither "asks men to change" (60). The failure to challenge assumptions embedded in current practices and policies means that women's activities and life patterns are not fully recognized or respected. Fraser rejects both models and proposes a third, that of "The Universal Caregiver": "a third possibility is to *induce men to become more like women are now*, namely, people who do primary carework" (60, her emphasis). Quoting the Swedish Ministry of Labor, Fraser finds support for the vision behind this model: "'To make it possible for both men and women to combine parenthood and gainful employment, a new view of the male role and a radical change in the organization of working life are required'" (62).

The Universal Caregiver model is meant to reveal and challenge the entrenchment of gender norms: "the construction of breadwinning and caregiving as separate roles, coded masculine and feminine respectively, is a principal undergirding [of] the current gender order" (61). Fraser's call for deconstructing gender is perhaps a tall order that says more about the deficiencies in the two models that currently structure liberal theory and policy than about how to reach this utopian vision of inducing "men to become more like women are now." That said, Fraser's account is instructive for highlighting the role of gender norms at the very heart of liberal institutions and structures. Yet, her account also falls prey to certain assumptions. Alison Weir agrees with Fraser's account of the two models that dominate liberal thinking and she also agrees that both are problematic and deficient. Yet, she argues that all three models, including Fraser's Universal Caregiver model, focus too exclusively on gender norms from the perspective of women in the USA. In other words, Fraser's account falls short because it fails to capture how gender norms operate in a global context in which relations of power at all levels of race, class, nation-state, and global markets shape how gender norms are utilized in particular contexts.

Weir situates care work in a global context and proposes that a more accurate account of the Universal Caregiver is one that "takes the perspective of the marginalized poorly-paid careworker" (2005, 311) as a starting point. For Weir, the perspectives of "immigrants and other marginalized workers who work for poverty-level wages" can help illuminate the exploitation involved in global care chains that have these women care for other people's children in order to care for their own children in their home countries. Moreover, market structures, capitalism, and globalization not only shape global care chains but they keep them in place in ways that allow privileged caregivers in North countries to exploit the racialized, gendered, and class-based aspects of carework. From the perspective of the "most marginalized and least empowered" (311), "care is not simply the underpaid labor they provide for others; care – for their own children and families – is what they are too often unable to provide, because the conditions of global capitalism deny them the right to care for their own children, and the freedom to live the lives they would choose" (312). Weir's model of the "Global Universal Caregiver" departs from Fraser's account in arguing that "global care chains can be unlocked only by radical change: only by a shift in our definition of the person, and the citizen, from independent worker to interdependent caregiver" (312). Thus, it will not only be men who need to change by rejecting the rational, independent, market-maximizing male as the norm for the social, economic, and political actor. What needs to be challenged and changed is the global order itself, one that supports oppression and domination in and through the intersections of race, gender, ethnicity, and class with respect to care work. While both the Fraser and Weir projects highlight what is missing or taken for granted in accounts of agency on offer in the liberal tradition, Weir's vision of the Global Universal Caregiver pinpoints features of interdependencies in a global context that provides a deep running challenge to the conceptions of agents and agency examined thus far. The challenge, as Weir notes, pushes in the direction of reconceptualizing the person and the citizen, the agent and agency itself, in terms of interdependence rather than independence.

Moving Beyond Liberal Theory: Expanding the *Concept* of Agency and Challenging Norms

As with Nussbaum, Sen's account can accommodate the idea that one's well-being *can* be tied up with caring for others and that this can enhance one's agency freedom. In other words, these need not be construed as irrational choices. Moreover, and as noted earlier, Sen cannot be said to ignore relational evaluations of well-being. Instead, the point is that in focusing on individuals and the kinds of freedoms that matter to them, Sen's account fails to be explicit about how and why lives and identities wrapped up in caring practices and in responsibilities for meeting the needs of others (for parts of every individual's life) often diminish agency and well-being freedoms for those who take on these responsibilities. Moreover, these caring practices can diminish an individual's freedom at the same time as those cared for must rely on caregivers for enhancing both their agency and well-being freedoms. These points need to be spelled out because values and practices associated with care do not have an easy fit with projects of enhancing one's own freedom. Moreover, they tend to be invisible and part of the assumed background against which theorists fall back on endorsing standard agency-enhancing solutions of having women work outside the home and be players in economic and political structures. Their being invisible and assumed means that possibilities for understanding the negative aspects of these values and practices or having their positive aspects reflected in public policy are inhibited by women's lack of voice and participation in debates or policies that could result in *real* challenge and change to the entrenched gender norms. These norms sustain the very inequalities that Sen wants to address – women's lack of agency and well-being freedoms to work outside the home, participate in debates, or be engaged in the making of public policy. These are some of the important insights to take from the Fraser and Weir projects of uncovering the norms underlying the frameworks at the heart of liberal theory and global market structures. Yet, I think we can do more than expose norms underlying models and overarching frameworks that have been on offer in mainstream liberal theory and policy.

A promising approach would involve taking a closer look at the notion of agency assumed by Sen and other liberal theorists so as to question institutions and structures built on norms that interpret caring practices and responsibilities for meeting the needs of others as *hin-drances* to agency. In other words, the liberal understanding of agency, a norm assumed in mainstream moral and political theory, may itself need to be challenged. This move is made by Sarah Clark Miller when she departs from standard accounts of agency in terms of a person's capacity to use reason to plan and control the course of one's life. Miller argues that agency also needs to capture the emotional and relational features of all agents who cannot but engage with others in moral decision-making processes that can harm or enhance agency and well-being freedoms for oneself and others.

As embodied creatures with physical, psychological, and emotional needs, Miller argues that agency can be compromised and result in harm to an agent when "people cannot act as agents in their own lives. Their rational, autonomous, emotional, and relational abilities are squandered. In short, the presence of unmet fundamental needs can render humans unable to function in the most basic of ways" (2012, 26). Facts about interdependencies and relationships have implications for how we actually engage and should engage with others. Miller differs from the accounts discussed thus far in that she connects her account of agential capacities to obligations *all* of us have for meeting the needs of others. She zeroes in on the significance of agency and the harm of compromised agency as that which accounts for the signifi-cance of needs and of moral responsibilities for responding to them. Agents have needs that are best met in and through interdependent networks of relationships in which agents make use of relational, emotional, and rational skills. Moreover, responding in morally appro-priate ways to another's needs requires that agents call on these agential capacities to know how to best enable these very same capacities in others. In short, Miller's enriched and expanded account of agency sets obligations on any and all to respond to the needs of others in ways that "establish, maintain, or restore human agency" (37) for ourselves and others.

There are a number of points to make in connection with Miller's expanded account of agency. It already moves us well beyond a focus on agents as rational choosers; it allows an examination of the com-plexity of lives affected in and through networks of relationships in a global context; and it ties obligations to an account of needs and of responsibilities to meet needs so as to maintain, restore, or strengthen agency. Agency is, thus, the hallmark of one's ability to care for oneself and for others. These are aspects of Miller's account that point to the fundamental fact and significance of interdependence.[1] The implications for agency are clear: all of us have relational, emotional, and rational capacities that we call on and should develop in order to be effective agents in our interactions with and obligations to others. The irony for the liberal theorist focused on the role of reason in shaping a rational plan of life is that this sort of agent also calls on emotional and relational capacities in the choices made to abstract from relationships and suppress emotions in learning to live a life one has reason to value.

Agency can be harmed or enhanced in and through relationships in which we find ourselves, are faced with choices, and make decisions about what to do. A critical analysis of networks within which personal and public relationships exist can show why developing each of the capacities in the triad of relationality, emotionality, and rationality is important at all levels; of individuals, families, communities, nations, and the global context. Miller is explicit about her project being focused on *moral* rather than *political* obligations and implications. She begins from "the point of view of individual moral agents making decisions about how to act and how to live" (138). I would argue that a thoroughgoing relational account of interdependencies in a global context makes the delineation of the moral and political and the focus on the moral hard to maintain. As Weir shows in her defense of the Global Universal Caregiver, agents reason about their own lives in the context of networks of relationships and emotional attachments in what are now complex global chains of interdependencies. Attention to these global chains not only highlights the intersectionality of race, gender, ethnicity, class, and so on, it also points to the need for a sophisticated and complex analysis of gender norms in a global context.

Conclusion: Tying It All Together

I began the chapter with Crocker: his following Sen on agency and his continued commitment to developing an account of public discussion and deliberation as vital to enhancing agency. I want to end by sketching some of the implications of using an expanded account of agents as relational, emotional, and rational and nested in a global context of interdependencies. To summarize what emerged from Sen, his account can be said to be multidimensional in its rejection of a too easy distinction between negative and positive freedoms; in its account of the interconnectedness and complementarity of agency and well-being freedoms; in its insistence that context matters to an account of unfreedoms and to the analysis of policies that will work to remove them; and in its defense of an inclusive and deliberative understanding of participation and of public discussion more generally.

I argued that Sen's account does not capture the full effects of gender norms assumed and entrenched in broader networks of relationships. Relationships at all levels of the personal, public, national, and global determine who engages in what activities and who has the power to dictate the meaning and value of those activities. Sen assumes rather than questions liberal understandings of the agent and liberal policies for what enhances agency. As against Sen, Crocker recognizes that more than encouragement to participate is needed to have those who are excluded and marginalized heard in ways that can shape public policy. Yet, his delineation of principles and conditions for deliberative participation still places his account in a liberal framework that assumes certain sorts of economic, social, and political actors and institutions. This is the actor that also features, in the end, in the Gasper and van Staveren and Nussbaum critiques of Sen. Devising strategies for ensuring participation in public discussion is important, but we need to be cognizant of how participation for some is undermined and restricted in ways that make it difficult for them to challenge let alone reshape public policy that can address the inequalities of the "most marginalized and least empowered" (Weir 2005, 311).

The path followed in this chapter had me arrive at a critique of liberal models and overarching frameworks from which emerged a reconception of the very account of agents and agency at the heart of the debates about what can enhance agency. The result was a clearer picture of how gender norms are implicated in accounts of agents and agency on offer in mainstream theory and policy. Miller's account of the rational, emotional, and relational capacities employed and needed by all agents to fulfill obligations to meet the needs of selves and others is an account of agency that makes the effects of gender norms on lives and policies visible. Placing Miller's account in the broader global context described by Weir adds additional levels of complexity by explaining how gender norms are also shaped by race, class, ethnicity, caste, and so on – and all in a global context in which liberal frameworks and policies dominate. I will end by sketching ever so briefly how the shape and direction of my arguments fit together by returning to a discussion of Sen's example of the unfreedoms of African Americans.

As discussed earlier, Sen's multidimensional account would take the history and ongoing discrimination of African Americans to be relevant to the analysis of data that show that African Americans have higher early mortality rates than many people in so-called developing countries. Conceiving of agents as having rational, emotional, and relational capacities can reveal features in addition to those Sen identifies in his examination of specific kinds of data. African Americans are indeed overrepresented in the ranks of the poor and in prison populations, but we also need to note the detrimental effect this has on families, on rates of single African American mothers living in poverty, on their ability to care for themselves and families, on ongoing racism that persists in policing and prison policies that too often remove African Americans from families and communities, and on high levels of apathy and alienation from democratic processes. Moreover, possibilities for effective agency are limited by institutional structures in a network of relationships that force many African Americans to be in relation with those who control social welfare programs, administer health-care plans, determine reproductive and child-care policies, set workfare rules, deal with domestic or community violence, or decide who has housing and where. These factors place a heavy emotional burden on individuals and relationships and they create and perpetuate fundamental needs that "render humans unable to function in the most basic of ways" (Miller 2012, 26). It is important to note that my account would not accept descriptions of African Americans as mere *victims* of racism and oppressive structures. They are agents who use and need to use relational, emotional, and rational capacities to make decisions about how to act and how to live in these very contexts that limit possibilities for effective agency.

Even when relationships at the public level determine how or whether agential capacities are thwarted rather than respected, agents can and must act in ways that make it possible for them to maintain, restore, or strengthen the ability to care for self and others in their communities. All that they do and need to do restricts their ability to participate in public discussion that can lead to meaningful change at the same time as it challenges norms of what it means to be an economic, social, and political actor. The account I provide takes the attention away from the normative implications of considering agents as planning and enacting a life they have reason to value – on their own and through standard policies designed to enhance agency and well-being freedoms. Instead, my account highlights the need to pay attention to inequalities and barriers to effective agency that emerge from oppressive norms and institutional structures. These norms and structures are especially important in understanding the racialized and class-based nature of gender norms in African-American communities and in the global context.

We have gone well beyond the theorists examined in this chapter on issues of how to enhance agency and well-being freedoms. An expanded notion of agency that incorporates the rational, emotional, and relational capacities of *all* agents can help identify whose voices are excluded from the public discussion that can shape and change public policy. As long as public discussion gives the rational agent who makes decisions on how to live a life one has reason to value center stage in economic and political matters, it will be difficult to hear what those who are "most marginalized and least empowered" in interdependent global chains of oppression say about their lives. It will take a lot of work and effort to reach the goal Crocker imagines in his account of public discussion and deliberative democracy that has a "vision of the ethically justified ends, means, and responsibilities of development in a globalized world – a vision not to be uncritically, mechanically, or slavishly applied but one to be democratically debated, criticized, adapted, and improved" (2008, 392).

Note

1. There is a vast and growing literature on relational theory from which Miller draws and develops her account of agency, but also from which feminists have developed accounts of justice and equality, for example, that challenge conceptions of these key concepts in traditional liberal theory (Koggel 2002, 2012). Two recent collections show the range and reach of this work: Downie and Llewellyn (2012) and Meynell, Campbell, and Sherwin (2009). The work of Iris Marion Young (2012) also makes use of relational insights in her account of a social connection model from which she criticizes liberal conceptions of justice and responsibility.

References

Crocker, David A. 2008. *Ethics of Global Development: Agency, Capability, and Deliberative Democracy*. New York: Cambridge University Press.

Downie, Jocelyn and Jennifer Llewellyn, eds. 2012. *Being Relational: Reflections on Relational Theory and Health Law*. Vancouver: University of British Columbia Press.

Fraser, Nancy. 1997. *Justice Interruptus: Critical Reflections on the "Postsocialist" Condition*. New York: Routledge.

Gasper, Des and Irene van Staveren. 2003. "Development as Freedom – and what else?" *Feminist Economics, Special Issue on the Ideas and Work of Amartya Sen* 9(2–3): 137–161.

Koggel, Christine M. 2002. "Equality Analysis in a Global Context: A Relational Approach." In *Feminist Moral Philosophy*, Samantha Brennan (ed.). *Canadian Journal of Philosophy*. Supplementary Volume 28: 247–272.

Koggel, Christine M. 2003. "Globalization and Women's Paid Work: Expanding Freedom?" *Feminist Economics, Special Issue on the Ideas and Work of Amartya Sen* 9(2–3): 163–183.

Koggel, Christine M. 2009. "Agency and Empowerment: Embodied Realities in a Globalized World." In *Agency and Embodiment*, Letitia Meynell, Sue Campbell, and Susan Sherwin (eds.). University Park: Pennsylvania State University Press.

Koggel, Christine M. 2012. "A Relational Approach to Equality: New Developments and Applications." In *Being Relational: Reflections on Relational Theory and Health Law*, Jocelyn Downie and Jennifer Llewellyn (eds.). Vancouver: University of British Columbia Press: 63–88.

Koggel, Christine M. 2015. "The Practical and the Theoretical: Comparing *Displacement by Development* and *Ethics of Global Development*." *Journal of Human Development and Capabilities* 16(1): 142–153.

Meynell, Letitia, Sue Campbell, and Susan Sherwin, eds. 2009. *Agency and Embodiment*. University Park: Pennsylvania State University Press.

Miller, Sarah Clark. 2012. *The Ethics of Need: Agency, Dignity, and Obligation*. New York: Routledge.

Sen, Amartya. 1999. *Development as Freedom*. New York: Anchor Books.

Sen, Amartya. 2009. *The Idea of Justice*. Cambridge, MA: Harvard University Press.

Weir, Alison. 2005. "The Global Universal Caregiver: Imaging Women's Liberation in the New Millennium." *Constellations* 12(3): 308–330.

Young, Iris Marion (2012). *Responsibility for Justice*. New York: Oxford University Press.

7 | "Reason to Value" *

Process, Opportunity, and Perfectionism in the Capability Approach

SERENE J. KHADER AND STACY J. KOSKO

Introduction

In pursuing the view of development as freedom, we have to examine ... the extent to which people have the opportunity to achieve outcomes that they value and have reason to value.

(Sen 1999b, 291)

From the capability perspective, to have well-being, to be and do well, is to function and to be capable of functioning in ways people have reason to value.

(Crocker 2008, 269–270)

Imagine that Amibesa is an illiterate woman in rural Ethiopia whose parents and siblings have never practiced family planning, despite having some knowledge about and access to contraception. Amibesa, like her neighbors, believes that children are an expression of God's will, and that she has a duty to respect her husband's desire for more children. She has never discussed family planning with her husband.[1] Despite her low income, and an alarmingly high risk of death in childbirth or from an unsafe abortion, Amibesa does not wish to pursue any of the family planning methods available to her.[2]

Although this example is fictional, real cases like Amibesa's can pose difficulties for Amartya Sen's variant of the capability approach. Sen argues that development is the expansion of freedom (Sen 1999b, see also 2002, 8). If freedom is the ability to pursue *what one values*, then

* We are indebted to our research assistants, Emma Velez and Jameson Spivack, for their invaluable contributions to this chapter, to four peer reviewers, and also to the participants of the 2015 Human Development and Capability Association conference in Washington, DC, for their enthusiastic and helpful conversation during and on the fringes of that meeting. The National Endowment for the Humanities 2013 Summer Institute on Development Ethics also provided fertile ground for us to begin this conversation.

178

the opportunity to control the number and spacing of her children does not count as development in Amibesa's case. Sen's phrase in the epigraph, echoed by David A. Crocker, has seemed to many to resolve this difficulty. Development is freedom, and freedom is the ability to pursue not only what one "values" but also what one "*has reason* to value." Amibesa has reason to value access to and knowledge of contraception (even if she elects not to use it).[3]

But, is the phrase "reason to value" really a solution to this difficulty? The idea that development is freedom, rather than access to some specific set of opportunities or goods, gains much of its appeal from promising to avoid certain paternalism and pluralism-related criticisms of development. Crocker defends his "agency-focused version of capability ethics" (2008, 1) as particularly respectful of differences in values that guide people to lead the kinds of lives they desire. "Authentic development," Crocker says, is something that "occurs when groups at whatever level become subjects who deliberate, decide, and act in the world rather than being either victims of circumstance or objects of someone else's decisions, the tool of someone else's designs" (2008, 339). For both Crocker and Sen, an "agent" is "someone who acts and brings about change, and whose achievements can be judged in terms of her *own values and objectives*, whether or not we assess them in terms of some external criteria as well" (Sen 1999b, 19, emphasis ours).

The paternalism and pluralism-related criticisms of the notion of development-as-freedom or agency suggest that development is something unacceptably imposed from without. They are commonsense worries, not articulated with a definition of paternalism or a particular defense of value pluralism in mind – and in fact they may be arrived at from a variety of philosophical perspectives.[4] One such worry is that development extends the legacy of colonialism by offering people "benefits" that they do not perceive as such (see Apffel-Marglin and Sanchez 2004; Escobar 1994; Rahnema 1997). Another is that development is coercive, a violation of the autonomy of both individuals and communities (Kapoor 2002). A third is that cultural homogenization is undesirable. The idea of development as freedom suggests that the "correct" types of interventions – that is, ones worthy of being described as "development" rather than "maldevelopment" (Penz, Drydyk, and Bose 2011) – do not prevent the beneficiaries from determining what types of lives they want to lead. As Wells summarizes in an autonomy-focused version of this line of defense, "Development can be understood as transformational and in the interests of those concerned only if people are treated as autonomous agents whose own valuation of the life they have *reason to value* is central to the evaluation of advantage and development" (Wells 2013, 11, emphasis ours).

But, something moves too fast here. Doesn't the very addition of the phrase "reason to value" suggest that people already value things they should not, or should value things that they do not – and thus that there are times where people's "own values and objectives" are not the only standard of judgment about what counts as development? Who decides what people have reason to value, and what kinds of interventions are acceptable when and if people's values conflict with it? The answers to these questions depend on what the phrase "reason to value" means. In the hands of his admirers, Sen's phrase has become something of a pointer, a way to signal to an audience in the know that one is engaging the capability approach, and usually his version of it. The phrase is rarely discussed in its own right.[5] Yet, Sen's version of the capability approach, now widely described simply as "*the* capability approach" (Nussbaum's is often referred to as "the capabili*ties* approach"), is now widely defined using it: It is the idea that development increases people's access to what they "value and have reason to value."

We argue in this chapter that, despite the intuitive strength and strategic value of the idea that development should be guided by people's own values, the phrase "reason to value" (or "R2V") incorporates additional normative commitments into the capability approach (CA). However, in our view, such commitments might be required for prospective judgments about what will enhance people's lives, or what they will come to value over time – judgments development practice cannot do without. The first section discusses the role the phrase currently plays in the CA literature. In each of the second, third, and fourth sections, we develop a potential interpretation of the phrase and assess (a) how well it harmonizes with other core commitments and goals of Sen's version of the CA as an approach to development practice and (b) how well it does at avoiding paternalism and disrespect for pluralism.

We draw only on commitments widely held by advocates of freedom and agency-focused versions of the CA (like Sen's and Crocker's).[6] In the fifth section, we argue that the only two interpretations of the phrase that permit the prospective value judgments that development practice requires also import perfectionist content into the CA. Thus, the idea of a CA whose only normative commitments are to respect for freedom and agency (at least of non-value-laden sorts) is untenable.

Reason to Value in Sen's Capability Approach

The phrase "reason to value" appears in the CA literature primarily in reference to cases where people's existing values seem deserving of criticism. This may be surprising given Sen's well-known reluctance to incorporate normative content into the CA, and his claims that incorporating normative content is paternalistic and inconsistent with respect for value pluralism. Sen's refusal to stipulate a list of valuable capabilities (Sen 2005, 158), his commitment to individuals' and communities' ability to identify and weight capabilities for themselves (see Robeyns 2003; Sen 2004), and his worries about grounding the value of the capabilities in an objective vision of the good life (Sen 2009, 49 fn) all attest to his desire to emphasize people's rights to live in ways they choose, and the desirability of their doing so to advance development. His arguments for focusing on capability over functioning also tend to focus on agency and choice rather than functionings. Having a range of substantive opportunities to be and do from which one might choose (capability) is, in his view, more important than being or doing in any particular way (functioning).[7]

Yet Sen's uses of the term "reasonable"[8] and "reason to value" point to a more normative strand in Sen's writing. Sen argues that reasonableness requires that behavior be more than simply goal-oriented, and uses the example of self-harm to demonstrate this (Sen 2002, 40). The phrase R2V is often invoked to justify questioning people's existing desires or going beyond people's existing desires in assessing well-being (Sen 1999b, 14, 18, 63, 152; 2002, 7, 13–14, 616). A need to question people's existing desires also seems built into Sen's commitment to fighting oppression of women and the poor, given that he argues that the "objective illusions" created by sexist, racist, and elitist ideologies can create adaptive preferences and make it difficult to identify accurately what oppressed and deprived people need (Sen 2002, 469–483). Even Sen's statement that "the 'freedom to lead lives that we have reason to value' cannot be independent of what we do value (on this see Sen 1982b, 1982c, 1985a)" (Sen 2002, 685) leaves room for nonidentity between what we value now and what we have reason to value. It may be objected that the value-laden remarks in this paragraph are not really part of the CA – and rather just parts of Sen's general body of political and economic thought. As Mozaffar Qizilbash (2012) argues, however, even though Sen sometimes defends only the narrow view that interpersonal comparisons of well-being should attempt to measure abilities to be and do rather than completed functionings or access to resources (a "capability perspective"), he also develops a unique theory of the role of capabilities, one that focuses heavily on choice and public reason (a "capability approach").

Whatever Sen's intentions, the phrase R2V operates in the secondary literature to restrict the range of abilities to be and do that count as constitutive of freedom. In an important CA handbook, Sabina Alkire and Séverine Deneulin make the notion of reason to value a defining one:

The capability approach contains three central concepts: functioning, capability and agency. A *functioning* is being or doing what people value and have reason to value. A *capability* is a person's freedom to enjoy various functionings – to be or do things that contribute to their well-being. *Agency* is a person's ability to pursue and realize goals she values and has reason to value. (Alkire and Deneulin 2009, 22)

In the work of Alkire and Deneulin, the idea that only a subset of abilities to be and do count as freedoms becomes explicit. The phrase "reason to value," especially in its longer form – "value and [have] reason to value" – seems meant to resolve conflicts between what people actually value and what they "should" value, where "should" means something like "have a reason" or "within reason." Alkire and Deneulin, for example, refer to "things (within reason) people value doing and being" (2009, 36). The idea of "reason to value" seems, in their work, to mark out the genuinely valuable functionings; it is unclear what work "value" is doing on its own.[9]

There is an alternative: that R2V expands, rather than restricts, what can count as an exercise of freedom. On this alternative, the set of valuable functionings includes two groups, those that one values and those one has reason to value. But, unless the functionings in the two groups never conflict, and can always be made equally available, this alternative view would undercut the CA's ability to provide principled reasons to oppose paternalism and protect value pluralism (the reason many are attracted to the notion of R2V to begin with). Consider a case where Amibesa believes that reproductive decisions are appropriately left to her husband, or that they simply ought to be outside of human control (i.e., left to God). If R2V is a notion that expands, rather than contracts, her freedom, then not controlling her fertility (what she values) and having control over the number and spacing of her children (what she has reason to value) are equally constitutive of her freedom. One problem with this view for pluralists or anti-paternalists is that, without a weighting of the various freedoms, neither alternative is better than the other. Pluralists and anti-paternalists who are attracted to the term R2V will find no reason to defer to Amibesa's actual desires in an expansive understanding of R2V, since it merely proliferates, and does not weight, objects that are constitutive of her freedom. Similarly, those who think Amibesa ought to have (substantive) access to contraception will find no reason to encourage this rather than respect her wishes.

More importantly, the use of the phrase R2V to *eliminate* "bad" capabilities from counting as valuable suggests that CA advocates like Alkire and Deneulin do not intend the "and" to be inclusive. In explanations of the phrase R2V, the focus is often on the CA's not being committed to expanding access to "harmful" – or what Alkire (2005) calls "horrid" – functionings, for example self-cutting, or more spectacularly, murder. Alkire interprets Sen as building "into the description of capabilities (and opportunity freedoms) the condition that they are valuable: The opportunities that matter for an assessment of freedom are those that people value and have reason to value. Opportunities that people have reason to find horrid, or irrelevant, or cumbersome are not to be expanded" (3). But what counts as a reason to value something, or find it horrid, as the case may be?

The Procedural Autonomy Interpretation

One potential interpretation of the phrase R2V states that one has reason to value what one values autonomously. Autonomy is the ability to form values that are genuinely one's own and live according to them.[10] On procedural accounts of autonomy, any set of values can be held autonomously, as long as they have been subject to some type of reflective *process*.[11] The procedural autonomy interpretation picks out as freedom-enhancing only the subset of capabilities an agent values on the basis of reflection, that she values, to borrow a phrase from Crocker, "not for *no* reason, based on a whim or impulse, but ... for *some* reason or to achieve a goal" (Crocker 2008, 157).

On *the procedural autonomy interpretation* of R2V, the idea that "Amibesa values and has reason to value X," means:

She has reasoned that X is valuable.

Procedural accounts differ about the type of reflective process required to make a set of values genuinely one's own. However, the value neutrality of procedural accounts of autonomy allows a wide variety of types of reasons to count as autonomous. A reason such as "because it is our custom," while perhaps unsatisfying to the outsider-evaluator who wishes for all "beneficiaries" to subject their values to critical scrutiny, nevertheless may be enough to demonstrate that Amibesa has reasoned that X is valuable. Many preferences that Sen describes as adaptive, such as women's self-sacrificing preferences, count as autonomous on procedural conceptions (see Khader 2011).[12]

The procedural autonomy interpretation, though intuitive, is inconsistent with many uses of R2V in capability literature. We have already seen that Sen and his interpreters tell us that a person who does not value a functioning, and whose other values are unknown, still has reason to value it and, conversely, a person who values a "horrid" functioning might not have reason to value it. But, surely a person can use their reason to come to value having their reproductive life determined by others, for example. Sen's typical recommendation for such cases is public deliberation or expansion of their capability set expanded with the aim of bringing that person to value (or devalue) that functioning, or with the expectation that she will come to (de-) value it.

Even CA scholars who seem to endorse the procedural autonomy interpretation give way to a more process-oriented view, often ending in a nudge toward public deliberation, when faced with the possibility of what seem to them to be unacceptable reasoning processes. A passage from Sabina Alkire and Séverine Deneulin (2009), for example, illustrates this slippage: "First, functionings are things people value. In other words, an activity or situation 'counts' as a functioning for that person only if that person values it" (2009, 32). Though the "only if that person values it" clause suggests the procedural autonomy interpretation, they go on in the same passage to discuss the wrongness of valuing murder. Their way of resolving the tension is to add that the phrase R2V "just acknowledges that, given our disagreements, we do need to make some social choices" (2009, 32). Their conclusion is that the CA offers public reasoning processes as useful methods for working out those choices (including by changing the internal valuation of individual participants), a more process-oriented view than the procedural autonomy interpretation alone allows.[13]

The Process Interpretation

A second interpretation of R2V, the process interpretation, suggests that one has reason to value what one values after deliberative processes, changes in one's opportunity set, or both. It is forward-looking and suggests that the term R2V tells us what people *would* value after undergoing certain changes. This is the interpretation that Crocker seems most committed to, both in his writing and in public lectures and discussion.

Crocker has done much to forward Sen's distinction between the process and opportunity aspects of freedom, a distinction that can help us get clearer about which processes, in addition to an agent's internal reasoning, are necessary for a person to come to have reason to value something: "[F]reedom is concerned with the *processes of decision making* as well as the *opportunities to achieve valued outcomes*" (Sen 1999b, 291). Exercise of political freedoms (like public discussion and free speech) or expansion of available opportunities (a change in one's circumstances that results in an expansion of one's real capability set) might be reason-giving processes. If having R2V something means one *would* value it following certain kinds of processes, then the function of R2V is largely to facilitate prospective judgments, allowing development practitioners to anticipate what Amibesa might, after an intervention, "have reason to value," irrespective of what she currently values.

We have identified two types of process that might make Amibesa's values count as reasoned: her participation in collective deliberation and an expansion of her capability set. According to the first, which we call the "deliberative-process" version of this interpretation, when we say that Amibesa values and has reason to value something, we are saying that:

Through a public, deliberative process, she has reasoned (or will
reason) that X is valuable.

Though this interpretation of R2V is largely absent in the secondary
literature on R2V it would be consistent with Sen's emphasis on the role
of political freedom in value formation, an emphasis Crocker
embraces.[14] Sen argues that the ability to participate in politics and
public discussions is valuable, not only because of its ability to motivate
governments to act in the public interest, but also because it plays
a constitutive role in development, by facilitating value formation.
Collective decision-making processes are central to the development,
evaluation, and evolution of weights and values that individuals might
place on ways of doing and being and on various goods (Sen 1999b,
152). Sen and Crocker both suggest that public deliberation transforms
the normative status of values; their being deliberated upon makes
them especially worthy of playing a role in development policy.
In many cases, Sen treats values that have not undergone scrutiny
through some kind of public process as in some way suspect, perhaps
unreliable as guides to the actual (uninformed, unregimented) values
a person holds: "We cannot, in general, take preferences as given
independently of public discussion, that is, irrespective of whether
open debates and interchanges are permitted or not" (Sen 1999b,
153). Crocker argues that agency, rather than the mere possession of
values, requires one to "deliberate, decide, act (rather than being acted
on by others)" (Crocker 2008, 270).[15]

A second version of the process interpretation, which we call the
"opportunity-process" interpretation, is well-rehearsed, particularly in
the work of Alkire and Ibrahim, although not always as an explicit
interpretation of R2V. It suggests that a person has reason to value
something if they come to value it "through the exercise of other freedoms," where freedoms include new options about how to live one's
life, rather than merely new opportunities to deliberate. According to
this opportunity-process version, if Amibesa values and has reason to
value something, we mean that:

Through exposure to greater opportunities, she has reasoned (or will
reason) that X is valuable.

Describing something like the opportunity-process view, Sen writes
"In examining a person's opportunities, it is possible to go beyond

the actual preferences used in her choice acts into the preferences she could have chosen to have" under different circumstances (Sen 2002, 616). Opportunity-process therefore relates to what Sen has called the *opportunity aspect of freedom.* According to the opportunity-process view, a set of capabilities that Amibesa might actually value need not be (is probably not) the same as the set of capabilities that she might have ("good") reason to value under different circumstances.[16]

The opportunity-process interpretation emphasizes that there are alternative ways of being and doing that Amibesa might come to value if she had different opportunities, but that the reason she does not currently value (or seem to value) them is that they are beyond her reach. Here the phrase R2V furnishes a prospective argument for expanding the capabilities of the deprived, irrespective of an agent's current values. In our example, Amibesa does not value access to family planning education and methods, but she might come to value – and even pursue – these goods if her larger circumstances change such that having control over the number and spacing of her children is now among the feasible freedoms before her (because, for example, she is less poor, or less dominated within the home, or the male child mortality rate or son preference declines, or she has been given the previously absent hope of availing herself of birth control without shame or judgment). This opportunity-process interpretation claims to respect agents' actual and *potential* evaluations. Alkire makes this explicit: "things that people actually value – as well as have reason to value" (Alkire 2008, 5).

The process interpretation, both its deliberative and opportunity versions, has the advantage of consistency with other normative commitments often appealed to by proponents of Sen's version of the CA. First, especially in its deliberative form, it is in line with Sen's emphasis on the process aspect of freedom and the role democratic processes play in enabling people to appreciate valuable functionings. Second, the opportunity-process version links the opportunity and process aspects of freedom together in a way Sen often does: The "valued outcomes" that Amibesa has *reason to value* are identified in part through the *process aspect of freedom*, while those that she already *values* can be pursued (or not) more immediately, provided that the *opportunities to achieve these valued outcomes* are available to her. (She may eventually have reason to value additional outcomes should her opportunities expand.) Third, both versions of the process interpretation can helpfully explain some of Sen's remarks on positional objectivity and his belief that deliberation and social change play corrective and constitutive roles in value formation. Fourth, and similarly, the process interpretation also seems consistent with the broad CA literature's apparent consensus that adaptive preferences should not be taken at face value.

However, consistent as the process interpretation seems to be with Sen's own remarks and the broader literature on adaptive preferences, it cannot furnish a view that does what users of the term R2V seem to want – one that rejects value for "horrid functionings" on one hand and refers only to agents' own values on the other. The deliberation version of the process interpretation seems to commit the CA to accepting people's rejection of valuable functionings if the rejection survives deliberation. If Amibesa does not value the ability to control her fertility after deliberation, she does not have reason to value it and never did. On the other side of this coin, it also seems to commit the CA to accepting people's embrace of horrid (or oppressive or harmful) functionings if the embrace survives deliberation. Finally, if, in responding to these two problems, CA proponents simply prescribe expanding people's capabilities irrespective of their current values (as in the opportunity-process view) – or insist that people keep deliberating until they have the "right" (the "reasonable") values – then they suggest that "experts" sometimes know what people have reason to value better than people themselves, thus importing values that agents do not already have.

The opportunity-process interpretation was probably never tenable without commitments to external values to begin with. *Which* opportunities must be available before people's values count as reasoned? The opportunity version seems to rely on external evaluators to select, or at least shape through facilitation, the relevant set of opportunities. Since the whole point of saying people need greater opportunities to know that they have reason to value something seems to be that their status quo views are distorted, the opportunity-process view seems designed to justify the importation of values besides freedom and agency into development. To say that we will only know whether Amibesa has reason to value contraception after she has been exposed to shame-free opportunities for family planning requires some reason to expose her to this particular opportunity. Conflicting opportunities (such as the opportunity to be regarded as a devout follower of a religion that rejects contraception) and trivial opportunities (such as the opportunity to become a better cricket player) are also opportunities, so what justifies choosing the particular opportunities involved in opportunity expansion?[17] If the process interpretation introduces values not held initially by the people involved, or wants to question "bad" preferences that survive deliberation, then the process interpretation may dissolve into the perfectionist interpretation below.

The Perfectionist Interpretation

What we call *the perfectionist interpretation* is a third and final interpretation of "reason to value." In philosophy, the term "perfectionism" has a broad and narrow usage. According to the broad usage, perfectionism is the idea that there is such a thing as an objective good for human beings; according to the narrower one, the human good is "the development of human nature" (Hurka 1993, 3).[18] According to the perfectionist interpretation, Amibesa values and has reason to value X because:

X is valuable.

Though many CA proponents reject the notion that the philosopher or the development practitioner or policy maker "knows best" what is valuable, perfectionism offers the most direct route to explaining the idea that the phrase R2V adds to the CA. There are two ways perfectionism might explain the meaning of the term R2V. The first, the broad perfectionist reason, is that the objective goodness of something just is reason to value it. The second, narrower perfectionist reason, is that, if it is human nature to desire the development of one's own potential (to some level at least), one will likely come to value that which will help a person flourish.[19] If this idea about human nature is correct, we should expect what is objectively good for human beings to overlap significantly with what they value after critical reflection, after social-level deliberation, and after being exposed to "better" opportunities. Lack of opportunity and social inequality may make people unaware of the consequences of exercising certain functionings, or failing to exercise others, and lack of reflection can prevent people from seeing the ways in which new opportunities are extensions of their existing systems of value. On the perfectionist interpretation, what adherents of the procedural autonomy and process interpretations call "reasoning processes" (including collective and individual deliberation, and perhaps even reflection following opportunity expansion) are vehicles for helping the agent recognize the (objective) value of certain capabilities. To put this less abstractly, the perfectionist interpretation says that if Amibesa comes to value (substantive, shame-free) access to family planning after a community meeting, or seeing the ways in which deliberate spacing of children impacts her friends' lives, or finally having the real opportunity to engage in a meaningful discussion about it with her husband, it is likely because these processes helped her see the worth of family planning – or the worth of the underlying capabilities to which control over one's fertility is a means.[20]

This perfectionist notion that reasoning processes will cause people to come to value what is actually valuable seems implicit in many uses of the phrase R2V. To see how this is the case, it will be useful to observe that development often requires making *prospective* judgments about what people will come to value. Prospective judgments concern what an agent will likely come to value and are made *before* the agent actually engages in deliberation or experiences opportunity expansion. Both the mere suspicion that a person's expressed values and desires are not the ones she has "reason to value" (we should wonder whether Amibesa really has a choice) and explicit arguments that a person has reason to value certain things she does not already value (we should make sure Amibesa has the opportunity to learn more about family planning and discuss it with her husband, whether she wants to avail herself of it right now or not) require such prospective judgments, which are difficult to make without perfectionist commitments.

If we did not have some sense of what *was* valuable and expect agents generally to value it, there would be no predicting what agents would eventually come to value through reasoning or opportunity-expanding processes. We would worry, for instance, that women who exercised reproductive self-determination in the status quo were not expressing their true values – and we would think it was likely that, after reasoning processes and opportunities to conceive of their reproductive lives as in the hands of fate, many of them would come to devalue reproductive self-determination. But, as we noted in the first section of this chapter, this is not what CA theorists actually say; the idea that one might have reason to value something other than what they do is only invoked when people's existing values are somehow harmful or limiting.

Further, if we did not have some reason to believe that people would come to want "the right" functionings, then adding *any* opportunities to their set or introducing them to *any* new ideas would equally promote their freedom. But, again, this is wildly inconsistent with usage. CA theorists do not say that that women should be led to question the value of education, or that well-nourished people should be told about the virtues of fasting, and so on. They say instead that certain capabilities, such as being educated or well-nourished, are inherently or instrumentally valuable.

It may be objected that the idea that there are functionings that are "right" and "wrong" to value is antithetical to the other elements of the CA – especially the CA's valorization of multiple realizability and public deliberation. It is first worth noting that, even if the objection were true, it would not provide a reason to continue the current use of the phrase R2V. It would instead count in favor of dropping the idea of R2V from the capability approach altogether or redefining valuable capabilities only as those that people *already* value.

A second line of response to the objection is that the belief that certain functionings are inherently valuable does not obviate the need for public deliberation or the possibility of multiple realizability,[21] the pluralist and anti-paternalist possibilities that seem most important to those who wish to define development as freedom. As Rutger Claassen (2014) argues, capability theorists often fail to distinguish objections to perfectionism from objections to paternalism. One can be a perfectionist and still value deliberation and a plural, context-sensitive understanding of capabilities. Arguments for the compatibility of perfectionism with pluralism, deliberation, and conservatism about the permissibility of coercion are well-rehearsed in the literature on perfectionism and liberalism. To canvass a few: the idea that there are objectively valuable functionings does not imply that they should be realized in the same way in all contexts (Nussbaum 2001) or that we need to commit to a view about the value of functionings above a basic welfare threshold (Claassen 2014; Khader 2011; Nussbaum 2001); the content of the list of valuable functionings itself can be a topic of public deliberation (Ackerly 2000; Alkire 2007; Khader 2011; Nussbaum 2001); public deliberation allows people to choose variants of the valued functionings that are most likely to be successfully realized in their contexts (Crocker 2008; Khader 2011; Nussbaum 2001); people's lives go better when their lives enact valued functionings *and* they endorse this fact (Crocker 2008; Khader 2011; Olsaretti 2005; Raz 1988; see also Sen 2009, 225), and public deliberation increases the likelihood that they will (Crocker 2008).

Conclusion: Process or Perfection?

If a certain level of perfectionism is compatible with deliberation and multiple realizability – and thus with commitments to some level of anti-paternalism and value pluralism – the contrast between the process and perfectionist interpretations is not stark. Both can place a high value on deliberation about values in public, and in the minds and intimate relationships of, individual agents. Both suggest that agents may have R2V functionings they do not in fact value, or reasons to reject functionings they currently do, and both endorse policies or procedures that attempt to modify people's existing values, or at least open to the door to modification. The conclusion that the *content* of an agent's values somehow tracks whether they are reasonable seems inescapable for both interpretations. This is clear enough with regard to the perfectionist interpretation, but recall that the process-deliberation interpretation threatens in practice to encourage deliberation until agents arrive at the "right" values (for surely anything less is evidence of coercion, exclusion, or manipulation between deliberators).[22] If the deliberative-process interpretation is going to be consistent with the uses of the term R2V to eliminate bad functionings, and the judgments of CA proponents that values formed because of oppression and deprivation are suspect, it is also going to have to license prospective judgments about what people will come to value after deliberation; it has to suggest that it is reasonable to think *before* any deliberation has occurred that Amibesa will come to value real access to family planning *afterwards*. The need for perfectionist and prospective judgments is even clearer in the case of the opportunity-process version. It clearly justifies expanding people's opportunities in ways they may not initially endorse (creating sexual education opportunities and encouraging spousal communication about number and spacing of children in Amibesa's community in hopes that she will ultimately see their value). We summarize these interpretations, their consistency with Sen's version of the CA, and their potential pluralism and paternalism implications in Table 7.1, below.

Table 7.1 *Summary of interpretations of R2V*

Interpretation	Definition of "Y values and has reason to value X"	Consistent with the commitments of Sen's version of the CA?	Problematic implications for anti-paternalism and value pluralism
Procedural autonomy	Y has reasoned that X is valuable.	• consistent with some remarks on positional objectivity and Sen's refusal to stipulate a list of valued functionings • inconsistent with repeated claims by Sen and others that a person can have R2V things she does not actually value (at least without the implausible view that "bad" values simply cannot be arrived at reflectively) • inconsistent with repeated claims by CA proponents that some functionings are unreasonable to value because of content	• none
Deliberative-process	Through a public, deliberative process, Y has reasoned (or will reason) that X is valuable.	• consistent with some of Sen's remarks on positional objectivity and refusal to stipulate a list of valued functionings	• requires CA to treat harmful functionings valued after deliberation as agency-expanding; especially problematic given

Table 7.1 (*cont.*)

Interpretation	Definition of "Y values and has reason to value X"	Consistent with the commitments of Sen's version of the CA?	Problematic implications for anti-paternalism and value pluralism
		• consistent with the value Sen places on the democratic and deliberative elements of the process aspect of freedom • consistent with CA proponents' claims that expressed desires for some harmful functionings are suspect • inconsistent with repeated claims by CA proponents that some functionings are unreasonable to value because of content • inconsistent with focus of others besides Sen on capability expansion providing R2V	• inadequacies of real-world deliberation • commits CA to development interventions that reject access to valuable functionings if the individuals involved do not want access to them even after deliberation • unclear when deliberation is finished/danger of treating value for the "right" functionings as an indicator of this (indistinguishable in practice from the perfectionist interpretation)
Opportunity-process	Through exposure to greater opportunities, Y has reasoned (or will reason) that X is valuable.	• consistent with Sen's remarks on positional objectivity	• no basis for knowledge of what would expand a person's agency until after her situation has been changed

	- consistent with CA proponents' claims that expressed value for harmful functionings is often suspect - inconsistent with repeated claims by CA proponents that some functionings are unreasonable to value because of content - inconsistent (because of the need to select valuable opportunities) with CA proponents' claims that an individual is the exclusive authority on what would make her life go well	- need for a conception of the good external to the individual to determine what counts as a valuable opportunity - no way to take seriously people's rejection of "opportunity"
Perfectionist X is valuable.	- consistent with repeated claims by CA proponents that some functionings are unreasonable to value because of content - consistent with CA proponents' claims that expressed desires for some harmful functionings are suspect - inconsistent with Sen's refusal to stipulate a capability list - inconsistent with CA proponents' claims that an individual is the CA's exclusive authority on what would make her life go well	- inconsistent with claims that an individual is the CA's exclusive authority on what would make her life go well - seems to some to be inconsistent with cultural diversity/cultural freedom - seems to some to license coercing people into exercising "good" functioning

Even if the process interpretation does not completely dissolve into the perfectionist interpretation, it raises similar concerns about paternalism. This leaves proponents of Sen's CA with two options, drop the phrase "reason to value" and simply aim to expand agents' access to what they already value (and abandon judgments about adaptive preferences, horrid functionings, and so on), or keep it and accept some level of paternalism.[23]

There are good reasons to prefer the latter. If part of the appeal of the CA is that it does not take people's preferences at face value and that it allows criticism of oppression and deprivation, it is difficult to see how it can do without at least some commitments about which functionings are valuable (see Khader 2011 and Khader 2018). Further, though we have not discussed this point at length, if the CA is going to license more than local-level judgments about deprivation, such as those embodied in the Human Development Report, or those embodied in the widespread claim that poverty is harmful, it is unclear how the CA can do without a general view of which functionings are valuable. Acknowledging that the phrase R2V imports objective normative content into the CA is key to the CA's ability to respond to adaptive preferences and to make large-scale, at-a-distance judgments about the presence of deprivation. If paternalism means the view that others sometimes have knowledge about what is good for us that we, in that moment, do not, the CA may not be able to avoid certain elements of paternalism.

We think it is important for proponents of the CA to be honest about this fact. A real danger in development practice is that the phrase R2V may mask conflicts between what people already value and what others think they should. Obscuring the fact that, in practice, the CA sometimes asks people to change their values – and even introduces them to functionings they claim not to want – may prevent us from recognizing the moral stakes of development interventions. If what we value and what we should value are equally constitutive of freedom, the harm of losing access to what we already value is easy to ignore. Thus, there are benefits to recognizing that the phrase R2V is a value-laden phrase, and one that imports value-laden content into Sen's CA.

The elements of paternalism entailed in the CA can be made less objectionable than they initially seem. Our reason is emphatically not that, if perfectionist development practices "seem to restrict people's freedom to live the way they choose, so much the better" (Deneulin 2002, 516).[24] Rather, we want to draw our moral attention to the inescapable and highly fraught character of power relationships between the practitioners (the aid worker, the policy maker ...) and "beneficiaries" in development, and the fact that interventions are often designed with little involvement from, let alone power exerted by, those individuals. The very term "beneficiary" can obscure the human being whose opportunities and well-being are the subject of these well-intentioned, but sometimes not beneficial, "interventions." Sen, Crocker, and other CA theorists share a concern that people – even and especially the very poor or oppressed – should wield agency in deciding what kinds of lives they want to lead, and whether and how to value the ways of being and doing that will allow them to lead such lives. In fact, they agree that individuals ought to wield "enlightened agency" or "informed critical agency," "the freedom to question established values and traditional priorities" (Drèze and Sen 2013, 232). Threats to this freedom might be characterized as "agency vulnerability: the risk of being limited in our ability to control the social and economic forces that affect us" (Kosko 2013, 1).

We share this desire to respect and cultivate (informed, critical) agency. Rather than denying the risk of objectionable paternalism or disrespect for value pluralism, we should be clear that the CA requires value commitments and that practitioners will sometimes encounter conflicts between these values and the existing values of beneficiaries, and build in reasons to respect agency and pluralism of value. One anti-paternalist commitment, long central to the CA in the form of the capability/functioning distinction, is avoidance of paternalistic coercion. We can say that agents' lives would go better with certain functionings – and that real opportunities to pursue them ought to be available (capabilities) – without saying that people should be coerced into exercising them. Second, as we mention above, saying that there are valuable functionings people may not recognize is far from saying that people's first-person reasons and local-level deliberative processes are irrelevant to development practice.[25] Knowing that some functionings are generally good is far from knowing whether and why people reject them, how it is effective to provide them in a given context, and how to combine them with people's existing systems of value. We can say that Amibesa's life would go better with the option to control the number and spacing of her children without saying that she should be forced to attend a family planning class and use contraceptives, and while acknowledging that her reasons for rejecting family planning provide important practical information. Further, democratic and deliberative processes are valuable for many reasons unrelated to their revealing of agents' true values: the prevention of tyranny, the development of capacities for self-representation, and the development of capacities to see others as equal, to name a few.

All plausible interpretations of the phrase R2V that cohere with the aims of Sen's version of the CA, and are consistent with its actual usage, suggest that it is sometimes acceptable to try to expand people's access to things they do not value. Given what R2V seems to us to bring to the CA, it also seems that the Sen/Nussbaum disagreement on the list of valuable, or "basic," capabilities is over-blown. It matters less that Nussbaum and her admirers are willing to stipulate a list of basic capabilities if, as is belied by the phrase R2V, inherent in Sen's version of the CA is an underlying assumption that certain capabilities are objectively (more, most) valuable.[26] Whatever the precise content of "the list," given what R2V really means and how it is used, the CA seems already committed to acknowledging that some ways of being and doing, and some opportunities, are objectively valuable irrespective of whether the individual or community articulates *today*, under present circumstances, that they are so. Alkire acknowledges as much in advocating for her minimally specified "open menu" approach to stimulating public discussion, in which the outside facilitator brings presumably valuable "dimensions" to the table in the hopes of "usefully spark[ing] conversation" (Alkire 2002, 38). The selection of these dimensions requires making certain assumptions about what members of the community have reason to value.

The motivation underlying the approach of "development as freedom" is not so much to order all states ... into one "complete ordering," but to draw attention to important aspects of the process of development, each of which deserves attention ... An adequately broad view of development is sought in order to focus the evaluative scrutiny on the things that really matter. (Sen 1999b, 33–34)

The difference between "what really matters" and what people "have reason to value" may not be so large after all.

Notes

1. Spousal communication is significantly correlated with women's family planning decisions in Ethiopia, decreasing the likelihood of unmet need for services by about 40 percent relative to those who have never discussed family planning with their partner (Korra 2002, 19).
2. In 2015, Ethiopian women faced a 1:64 lifetime risk of maternal mortality (The World Bank Group 2017), with 32 percent of all maternal deaths attributed to unsafe abortions in 2011 (Central Statistical Agency [Ethiopia] and IFC International 2011). For a detailed empirical study of "Family Planning Knowledge, Attitude and Practice among Married Couples in Jimma Zone, Ethiopia," see Tilahun et al. 2013. Among other things, the study concludes "that mere physical access (proximity to clinics for family planning) and awareness of contraceptives are not sufficient to ensure that contraceptive needs are met." Meanwhile, Dennis P. Hogan, Betemariam Berhanu, and Assefa Hailemariam (1999) find that "[w]omen's literacy and autonomy are, by far, the most significant forces in the movement toward lower fertility" in Southern Ethiopia.
3. The claim that Amibesa's well-being would be improved by her ability to access and discuss family planning should be distinguished from the claim that population control is a proper aim of development policy, or that women's reproductive decision-making is primarily of instrumental value. See Sen 1994 for a discussion of why women's empowerment is superior to population control and Wilson 2015 for a discussion of how policies officially aimed at women's empowerment can become coopted for population control aims.
4. For more technical philosophical work on the capability approach and paternalism, see Carter 2014, Claassen 2011, and Khader 2018.
5. Notable exceptions to this are Sabina Alkire, Solava Ibrahim, and Séverine Deneulin (especially their work with Alkire), discussed later in this chapter, Christine Koggel (Chapter 6 in this volume), the joint work of Jean-Michel Bonvin and Nicolas Farvaque, and Tom G. Palmer.
6. Nussbaum's version of the CA is mostly outside the scope of this chapter, because of its conception of capabilities as the topic of an overlapping consensus on a flourishing life, rather than as what matters in light of people's own values and objectives. See Khader (2018) for a discussion of how the deep normative commitments of the CA are currently up for normative debate.
7. For a lucid discussion of the distinction between capabilities and functionings, see Crocker 2008 and Crocker and Robeyns 2009.

8. Sen also often uses the term "reasonable" in the Rawlsian sense, but this is outside of the scope of our analysis.

9. See Christine Koggel's chapter in this volume (Chapter 6), in which she understands this full version of the phrase somewhat differently, as mapping onto the distinction that Crocker also makes between agency and well-being freedoms.

10. In this use, autonomy and agency understood as the ability to form and act upon one's values are largely the same. For a useful discussion of the concept of "agency" in Sen's work, see Part II of Crocker and Robeyns (2009). For a discussion of the role of one's "highest values or moral principles" in the exercise of agency, as well as its relationship to Adela Cortina's, Flavio Comim's, and Rob Reich's concepts of autonomy, see Crocker 2008, chapter 7, especially footnote 12, 249–250. See also Reich (2002), chapter 4, on "minimalist autonomy."

11. Procedural accounts of autonomy are not the only available accounts. We do not handle substantive accounts in a separate section, because their incorporation of perfectionist content makes them versions of the perfectionist interpretation – albeit ones with unnecessary problematic consequences about how to treat individuals who do not value what it is objectively good for them to value.

12. See Sen 2002 for the related concept of "positional objectivity."

13. The bulk of Alkire's work, however, alone and together with Deneulin and Ibrahim, emphasizes the importance of opportunity-expansion in the evolution of what individuals have reason to value, with less attention to public deliberation.

14. Palmer is an exception. He develops – and critiques – this interpretation (Palmer 2009, 36–37).

15. See Crocker 2008 (300) and Sen 1999a (10) on the instrumental value of political participation in helping societies arrive at consensus about valued public goods.

16. Similar lines of reasoning can be found in the work of Jean-Michel Bonvin and Nicolas Farvaque (2005), Sabina Alkire, Solava Ibrahim, and Séverine Deneulin (for example Alkire and Deneulin 2009 and Alkire and Ibrahim 2007), and Martha Nussbaum (2001).

17. For a related discussion, albeit not explicitly linked to R2V, see Alkire 2007 for a review of five possible processes through which dimensions of a multidimensional poverty index might be selected. Among them, she considers a deliberative participatory process.

18. The perfectionist commitments central to the perfectionist interpretation of R2V are not foundational and are compatible with a variety of metaethical views, including constructivism.

19. An additional feature of some perfectionist moral and political theories is that social distribution should aim at promoting human excellence. The perfectionist interpretation of R2V does not include this latter claim.

20. The perfectionist interpretation does not imply that the political freedoms exercised in deliberative processes are *merely* means to recognizing what would be required for one's own flourishing. Political freedoms can be important in expanding an agent's ability to recognize what is of value to her – and valuable for a host of other reasons.

21. Note that this position already picks out public deliberation as a valuable functioning.

22. See Crocker 2008, chapter 10, for a thorough discussion of this view, and possible responses.

23. It is worth noting that simply dropping this phrase would not itself eliminate all concerns about paternalism from Sen's version of the CA. It would, however, eliminate this source.

24. Here, Deneulin wishes to make clear that she sees "paternalism as non-indifference to the suffering of people lacking the conditions for living dignified human lives" (16).

25. See Khader 2011 for a discussion of why respect for people's first-person input is consistent with a critique of their values.

26. See Claassen 2011 for further discussion of why less is at stake in the Sen/Nussbaum disagreement over lists than is often thought.

References

Ackerly, Brooke. 2000. *Political Theory and Feminist Social Criticism.* Cambridge University Press.

Alkire, Sabina. 2002. *Valuing Freedoms: Sen's Capability Approach and Poverty Reduction.* New York: Oxford University Press.

    2005. "Measuring the Freedom Aspects of Capabilities." Cambridge, MA: Self. Accessed August 31, 2016. www.researchgate.net/profile/Sabina_Alkire/publication/228355513_Measuring_the_Freedom_Aspects_of_Capabilities'/links/004635231a3c0cbad8000000.pdf.

    2007. "Choosing Dimensions: The Capability Approach and Multidimensional Poverty." In *The Many Dimensions of Poverty,* Nanak Kakwani and Jacques Silber (eds.). New York: Palgrave Macmillan.

    2008. *The Capability Approach to the Quality of Life.* Background report. Paris: The Commission on the Measurement of Economic Performance and Social Progress.

Alkire, Sabina, and Séverine Deneulin. 2009. "The Human Development and Capability Approach." In *An Introduction to the Human Development and Capability Approach: Freedom and Agency*, Lila Shahani and Séverine Deneulin (eds.). London: Earthscan, 22–48.

Alkire, Sabina, and Solava Ibrahim. 2007. "Agency and Empowerment: A Proposal for Internationally Comparable Indicators." *Oxford Development Studies* 35(4): 379–403.

Apffel-Marglin, Frederique, and Loyda Sanchez. 2004. "Developmentalist Feminism and Neocolonialism in Andean Communities." In *Feminist Post-Development Thought: Rethinking Modernity, Postcolonialism and Representation*, Kriemild Saunders (ed.). London: Zed Books, 159–197.

Bonvin, Jean-Michel, and Nicolas Farvaque. 2005. "What Informational Basis for Assessing Job-Seekers?: Capabilities vs. Preferences." *Review of Social Economy* 63(2): 269–289.

Carter, Ian. 2014. "Is the Capability Approach Paternalist?" *Economics and Philosophy* 30: 75–98.

Central Statistical Agency (Ethiopia) and IFC International. 2011. *Ethiopia Demographic and Health Survey 2011*. Addis Ababa, Ethiopia and Calverton, MD, USA: Central Statistical Agency (Ethiopia) and IFC International.

Claassen, Rutger. 2011. "Making Capability Lists: Philosophy versus Democracy." *Political Studies* 59: 491–508.

Claassen, Rutger. 2014. "Capability Paternalism." *Economics and Philosophy* 30(1): 57–73.

Crocker, David A. 2008. *Ethics of Global Development*. Cambridge University Press.

Crocker, David A., and Ingrid Robeyns. 2009. "Capability and Agency." In *Amartya Sen*, Christopher Morris (ed.). Cambridge University Press, 60–90.

Deneulin, Séverine. 2002. "Perfectionism, Paternalism, and Liberalism in Sen and Nussbaum's Capability Approach." *Review of Political Economy* 14(4): 498–518.

Drèze, Jean, and Amartya Sen. 2013. *An Uncertain Glory: India and its Contradictions*. Princeton University Press.

Escobar, Arturo. 1994. *Encountering Development: The Making and Unmaking of the Third World*. Princeton University Press.

Hogan, Dennis P., Betemariam Berhanu, and Assefa Hailemariam. 1999. "Household Organization, Women's Autonomy, and Contraceptive Behavior in Southern Ethiopia." *Studies in Family Planning*. Accessed June 29, 2017. http://onlinelibrary.wiley.com/doi/10.1111/j.1728–446 5.1999.t01-2-.x/full.

Hurka, Thomas. 1993. *Perfectionism*. New York: Oxford University Press.

Kapoor, Ilan. 2002. "The Devil's in the Theory." *Third-World Quarterly* 23 (1): 101–117.

Khader, Serene J. 2011. *Adaptive Preferences and Women's Empowerment*. Oxford University Press.

Khader, Serene J. 2018. "Should the Capability Approach Be Paternalistic?" In *Routledge Handbook to the Philosophy of Paternalism*, Kalle Grille and Jason Hanna (eds.). New York: Routledge, 206–220.

Korra, Antenane. 2002. *Attitudes towards Family Planning and Reasons for Nonuse among Women with Unmet Need for Family Planning in Ethiopia*. CARE-Ethiopia.

Kosko, Stacy J. 2013. "Agency Vulnerability, Self Determination, and the Participation of Indigenous Peoples." *Journal of Global Ethics* 9(3): 293–310.

Nussbaum, Martha. 2001. *Women and Human Development: The Capabilities Approach*. New York: Cambridge University Press.

Olsaretti, Serena. 2005. "Endorsement and Freedom in Amartya Sen's Capability Approach." *Economics and Philosophy* 21: 89–108.

Palmer, Tom G. 2009. *Realizing Freedom: Libertarian Theory, History, and Practice*. Washington, DC: Cato Institute.

Penz, Peter, Jay Drydyk, and Pablo S. Bose. 2011. *Displacement by Development: Ethics, Rights and Responsibilities*. Cambridge University Press.

Qizilbash, Mozafar. 2012. "The Capability Approach: Its Interpretation and Limitations." In *The Capability Approach: Development Practice and Public Policy in the Asia Pacific Region*, Katharine Gelber and Francesca Panzironi (eds.). London: Routledge.

Rahnema, Majid. 1997. "Development and the People's Immune System: The Story of Another Variety of AIDS." In *The Post-Development Reader*, Majid Rahnema (ed.). London: Zed Books.

Raz, Joseph. 1988. *The Morality of Freedom*. Clarendon Press of Oxford University Press.

Reich, Rob. 2002. *Bridging Liberalism and Multiculturalism in American Education*. Chicago University Press.

Robeyns, Ingrid. 2003. "Sen's Capability Approach and Gender Inequality." *Feminist Economics* 9(2–3): 61–92.

Sen, Amartya. 1994. "Population: Delusion, and Reality." *The New York Review of Books*, September 22.

  1999a. "Democracy as a Universal Value." *Journal of Democracy* 10(3): 3–17.

  1999b. *Development as Freedom*. New York: Anchor Books.

  2002. *Rationality and Freedom*. Cambridge, MA: Belknap Press.

2004. "Capabilities Lists and Public Reason." *Feminist Economics* 10: 77–80.

2005. "Human Rights and Capabilities." *Journal of Human Development* 6(2): 151–166.

2009. *The Idea of Justice*. Cambridge, MA: Harvard University Press.

The World Bank Group. 2017. *Trends in Maternal Mortality: 1990 to 2015*. Accessed October 30, 2017. http://data.worldbank.org/indicator/SH .MMR.RISK.

Tilahun, Tizta, Gily Coene, Stanley Luchters, Wondwosen Kassahun, Els Leye, and Marleen Temmerman. 2013. "Family Planning Knowledge, Attitude and Practice among Married Couples in Jimma Zone, Ethiopia." *PLoS ONE* 8(4): e61335. https://doi.org/10.1371/jo urnal.pone.0061335.

Wells, Thomas R. 2013. "Reasoning about Development: Essays on Amartya Sen's Capability Approach." Thesis to obtain the degree of Doctor. Rotterdam: Erasmus University Rotterdam.

Wilson, Kalpana. 2015. "Towards a Radical Reappropriation: Gender, Development, and Neoliberal Feminism." *Development and Change* 46(4): 803–832.

8 The Multidimensionality of Empowerment

Conceptual and Empirical Considerations

JAY DRYDYK, ALEJANDRA BONI, ALEXANDRE
APSAN FREDIANI, MELANIE WALKER, AND
AURORA LÓPEZ-FOGUÉS

The theory and practice of empowerment and participatory development have attracted the attention of a few philosophers along with a multitude of social science researchers. Rarely, though, do they collaborate as directly as the authors of this chapter have done. In this chapter we begin with a philosopher's analysis of what 'empowerment' has meant in development discourse over the past three decades, identifying agency, well-being, and power relations as dimensions making a process more empowering or less so. We continue by treating this as a research question: Is there any evidence that empowerment is multidimensional in this way? Two case studies assess agency, well-being, and power relations as dimensions of change in participatory projects in Spain and Kenya. A third case study in South Africa investigates a learning process that 'connects the dots' to bring such changes about: an epistemically inclusive, dialogical exchange of reasons that recognizes and values participants' identities.

1 The Life and Times of the Concept of Empowerment

The importance of empowerment has long been recognized within the human development approach and within development ethics. More than twenty years ago, Mahbub ul Haq included empowerment as one of the four pillars of the human development approach, distinguishing it as a people-first approach from the paradigm of development as growth (Haq 1995, 16). More recently, empowerment has been included in a comprehensive development ethics framework as one of seven values distinguishing worthwhile development from undesirable maldevelopment (Penz, Drydyk, and Bose 2011, 116–51).

Over this time span, empowerment may seem to have received a favourable reception among development institutions. However, this apparent agreement on the value of empowerment has concealed important differences regarding its true nature and scope (Eyben and Napier-Moore 2009). Indeed, a noticeable conceptual shift has taken place since the introduction of 'empowerment' to the discourse of international institutions in 1995 at the Fourth World Conference on Women, held in Beijing. There the focus was on gender relations, including relations of power (Batliwala 2007, 559; Eyben and Napier-Moore 2009, 287), and, remarkably, the official discourse embraced the wider usage of civil society organizations that 'defined empowerment as a process, and the results of a process, of transforming the relations of power between individuals and social groups' (Batliwala 2007, 560; cf. Batliwala 1993). As 'empowerment' was taken up by development institutions, however, this transformative, relational conception was abandoned. The result, according to one study, is that 'Today, most frequently, empowerment is about choice, decision-making, realising opportunities and potential, and community action' (Eyben and Napier-Moore 2009, 291). The central idea has become choice expansion, and while this may be transformative for individuals, it need not be transformative of gender relations, other social relations, or power. So one is now able to advocate empowerment without advocating social change.

The institutionally accepted conception of empowerment as choice expansion has been articulated further by David Crocker as an agency-based analysis of empowerment. Initially Crocker conceived of empowerment as comprising 'those conditions and processes that enable individuals and groups to strengthen and exercise their agency' (Crocker 2008, 19), though in more recent work he has adopted a more complex conception (Crocker 2014, 247) that includes some of the additional ideas presented in the rest of this section. Building on the work of Sabina Alkire, Crocker begins with Amartya Sen's distinction between agency freedom and well-being freedom. The scope of our well-being freedom extends to all those ways of functioning which we have reason to value as aspects of living well, and which we could actually manage to achieve. Agency freedom extends to all goals valuable and achievable to us, whether or not they pertain to our own well-being, thus also including what we would like to bring about for others (even when this is risky to our own well-being). But according to Crocker, Sen has an 'ideal of agency' that goes beyond this (Crocker 2008, 153ff.).

A person is an agent with respect to action X just in case she (1) decides for herself (rather than someone or something else forcing the decision) to do X; (2) bases her decisions on reasons, such as the pursuit of goals; (3) performs or has a role in performing X; and (4) thereby brings about (or contributes to the bringing about of) change in the world. (Crocker 2008, 157)

The first two are qualities of choice-making, but the second two pertain to carrying choices out within one's social environment. Consequently, there is more to expansion of agency than expansion or enhancement of choice-making; to have greater agency people must also have more opportunities 'to translate their choices into desired actions and outcomes' (Alsop and Heinsohn 2005, 6).

Although Alsop, Bertelsen, and Holland confine 'agency' to the 'ability to make purposeful choices' (2006, 10), Ibrahim and Alkire show that most other authors who define 'agency' include performance and effectiveness as well (2007, 384). Nevertheless, all four aspects can be accommodated within the idea of empowerment as expanded choice expansion, so long as this means not just *making* more and better choices but *having* more such choices that can be realized.

This conception of empowerment as agency expansion has given rise to many valuable indicators making the underlying idea of expanded choice more concrete and measureable. But, as we have seen, these gains have come at a cost: no longer is empowerment seen as a change in social relations and power, and this is open to much philosophical, political, and explanatory criticism (Batliwala 2007; Drydyk 2008; Eyben and Napier-Moore 2009). While these criticisms are weighty, so are the gains that have been made in our capacity to know and measure people's agency, and these too are significant from an ethical and political perspective: at the end of the day, change in social relations and power should not be valued over and above its impact on people's freedom to shape their own lives and circumstances for the better. With these concerns in mind, I set out to bring power back in to the picture (Drydyk 2013) by harmonizing the concept of power with concepts of agency and choice.

The first step is to define 'power' in terms of *choice*. The core idea is that a power relation exists between groups A and B if choices *made* by A determine or limit the choices that members of B *have*. Thus, legislative power exists when legislation chosen by legislators limits the choices that citizens and residents have: for example, they can still choose to assault one another, but they lose the choice of assaulting someone and likely going unpunished. One simple variation (among many): in a functioning democracy, legislative power is balanced by electoral power, in which the choices that voters make limit the choices that legislators have (for more complex variations, see Drydyk 2013).

The second step is to conceive of empowerment as expansion not just in one domain but in three: (1) *Expansion of agency* is necessary for empowerment. If a paternalistic band of Martians invades Earth and hypnotizes humanity to live better lives, this may enhance our well-being, but it does not empower us. (2) Conversely, if the captain of the *Titanic* informs passengers that they may now arrange the deck chairs as they see fit before impact with the iceberg, their agency has been expanded, but learning evacuation procedures would have expanded their agency in ways more useful and relevant to their well-being. So, we must judge expansion of agency more empowering to the degree that it *enhances well-being freedom* as well as agency. (3) Similarly, *gaining in power* can also render gains in agency and well-being freedom more empowering. One reason is that power can limit vulnerability: as Sen has shown, the electoral power of citizens in a functioning democracy compels quick responses to food shortages and other disasters, and it is the paramount goal of disaster relief to restore and secure victims' agency and well-being freedom (Sen 1999, 51–3, 160–88; Sen 2000; Sen 2009, 338–45; Drydyk 2014).

The key finding of this conceptual analysis is that empowerment is multidimensional: agency expansion is central, but how these choices expand well-being freedom is another important dimension, and how expanded choice results from gains in power is another. In the following sections, we examine evidence for this multi-dimensionality in three participatory research projects.

2 Participatory Video and Youth Empowerment

In this case study, we analyse a participatory video (PV) process that took place in Quart de Poblet (a municipality of 25,000 inhabitants, close to Valencia, Spain) from February to April 2014. The participants were eleven adolescents between sixteen and twenty-four years old, hit by the economic crises that severely shocked Spain in the previous few years. Over a period of three months, the group of youngsters engaged in a PV process to reflect on their aspirations and visions on relevant issues they identified: migration, education, and youth participation.

We proposed the PV methodology as a way to engage with the interests and motivations of this group of youth who were, at the time of starting our PV process, involved in different activities promoted by the municipality. This process was a part of a three-year FP7-European project, called 'SocIEtY' (Social Innovation | Empowering the Young for the Common Good), which aimed to explore what can be done to create social and institutional opportunities for youth and to develop a broad knowledge to foster socially innovative policy making.

In our analysis of the PV process conducted in Quart de Poblet, we investigate the following elements of multidimensional empowerment: (1) power defined in terms of choice – the central idea being that a power relation exists if choices made by one person or one group determine or limit the choices that other members have; and (2) that expansion of agency is necessary for empowerment, and we must judge expansion of agency more empowering to the degree that it enhances well-being freedom or capabilities as well as agency.

The main question to be answered at the end of our discussion is: Has the PV process expanded agency and capabilities of the youngsters of Quart de Poblet? If the answer is positive, can we say that these expansions have brought more empowerment to the youngsters, understood as an increase of their choices?

In the next section, we will very briefly present a description of the methodology and the participants; then we will discuss some of the evidence for multidimensional empowerment. Two different sources were used: (1) primary materials included the three final short videos made by each participant group, a video-interview made with each participant, and notes from the discussions held in the group sessions; (2) secondary material included videos, documents, news, and other types of information shared by the research team but also by the participants and posted in social networks (WhatsApp and Facebook).

Participatory Video in Quart de Poblet

The youth participants were all volunteers, selected due to their engagement with the municipal youth area. They were:

(1) Interns of Quart Jove (Youth Department of Quart): five participants (three female and two male). Ages: between twenty and twenty-two. Level of studies: vocational and university.
(2) Cremant: three participants who are part of a local social enterprise promoting audio-visual projects (two female, one male). Ages: twenty-two to twenty-four. Level of studies: university.
(3) Esplai: three participants of a youth club promoting recreational activities (one female, two male). Ages: sixteen to eighteen. Level of studies: secondary.

In the context of our research, PV was selected as a research method to articulate the voice and aspirations of young people on issues that are relevant for them (Olivier et al. 2012). Moreover, it aimed to create a learning space to reflect on those issues and a way to influence policy makers, both at the local and European level. At the local level, we did a public presentation of the short videos to local policy makers; at the European level, we showed one of the videos at the European Parliament in the final conference of the Society project of which our PV was a part.

The PV started with a *diagnosis* phase that lasted 1.5 days and was developed in a first workshop. Its goals were to introduce the participants to each other and to the facilitators, to explain the potentialities of media to get a message across, and to identify key issues that the group of participants considered relevant for them as young people. The second phase was *planning*. For two weeks, each group worked autonomously to agree on their story board and to clarify the roles of each group member in relation to the project (editor, director, interviewer, etc.). The third phase was *production* and lasted two weeks. Alongside the process, all the groups learned the technique of filming and its use as a social tool. The fourth phase was *curation*, which also

Table 8.1 *Main characteristics of the PV produced*

Group	Title	Keywords	Intention of the video*	Link
Quart Jove	*Adiós España (Good-Bye Spain)*	Youth opportunities Entrepreneurship Migration	'To show that young people have ideas but not enough opportunities and that there is something to be done about it' (P3, 12 February)	https://vim eo.com/14 5614948
Cremant	Educational laws	Legal instability Politics Education Conservatism Religion Segregation Social justice	'They change the law all the time as they want, and ask for more money or for more years, and we cannot do anything about it' (P6, 12 February)	https://vim eo.com/12 8790965
Esplai	*Esplai*	Participation Voluntarism Young people Monitors Free time	'The good and the bad things of being a volunteer and the values attached to it' (P4, 25 February)	https://vim eo.com/12 6901812

* According to some of the participants

lasted two weeks. Finally, we had the two public presentations mentioned above, at the local and the European level.

The three final videos obtained are summarized in Table 8.1.

Capabilities and Agency Enhanced During the PV Process

We observed that that three capabilities were fostered: first, the capability for voice (Bonvin and Farvaque 2006), understood as the real opportunity people have to express their opinions and perspectives; second, the awareness capability that includes being able to carry out self-critical investigation and analysis of their own reality (Gaventa and Cornwall 2008), and, third, the capability to aspire (Appadurai 2004), which encompasses the capability to envision a desired future and a way to achieve it, at least in part, through research processes (Frediani 2015).

These three capabilities were enhanced during the research process, during group dynamics and in the interaction with facilitators. Also, the contents of the three videos reveal elements of those three capabilities, especially in their understanding of how structural conditions limit the expansion of real opportunities of youth in the local and national contexts. The video of Quart focused on difficulties of pursuing a vocation in Spain and the need to migrate, hence, difficulties in achieving the capability for work. The video revealed three barriers to developing that capability, and situated a power imbalance aggravated by governmental interventions: unemployment plans, impunity of the banking system, and the fraudulence of entrepreneurship programmes. The video of Cremant focused on the instability of educational laws and their use as a political tool. It is a thoughtful analysis of the strategic use of education, its current conservative path, and its influence on the genuine choices of young people in Spain in terms of equity and heterogeneity. Finally, the video of Esplai (produced by the youngest group) identified Esplai and the tutors as people in their lives whom they wanted to emulate because of their ethics and their positive influence.

Whilst the Esplai video is the only of the three videos that takes a positive perspective, in all three, aspiration is central as far as it has to do with how individuals frame a desirable future and what they regard a 'good life' (Baillergeau and Duyvendak 2013). In this sense, the three videos understand a good life as one that favours people and give them power to choose their life (Quart), avoids the instrumentalization of education for an ideological purpose (Cremant), and uses the methodology of learning and play for creating an inclusive society (Esplai).

With regard to agency, we can say that the expansion of those three capabilities during the process and the production of the three videos make, to some extent, those young people agents of change. Videos are the way in which they decide to act as change makers and, at least, express their own views for a better world, with fairer opportunities for young people to pursue the life they have reason to value and with a clear idea for reducing power relations to the extent that their choices may be limited by others.

The videos were the outputs of a predefined process controlled by facilitators; thus, the autonomy of the youngsters was to some extent restricted. However, all the participants agreed to participate freely in the PV, and they decided with total independence on the narrative of the three videos according to their own aspirations and perspectives. In that sense, this PV contributed to expanding the agency of the young people; as they had the opportunity to express their own views, they chose to do it through the videos and they were able to make their own decisions.

Nevertheless, this process could have brought more agency to the young people if the PV process had incorporated more active participation in the curation and public screening phases. Presumably, a more active involvement in those stages would have brought the participating youth a deeper understanding of themselves as agents of change with the opportunity to put it into practice.

Multidimensional Empowerment

What can be said about the empowerment of youth? In the processes of reflection and video making, they have expressed their opinions and aspirations, reflected on power relations, raised their voices, and exercised their capability to be agents of change. Can we say, in keeping with a multidimensional conception of empowerment, that the youth participants in this project have been empowered?

We can answer from at least three different perspectives. First, it is clear that the involvement of youth participants during the PV process has expanded their choices. They choose to be researchers, to elaborate a video, to reflect on their aspirations, to raise their voices both through the process and in the video narratives, to be agents of change. But, second, the PV process could not remove structural barriers that limit young people's choices, as the participants reflected in the video narratives. In that sense, the empowerment is limited. And, third, what PV has brought to the participants is the opportunity to have more choices in the future. They have acquired a valuable experience as researchers; they are equipped with a tool that can be useful for raising their (or other) voices in the future in a participatory way.

In that sense, the idea of multidimensional empowerment to analyse participatory processes allows us to highlight both actual and potential positive effects of a process without forgetting the structural barriers that are hindering empowerment expansion and, consequently, are limiting the choices of youth participants.

3 What Is the Potential of Action Learning Initiatives in Supporting Empowerment Processes? The Case of the Practical Action Partnerships

In a second case study, we applied the multidimensional concept of empowerment to analyse the process and outcomes of action learning focusing on participatory approaches to informal settlement upgrading in Kisumu, Kenya. From 2008 to 2013, Practical Action (PA), Shelter Forum (SF), and Kisumu Urban Apostolate Programme (KUAP) implemented a development project funded by Comic Relief called 'Peoples' Plans into Practice (PPP): Building Productive and Livable Settlements with Slum Dwellers in Kisumu and Kitale'. The project aimed to improve the well-being, productivity, and living conditions of poor people living in informal settlements in Kenya and the East African region. Specifically, the project intended to achieve this by setting up and strengthening Neighbourhood Planning Associations (NPAs) to ensure that residents of informal settlements could enhance their participation in the planning and development processes of the local authorities and service providers.

In 2012, a partnership was set up between the implementing nongovernmental organizations (NGOs) and representatives of NPAs in Kisumu with The Bartlett Development Planning Unit (DPU) of University College London (UCL) to conduct a student-led research initiative exploring the outcomes and learning generated by this Practical Action Partnership project. This action learning initiative was conducted as an assignment in the practice module of the MSc in Social Development Practice. The three-year partnership consisted in carrying out a research project slightly different each year but with a complementary focus – which included three months of desk research and a two-week field trip (see Table 8.1, with the title of each research project).

Within this initiative, action learning was understood as a pedagogical approach of the master's programme, which aimed to embed the student learning process within struggles for social change. Drawing on principles of co-learning, our pedagogical approach focused on enabling collective processes of reflection, involving local as well as international partners. Apart from the learning motivations, the process and outputs were action-oriented and were planned to support ongoing processes aimed at securing the rights of residents living in informal settlements in Kisumu.

Table 8.2 *Research projects*

Year	Focus of research
2013	Examination of the well-being impacts of four water and sanitation projects implemented in different informal settlements funded by the PPP project.
2014	Analysis of the activities of the NPAs and their role in deepening democratic practices in the city of Kisumu.
2015	Assessment of key urban development challenges faced by residents of informal settlements when securing their citizenship rights in Kisumu and participating in policy and planning processes.

The empowerment outcomes and process of this initiative will be explored through the lens of three key components of multidimensional empowerment: agency, well-being freedom, and power relations.

The concept of *agency* is understood as the expansion of choice, especially through collectively and critically reflecting on one's realities. For this action learning process, a key question that emerges is the extent to which it improved the abilities of students, NPAs, and implementing NGOs to engage with decision-making processes. From the students' perspective, their personal reflections after the field trip outline the various learning outcomes generated by this experience. Those included better understanding of the challenges of development practices and meaningful participatory processes. They also expanded their choices as social development practitioners by deepening their critical understanding of the role of social development practitioners, being able to identify more precisely the scope, threats, and opportunities for meaningful engagement.

From the vantage point of NPA representatives, the research activities made them more aware of the social realities of people living in informal settlements. Each student group worked in close partnership with two representatives from NPAs. A particular issue that emerged from the research activities, and was discussed collectively, was the forms of exclusion and stigmatization that people with disabilities and their families are experiencing in informal settlements. Meanwhile, the action learning process was able to strengthen the alliance between different civil society groups focused on the rights of the urban poor in

Kisumu and struggling for more recognition in urban development plans and processes. Through the engagement with the field trip activities, the NPA groups decided to formalize the umbrella organization called the Kisumu Informal Settlement Network (KISN). At the end of each field trip a public meeting was organized involving all the stakeholders that took part in research activities. In the third year, this has led to a productive discussion around the extension of KISN, to also incorporate the organization of informal traders (Kisumu National Alliance of Street Vendors and Informal Traders) as well as people with disabilities (Association for the Physically Disabled of Kenya).

Meanwhile, the action learning process identified some important limitations around the way within which some issues facing informal settlements were framed, but could not be contested effectively. For example, in relation to housing, the research identified that most stakeholders approached housing rights as an economic issue, thus leading to recommendations around home-ownership. However, research findings demonstrate that the current practices around home-ownership were not able to include the poorest and reinforced trends of gentrification within informal settlements. In other words, under these conditions, a home-ownership focus expanded housing choices for some, but not for the poorest. Due to the limited scope and time-frame of the field trip engagement, activities were not able to produce alternative framings to the housing questions and further work is needed to move the current dominant diagnosis from an economic orientation to one focused on a lack of entitlements.

The second aspect of multidimensional empowerment is *well-being* freedom, approached as the expansion of people's abilities and opportunities to bring about well-being achievements. In the context of the action learning initiative, this calls for a reflection on the role of the engagement in improving the well-being freedom of the urban poor. After each of the three research projects was conducted, the academic staff edited the work of the students and produced reports outlining the main research findings. Copies were printed and sent to partners in Kisumu, Practical Action office in Kenya and in the UK and were also made available to the public on The Bartlett Development Planning Unit website. A key finding of the report has been around the limitations of market-driven approaches to informal settlement upgrading. These limitations have specific programmatic implications to Practical Action activities and other NGOs working in this field. The lessons learned were shared with key Practical Action staff members and trustees. Meanwhile, the reports also outline methodological mechanisms to implement a well-being approach to the programming of development projects.[1]

However, so far, these findings have had limited impacts on policies and practices of upgrading in Kisumu. This engagement in isolation has been unable to create the conditions to influence the strong emphasis on market-driven approaches to urban governance and international donors' drive towards cost-recovery through shifting development financing from grants towards loans.

Relations of power are the third component of multidimensional empowerment. This third component emphasizes the need to reflect on the implications of the action learning process for renegotiating the relations of power within and among groups in ways that reduce asymmetries of vulnerability. Throughout the field activities, meetings, public events, and dissemination of findings, the action learning process supported recognition of the needs of particular vulnerable groups. For example, due to the students' research emphasis on issues around disabilities, NPAs have become more inclusive by addressing some of the barriers to the representation of people with disabilities.

The field trip activities have strategically attempted to unlock entry points for conversation between NPAs and government authorities. By using the leverage generated by a visit by an international university, meetings were established with key government officials. As NPA representatives were attending the meetings together with the UCL staff and students, they were able to enhance their visibility with government authorities, ask questions, and access information that was otherwise very challenging to gain. Also, with the objective to improve the recognition of these organizations, the final printed reports were used by NPA representatives to enhance their legitimacy and visibility with other stakeholders.

Nevertheless, after the three action learning initiatives in Kisumu, NPA representatives have still not been more meaningfully recognized in urban development policy and planning processes. When invited to participate in particular initiatives, their role remains purely consultative. Due to scarce resources available for social mobilization, NPAs had to rely on Practical Action's support to continue operating. Thus, in the long term, the action learning process was not able to substantially address the barriers for meaningful participation with government authorities and could end up reinforcing the dependency of neighbourhood organizations on external NGO support and funding.

The empowerment lens to reflect on the process and outcomes of this action learning initiative has generated a productive analysis of its achievements and limitations. It reveals the importance to think across scales, of flows of empowerment from the local to international level. The framework enables a reflection on roles of action learning beyond the lessons learned to the participants, including the implications to the wider relations of power being supported or disrupted. Finally, this reflection has highlighted the importance of longer-term and dynamic action learning partnerships. After the three field trips, the DPU partnership with Practical Action and NPAs in Kisumu requires adaptation and new practices, in ways that it can respond to ongoing challenges for empowerment.

4 Participatory Action Research in a South African University

We began this chapter with an analytical critique of a reduced notion of empowerment consisting in the expansion of choices, and agency as comprising having more realizable choices (which may or may not be better choices). The concern emerging from this critique is to revive richer notions of empowerment constituted by the expansion of agency as a necessary condition, underpinned by enhanced well-being freedoms, and, third, gains in power which expand agency and well-being freedoms. How might power play out in actual situations? The example we will discuss in this section highlights the empowerment work that process necessarily does in advancing agency, capabilities, and reconfiguring power in the specific pedagogical space of a participatory action research (PAR) project conducted in 2015. The project focus was gender equity at the rural QwaQwa campus of the University of the Free State in South Africa, involving thirteen undergraduate students and two facilitators over eight months. The students were all black, but from different cultural and ethnic backgrounds – either Zulu or Sotho – and more or less evenly split between men and women volunteers.

This education example on how empowerment is actually done adds practically to our initial analytical arguments by considering how well-being and agency are expanded in and through pedagogical practice, which in turn is always suffused with power relations inherent in biographies and interactive communicative arrangements. The process means to empowerment and the empowerment outcomes are interwoven. Through a development (education) process, well-being freedoms are formed and agency exercised under conditions of power; agency requires actions, in our case pedagogical actions, knowledge actions, participation actions, and public dissemination actions. Nor are the empowerment outcomes at one point in time assumed to be all there is; learning, like empowerment, is neither linear nor static but dynamic and evolving often in unexpected ways so that tri-dimensional empowerment needs also to be understood in dynamic terms.

In our PAR process, a dialogic pedagogical process was envisaged as a key conversion factor and the research process as the space in which it could be operationalized. The pedagogy we (the two facilitators) had in mind required: (1) *epistemic inclusion* – all voices and perspectives are heard and gaps and new understanding debated; (2) *identities recognition* and equal valuing is crucial (e.g. of men and women, black and white, Zulu and Sotho participants); and (3) a *dialogical*, voice-affirming, cooperative process of exchanging reasons in order to co-construct knowledge through interpersonal coordination and cooperation. Such dialogue reinforces public values of respect, tolerance, and so on, and requires that we are accountable to each other as we must justify and scrutinize our reasoning. Together these three features (epistemic inclusion, identities, and dialogue/voice) constituted the process features for the formation of key well-being freedoms, expanded agency, and empowerment. The pedagogical dimensions anticipate capabilities that include knowledge, affiliation, and public reasoning.

Turning now to more detail about the project itself, the theme was specified (gender equality) rather than leaving it open, but students (all undergraduates) volunteered to participate and did so only if this theme interested them. The broad aim was to explore how a PAR can challenge gender inequalities and empower young people to bring about change on the university campus and in their own lives. There was negotiation around research questions, but not complete freedom to change what we had drafted. Meetings took the form of four weekend-long workshops and included opportunities for the collection and analysis of interview and visual data. Using participatory pedagogical methods, students discussed and reflected on gender norms, stereotypes, and identities (in the context of the patriarchal culture of the country), challenging who 'looks like a woman' and the parenting role of men, but also examining intersections of gender and ethnicity, and gender and income, in their own lives as much in as the lives of other students. There were extended discussions among the students on what gender inequality is, with students examining their own beliefs about gender and related inequalities. Acquiring gender awareness knowledge was therefore crucial. This developing awareness was then iteratively re-encountered through speaking to other students, conducting interviews, taking photographs, and analysing this evidence together.

Three public deliberation steps were planned and implemented by student groups working in small task teams: to write a policy brief for discussion with the dean of student affairs about a gender policy for students; an open discussion forum for students and staff on gender issues; and a public event on the QwaQwa campus comprising music and drama. Students designed project t-shirts to be worn and handed out at the cultural event as part of the dissemination of knowledge process. They hoped the T-shirts would continue to provoke debate after the event. On the front of the black T-shirt white letters said 'Gender Equality ...' while the back read variously 'is liberating'; 'makes a better society'; 'is for everyone'.

On acquiring more and better knowledge about gender inequalities and shifting in their own taken-for-granted gender assumptions, students commented, for example, that 'It's impossible to have female SRC president on our campus. It's not something that you will be restricted from but it's something that we just think' (Ntombi, female), but with more awareness and education women would 'know when you are robbing them' (Solo, male). They were more knowledgeable about forms of power, saying things like: 'Competent and confident women will arise and hidden power will start to shift away slowly but surely ... PAR challenged me and I thought it would be good to have programmes in place that change people's perception of gender ... because we are so diverse and our encounters are different, there will always be wrong here and there' (Teboho, male). As Kay (female) said, 'it [PAR] was really an eye-opener'. The participatory discussions in which all voices could be expressed and heard shifted power from the facilitators who provided pedagogical structure and greater knowledge input at the outset to student voices but also enabled gender shifts among group members. In the interactive and communicative common space, 'it's not just about your individual thoughts, your individual abilities, you're able to come together and sit with others and work together, share your thoughts, be in a position to be corrected, you give others the chance, you listen, because you also want to be listened to', Ntombi (female) explained. Langa (male) remarked that working participatively went beyond 'involvement', it was more like 'living the project . . . it was more than sitting around the table discussing, it was like you are now living, you're changing the way you do things'. With regard to working with others he remarked, 'Some people I did not know [before the PAR], now I do know them, and to share ideas about something, because when you're alone, it's just your ideas, and you think that's right and that's correct . . . it changed the way we view the future.' At first he felt that there had not really been gender-equal social relations in the group – 'we were doing that inequality' – but towards the end, 'we changed, we changed the way we looked at things'.

Thus, the foundational well-being freedom that emerged through the research process was that of knowledge – awareness-raising, critical knowledge about self and others and about society, including structures of power and advantage that hinders the expansion of capabilities. We also paid attention to history as a significant conversion factor – an analysis of how gendered conditions have shaped students' own gendered and cultural assumptions about what women and men can do in society and what is possible for them. Equally significant was the interactive and relational development of participation and public deliberation well-being freedoms, working together and across knowledge. Moreover, by taking their new knowledge to a wider constituency – from the dean of students to their peers – the research was more widely shared and the space of deliberation expanded (although not in uncontested ways). Thus, knowledge was the 'trigger' capability. It underpinned everything else but equally what was crucial was that knowledge was acquired through relationships, participation, discussion, and voice in a research process of data collection and analysis. The women students in particular came to recognize their inherent worth although older gendered patterns persisted, while the men who already recognized their own self-worth went quite some way to acknowledging the fundamental equality of all human beings. Through their new knowledge students recognized their ability and responsibility to contribute to personal and social change among their peers.

But the project also raised key education questions which relate to empowerment as process and outcome. What kind of research do we need so that students can act? Can students come into being as empowered persons if research is conceived and practised only as an academic expert process? Thus universities (and the research that goes on in them) – which show no interest in how students think or feel, where there is no place for students to take initiatives, where knowledge is fed into heads, and where there is no attention to how actions affect the opportunities of others–are places where empowerment would struggle because well-being freedoms would be constrained and agency held back. This has implications for any development process which has as its aim the empowerment of participants. In our experience the multidimensional framework of agency, well-being, and power is rather essential for the process.

What integrated the dimensions for us was a modality of education which in itself seeks epistemically and pedagogically to reshape unjust social and political relations and the distribution of power across a PAR project. Through our PAR project we gave substantive practical content to the concept of empowerment involving: well-being freedoms (and we need to identify which matter situationally – in our case knowledge, participation, and deliberation); an agency expansion process for wider choices (to act in more gender-fair ways, to treat women with respect, to go for leadership roles) with responsibility to inform others about gender equality, and the acknowledgement of power in pedagogical processes, including among men and women peers. In this way, we connected the conceptual dots in practice.

In short, then, a multidimensional empowerment framework of well-being freedoms, agency, and power is useful, but still needs connecting up in the context of real practices, and in our case, it also needed some capabilities specification. How we get to the empowerment outcome we think also matters as much as the outcome itself, not either-or but comprehensively both-and. As Sen (2009) reminds us, comprehensive outcomes require attention to the development process as much as to the development outcome, and both should be more rather than less just.

5 Conclusions

"When *I* use a word,' Humpty Dumpty said, in rather a scornful tone, 'it means just what I choose it to mean – neither more nor less" (Carroll [1871]1981, 178). Outside of Wonderland, however, arbitrary definitions and conceptual changes are more troublesome. In the context of development, the changing meaning of 'empowerment' has been very troublesome. What motivated us to consider a multidimensional conception of empowerment was that previous changes in the meaning of 'empowerment' seemed to narrow its focus arbitrarily. Initially, at the time of the Beijing Conference, 'empowerment' of women implied a transformation of gender relations, especially of patriarchal power. Yet when discussion of empowerment was taken up within development institutions, what people there chose to mean by it was neither more nor less than expansion of women's choices. This made it possible to think about women's empowerment without giving any thought to transforming patriarchal power relations – which some people evidently considered a useful simplification.

The multidimensional conception of empowerment is meant to block this kind of oversimplification by reintroducing two further dimensions, in addition to agency, as dimensions along which people could be comparatively empowered or disempowered. One is well-being (or, in capability terms, well-being freedom). Expanding important life-choices that impact on people's freedom to live well constitutes greater empowerment than expanding choices in less consequential ways. The other dimension is power: choice expansion that results from changes in power relations also has greater claim to be called 'empowering'.

These arguments against the choice conception and in favour of the multidimensional conception are partly intuitive, partly methodological. They are intuitive in relying on the intuitions of speakers and writers about what are plausible or implausible ways of using the word. They are methodological in claiming that some usages bring to light possibilities that other usages hide from view. These are the accustomed tools of 'armchair' philosophy. The co-authors of this chapter began working together because we believed we had another tool that could move this issue out of the armchair, and into community life. This tool is participatory action research.

Our research question, broadly understood, was whether distinguishing between agency, well-being freedom, and power as dimensions of empowerment was merely an armchair activity, or whether drawing these kinds of distinctions matters to people as they struggle for their own empowerment in the context of development. Our preliminary finding, based on three case studies, is that these distinctions do matter to people.

The participatory video project created an initial expansion of choices just by bringing young people into the project as researchers, giving them a new capability to reflect on their own aspirations, to raise their voices both through the process and in the video narratives, to be agents of change. At the same time, the participants were reflexively aware that their life-choices, outside the project, remained limited. The participants in Quart focused on limitations on future livelihoods; in Cremant this focus narrowed to limitations and instability of young people's educational opportunities. In neither case were the power dimension and the well-being dimension clearly distinguished from each other; what the participants perceived was their own powerlessness mixed in with other conditions limiting their ability to shape their own lives for the better. One insight revealed in these projects was a contrast between the presence of choice expansion within the project and absence of choice expansion in the wider world.

In the second case study, participatory action research included representatives of NPAs from informal settlements in Kisumu, Kenya. One of their salient discoveries was that choice expansion can be terribly uneven: when the goal of upgrading housing was framed as home-ownership, this did not expand the choices or improve the housing of poorer people in the settlement. Another key finding was that market-based approaches to upgrading of settlements had only very limited impacts on people's well-being. What was evident here was a contrast between the extent of choice expansion through market measures and the much lesser extent of resulting improvements in well-being, a contrast between the dimension of choice and that of well-being freedom. The project leveraged the participation of an international university to facilitate meetings between stakeholders and power-holders, such as the Governor of Kisumu. The experience of the stakeholders was again one of contrast: the opportunity to engage with power-holders such as the Governor himself constitute an expansion of choice, and yet this yielded no expansion of influence – a striking contrast between the dimensions of agency and power.

The third case study revealed a further dimension of empowerment, a dimension of knowledge, which can be essential for a group to move forward in the other three dimensions. Chronically unequal power relations such as gender inequality are reproduced in part by diminishing self-worth, self-respect, and self-confidence among the powerless group. These are barriers to agency as a deep capacity, and 'giving' people choices without building this deep capacity is not empowering. This points to the importance of awareness-raising, critical knowledge about self and others and about society, including structures of power and advantage that hinder the expansion of capabilities. In particular, this knowledge dimension of empowerment has dual value: intrinsically, it constitutes an expansion of people's well-being freedom and their real agency; instrumentally, it triggers action by individuals and groups in the three other dimensions. A group's process of deliberation can promote this knowledge dimension insofar as it includes group members' points of view, affirms their identities, and produces shared knowledge by give-and-take of reasons.

In all three cases, providing spaces for deliberation and dialogue proved to be essential for the expansion of capabilities, agency, and (within limitations) empowerment. Deliberation and dialogue were key for all the participants in the research process but also for trying to influence decision makers. In none of these cases did the participants get so far as to actually shifting power relations with those decision makers; nevertheless, they perceived different aspects of the deliberative experience as preparing them to continue the struggle.

These last observations yield a result that will be unexpected to many who have discussed 'empowerment'. The three characteristics of empowering deliberation bear striking similarities to the ideals of democratic deliberation that David Crocker has so carefully delineated (2008, 338–45). This is far from the thinking of those who appropriated 'empowerment' to confine it to choice expansion without regard to relations of power. Who knew that public reasoning and democratic deliberation could be empowering? Well, David Crocker did, and we would do well to carry this insight forward in the next phases of conceptual analysis and participatory research on empowerment.

Note

1. To download reports, access website: www.bartlett.ucl.ac.uk/dpu/pro grammes/postgraduate/msc-social-development-practice/Overseas-fieldwork.

References

Alsop, Ruth, and Hina Heinsohn. 2005. 'Measuring Empowerment in Practice: Structuring Analysis and Framing Indicators'. World Bank Policy Research Working Paper 3510. Washington, DC: World Bank.

Alsop, Ruth, Mette Frost Bertelsen, and Jeremy Holland. 2006. *Empowerment in Practice: From Analysis to Implementation.* Washington, DC: World Bank.

Appadurai, Arjun. 2004. 'The Capacity to Aspire: Culture and the Terms of Recognition'. In *Culture and Public Action*, Vijayendra Rao and Michael Walton (eds.). Stanford University Press, 59–84.

Baillergeau, Evelyne, and Jan Willem Duyvendak. 2013. 'Aspirations of Young People and Social Inequality in Europe. Final Conceptual Report for Addressing Inequality, Disadvantage, Social Innovation and Participation'. Accessed 28 September 2015. www.society-youth .eu/about-us/78-society/131-aspirations-of-young.

Batliwala, Srilatha. 1993. *Women's Empowerment in South Asia: Concepts and Practices.* New Delhi: United Nations Food and Agriculture Organization, Asia South Pacific Bureau of Adult Education.

Batliwala, Srilatha. 2007. 'Taking the Power out of Empowerment – An Experiential Account'. *Development in Practice* 17(4–5): 557–65.

Bonvin, J., and Farvaque, N. 2006. 'Promoting Capability for Work: The Role of Local Actors'. In *Transforming Unjust Structures: The Capability Approach*, S. Deneulin, M. Nebel, and N. Sagovsky (eds.). Dordrecht: Springer, 121–42.

Carroll, Lewis. [1871]1981. *Through the Looking-Glass.* In *Alice's Adventures in Wonderland and Through the Looking-Glass.* New York: Bantam Dell.

Crocker, David. 2008. *Ethics of Global Development: Agency, Capability, and Deliberative Democracy.* Cambridge University Press.

Crocker, David. 2014. 'Development and Global Ethics: Five Foci for the Future'. *Journal of Global Ethics* 10(3): 245–53.

Drydyk, Jay. 2008. 'Durable Empowerment'. *Journal of Global Ethics* 4(3): 231–45.

Drydyk, Jay. 2013. 'Empowerment, Agency, and Power'. *Journal of Global Ethics* 9(3): 249–62.

Drydyk, Jay. 2014. 'Is Social Inclusion Sufficient for Justice?' In *Pensamiento Económico y Cambio Social: Ensayos en Honor a Javier Iguíñiz*, José Carlos Orihuela and José I. Távara (eds.). Lima: Fondo Editorial del Pontificia Universidad del Peru, 143–74.

Eyben, Rosalind, and Rebecca Napier-Moore. 2009. 'Choosing Words with Care? Shifting Meanings of Women's Empowerment in International Development'. *Third World Quarterly* 30(2): 285–300.

Frediani, Alexandre Apsan. 2015. 'Participatory Capabilities in Development Practice'. DPU Working Paper 178. Accessed 28 September 2015. www.bartlett.ucl.ac.uk/dpu/latest/publications/dpu-working-papers/WP178.pdf.

Gaventa J., and A. Cornwall. 2008. 'Power and Knowledge'. In *Sage Handbook of Action Research: Participative Inquiry and Practice*, P. Reason and H. Bradbury (eds.). 2nd edition. London: Sage Publications, 71–81.

Haq, Mahbub ul. 1995. *Reflections on Human Development*. New York: Oxford University Press.

Ibrahim, Solava, and Alkire, Sabina. 2007. 'Agency and Empowerment: A Proposal for Internationally Comparable Indicators'. *Oxford Development Studies* 35(4): 380–403.

Olivier, T., de Lange, N., Creswell, J. W., and Wood, L. 2012. 'Mixed Method Research in Participatory Video'. In *Handbook of Participatory Video*, E. J. Milne, C. Mitchell, and N. De Lange (eds.). Lanham, MD: AltaMira Press, 131–48.

Penz, Peter, Drydyk, Jay, and Bose, Pablo. 2011. *Displacement by Development: Ethics, Rights, and Responsibilities*. Cambridge University Press.

Sen, Amartya. 1999. *Development as Freedom*. New York: Random House.

Sen, Amartya. 2000. 'Why Human Security?' Presented to International Symposium on Human Security, Tokyo, 28 July.

Sen, Amartya. 2009. *The Idea of Justice*. Cambridge, MA: Harvard University Press.

9 Agency, Income Inequality, and Subjective Well-Being*
The Case of Uruguay

GONZALO SALAS AND ANDREA VIGORITO

1 Introduction

This chapter provides an empirical illustration of the evolution of agency levels and inequality in Uruguay and its association with subjective well-being. Specifically, we explore whether improvements in the control of economic resources translates into increases in agency levels and declines in preexisting disparities. We also analyze whether those agency level variations are correlated with variations in different aspects of life satisfaction levels. The exercise is carried out for the period 2006–12.

The recent evolution of living standards and development policies in Latin America, and specifically in Uruguay, provides a very interesting scenario to assess the interrelation between economic growth, income redistribution, agency levels, and subjective well-being. While the region still experiences high inequality levels, most countries have faced rapid economic growth in the last fifteen years, coupled with falling poverty and inequality (Cornia 2010; López-Calva and Lustig 2010; Gasparini and Lustig 2011).

* This research has been carried out as part of the interdisciplinary *Ethics, Economics and Justice Research Group* (Universidad de la Republica, Uruguay), for which David Crocker's writings have been an illuminating reference. He has also been enthusiastically supporting the Latin American and the Caribbean Association for the Study of Human Capabilities (ALCADECA, by its Spanish acronym) since its creation in 2006 at Mexico City, generously devoting his time to participate in our meetings and encourage the network to continue its work. More recently, David Crocker provided relevant insights to a research project that our group carried out in the last four years, based on his work on deliberative democracy. Such project attempted to identify the dimensions of development valued by Uruguayans. We are very grateful for the detailed comments and suggestions to improve this chapter provided by Lori Keleher, Stacy Kosko, and three anonymous referees. All remaining errors are our own.

In this context, the Uruguayan case is of particular interest. We study a period that followed a severe economic crisis, and was characterized by substantial economic growth, the introduction of an ambitious package of redistributive reforms, and the rise of a center-left coalition government (*Frente Amplio*). This period is also characterized by a reduction in income inequality and poverty (Amarante, Colafranceschi, and Vigorito 2014).

A crucial point from a human development and capability perspective is to evaluate whether the previous improvements also implied well-being and agency gains, enhancing freedoms and achievements (Sen 1985; Crocker and Robeyns 2009).[1] With regard to well-being achievements (functionings), inequality fell in those dimensions related to income and access to resources, while health and educational disparities did not decrease in the last decade (see ECLAC 2015 for Latin America and Colafranceschi, Failache, and Vigorito 2014 for Uruguay). Nevertheless, there are scarce studies assessing the evolution of well-being freedoms (capabilities) for Latin America.[2]

In this chapter we focus on agency understood as the ability of individuals to choose and achieve valued goals, constrained by the opportunity, social, and political structures in which they live (Sen 1992; Crocker 2008; Keleher 2014). This aspect has deserved less attention than well-being in applied work within the capability approach, particularly in Latin America. However, agency is a very relevant aspect in order to direct development evaluations and policies (Crocker 2008; Crocker and Robeyns 2009). In his writings, David Crocker has pointed out that agency freedom is the nuclear point in Sen's work, and emphasizes the difference between agents and patients in normative thinking and development policies: While the former carry out the actions they decide to be involved in, the latter are those who suffer these actions (Crocker 2008). Cortina (2009) also argues that agency freedom is a key element in Sen's work.

In the last two decades, mainstream economics has been increasingly interested in studying subjective well-being as a new way of carrying out cardinal utility comparisons (Clark, Fritjers, and Shields 2008). As the capability approach, this perspective also challenges income-based well-being assessments (Comim and Teschl 2005; Comim 2008). However, scarce specific studies have addressed the relation between agency and subjective well-being, although cross-sectional studies present conflicting evidence on these links (Verme 2009; Anand,

Krishnakumar, and Tran 2011; Graham and Nikolova 2015). At the same time, even less research has been directed to analyze processes of adaptation to bad life circumstances, which is a traditional criticism of capability theorists to utilitarianism (Clark 2009). More specifically, limited research has also been targeted toward the analysis of how they relate to agency level variations. Among the dimensions comprising subjective well-being, assessing life as a whole is the one of interest for this chapter.[3]

Agency is a complex and difficult concept to operationalize because it is multidimensional and entails comparing individual goals and their fulfillment (Gasper 2007). At the same time, agency assessments require longitudinal data in order to prevent problems related to adaptive preferences (Burchardt 2009). In this chapter, we contribute to the existing literature by providing new evidence on the evolution of agency levels and inequality and its relation to subjective well-being for a developing country. To our knowledge, there are few empirical studies providing quantitative assessments of agency, and even less that are able to follow up individuals through time.

We build agency indicators based on three domains: economic control and choice, potential for change, and impact in the community. This is an adaptation of a proposal by Alkire and Ibrahim (2007). The data we use come from the longitudinal study *Estudio Longitudinal del Bienestar en Uruguay* (ELBU). The sample is representative of children that were attending first grade at primary public schools in 2004 and their families (85 percent of the cohort) in urban areas, which account for 87 percent of the Uruguayan population. This chapter is based on the 2006 and 2011/12 waves and covers Montevideo and its metropolitan area (60 percent of the total population).

We find that overall agency and economic control and choice show a pro-poor redistribution in the period under study. Moreover, the potential for change domain shows higher increases in the middle of the income distribution, while impact in the community exhibits a regressive pattern. Our results also show that there is not a strong correlation between agency and subjective well-being. However, when this association is statistically significant, it exhibits a positive sign, ruling out the adaptive preferences hypothesis.

The chapter is organized as follows. Section 2 presents a general framework and a brief review of the empirical literature. Section 3 contains methodological details. Section 4 presents the main results and Section 5 offers some final remarks.

2 Agency, Adaptive Preferences, and Subjective Well-Being

Capability theorists highlight that the distinction among well-being and agency on the one side, and freedom and achievement on the other, are key elements to carry out development evaluations based on Sen's perspective (Crocker 2008; Keleher 2014). In the case of well-being, freedoms refer to capabilities, understood as potential opportunities of beings and doings that a person faces. Achievements, on the other hand, refer to functionings, which reflect the quality of life or actual beings and doings. Moreover, in the agency aspect, freedom to achieve refers to the choice of goals that a person has reason to value, and achievement to their realization (Sen 1985). In the presentation of her list of universal combined capabilities, Nussbaum (2000) argues, in opposition to Sen, that the concept of capabilities itself, and particularly practical reason and affiliation, has a clear agency content.[4]

In his often-quoted Dewey lectures, Sen presents an initial definition of agency: "what the person is free to do and achieve in pursuit of whatever goals or values she regards as important. A person's agency aspect cannot be understood without taking note of his or her aims, objectives, allegiances, obligations, and – in a broad sense – the person's conception of the good" (1985, 203).

In his first formulations, Sen differentiated agency success (which can be due to others) from instrumental agency (due to one's own effort or participating in a joint initiative). Later in his writings, however, he acknowledges that for agency freedom to hold, the person needs to be involved in the process (Sen 1999; Crocker 2008). Agency goals might be self-regarding or other-regarding. Crocker (2008) specifies four requirements for a person to be an agent: (i) self-determination; (ii) reason, deliberation, and orientation to base his decision; (iii) action – to have an active role; (iv) impact to contribute to change. "Although they are interconnected, agency freedom can reinforce or contradict well-being freedom: one's well-being does not exhaust one's motivations or objectives and agency freedom provides normative space for the sacrifices individuals may do in order to achieve goals that they value" (157). Hence, interpersonal rankings might differ depending on whether they focus on well-being or agency.[5]

Rather than a dichotomous condition, agency can be thought as a continuum (Reich 2002, quoted in Crocker and Robeyns 2009). Another relevant characteristic of agency is that it can vary throughout the life course and is sensitive to political and social transformations (Drèze and Sen 1995). Specifically, individual agency is generated and achieved in a certain socioeconomic context that might foster or deter its development (Alsop, Bertelsen, and Holland 2006). Based on the previous discussion, in this chapter we understand agency as the ability of individuals to choose and achieve valued goals, constrained by the opportunity, social, and political structures in which they live (Sen 1992; Crocker 2008; Keleher 2014).

Referring to the links between subjective well-being and agency, Gasper (2007) points out that "freedom not matched by achievement would often be a source of frustration, subjective ill-being, so that agency freedom and subjective well-being can easily move in opposite directions" (p. 355). If prospects of living a better life are raised but not materialized due to opportunity constraints, frustration might arise (Graham and Behrman 2010; Bart et al. 2013).

The opposite phenomenon can be understood in the light of the varied versions of adaptive preferences (Elster 1983; Sen 1999; Nussbaum 2000). In this perspective, adaptation to bad circumstances might cause well-being to be higher for those experiencing more agency deprivation. Khader (2011) argues that it is hard to find a general and comprehensive definition of adaptive preferences that goes beyond criticisms to utilitarianism and accounts for specific features. She proposes the following definition: "preferences inconsistent with basic flourishing that a person developed under conditions non-conducive to basic flourishing and that we expect them to change under conditions conducive to basic flourishing" (p. 18).

In the subjective well-being literature, the issue of adaptation has also been discussed, arriving at mixed conclusions. Although some authors believe in automatic adaptation to changing conditions, recent studies find that people do not completely adapt to events such as divorce, unemployment, disability, and widowhood. These experiences generate permanent changes in subjective well-being (Layard 2007; Lucas 2007; Clark 2016). Finally, a third possibility is that agency changes might have no effects on subjective well-being. In what follows we analyze their empirical association for the case of Uruguay.

2.1 Operationalizing Agency

As the preceding section illustrates, agency is a complex concept that is difficult to operationalize. These difficulties contribute to explain the scarcity of quantitative research on agency indicators, although agency measurement has received considerable attention in the empowerment literature. Narayan (2005), Alkire and Ibrahim (2007), and Alkire (2008) address the complexities of building such indicators and present some criteria and proposals, mainly focused on developing international comparisons.

A first decision refers to whether we focus on measuring agency freedom or achievement. Difficulties involved in measuring freedom to achieve entail interpersonal comparisons of goals and their fulfillment (see for example Pogge 2002; Gasper 2007; Burchardt 2009). In this chapter, we combine indicators reflecting agency achievement and agency freedom. Another relevant issue refers to the use of subjective information and its potential biases. Bart et al. (2013) differentiate "agency beliefs" (referring to psychological and personal characteristics) and observed agency. Burchardt (2009) argues in favor of basing agency assessments on panel data to understand its dynamics. For her, cross-sectional appreciations of agency and well-being are potentially problematic due to adaptation. As in the case of utility, accomplishment of aspirations can be easier if goals are lowered, and hence, subjective information might present severe drawbacks to carry out interpersonal comparisons of advantage.

A bulk of proposals focuses agency assessments on direct control. However, excessive control can even be deleterious to agency and well-being achievements (Keleher 2014), and might not reflect effective power. Moreover, a main caveat of these measures is that it is not known whether choice brings about the desired results or not.

To overcome the limitations of control-based measures, other researchers have been exploring developments that come from the psychological literature. Effective power can be approximated on the basis of efficacy measures (Bandura 1989) aiming at capturing to what extent people select the resources they want to mobilize. Additionally, an interesting framework derives from self-determination theory, which states that behavior goes from a continuum from more to less autonomy, with intrinsic motivation in one extreme and external control in the other (Ryan and Deci 2000). In the first case, individuals act according to their own interest, whereas in the second one, they are driven by punishment or external reward. For example, Verme (2009) operationalizes freedom of choice and Bart et al. (2013) proxy agency beliefs based on locus of control indicators. In the present chapter, we include a dimension reflecting external/internal control.

A set of studies operationalize agency based on perceived situation and satisfaction indicators. Graham and Nikolova (2015) use satisfaction with one's freedom to choose as an agency indicator, while Anand and van Hees (2006) draw on perceived sense of achievement in a set of dimensions. Anand, Krishnakumar, and Tran (2011) base their agency assessments on self-reported perceptions on religious, political expression and imagination, and thought freedom.

Other proposals are based on dimensions drawn from Nussbaum's list. Anand et al. (2009) present a comprehensive proposal of capability-based indicators. In the cases of affiliation and practical reason, they include appreciation for other people, social interactions, identification with other people's situations, idea of a good life, internal/external influences, and having life plan as indicators. Ruesga and Pick (2014) also operationalize agency specifically oriented to interventions and policy design.

Finally, based on previous work by Rowlands (1997), Alkire and Ibrahim (2007) propose four domains of interest to build agency and empowerment indicators systems: (i) *control* over personal decisions, (ii) *choice* referred to autonomy in specific domains and household decision-making, (iii) *changing* aspects in one's life at the individual level, and (iv) in the community.

Combining the four properties of agency set by Crocker and adapting the Alkire and Ibrahim (2007) proposal we consider three domains: economic control and choice, potential for change, and impact in the community.

2.2 Previous Findings

This section reviews recent studies that have addressed the association between agency and subjective well-being.[6] Three cross-country studies find a positive correlation between agency indicators and subjective well-being. Using survey data from university students in four countries, Chirkov et al. (2003) find a positive correlation between autonomy (measured as degree of internalization) and subjective well-being. Based on pooled data from the World and European Values Surveys, Verme (2009) finds that locus of control is a very strong predictor of subjective well-being. Graham and Nikolova (2015), drawing on data from the Gallup Poll, find a positive correlation among subjective well-being and agency, even stronger than in the case of life satisfaction.

Evidence of a positive and significant correlation between agency and subjective well-being is also available for other cross-sectional studies at the country level, such as Anand and van Hees (2006), Anand et al. (2009), Anand, Krishnakumar, and Tran (2011), and Klein (2014).

Other studies present mixed results or conflicting evidence. In their research for Mozambique, Bart et al. (2013), observe that at a given level of wealth, people with higher agency tend to report higher subjective well-being.[7] However, at a given agency level, those interviewees with lower control over economic resources report less subjective well-being than those with higher control (frustrated freedom hypothesis). Based on the 1970 British Cohort, Burchardt (2009) finds that, among young people, aspirations and their fulfillment are highly correlated to intergenerational advantage. She argues that agency goals are subject to adaptive preferences and, as in the case of utility and subjective well-being, interpersonal comparisons are problematic.

Two cross-sectional studies address agency indicators in the case of Uruguay based on the 2006 ELBU wave. Drawing on Nussbaum's list, Burdín et al. (2008) find that agency levels are higher for men, the more educated and nonpoor households. Burstin et al. (2010) find very similar results. Although the latter study rejects the adaptive preferences hypothesis, it finds weak evidence supporting the view that those groups with lower agency levels are more prone to adaptation. The previous review shows that there is mixed evidence regarding the links between agency levels and subjective well-being. However, due to the lack of panel data, issues connected to the evolution of agency and adaptation at an individual level have been scarcely analyzed.

3 Methodology

We first describe the database used in this study (3.1). After that, we present the indicators used to build the agency index (3.2), and the corresponding aggregation methods (3.3).

3.1 Data

This empirical exercise is based on two waves of the longitudinal study ELBU, carried out by *Instituto de Economia*. The study follows a representative sample of households with children attending the first year of primary school at public institutions in Montevideo and urban areas in 2004.[8] Eighty-five percent of the children living in these areas attended public schools at baseline. Thus, this study is probably under-estimating the highest income deciles. The sampling framework corresponds to the 2002 Height Census undertaken in all public schools in Uruguay. To date, four ELBU waves (2004, 2006, 2011/12, and 2017) have been completed.

This chapter is based on the 2006 and 2011/12 waves, as questions on agency were included for the first time in the 2006 wave, which covered Montevideo and its metropolitan area. In that year, 1,185 households were interviewed. For the 2011/12 wave, 758 of those households were found and reinterviewed. Panel attrition is 30.08 percent and there are no substantial biases due to the loss of households between panels in terms of socioeconomic characteristics, although the probability of finding elder household heads and households outside Montevideo was slightly higher on the second wave (Failache, Salas, and Vigorito 2016).

Table 9.1 depicts the main sample characteristics. It can be noticed that most respondents were women and there is a heterogeneity in terms of age, education, and income.

The survey questionnaire gathered information on socioeconomic characteristics and a wide range of questions on agency, well-being, attitudes, and opinions of the respondent, which was the adult in charge of the first-grader.[9]

3.2 Agency Dimensions and Operationalization

As mentioned above, this analysis is an adapted version of the three domains proposed by Alkire and Ibrahim (2007): economic control and choice, potential for change, and impact in the community. Table 9.2 presents the list of questions, variables, and indicators used in this study. Economic control and choice identifies control over resources. Economic control is proxied by autonomous income and by permanent income and surrounding household conditions. The first one reflects

Table 9.1 *Sample characteristics, ELBU*

	Obs.	Mean	SD	Min	Max
Age (2006)	739	41.09	7.85	16	70
Sex (% male respondents)	740	0.044	0.205	0	1
Region (% outside Montevideo)	740	0.214	0.41	0	1
Marital status (%)					
Divorced/Separated (2011/12)	740	0.198	0.391	0	1
Divorced/Separated (2006)	740	0.151	0.358	0	1
Widow (2011/12)	740	0.033	0.189	0	1
Widow (2006)	740	0.027	0.164	0	1
Average years of education (adults aged twenty-two or more)	740	10.19	3.474	2	18
Persons per room		1.736	1.091		
2011/12	740			0.33	14
2006	740	1.922	1.361	0.02	13
Employment rate among respondents					
2011/12	740	0.730	0.439	0	1
2006	740	0.581	0.491	0	1
Log. per capita household income				5.19	
2011/12	740	9.742	0.853	5.19	11.88
2006	740	9.337	0.987	4.59	11.75

Source: own elaboration based on ELBU data.

individual income generating capacity and includes labor, pension, and capital income. For the second one, we include a composite index reflecting access to a set of durable goods (Filmer and Pritchett 1998). Weights for each item are depicted in Table A9.1. Choice is a proxy for bargaining power within the household and it is operationalized as the share of the respondent's autonomous income over household income.

Although this dimension is insufficient to describe overall agency (Gasper 2007), generation and control over resources are necessary conditions to exert agency in a market society (Bojer 2000). This dimension can be connected to action, which is the third requirement of agency proposed by Crocker (2008).

The second domain, potential for change, reflects self-perceived degree of command over one's life. People with internal locus of control believe they control their own fate and are responsible for their actions

Table 9.2 *Dimensions, variables, and indicators*

Dimension	Variable/question	Indicator
Economic control and choice	Autonomous income	Respondent's labor +pension+capital income
	Durable goods composite index	Goods included and weights in Table A9.1
	% autonomous income in household income	Share (%)
Potential for change	Who do you think will contribute to a change in your life?	You; Family; Another person/group of persons; Local/National government; God/Religion; Other/N.A.
	To what extent do you believe you can decide your own destiny?	Destiny; Mainly destiny; Half destiny, half ourselves; Mainly ourselves; We determine our own fate.
Impact in the community	Have you recently felt that you play a relevant role in family events or in your community?	No 0 Yes 1
	Were you prevented from taking part in a social event due to not having the appropriate clothes?	No 0 Yes 1
	Do you feel that your opinions are considered among your family members, neighbors, or friends?	No 0 Yes 1
	Imagine a nine steps ladder. In the lower level, those with no power are located, while in the highest level, there are those people who have a lot of power. Where would you place yourself?	Scale ranging from 1 to 9

Source: own elaboration based on ELBU data.

(Rotter 1966). Meanwhile, those with external locus of control believe that their lives are the result of destiny designs. Hence, this dimension reflects a potentiality, rather than a direct achievement and it is closely connected to the first agency requirement proposed by Crocker (self-determination).

This dimension is based on two sets of indicators. The first one reflects who the respondent thinks will contribute more to a change in her life. The second refers to the role of destiny versus one's own command over one's life (fatalism).

Finally, the third domain, impact in the community, gathers aspects reflecting one's place in relation to others and self-perceived capacity of changing things in one's context and environment. Indicators for this domain refer to four different areas: (i) family, (ii) neighbors and friends, (iii) reference group and colleagues, and iv) community in general. This dimension can be connected to impact in the community, which is the fourth agency requirement proposed by Crocker.

3.3 Methods

In order to analyze agency levels, we created a composite index that combines the three previously mentioned domains. To operationalize agency as a continuum, we base our analysis on fuzzy sets logics (Zadeh 1965; Ragin 2008). This methodology has been extensively used to carry out poverty and vulnerability analysis from the capability perspective (Betti et al. 2006).

Fuzzy set theory replaces the traditional approach – defined as the demarcation of a certain condition based on a binary function. It instead uses a generalized function, which varies between zero and one. Methodological details and robustness check based on principal components analysis can be found in Salas and Vigorito (2019). Given that we don't have an a priori hypothesis on the relative importance of each dimension, we assigned equal weight to the three vectors when computing overall agency index (0.33). Finally, the last step to build fuzzy sets-based agency indicators is to determine the lower and upper thresholds by dimension, indicating no agency or full agency. That can be seen in Table 9.3.

Table 9.3 *Upper and lower threshold by dimension*

	Lower bound (=0)	Upper bound (=1)
Durable goods index	25th percentile	75th percentile
Autonomous income	50% of the median	150% of the median
Autonomous income share	50% of the median	150% of the median
Fatality	Everything is determined by fate	We make our destiny
Role in changing own life	God	You
Role in family and community	0	1
Participation in social events	0	1
Opinions	0	1
Power ladder	1	9

4 Main Results

In this section, we first describe the evolution of agency and subjective well-being (4.1). Then, we carry out a multivariate analysis on the determinants of agency levels (4.2). Finally, we investigate the association between agency and subjective well-being (4.3).

4.1 Agency and Subjective Well-Being: Levels and Trends

The low correlation coefficients among the three agency domains in the two periods analyzed indicate they are capturing different aspects (Table A9.2). Potential for change and impact in the community present a low but negative relation.[10] We first explore the levels and rate of change of Overall Composite Agency Indicator (OCAI) and its distribution (Figure 9.1). Panel A depicts agency levels by OCAI centile in each period. The 2011/12 distribution dominates the 2006 one until the median, indicating larger improvements in agency for the lower fractiles. In particular, while average rate of change is around 4.25 percent (black horizontal line), the rate of change for the first quintile ranges from 25 to 5 percent, and falls to 0 percent for those strata above the median (panel B).

Figure A9.1 depicts average agency levels by 2006 per capita household income, in the two periods. Total agency exhibits an upward sloping gradient, ranging from 0.4 to 0.7 with the highest levels for the richest sectors. Unsurprisingly, this means that an individual's

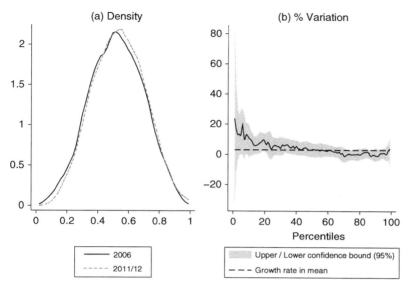

Figure 9.1. Agency kernel density function and variation by percentile, 2006–2011/12.
Source: own elaboration based on ELBU data.
Note: in panel (a) the horizontal axis represents agency percentiles and the vertical axis represents agency levels; in panel (b) the horizontal axis corresponds to agency percentiles and the vertical axis depicts the average variation in agency between 2006 and 2011/12 as a proportion of the 2006 average agency level.

position in the income distribution is correlated with higher agency levels. However, there are considerable differences by domain. Economic control and choice is the most unequal dimension, with average values ranging from around 0.15 in the bottom percentiles to almost 0.80 in the top ones. Meanwhile, potential for change and impact in the community show a comparatively reduced gradient (0.4 to 0.7), indicating a more equal pattern.

Regarding the 2006–2011/12 rate of change in per capita household income percentile, OCAI exhibits a monotonic progressive pattern with higher improvements for the lower percentiles, while the richer ones remains constant or slightly decline (Figure 9.2). Economic control and choice present a progressive pattern, in line with the recent evolution of income inequality. Meanwhile, potential for change exhibits an intermediate situation, with more gains in the middle of the

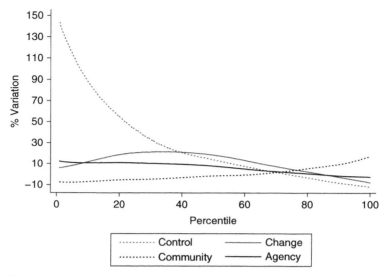

Figure 9.2. Average agency variation by domain and 2006 per capita household income percentile, 2006 and 2011/12.
Source: Own elaboration based on ELBU data.

distribution. Finally, impact in the community shows a regressive trend, with higher increases for richer sectors.

4.2 Socioeconomic Determinants of Agency

To single out the variables associated with agency, we run ordinary least squares (OLS) for OCAI and each domain on the covariates of 2011/12 agency levels. As part of those covariates, we include a set of demographic and socioeconomic variables and, in a second stage, a group of lagged (2006) agency variables (Table 9.4 depicts the regression outputs including lagged variables and Table A.2.7 in Salas and Vigorito [2017] presents the same results, excluding them). Demographic variables include sex, age, marital status in 2011/12 and 2006, and current region of residence. Moreover, socioeconomic covariates comprise current and past income, average years of schooling of adults in the household, past and present employment status of the interviewee, and past and present crowding. In most cases, the coefficients maintain their significance and magnitude in the two specifications, suggesting that past agency levels reflect an independent effect from the remaining covariates. Finally, the

Table 9.4 *Regression analysis: agency levels, estimated coefficients, OLS*

| | 2011/12 levels | | | |
	Pot. for change	Ec. control	Impact in community	OCAI
	(1)	(2)	(3)	(4)
Lagged agency in	0.073	0.277***	0.142***	0.138***
domain (2006)	(0.047)	(0.045)	(0.048)	(0.046)
Age	−0.005**	0.001	0.003*	0.0004
	(0.002)	(0.001)	(0.001)	(0.0008)
Sex (1=Male)	0.067	0.078***	−0.039	0.030
	(0.068)	(0.026)	(0.044)	(0.037)
Region	−0.007	−0.013	0.075***	0.014
(1=Canelones)	(0.033)	(0.020)	(0.028)	(0.016)
Marital status				
(1=Yes)				
Divorced (t)	0.047	0.023	−0.040	0.010
	(0.035)	(0.025)	(0.030)	(0.018)
Divorced (t-1)	0.076**	0.002	−0.003	0.036*
	(0.038)	(0.027)	(0.030)	(0.021)
Widower (t)	0.037	0.007	−0.019	0.012
	(0.059)	(0.049)	(0.067)	(0.030)
Widower (t-1)	−0.044	0.120***	0.012	0.041
	(0.082)	(0.042)	(0.094)	(0.041)
Log. p.c. hh.	−0.015	0.086***	0.005	0.039***
income (t)	(0.011)	(0.015)	(0.009)	(0.010)
Log. p.c. hh.	0.009	−0.012	0.025**	0.006
income (t-1)	(0.017)	(0.010)	(0.011)	(0.008)
Ed. climate	0.011***	0.007***	0.011***	0.007***
	(0.004)	(0.003)	(0.003)	(0.002)
Overcrowding (t)	−0.018	−0.022***	−0.007	−0.016***
	(0.013)	(0.006)	(0.010)	(0.005)
Overcrowding (t-1)	−0.007	−0.009	−0.012	−0.013**
	(0.009)	(0.009)	(0.009)	(0.005)
Employment (t)	0.022	0.298***	0.005	0.112***
	(0.033)	(0.019)	(0.025)	(0.015)
Employment (t-1)	0.010	−0.081***	−0.029	−0.018
	(0.031)	(0.024)	(0.023)	(0.017)
Constant	0.663***	−0.632***	0.023	−0.099
	(0.186)	(0.149)	(0.141)	(0.095)
Observations	666	725	645	582
R-squared	0.067	0.572	0.125	0.365

Source: own elaboration based on ELBU data.
Note: Robust standard errors in parentheses, *** $p<0.01$, ** $p<0.05$, * $p<0.1$.

explanatory power varied significantly by domain: R2 coefficients are very low in the case of potential for change, suggesting that socioeconomic variables are not its main driver.

Excepting potential for change, past agency in the specific domain exhibits a positive sign and is significant in all cases, reflecting a certain degree of persistence throughout the life cycle. The magnitude of the coefficient ranges from more than one-third in the case of economic control and choice to around 13 percent in OCAI. Regarding demographic variables, age is significant and exhibits a positive sign only in the case of potential for change, indicating more internalizing positions for younger adults. Being a male respondent is associated with higher agency levels only in the case of economic agency, probably reflecting wage differentials by gender.

Household income variables are significant in all cases, except for potential for change. This might suggest that its main determinants are not socioeconomic. Lagged income is significant and exhibits a positive sign only in the case of impact in the community. Meanwhile, contemporary household income is significant and positive in the cases of economic control and choice (8 percent) and OCAI (4 percent). Average years of education of the adults in the household has a positive effect on OCAI and by domain, with a higher effect in the cases of potential for change and impact in the community. Finally, lagged employment status is significant and negative in the case of economic control and choice, while present employment is also significant for OCAI, exhibiting a positive sign in both cases.

To sum up, the determinants of agency levels and persistence of agency vary significantly by domain, suggesting different rigidities and evolution patterns in the period analyzed. In the case of potential for change, the impact and explanatory power of the whole specification is considerably low. Moreover, results suggest that the OCAI gap by socioeconomic stratum has narrowed during the time frame analyzed in this chapter, which is consistent with the reduced income inequality experienced in the region. However, this situation varies by domain, with impact in the community presenting a regressive pattern. In conclusion, it is important to highlight that general economic environment effects and changes in political regimes and public policies, among other factors, need to be analyzed in depth to understand the evolution of this component.

4.3 Agency, Subjective Well-Being, and Adaptive Preferences

In this section we address the relationship between agency and evaluative subjective well-being. At the same time, adaptation processes will be explored, given the longitudinal nature of the data. ELBU contains information on life satisfaction in general and for specific domains, such as economic situation, social participation, and household decision-making in a scale from 1 (not satisfied at all) to 5 (very satisfied).

Life satisfaction levels did not present a significant gradient by OCAI (Figure 9.3, panel D).[11] However, increases were higher among individuals in lower OCAI strata. Economic situation presents a similar but more pronounced gradient (Figure 9.3, panel b). Specifically, variations were substantial and increases among low OCAI percentiles particularly striking. Decision-making in the household levels presents a flat levels curve, although increases in satisfaction were slightly higher among lower OCAI strata. Finally, social participation (Figure 9.3, panel a) resembles the other domains in the scarce gradient, although increases were higher for the richer sectors.

To assess persistence in evaluative subjective well-being by domain, we run the model for 2011/12 including the lagged variable for satisfaction in each respective domain as an independent variable, along with the socioeconomic and demographic controls used in the previous section (Table 9.5). The coefficients for the lagged satisfaction (2006) are always positive and significant, except in the case of participation, where the coefficient is 0.14 but the estimate is not significant. Persistence is higher in the cases of life satisfaction and economic situation (around 0.35), while in decision-making it is 0.19. Thus, persistence in life satisfaction varies by domain.

We also analyzed the correlation between subjective well-being by domain, both in levels and growth rates, and the demographic and socioeconomic variables considered in the previous section, which are the standard predictors identified in the related literature (Verme 2009; Graham and Nikolova 2015). We also added contemporary and lagged variables for OCAI in the level model, and its variation in the growth rate model (Table 9.6). Additionally, in separate specifications, we included as independent variables the three agency domains, to assess whether they have different and independent effects (see Table A2.8 in Salas and Vigorito 2019). Moreover, to better understand the effects of

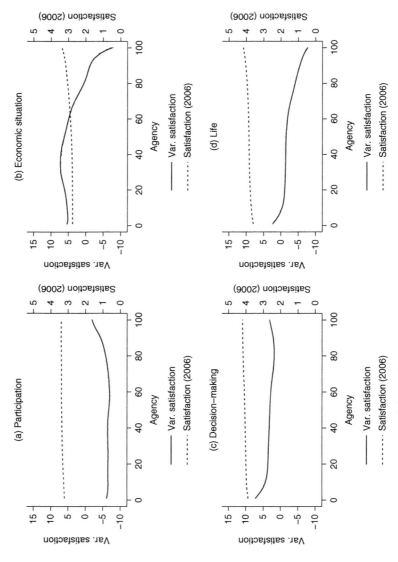

Figure 9.3. Average 2006 life satisfaction level and 2011/12–2006 variation by domain and OCAI percentile. Source: Own elaboration based on ELBU data.

Table 9.5 *Persistence in life satisfaction by domain, estimated coefficients*

	Life	Participation	Economic situation	Decision-making
Lagged satisfaction in the domain (2006)	0.394*** (0.065)	0.140 (0.103)	0.369*** (0.053)	0.196*** (0.070)
Observations	582	487	581	576
R-squared	0.197	0.094	0.255	0.076

Source: own elaboration based on ELBU data.
Notes: Robust standard errors in parentheses, *** $p<0.01$, ** $p<0.05$, * $p<0.1$.
Control variables include age, sex, marital status, education, region, present and past income, employment, and crowding.

the potential for change and impact in the community indicators, we run separate equations including all single indicators instead of the domain index (see Table A.2.9 in Salas and Vigorito 2019). In all cases, the coefficients of the demographic and socioeconomic variables did not change when the agency variables were added to the estimations.

As shown in the literature, divorce and widowhood are negatively related to general life satisfaction levels. Age and sex are not significant, and average years of education completed by the household's adults are only significant and positively related to satisfaction in the case of decision-making. Current per capita household income is significant and positively associated to subjective well-being levels only in the case of economic satisfaction. Lagged income is also positive and significant but exhibits a lower effect. However, in the case of participation, current income yields a negative sign, with a big size effect (0.384), reflecting that lower income strata are relatively happier in this dimension. In the remaining dimensions (life and decision-making), income variables are not significant. In terms of growth rates, results are similar for participation and lagged income becomes significant in the case of life satisfaction, indicating higher gains in lower strata. Agency variables and lagged OCAI exhibit a strong and positive relation with life satisfaction levels in all domains, although in decision-making estimates are imprecise. Contemporary OCAI is not significant for every

Table 9.6 *Regression results – dependent variable: subjective well-being by domain, levels and variations*

| | 2011/12 levels | | | | Variations (2011/12–2006) | | | |
| | Life | Participation | Economic situation | Decision-making | Life | Participation | Economic situation | Decision-making |
	(1)	(2)	(3)	(4)	(5)	(6)	(7)	(8)
OCAI (t)	0.224	0.293	-0.354	0.291				
	(0.410)	(0.642)	(0.432)	(0.306)				
OCAI (t-1)	0.710*	1.906***	0.843**	0.483	0.285	1.669**	-0.382	0.138
	(0.386)	(0.578)	(0.407)	(0.315)	(0.521)	(0.830)	(0.592)	(0.455)
Var. OCAI	0.610	1.626***	0.166	0.451				
	(0.413)	(0.616)	(0.464)	(0.360)				
Age	-0.001	0.019*	-0.009	0.006	-0.004	0.021*	0.002	0.002
	(0.007)	(0.011)	(0.008)	(0.006)	(0.008)	(0.012)	(0.008)	(0.007)
Sex (1=Male)	0.004	-0.140	-0.200	-0.127	0.009	0.307	-0.131	-0.123
	(0.247)	(0.373)	(0.180)	(0.271)	(0.332)	(0.478)	(0.279)	(0.271)
Region (1=Montevideo)	-0.014	0.282	0.325**	0.121	-0.160	0.351	0.231	-0.040
	(0.150)	(0.224)	(0.155)	(0.115)	(0.150)	(0.264)	(0.157)	(0.122)
Marital status (1=Yes)								
Divorced (t)	-0.450***	-0.277	-0.459***	0.177	-0.457***	-0.274	-0.730***	0.216
	(0.152)	(0.238)	(0.150)	(0.138)	(0.153)	(0.253)	(0.181)	(0.140)
Divorced (t-1)	-0.282	-0.087	-0.101	-0.459**	0.164	0.046	0.201	-0.464**
	(0.181)	(0.254)	(0.180)	(0.185)	(0.187)	(0.291)	(0.202)	(0.187)
Widower (t)	-0.678***	0.119	0.0847	0.256	-0.765***	-0.446	-0.010	0.583
	(0.203)	(0.503)	(0.262)	(0.290)	(0.263)	(0.397)	(0.340)	(0.427)

	(1)	(2)	(3)	(4)	(5)	(6)	(7)	(8)
Widower (t-1)	0.697***	-0.470	0.406	-0.369	0.960***	-0.0319	0.939**	-0.628
	(0.250)	(0.711)	(0.305)	(0.422)	(0.296)	(0.523)	(0.473)	(0.447)
Log. per capita household income (t)	0.013	-0.384***	0.210**	-0.009	0.028	-0.449***	0.090	-0.032
	(0.084)	(0.133)	(0.104)	(0.081)	(0.100)	(0.156)	(0.103)	(0.101)
Log. per capita household income (t-1)	-0.0628	-0.058	0.148**	-0.052	-0.183***	0.006	-0.045	-0.064
	(0.065)	(0.105)	(0.066)	(0.051)	(0.068)	(0.126)	(0.075)	(0.055)
Educational environment	0.033*	0.016	0.027	0.035**	0.029*	0.021	0.039*	0.038**
	(0.018)	(0.026)	(0.021)	(0.016)	(0.018)	(0.028)	(0.021)	(0.017)
Overcrowding (t)	-0.091	0.066	-0.133***	0.007	-0.005	0.060	-0.029	0.032
	(0.062)	(0.074)	(0.044)	(0.044)	(0.052)	(0.076)	(0.065)	(0.051)
Overcrowding (t-1)	-0.061	-0.168***	0.011	-0.002	-0.043	-0.164**	-0.023	-0.044
	(0.041)	(0.062)	(0.054)	(0.034)	(0.040)	(0.075)	(0.049)	(0.032)
Employment (t)	-0.117	-0.317	-0.080	0.040	-0.094	-0.134	-0.035	0.080
	(0.142)	(0.205)	(0.153)	(0.123)	(0.138)	(0.217)	(0.156)	(0.134)
Employment (t-1)	-0.097	0.089	-0.086	-0.167	-0.025	-0.066	-0.004	-0.107
	(0.124)	(0.195)	(0.141)	(0.110)	(0.122)	(0.205)	(0.150)	(0.122)
Constant	3.935***	5.710***	-0.355	3.798***	1.283	2.483	-0.509	0.500
	(0.896)	(1.330)	(0.935)	(0.826)	(1.036)	(1.574)	(1.074)	(0.951)
Observations	582	499	582	580	582	487	581	576
R-squared	0.122	0.091	0.163	0.062	0.07	0.073	0.088	0.053

Source: own elaboration based on ELBU data.

Note: Robust standard errors in parentheses, *** $p<0.01$, ** $p<0.05$, * $p<0.1$.

case. Variations only exhibit a large positive association in participation satisfaction.

Contemporary impact in the community agency is positively related to all domains, with large coefficients, exhibiting larger effects on social participation satisfaction. At the same time, the lagged indicator is significant and positive only in the cases of life and decision-making satisfaction. In terms of growth rates, it maintains a strong and positive association only in the case of participation. Meanwhile, potential for change and economic control and choice are never significant.

The strong effect of contemporary impact in the community poses questions regarding which indicator might be explaining the results. In order to test for that, we run separate equations for each single indicator (Table A.2.9 in Salas and Vigorito 2019). We did the same in the case of change, as the previous literature suggested a strong and positive relation to life satisfaction (Verme 2009).

In the case of community indicator, the main explanatory variables are the power ladder variable and prevention from participation in social events due to clothing. These findings indicate that positionality with respect to public life is driving the results. In the case of potential for change, single indicators are not significant in most cases, even though individuals who are more fatalistic in 2006 tend to be more satisfied with their economic situation. In the case of decision-making in the household, external individuals are more satisfied.

This section illustrates that, in most cases, correlation between OCAI and contemporary evaluative subjective well-being are positive or nonsignificant. Results on lagged agency and income variables also tend to positive or nonsignificant relations, ruling out the adaptive preferences hypothesis.

5 Concluding Remarks

The empirical exercise carried out in this chapter shows that, in the case of Uruguay, agency levels are unequally distributed in favor of those individuals with higher socioeconomic advantage. In the period under study, characterized by a significant reduction in poverty and inequality, agency evolution showed a progressive pattern in those domains related to control over resources. However, in terms of self-determination and, particularly, in the impact in the community domain, those individuals in the middle and higher strata of the income distribution in 2006 accrued larger gains. Hence, increased agency in terms of control over resources coexists with a retraction in power in the public sphere. A regressive variation pattern is observed in those agency domains related to public life that needs to be further explored.

Our findings show that agency is not a static condition. The fact that income redistribution can be coupled with a regressive pattern in terms of impact in the community is a relevant finding from a capability perspective – related to how to evaluate and design development policies. Even though the reasons explaining these results need to be further analyzed, these findings suggest that public policies that redistribute resources need to be coupled with agency enhancing interventions, particularly in the sphere of participation and empowerment in the public sphere.

This chapter also shows that the correlation among subjective well-being and agency levels and their variations is weak. However, in most of the cases in which the association was statistically significant, it exhibited a positive sign. The same observation holds for lagged and contemporary income. These findings are not consistent with the adaptive preferences hypothesis but need to be further studied. Moreover, regarding the domains, it must be noticed that impact in community agency was positively correlated with satisfaction levels and gains in most of them, and that the drivers of these effects were those indicators more connected to public life. These results need to be further studied to assess their stability and robustness considering new ELBU waves.

Although the panel nature of the dataset used in this study allows for assessing the role of lagged variables and not only contemporary ones, reverse causality problems might still persist as more satisfied individuals might be more likely to enhance their agency and improve their income (Anand, Krishnakumar, and Tran 2011). At the same time, more research is needed in order to assess the stability of these findings in periods of economic decline or increasing income inequality and to understand whether these results can be extended among other population groups and countries.

Notes

1. We come back to this point in Section 2.
2. Anand, Krishnakumar, and Tran (2011) and Krishnakumar and Nogales (2016) carry out cross-sectional empirical studies on capabilities for Argentina and Bolivia respectively.

3. Evaluative, hedonic, and eudemonic aspects can be distinguished within subjective well-being (Clark 2016; Graham and Ruiz Pozuelo 2017).
4. There are different views on the potential consequences of this point. While Crocker (2008) states that disregarding the capability-agency distinction is problematic, Keleher (2014) argues that both Sen and Nussbaum's versions of the capability approach account for agency and the role of empowerment in human development.
5. Again, differentiating achievements from freedoms.
6. We restrict our literature review to those papers that explicitly address agency.
7. They assess agency belief operationalized as a combination of a question on fatality and gender power in the household.
8. Information on this dataset, survey questionnaires, and micro-data can be found at www.fcea.edu.uy/estudio-del-bienestar-multidimensional-en-uruguay.html.
9. A comparative analysis of the ELBU data with the information from the official household survey (Encuesta Continua de Hogares, or ECH) run by the local statistical office (Instituto Nacional de Estadistica, or INE) in terms of income, labor force attachment, and other socioeconomic variables shows very similar results (see Failache, Salas, and Vigorito 2016 for details). As most household surveys, comparisons with income tax records show that labor earnings and pensions are well captured in ECH, whether top and capital incomes are underreported (Burdín, Esponda, and Vigorito 2015). Informal income is included in ECH and in ELBU. In the period under analysis, informality was low: workers contributing to the social security accounted for 80 percent of the labor force (INE 2017).
10. We ran a principal component analysis robustness check to assess how the indicators belonging to these two domains are grouped, and we found two clear separate vectors.
11. As in the case of the graphs on agency domains, the graphs are smoothed using nonparametric regressions.

References

Alkire, S. 2008. "Concepts and Measures of Agency." In K. Basu and R. Kanbur (eds.), *Arguments for a Better World: Essays in Honor of Amartya Sen: Volume I: Ethics, Welfare, and Measurement*. Oxford University Press.

Alkire, S. and S. Ibrahim 2007. "Agency and Empowerment: A Proposal for Internationally Comparable Indicators." *Oxford Development Studies* 35(4): 379–403.

Alsop, R., M. Bertelsen, and J. Holland 2006. *Empowerment in Practice from Analysis to Implementation.* Washington, DC: World Bank Publications.

Amarante, V., M. Colafranceschi, and A. Vigorito 2014. "Uruguay's Income Inequality and Political Regimes over the Period 1981–2010." In *Falling Inequality in Latin America: Policy Changes and Lessons.* A. Cornia (ed.), Oxford University Press, 118–139.

Anand, P. and M. van Hees. 2006. "Capabilities and Achievements: An Empirical Study." *The Journal of Socio-Economics* 35: 268–284.

Anand, P., J. Krishnakumar, and N. B. Tran. 2011. "Measuring Welfare: Latent Variable Models for Happiness and Capabilities in the Presence of Observable Heterogeneity." *Journal of Public Economics* 95: 205–215.

Anand, P., G. Hunter, I. Carter, K. Dowding, F. Guala, and M. van Hees. 2009. "The Development of Capability Indicators." *Journal of Human Development and Capabilities* 10(1): 125–152.

Bandura, A. 1989. "Human Agency in Social Cognitive Theory." *American Psychologist* 44(9): 1175–1184.

Bart, V., E. Fischer, B. Cooil, A. Vergara, A. Mukolo, and M. Blevins. 2013. "Frustrated Freedom: The Effects of Agency and Wealth on Wellbeing in Rural Mozambique." *World Development* 47: 30–41.

Betti, G., B. Cheli, A. Lemmi, and V. Verma. 2006. "On the Construction of Fuzzy Measures for the Analysis of Poverty and Social Exclusion." *Statistica and Applicazioni* 4(1): 77–97.

Bojer, H. 2000. "Children and Theories of Social Justice." *Feminist Economics* 62: 23–39.

Burchardt, T. 2009. "Agency Goals, Adaptation and Capability Sets." *Journal of Human Development and Capabilities* 10(1): 3–19.

Burdín, G., M. Leites, G. Salas, and A. Vigorito 2008. "Agencia, pobreza y bienestar. Una propuesta para su operacionalización." In *Pobreza y Libertad.* A. Cortina and G. Pereira (eds.), Madrid: EdTecnos.

Burdín, G., F. Esponda, and A. Vigorito. 2015. "Desigualdad y altas rentas en el Uruguay: un análisis basado en los registros tributarios y las encuestas de hogares del período 2009–2011." In *Desigualdad, concentración del ingreso y tributación sobre las altas rentas en América Latina.* J. P. Jiménez (ed.), Santiago de Chile: CEPAL.

Burstin, V., A. Fascioli, H. Modzelewski, G. Pereira, A. Reyes, G. Salas, and A. Vigorito. 2010. *Preferencias adaptativas entre deseos, frustración y logros.* Montevideo: Ed. Fin de Siglo.

Chirkov, V., R. Ryan, Y. Kim, and U. Kaplan 2003. "Differentiating Autonomy from Individualism and Independence: A Self-Determination Theory Perspective on Internalization of Cultural

Orientations and Well-Being." *Journal of Personality and Social Psychology* 84(1): 97–110.

Clark, A. 2016. "Adaptation and the Easterlin Paradox." In *Advances in Happiness Research: A Comparative Perspective*. T. Tachibanaki (ed.), New York: Springer.

Clark, A., E. Frijters, and M. A. Shields. 2008. "Relative Income, Happiness, and Utility: An Explanation for the Easterlin Paradox and Other Puzzles." *Journal of Economic Literature* 46(1): 95–144.

Clark, D. 2009. "Adaptation, Poverty and Well-Being: Some Issues and Observations with Special Reference to the Capability Approach and Development Studies." *Journal of Human Development* 10(1): 21–42.

Colafranceschi, M., E. Failache, and A. Vigorito 2014. "Desigualdad multidimensional y dinámica de la pobreza en Uruguay en los años recientes." *El Futuro en Foco. Cuadernos sobre Desarrollo Humano* N°2. PNUD Uruguay.

Comim, F. 2008. "Capabilities and Happiness: Overcoming the Informational Apartheid." In *Capabilities and Happiness*. L. Bruni, F. Comim, and M. Pugno (eds.), Oxford University Press.

Comim, F. and M. Teschl. 2005. "Adaptive Preferences and Capabilities: Some Preliminary Conceptual Explorations." *Review of Social Economics* 63(2): 229–247.

Cornia, A. 2010. "Income Distribution under Latin America's New Left Regimes." *Journal of Human Development and Capabilities* 11(1): 85–114.

Cortina, A. 2009. "La pobreza como falta de libertad." In *Pobreza y Libertad*. A. Cortina and G. Pereira (eds.), Madrid: Ed Tecnos.

Crocker, D. 2008. *Ethics of Global Development: Agency, Capability, and Deliberative Democracy*. Cambridge University Press.

Crocker, D. and I. Robeyns. 2009. "Capability and Agency." In *Amartya Sen*. C. Morris (ed.), Cambridge University Press.

Drèze, J. and A. Sen. 1995. *India: Economic Development and Social Opportunity*. Oxford: Clarendon Press.

ECLAC. 2015. "Pactos para la igualdad: Hacia un futuro sostenible." Documento del Período de Sesiones. http://repositorio.cepal.org/bit stream/handle/11362/36692/6/LCG2586SES353s_es.pdf.

Elster, J. 1983. *Sour Grapes: Studies in the Subversion of Rationality*. Cambridge University Press.

Failache, E., G. Salas, and A. Vigorito. 2016. "La dinámica reciente del bienestar de los niños en Uruguay. Un estudio en base a datos longitudinales." *DT IECON 11/16.*

Filmer, D. and L. Pritchett. 1998. "The Effect of Household Wealth on Educational Attainment around the World: Demographic and Health Survey Evidence." World Bank.

Gasparini, L. and N. Lustig. 2011. "The Rise and Fall of Income Inequality in Latin America." In *Handbook of Latin American Economics*. J. A. Ocampo and J. Ros (eds.), Oxford University Press.

Gasper, D. 2007. "What Is the Capability Approach? Its Core, Rationale, Partners and Dangers." *The Journal of Socio-Economics* 36(3): 335–359.

Graham, C. and J. Behrman 2010. "How Latin Americans Assess Their Quality of Life: Insights and Puzzles from Novel Metrics of Well-Being." In *Paradox and Perception: Measuring Quality of Life in Latin America*. C. Graham and E. Lora (eds.), Washington, DC: Brookings Institution Press.

Graham, C. and M. Nikolova. 2015. "Bentham or Aristotle in the Development Process? An Empirical Investigation of Capabilities and Subjective Well-Being." *World Development* 68: 163–179.

Graham, C. and J. Ruiz Pozuelo. 2017. "Happiness, Stress, and Age: How the U Curve Varies across People and Places." *Journal of Population Economics* 30(1): 225–264.

INE. 2017. www.ine.gub.uy/web/guest/actividad-empleo-y-desempleo.

Keleher, L. 2014. "Sen and Nussbaum: Agency and Capability-Expansion." Ethics and Economics 12(June): 54–70.

Khader, S. 2011. *Adaptive Preferences and Women's Empowerment*. Oxford University Press.

Klein, E. 2014. "Psychological Agency: Evidence from the Urban Fringe of Bamako." *World Development* 64: 642–653.

Krishnakumar, K. and R. Nogales 2016. "Skill Formation and the Potential to Have a Good Job." Paper presented at the 6th Conference on ALCADECA in Montevideo.

Layard, R. 2007. "Happiness and Public Policy: A Challenge to the Profession." In *Economics and Psychology: A Promising New Cross-Disciplinary Field*. B. Frey and A. Stutzer (eds.), CESifo Seminar Series. Cambridge, MA: MIT Press.

López-Calva, L. F. and N. Lustig. 2010. *Declining Inequality in Latin America*. New York: UNDP and Brookings Institution Press.

Lucas, R. E. 2007. "Adaptation and the Set-Point Model of Subjective Well-Being: Does Happiness Change after Major Life Events?" *Current Directions in Psychological Science* 162: 75–79.

Narayan, D. (ed.) 2005. *Measuring Empowerment: Cross-Disciplinary Perspective*. Washington, DC: World Bank Publications.

Nussbaum, M. 2000. *Women and Human Development: The Capabilities Approach*. Cambridge University Press.

Pogge, T. 2002. "Can the Capability Approach Be Justified?" *Philosophical Topics* 302: 167–228.

Ragin, C. 2008. *Redesigning Social Inquiry: Fuzzy Sets and Beyond*. University of Chicago Press.

Rotter, J. 1966. "Generalized Expectancies for Internal versus External Control of Reinforcement." *Psychological Monographs* 33: 300–303.

Rowlands, J. 1997. *Questioning Empowerment: Working with Women in Honduras*. London: Oxfam.

Ruesga, C. and S. Pick 2014. "Agencia personal, empoderamient agéntico y desarrollo humano: una perspectiva empírica." In *Desarrollo como libertad en América Latina*. M. Nebel, P. Flores-Crespo, and M. Herrera (eds.), Mexico City: Universidad Iberoamericana.

Ryan, R. and E. Deci. 2000. "Self-Determination Theory and the Facilitation of Intrinsic Motivation, Social Development, and Well-Being." *American Psychologist* 55: 68–78.

Salas, G. and A. Vigorito. 2019. "Agency, Income Inequality and Subjective Well-Being. The Case of Uruguay." Extended version. *DT IECON X/ 17*.

Sen, A. 1985. "Well-being, Agency and Freedom: The Dewey Lectures 1984." *The Journal of Philosophy* 82(4): 169–221.

Sen, A. 1992. *Inequality Reexamined*. Oxford University Press.

Sen, A. 1999. *Development as Freedom*. New York: Alfred Knopf.

Verme, P. 2009. "Happiness, Freedom and Control." *Journal of Economic Behavior & Organization* 71(2): 146–161.

Zadeh, L. 1965. "Fuzzy Sets." *Information and Control* 8: 338–353.

Appendix

Table A9.1 *Variables and weights used to build the wealth index–Principal Component Analysis.*

	Variable	Weights
	2006	2011/12
Boiler	0.296	0.375
Cooker	0.123	0.069
Microwave oven	0.319	0.306
Music equipment	0.208	0.170
Dishwasher	0.113	0.101
Clothes iron	0.233	0.246
Vacuum cleaner	0.283	0.256
Car	0.245	0.256
Telephone (landline)	0.264	0.293
Mobile telephone	0.196	0.063
Video or DVD	0.284	0.210
Refrigerator	0.185	0.151
Washing machine	0.312	0.305
TV	0.193	0.242
Computer	0.294	0.354
Internet connection	0.161	0.349
Heater	0.275	0.202

Table A9.2 *Correlation between agency dimensions, 2006 and 2011/12*

	Control and choice	Change	Community	Agency
2006				
Control	1.000			
Change	0.077			
Community	0.073	−0.004	1.000	
Agency	0.705	0.603	0.492	1.000
2011/12				
Control	1.000			
Change	0.070			
Community	0.120	−0.051	1.000	
Agency	0.667	0.632	0.500	1.000

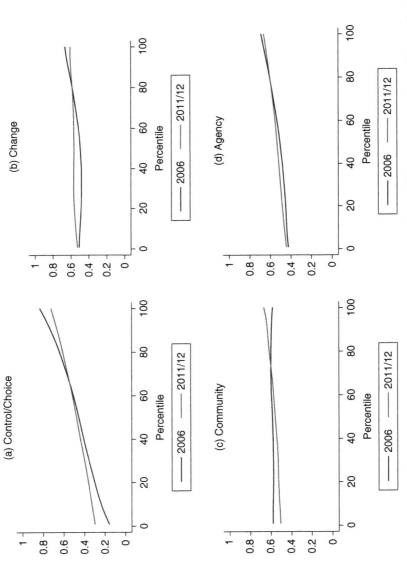

Figure A9.1. Average agency level by domain and 2006 per capita household income percentile, and inequality indexes, 2006 and 2011/12.

Source: own elaboration based on ELBU data.

10 The Legal Status of Whales and Dolphins

From Bentham to the Capabilities Approach

RACHEL NUSSBAUM WICHERT AND
MARTHA C. NUSSBAUM

1 From Suffering to Personhood

The 2013 documentary *Blackfish*,[1] whose success ultimately led
SeaWorld to discontinue its orca (killer whale) program, revealed
the conditions under which orcas are kept in marine parks. One
disturbing aspect is that the whales are placed in an alien environment without stimulation. As one trainer interviewed for the film
remarked, "It just can't be good for an animal that is so intelligent to
do the same thing every day."[2] The whales' frustration led to aggressive behavior against each other. Deprived of the social environment
they were used to, one expert claims that the orcas became "mentally
disturbed."[3]

Our chapter addresses the issue of cetaceans (whales and dolphins)
and whether they can be accorded legal status in some situations. Some
major issues involved here are the situation of cetaceans in captivity
and their use in scientific experiments. These cases raise questions of
animal welfare and seem to us to involve a broader concept of animal
rights or entitlements. Many animal rights activists have opposed both
these practices because of the suffering of the animals involved, stating
that the rights of particular animals should not be dependent on
whether or not they are "like" humans. While we agree that suffering
is an important criterion, it cannot be the only one. We argue that
intelligence and the ability to be social are qualities that are at least as
important. Indeed, there is a strong case for considering cetaceans
"non-human persons" and according them legal rights, most importantly standing to sue in their own right.

Why is this focus pertinent to development ethics? First of all, the case of marine mammals is a very good lens through which to examine more generally the treatment of a group of creatures with complex capacities and cultural formations.[4] This focus will help us to pose questions later about the adequacy of different theoretical approaches. But, there are also urgent practical issues. Developing countries are homes to most of the world's wildlife, and almost all of its large mammals. Developing nations control much of the territory that marine mammals, especially dolphins, inhabit.[5] Many developing countries manage theme parks and wildlife preserves that are basically large zoos, where animals are under human domination and are managed, typically, for human entertainment without sufficient ethical deliberation about the effect of this management on animal life opportunities. Moreover, these same countries routinely ship large mammals to zoos in developed countries without adequate ethical thought or quality-of-life safeguards.[6] The global community agrees in opposing poaching and trophy hunting, and developing countries at least try to limit these cruel practices, although not hard enough. The issue of adequate habitat and decent living conditions is the next frontier for the animal movement, and developing countries have not yet adequately faced it. It is time to face it now, with the best theoretical approach we can find.[7] Our argument takes cetaceans as its central example, but its conclusions apply also to those elephants shipped from Swaziland to zoos in Kansas and Nebraska, to the confinement of tigers in tourist theme parks in India, and to the treatment of elephants as tourist attractions (whether at temples or giving rides to tourists) all over South and Southeast Asia – all allegedly to benefit the animals themselves. Development ethics so far has paid far too little attention to animal ethics, and therefore to the important question of choosing an appropriate theoretical approach – while developing countries are daily making a range of choices that have a decisive impact on animal lives.

2 Cetaceans in Captivity

Since our approach will ultimately discuss both suffering and intelligence, we begin by discussing evidence indicating that whales and dolphins suffer in captivity precisely because of their highly developed intelligence and ability to reason. Aquariums and marine theme parks generally do not have settings that are in any way similar to what cetaceans experience in the wild. It is therefore likely that they are not behaving in a "natural" way in these settings. Thomas White, for example, in his *In Defense of Dolphins*, points out that dolphins have complex intelligence and social abilities, and argues that there is evidence that they have a culture. As he puts it, a dolphin is "a someone who perceives the world and makes decisions in a way similar to how we humans do."[8] White presents evidence that dolphins, along with many other non-human species, feel pain in a way that scientists have not understood until recently.[9] He also proposes that cetaceans might have "different rights" owing to the fact that they have intelligence, even if it is not human intelligence.[10] He goes on to discuss several different issues involving dolphins, such as fishing practices that inevitably endanger them. He proposes that dolphins are treated by humans as property, and that this is inconsistent with an ethical position on animals.[11] "Captivity is so controversial," writes White, "because it provides such a mixed picture of possible benefits and harms."[12] These facilities feed the animals well and provide them with entertainment, but the question is: Who benefits? It is possible that humans are generally the ones who benefit. It may be positive for people to visit theme parks in order to learn more about cetaceans, and this may have an impact on how they regard animals and the environment. However, the animals themselves may not be faring so well. "Perhaps the most important question is whether the social conditions in which captive dolphins live are sufficient to provide a satisfying and appropriate life ... significant relationships and meaningful group membership may be as critical to the well-being and development of dolphins as individual liberty and a sense of autonomy are to humans."[13]

Activists have also expressed concerns over the plight of orcas in captivity. The various locations of SeaWorld, for example, have repeatedly claimed that keeping the animals provides an opportunity to do scientific research.[14] Independent orca researchers have questioned this, however, claiming that SeaWorld provides little additional knowledge about orcas and that researchers affiliated with the park have failed to conduct peer-reviewed scientific studies on captive whales that would support their allegations.[15] Orcas are listed as endangered in both the United States and Canada. In conditions such as those prevailing at SeaWorld, they are forced to live in unnatural conditions and must do tricks for the entertainment of visitors. In addition, they cannot sustain the social networks that are crucial to them.

In fact, a member of the California state assembly, Richard Bloom, has introduced a bill to outlaw orca shows.[16] The Orca Welfare and Safety Act would provide for the rehabilitation of the orcas and return them to the wild where possible. If not, they would be "transferred and held in a sea pen that is open to the public and not used for performance or entertainment purposes."[17] While lawmakers in other states have passed similar legislation, these laws are purely symbolic as there are no facilities for captive orcas in their states. The situation in California, by contrast, would send a much more powerful message. Supporters of the bill contend that orcas are a "highly intelligent and social species" and should not be subjected to such treatment.[18] Five countries – India, Croatia, Hungary, Chile, and Costa Rica – have already banned all cetacean captivity.[19]

Many of these efforts were inspired by the success of the documentary *Blackfish* that documents the conditions at SeaWorld and the dangerous conditions for the trainers.[20] The film's director, Gabriela Cowperthwaite, was inspired by an article that appeared in the magazine *Outside* in 2010.[21] The article described the circumstances surrounding the death of Dawn Brancheau, an experienced trainer at SeaWorld in Orlando, Florida, who was killed by an orca attack in February 2010. Despite her extensive experience with the animals and commitment to their well-being, it appears Brancheau could not fight the conditions at SeaWorld that led to her death. Principally, the article argues, audiences were attracted by "the sight of one of the ocean's top predators performing like a circus animal."[22]

Indeed, until the 1960s, there were no orcas in aquariums and they certainly did not perform in shows.[23] The article credits the owners of the Seattle Aquarium with introducing the idea of capturing orcas in the wild and selling them. They started in Puget Sound, often using brutal methods including air attacks and explosives.[24] SeaWorld managed to net several hundred orcas during the 1960s and early 1970s. The Marine Mammal Protection Act became law in 1972 and forbade these activities, but SeaWorld continued to receive an exception for the purposes of educational display.[25] However, the state of Washington filed suit and prevented SeaWorld from capturing orcas in its waters. The two SeaWorld entrepreneurs continued their activities in Iceland.[26] One of the whales captured there was Tilikum, the male orca responsible for the death of Brancheau.

While SeaWorld's facilities are probably superior as far as marine parks go, the problems continued. There were continual incidents of attacks on trainers. In the film *Blackfish*, numerous trainers are interviewed stating that they had not been informed about these incidents and that they were genuinely unaware of the dangers they faced.[27] In addition, most trainers stated that they had little background or experience with marine mammals, and instead got their jobs because they had pleasant personalities and could swim well.[28] While working at SeaWorld they repeated information about such subjects as the life spans of orcas in the wild that was patently incorrect.[29] While even opponents of SeaWorld concede that their activities may have a legitimate educational function, whale researchers such as Naomi Rose question just how effective this education is. She states:

After they've just had a great day, most people are going to say, "Sure, you guys are great. You betcha I learned a lot." But what do they know after a visit? What do they do afterward? Public display doesn't actually teach people much. It just makes them feel good, which actually leads to less conservation action rather than more.[30]

Thus, while there may be some educational benefit, this brings us back to our original inquiry: Is it ethical to keep animals of such high intelligence in captivity? Furthermore, this practice has resulted in the deaths of humans.

Brancheau's death led to a suit against SeaWorld by the Occupational Safety and Health Administration. An initial ruling in May 2012 mandated that in the future the orcas would have to be separated from trainers.[31] SeaWorld appealed and the Court of Appeals for the District of Columbia Circuit ruled in favor of OSHA (Occupational Health & Safety) on April 11, 2014.[32] This decision, however, was fairly limited. Judge Judith W. Rogers stated that "The remedy imposed for SeaWorld's violations does not change the essential nature of its business ... There will still be human interactions and performances with killer whales; the remedy will simply require that they continue with increased safety measures."[33] The animal welfare issues thus remained largely unaddressed, but the case and the film undoubtedly brought greater publicity to the situation of orcas.

3 Legal Interventions and the Problem of Standing

Considerations such as these animated members of People for the Ethical Treatment of Animals when they sued SeaWorld's facilities in Orlando and San Diego over their treatment of orcas in captivity. Notably, this case involved Tilikum, the subject of the controversy. The group Next Friends, composed of members of PETA, filed a complaint for declaratory and injunctive relief, "seeking a declaration that the named wild-captured orcas are being 'held by the Defendants in violation of Section One of the Thirteenth Amendment to the Constitution of the United States, which prohibits slavery and involuntary servitude.'"[34] Next Friends emphasized that "the confinement of the orcas in barren concrete tanks negatively impacts them in many ways, including the suppression of Plaintiffs' cultural traditions and deprives them of the ability to make conscious choices and of the environmental enrichment required to stimulate Plaintiffs mentally and physically for their well-being."[35] While the orcas were born free, Next Friends argued that they were equivalent to slaves because they were

(1) held physically and psychologically captive; (2) without the means of escape; (3) separated from their homes and families; (4) unable to engage in natural behaviors and determine their own course of action or way of life; (5) subjugated to the will and desires of SeaWorld; (6) confined in unnatural, stressful and inadequate conditions; and (7) subject to artificial insemination or sperm collection for the purposes of involuntary breeding.[36]

SeaWorld argued that the plaintiffs lacked Article III standing to bring the action. This was a case of first impression because there were no authorities applying the Thirteenth Amendment to non-persons.[37] The court agreed and explained its reasoning as follows: "The only reasonable interpretation of the Thirteenth Amendment's plain language is that it applies to persons, and not to non-persons such as orcas."[38] The claim was therefore dismissed under Rule 12 (b) (1) for lack of subject matter jurisdiction.[39] However, the court emphasized that "Even though Plaintiffs lack standing to bring a Thirteenth Amendment claim, that is not to say that animals have no legal rights."[40]

The court in *Tilikum* concluded that orcas do not have standing to sue under Article III. The court in *Cetacean Community* v. *Bush* reached a similar conclusion.[41] This was a case in which an invented group, "the world's cetaceans," sought to bring suit under the Endangered Species Act (ESA), the Marine Mammal Protection Act (MMPA), the National Environmental Protection Act (NEPA), and the Administrative Procedure Act (APA).[42] The impetus for the suit was the US Navy's use of sonar to detect submarines. This has been proven to have negative effects on marine mammals: The practice "harms them by causing tissue damage and other serious injuries, and by disrupting biologically important behaviors including feeding and mating."[43] The Ninth Circuit ruled, however, that the cetaceans did not have standing to sue under any of these statutes, and that the district court was correct to dismiss the case under Rule 12 (b) (6) for failure to state a claim.[44]

Here, the Court considered some previous cases involving animals that appeared to hold that an endangered species has standing to sue. However, it concluded that the relevant statements in these cases are nonbinding dicta.[45] In the case of a suit to enforce the ESA, *Palila v. Hawaii Department of Land and Natural Resources*, the Ninth Circuit stated that the Hawaiian Palila bird had legal standing.[46] However, in the case of the cetaceans, the court concluded that these statements "were little more than rhetorical flourishes. They were certainly not intended to be a statement of law, binding on future panels, that animals have standing to bring suit in their own name under the ESA."[47]

However, the court in *Cetacean Community* also stated that "nothing in the text of Article III explicitly limits the ability to bring a claim in federal court to humans."[48] There are many federal and state laws that protect animals, but these generally concern more obvious abuses of animals and are already prohibited by statute.[49] Instead, the concern seems to be that Congress has never authorized a suit in the name of an animal.[50] None of the several statues mentioned – the ESA, the MMPA, NEPA, and the APA – explicitly authorize lawsuits. Associational standing is also not adequate, because "A generic requirement for associational standing is that an association's 'members would otherwise have standing to sue in their own right.'"[51] The Cetacean Community could therefore not prevail in this case, because its members did not have standing to sue.

The major problem here is that no court has decided that animals have standing comparable to that of persons. In the absence of any such decision, animals are not considered to have any sort of legal status comparable to "personhood." In this situation, it does not matter whether their legal disadvantage is based on the principle of reason or is instead based on suffering. Until these statutory issues are resolved, there cannot even be any discussion.

4 Non-Human Personhood: Bentham and the Rationale of Suffering

How might cetaceans be able to demonstrate a status as "non-human persons"? We now consider three possibilities: a Utilitarian approach based on suffering, an anthropomorphic approach based on reason and intelligence, and finally, a capabilities approach based upon the striving of these creatures to live a flourishing life characteristic of their species.

Jeremy Bentham departed from the conventional Judeo-Christian view of animals when he discussed their plight in his *Introduction to the Principles of Morals and Legislation*. In discussing the criminal branch of legislation, Bentham argued that ethics is "the art of directing men's actions to the production of the greatest possible quantity of happiness, on the part of those whose interest is in view."[52] Men can direct either their own actions or those of other agents, a group that includes "Other animals, which, on account of their interests having been neglected by the insensibility of the ancient jurists, stand degraded into the class of <u>things</u>."[53] While some religions have addressed the situation of animals, Bentham argues that the law of his day has completely neglected them. He does not see any justification for this. In his day, public discourse had evolved considerably on the topic of slavery, and there is no reason why animals should not receive the same consideration:

The day has been, I grieve to say in many places it is not yet past; in which the greater part of the species, under the denomination of slaves, have been treated by the law exactly upon the same footing as, in England for example, the inferior races of animals are still. The day *may* come, when the rest of the animal creation may secure those rights which never could have been with-holden from them but for the hand of tyranny.[54]

Bentham does not base his advocacy for animals on the idea that some species can reason in ways that are at least close to humans. The focus of his inquiry is different. He points out that even if the correct standard were the possession of reason, this standard would not defend the species line: "[A] full-grown horse or dog is beyond comparison a more rational, as well as a more conversable animal, than an infant of a day." But, in fact, reason is not the correct standard: "The question is not, Can they <u>reason</u>? nor, can they <u>talk</u>? but, can they <u>suffer</u>?"[55] This is an approach currently followed by many prominent animal rights activists, notably Peter Singer, who also bases his arguments on suffering.[56] And, this is what Bentham believes to be relevant in thinking about human action as well. Throughout his philosophical work, he consistently argues that pleasure and pain are simple sensations, varying in (a) intensity, (b) duration, (c) certainty or uncertainty, and (d) propinquity or remoteness. Pleasures and pains have many different sources, but pleasure itself contains no qualitative variations.

Bentham was especially eager to reject the familiar Christian view that there are "higher pleasures" and "lower pleasures" and that the pleasures of the body were inferior to the pleasures of the mind. In work that was not published during his lifetime, but has only very recently become available from the Bentham Project at University College London, he argues strongly for the decriminalization of homosexual relations, using the view of pleasure to argue that the source of a pleasure makes no difference at all to its quality as pleasure, and that there is no rational argument for restrictions on consensual sexual expression.[57]

Thus, we can now see that Bentham's insistence on the similarity between animals and humans in respect of pain and pleasure is part of a far-reaching program of repudiating puritanical British attitudes to the body, which surely underlay Victorian views of the human–animal divide.[58] But, the interest in animals was very genuine: Numerous remarks of Bentham himself and his devoted editor John Bowring testify to his fondness for a wide range of animals, including cats, donkeys, pigs, and mice. He cultivated a friendship with a pig who used to follow him around on his walks. A cat whom he named Reverend John Langborn used to eat macaroni at the table with him. He loved to have mice play in his study and eat crumbs from his lap. "I love everything that has four legs," he wrote. He used to recall with dismay the cruelties that he himself had inflicted on animals as a child, and the salutary effect that his uncle's reproaches had on him.[59]

Bentham's position was not radical in our contemporary terms. While he opposed the gratuitous infliction of pain on animals, and hence rejected hunting and fishing for sport, he did not oppose all killing and eating of animals. He reasoned that a painless death was not a harm to an animal, since such a death was less painful than the death that animals would meet in the course of nature.[60] But, the position had radical potential: Had he known of factory farming, he surely would have rejected it as a form of torture. And, his position was certainly radical for his day, as Gary Francione explains:

Bentham's position marked a sharp departure from a cultural tradition that had never before regarded animals as other than things devoid of morally significant interests ... For Bentham, our treatment of animals matters because of its effect on beings that can suffer, and our duties are owed directly to them. Bentham urged the enactment of laws to prevent animals from suffering.[61]

Indeed, many early animal welfare acts were inspired by Bentham's views.[62] However, Bentham did not question the traditional view of animals as property, something that limited the force of his argument.[63] No doubt the failure to raise this issue is explained by the fact that the defense of animals is in a lengthy footnote in what is otherwise a treatise on the criminal law, not on property law.

It can be argued, however, that this avoidance of the property issue undermines the cause of animal welfare as well as animal rights. As Francione concludes:

The property status of animals renders meaningless any balancing that is supposedly required under the humane treatment principle or animal welfare laws, because what they really balance are the interests of property owners against the interests of their animal property ... We are allowed to impose any suffering required to use our animal property for a particular purpose even if that purpose is our mere amusement or pleasure.[64]

Bentham's comparisons to slavery highlight the problem, for in order to make the case for slavery as a moral wrong, it is necessary not to be swayed by arguments that some slaveholders treated their slaves well.[65] While Bentham regarded the concept of rights as "metaphysical nonsense," he did recognize that people had the right not to be treated as property. His arguments regarding animals were primarily based on the idea that animals did not have self-awareness, and no significant interest in their own existence beyond avoiding suffering.[66] It is unclear whether his simple form of hedonism can even deal adequately with the wrongfulness of slavery; subsequent Utilitarians have struggled with this problem. Putting that question to one side, we argue here that simple hedonism is not an adequate basis for an account of animal entitlements, if these include not just the right not to be tortured but also the right not to be used as property.

The Benthamite conception of animal welfare has obvious appeal in US law, where it has long been recognized that a – if not *the* – major obstacle to legal progress in this area is the doctrine of standing. In order to have standing to go to court, a creature needs to be directly affected by the conduct in question. And, suffering is remarkably direct! For this reason legal theorist Cass R. Sunstein has argued that suffering provides the best basis for making progress on the thorny issue of standing for animals, and that it is a sufficient basis, without resolving the property issue. The relatively small number of cases brought on behalf on animals might seem to suggest that the standing issue cannot be resolved without first resolving the property issue. And, the image of animals as human property is one that many animal advocates have historically found difficult to overcome. However, Sunstein argues that the conflict of property with the standing issue is not necessarily an insuperable obstacle. In a well-known article, he questions the idea that regarding animals as property is an automatic bar to according them legal standing:

If the status of property means the status of mere means to the ends of others, or a status of human domination and control, animals should not have the status of property. But even inanimate objects can be, and are, protected against full domination and control ... I do not believe that it is necessary to consider animals to be persons, or to insist on certain cognitive powers in order to say that, by virtue of their capacity to suffer, they deserve legal rights against cruelty, abuse and neglect.[67]

Theoretically, then, it should not matter whether animals are entitled to a status comparable to that of humans. Suffering should be enough. However, as Sunstein goes on to say, "the rhetoric does matter. In the long term, it would indeed make sense to think of animals as something other than property, partly in order to clarify their status as beings with rights of their own."[68] And, in practice, the appeal to suffering has clearly not proved to be adequate. A response to Sunstein's article, written by Elizabeth DeCoux, reveals more about why the rationale of suffering will not be successful in courts.[69] DeCoux rightly states that courts' treatment of animal standing has been extremely inconsistent.[70] Federal statutes have failed to resolve this problem.[71] She suggests that more humane means of keeping animals in captivity, or experimenting on them, are an illusion, and that the laws established for these purposes are essentially an excuse for further abuse of animals.[72] Thus, she suggests that an approach focusing on suffering – even if it did resolve the standing issue – would be insufficiently radical to effect productive change. Even when courts have recognized standing, they did not explain the reasoning for their decision, "thus leaving the law regarding the standing of animals sufficiently unclear so as to allow room for equally unexplained decisions reaching the opposite result."[73]

Bentham's hedonism has one big appealing feature: its universal concern for bodies and for bodies in pain. Bentham really did see the world as populated by a wide range of sentient beings, all deserving a happy existence. His opposition to qualitative distinctions between pleasures was motivated by a concern to return ethics to the body, and this concern embraced all animal bodies. In the end, however, the theoretical apparatus of the position has grave limits. We have pointed to some of the practical limits, in terms of the law. We now turn to the theoretical limits.

5 The Rationale of Intelligence

John Stuart Mill, Bentham's great Utilitarian pupil and partial follower, argued that Bentham's hedonism was too simple: for pleasures differ in quality as well as in quantity.[74] In this important critique, Mill unfortunately blurs two completely different issues: (a) do pleasures differ in quality as well as quantity? and (b) are some pleasures "higher" or "lower" than others? Mill might have said "yes" to the first question while saying "no" to the second. In other words, he might have said, plausibly and truly, that the pleasure of eating a peach is different from the pleasure of chatting with a friend, but that there is no sensible reason to rank one above or below the other. In that way, Mill would have kept Bentham's radical assault on puritanical British prudery about the body while making his doctrine more subtle. But, being a product of the Victorian era, he blurred the two questions together. He suggests that it is only by showing that mental pleasures are superior to bodily pleasures that one can show that pleasures differ in quality.

Mill ignores an important option of great interest to the theorist of animal entitlements, then, when he insists on the primacy of mental pleasures. He was intensely concerned with animal suffering, leaving the bulk of his estate at his death to the Society for the Prevention of Cruelty to Animals. And in his "Reply to Whewell,"[75] he effectively assails the Christian conservative's position that the human being is made in God's image and therefore properly dominates the entirety of creation. Nonetheless, he retains an important part of Whewell's conservative position when he asserts that mental pleasures (that he thinks peculiar to human beings) are "higher." He retains the traditional image of a "ladder of nature" that demotes animals.

Mill's position is inadequate as a basis for animal entitlements. Still, it must be admitted that the Victorian era has not really ended in this regard: Most people do think that humans are superior to animals on account of their mental powers. Having already ranked the mental above the bodily, they then deny that animals partake in the mental. This is probably the most common type of position in contemporary ethical thought, and it has been used in just the way Bentham would have predicted, to rank all animals below all humans.[76]

There are two errors in this position: the ranking of the mental above the bodily, and the denial that animals partake in the mental. Since the first error is very difficult to dislodge, and since lawyers need to deal with real judges, who (in our post-Victorian Judeo-Christian culture) are almost certain to agree with Mill and disagree with Bentham, it might make sense to focus on the second error, the denial of intelligence and cognitive capacity to animals.[77]

The fact that animals of many types exhibit intelligence and cognitive capacity of many types has been known for a long time. Aristotle's keen observations of animals led him to recognize many types of commonality between humans and animals with respect to goal-directed practical reasoning and cognitively rich emotions.[78] But, the intervening ascendancy of the Judeo-Christian tradition in the West (abetted by Greco-Roman Stoicism, which asserted that non-human animals were mere "brutes" without intelligence) caused the eclipse of these promising insights in Europe and North America.[79] Recently, however, a flood of new research on the cognitive capacities of animals has made Aristotle's insights impossible to deny. Animals as allegedly "low" as rats and mice exhibit complicated forms of practical reasoning, as well as the beginnings of complex emotions.[80] Even in Kantian moral philosophy, which has traditionally split the world into rational beings, who have a "dignity," and sub-rational beings, who have a "price," the insight that animals are our "fellow creatures," sharing many commonalities with us and partaking in goal-directed behavior, has now become firmly entrenched thanks to the pioneering work of philosopher Christine Korsgaard.[81] These new/old insights seem potentially productive for law.

For some time, legal scholar and animal advocate Stephen Wise has urged that lawyers pursuing animal rights focus their attention on the obvious attributes of personhood that a few animal species, such as chimps and other apes, can be seen to share, and use these evident commonalities as a wedge in order to get the law to recognize some species of animals as persons for legal purposes.[82] It would be easy, in the light of recent research, to broaden Wise's approach, admitting quite a few more species into the category of "persons."

Back, now, to the standing debate: DeCoux alleges that Sunstein is incorrect when he concludes that the words "person" and "individual," as expressed in statutes, necessarily exclude animals.[83] It is also likely, as she alleges, that federal judges are unwilling to examine their own prejudices in such a way as to reconsider the situation of animals. But, perhaps they can be led to do so through judicious use of evidence and example. Activists can stress the "person" aspect of this debate, using appeals to cognition, intelligence, and even culture. Such an approach can provide a much more solid basis to standing for animals. One court in India, the High Court of Kerala, has already recognized a wide range of animals as persons within the meaning of the term "person" in the Indian Constitution. "Though not homo sapiens," the court concludes, "they are also beings entitled to dignified existence and humane treatment . . . Therefore, it is not only our fundamental duty to show compassion to our animal friends, but also to recognize and protect their rights . . . If humans are entitled to fundamental rights, why not animals?"[84] It is not surprising that an Indian court would take this step before courts in Europe and North America, where the Judeo-Christian tradition has long impeded recognition of common personhood. Still, the knowledge we currently have is undeniable, and it strongly supports this recognition.

A modified Millean proposal, then, could retain the focus on intelligence and cognitive capacity as hallmarks of legal personhood, but insist that some species of animals possess these characteristics. This approach seems particularly well suited to winning legal rights for marine mammals, since dolphins have long been recognized as a species extremely high in intelligence. They are able to pass the "mirror test"[85] and exhibit resourceful goal-directed behavior to at least as high a degree as chimps and bonobos. Whales too, though more mysterious to humans and difficult to study, have long been recognized as having an extremely high level of intelligence, including a signaling system that lies close to language and complex forms of socially learned interaction that amount to culture.[86] Whales and dolphins cannot be said to be "like" humans in terms of DNA, but they have their own form of intelligence and deserve protection under the law.

We do not wish to deny that this approach is legally promising, and perhaps it is the most legally promising approach to the treatment of marine mammals under current conditions. Recognizing these creatures' intelligence and social capacity, the law would also recognize that they are entitled not to be deprived of conditions necessary to the unfolding of these capacities. This approach moves beyond Bentham in the sense that not only manifest physical suffering, but also deprivation of free movement and community, would count as deprivations of which the law could take cognizance. Judges could, we believe, be persuaded of this without large-level cultural changes.

Nonetheless, we believe that this approach has two related defects that make it ultimately inadequate. First is the defect identified by Bentham in the moralities of his time: the exaltation of mental life to "higher" status and the demotion of bodily feeling to "lower" status. In the end, it is difficult to craft an adequate theoretical approach to the situation of animals as long as we permit anxiety and disgust about the body to influence our legal judgments. Theorists who study the influence of disgust in society and law have concluded that the roots of disgust toward marginalized groups (whether lower castes in India or racial minorities in the United States) lie in the dominant group's anxiety about its own animality and mortality. The characteristics that are rejected and imputed to disfavored groups are precisely those characteristics that humans tend to associate with animal bodies (smells, fluids, excretion, blood, etc.). And they hold that it is because humans shrink from acknowledging their own animality that they create groups of disfavored humans who are characterized as "mere animals," and potential contaminants to "higher" humans.[87] How perverse, then, it would be to upgrade the status of animals precisely by focusing on traits that we associate with the exalted above-the-animal status of the human (us). It's like saying: "Most animals are foul and smelly and mere bodies, but these animals, by contrast, are have nice clean minds." This self-deceptive strategy, which denies a great part of what we actually are, can hardly be a good basis for respecting our fellow creatures.

The second related problem with the "intelligence" approach is that it values animals because and only insofar as they are similar to us; it thus fails to respect them in their own right. It takes no interest in their distinctive forms of life and intelligence. And, of course, it will end up giving adequate protections only to those who can demonstrate quasi-humanness, thus not to a wide range of animal species. This may be the best we can do in the law right now, pragmatically. But, the downside of this strategy is that it could set back efforts to protect all but a few chosen species.

6 From Bentham to the Capabilities Approach

Our study of Bentham and Mill has given us some parameters for a truly adequate legal approach. Like Bentham, such an approach should take suffering extremely seriously. Like Mill, however, it should recognize a wide range of activities and experiences, differing in quality and not reducible to simple pains and pleasures. Like Bentham, it should refuse a ranking of lives and experiences, and should be especially skeptical of any ranking that encodes conventional anxieties about the body. Like Mill, however, it should refuse to reduce all value to pleasure and pain, simply understood, and should recognize the dignity of a wide range of forms of life.[88] In short, the approach should have Mill's inclusiveness and his sensitivity to qualitative differences without Mill's Victorian prejudices. It should have Bentham's radical edge without Bentham's reductivism.

And, there is one more thing such an approach must contain: a concept, or rather concepts, of animal agency–the idea, that is, that animals are not merely passive recipients of experience, but shapers of lives.[89] To be adequate to the complexity and variety of animal lives, the notion of agency must be developed in a flexible and species-specific way, and this will require intimate and detailed knowledge of each animal species. But, for all, there is something that is it to be a maker of a life. And, in political terms, although animals will not be democratic citizens along the lines of familiar human models of democracy, there is something to respecting animals as democratic agents, participants in the shaping of the world we share with them.[90] Respect for agency is lacking in Utilitarian approaches and underdeveloped in approaches that focus on intelligence. Rights-based approaches do better.[91] And, the Capabilities Approach is one species of a rights-based approach, in that it argues for fundamental entitlements grounded in justice. But, the challenge for such an approach is to develop a notion, or notions of agency in terms of an Aristotelian notion of a form of life actively striving for its characteristic end.[92]

The Capabilities Approach is able to take on this challenge. Like Bentham, it values all sentient beings and their lives: Animals for us, as for Bentham, are "friends," not servants or property. Lives are not ranked in a vertical hierarchy; instead, there is curiosity and respect for the lives of all, as they are, exhibiting in each case the distinctive capacities and activities of each. Bentham never spoke of wonder, and he might have made fun of that idea, but he did exhibit what we regard as morally inflected wonder when he valued the complexity – and the dignity – of animal lives and formed respectful friendships with animals of many types.[93]

This approach has Bentham's radicalism, but it rejects his reductivism. Sentience is important, pain is very important, but so too are a wide range of other opportunities for functioning: free and characteristic movement, access to relationships with other species members, opportunities for cognitive stimulation, variety, and delight, protection of bodily integrity. In each case, we need to learn enough to form a normative picture of the flourishing life of a creature of the appropriate type, and then to see clearly what real-world conditions unjustly impede flourishing. Nussbaum's capabilities list gives abstract guidance, but in each case the capabilities to which animals are entitled must be fleshed out in terms of species-specific ideas of opportunities for active functioning.

The Capabilities Approach does not hold that every capacity a creature has must be developed. Instead, it operates with a normative picture of flourishing for each type, trying to figure out, as well as possible, what opportunities for active functioning are essential. Thus, it is a likely result of such an approach that chimps do not need to be taught sign language: They can learn it and that fact is of scientific interest – to humans, but it does not form part of a chimpanzee form of flourishing life. Other communicative modalities are favored by chimps in their own community.

The Capabilities Approach recognizes that animals may not suffer consciously when deprived of an opportunity for some type of valued functioning and agency. Like humans, they can exhibit "adaptive preferences," going along with a deprivation of movement, or society, without forming a clear picture of what is missing. So the Capabilities Approach in that way goes beyond even Mill's Utilitarianism, recognizing that suffering is not the only thing to be avoided, even once we adopt a variegated and expanded notion of suffering. Once again, the idea of animals as intelligent agents is crucial: Not just receptacles of experience, they are, and should be seen to be, makers of their own lives.

Can such an approach guide law? Obviously it is slippery and complicated, but it has the advantage of being the way scientists think about the complexity of animal lives, and the way that ethically sensitive people think too, once they begin to think. Animal lives are unfolding stories of striving, and it is very intuitive to think this way. When people think about marine mammals, big abstractions such as "personhood" and "suffering" are difficult to think with, but the story of a life-form that seeks certain types of activity and strives for a variegated interactive social life is intuitively compelling. So, we believe that courts could ultimately think this way, infusing the legal notion of "personhood" with rich species-specific content. This in effect is what the Indian court did, when it ruled that confining circus animals in a tiny space and making them perform silly tricks was an infringement of the personhood and dignity of beings who are not human and have their own form of life. Another apt example of such an approach, with potential implications for law, is the work of Thomas White on dolphins, which we have already discussed in Section 2. Although White is not a theorist, his approach dovetails well with the Capabilities Approach, and shows how such an approach can be adapted to the needs of law.

What this approach means in general is that orcas, other whales, and dolphins are entitled to opportunities to exercise their major capabilities, social and physical, which means at least: to move freely in a large space, to interact regularly and in an unforced way with other species members, to be free from intrusions into their bodily integrity. Confinement makes the fulfillment of these conditions difficult, but perhaps not impossible if the facility is, for example, a large wildlife park with ample free space. Zoos almost never afford sufficient protection for the capabilities of large mammals. But, for marine mammals, White's work with dolphins suggests that captivity is particularly objectionable because of the capability deprivation it involves. Many criticisms of captivity focus only on substandard facilities. White raises the question "whether even the best facilities operate in a way that is ethically defensible. That is ... it should be apparent that dolphins are sophisticated beings with a complex set of needs. Can captive facilities provide the conditions that would have to be met so that dolphins who inhabit them are able to meet the fundamental needs of their species?"[94] Defenders of captivity point out that it provides benefits to both cetaceans and humans. These arguments are not utterly pointless, but they are not sufficient. Cetaceans in captivity are not able to engage in the social networks they create in the wild. The Capabilities Approach helps us see what is wrong with such facilities. Agency, not just passive welfare, is at issue.[95]

Furthermore, the main purpose of captive facilities is human entertainment. White concludes that "The idea of treating a species of self-aware beings with a sophisticated consciousness as 'property', not 'persons', and breeding them with an eye toward the traits that will make them most useful commercially has chilling similarities with the practice of human slavery."[96] Both in this case and in others, the most difficult question our approach will face in the area of marine mammals in confinement is the one the Indian court faced: teaching tricks that amuse humans. With symbiotic species such as dogs and horses, some of the characteristic functions of the species are interactive, and some involve learned forms of athletic excellence. There is nothing wrong with training, and a horse humanely trained to jump over fences may achieve a type of flourishing unavailable to a horse that is let out to pasture its entire life. But, with non-symbiotic species, the question is far more difficult. An elephant wearing a pink tutu seems clearly objectionable, a way of amusing humans by offending against the dignity of the animal. But, what about an elephant elaborately body-painted and taught to greet visitors to a Hindu temple? An elephant that uses its strength to roll logs, and is lovingly trained and kept in excellent conditions?[97]

Marine mammals pose many such difficult questions. Are dolphins more like horses, exhibiting athletic excellences with delight and alacrity? Or, are these tricks more like putting an elephant into a pink tutu? Should we be delighted that dolphins form interactive cultures with humans in some fishing communities, or should we see these cultures as unjustified interventions into animal lives?[98] Should orcas be kept from all symbiotic contact with humans, or should friendship be encouraged?[99] These questions can only be answered well once we have a comprehensive understanding of the forms of life of these creatures, which we do not yet have. But, the Capabilities Approach shows us the right questions to ask. Once we have a normative account of orca and dolphin lives, we can assess the damages done by SeaWorld and other related organizations, damages that include suffering, but go well beyond that. And then, some day, we can ask judges to use their moral imaginations to consider the entirety of these forms of life and to hold human beings accountable for protecting animal capabilities.

Postscript, July 15, 2016

We have happy confirmation today of our contention that US courts are able to move in the direction of the approach we recommend. In *Natural Resources Defense Council* v. *Pritzker*,[100] the US Court of Appeals for the Ninth Circuit ruled that the US Navy violated the law in seeking to continue a sonar program that impacted the behavior of whales. To some extent the opinion is a technical exercise in statutory interpretation of the Marine Mammals Protection Act. The court says that the fact that a program has "negligible impact" on marine mammals does not exempt it from a separate statutory requirement, namely that it establish means of "effecting the least practicable adverse impact on" marine mammal species. What is significant, and fascinating, is that the argument relies heavily on a consideration of whale capabilities that the program disrupts:

Effects from exposures below 180 dB can cause short-term disruption of abandonment of natural behavior patterns. These behavioral disruptions can cause affected marine mammals to stop communicating with each other, to flee or avoid an ensonified area, to cease foraging for food, to separate from their calves, and to interrupt mating. LFA sonar can also cause heightened stress responses from marine mammals. Such behavioral disruptions can force marine mammals to make trade-offs like delaying migration, delaying reproduction, reducing growth, or migrating with reduced energy reserves.[101]

The opinion does not give whales standing; no such radical move is necessary to reach the clear result that the program is unacceptable. But, it does recognize whales as beings with a complex and active form of life that includes emotional well-being, affiliation, and free movement: in short, a variety of species-specific forms of agency. The opinion goes well beyond Bentham, and it also eschews the anthropocentric approach. It is a harbinger, we believe, of a new era in the law of animal welfare.

Notes

1. *Blackfish*, directed by Gabriela Cowperthwaite (Cowperthwaite 2013).
2. *Ibid.*
3. *Ibid.* In 2016, after several years of declining attendance, SeaWorld announced that it was discontinuing its orca breeding program; the current generation would be the last to be kept there.
4. For a philosophically sophisticated analysis of the notion of culture in connection with marine mammals, but with more general implications, see Hal Whitehead and Luke Rendell, *The Cultural Lives of Whales and Dolphins* (Whitehead and Rendell 2015).
5. See *ibid.*, esp. 110–13, on dolphin–human interactions in a variety of fishing-dependent developing countries, including India, Mauritania, Burma, and Brazil. Another development ethics issue, inside the jurisdiction of some developed countries, is the interaction of marine mammals with indigenous communities, for example Inuit communities in Canada. See Wichert and Nussbaum, "Legal Protection for Whales: Capabilities, Entitlements, and Culture," in *Animals, Race and Multiculturalism: Contemporary Moral and Political Debates*, ed. Cordeiro Rodrigues (Wichert and Nussbaum 2017).
6. A typical case is the importation of elephants from Swaziland to US zoos, in which both authors of this chapter were involved: Friends of Animals, the organization with which Wichert works as a research attorney, sought an injunction against the importation. Wichert helped draft the motion and M. Nussbaum filed an amicus brief. Nonetheless, the elephants were imported in the dead of night, while the motion was still pending in a US federal court. See Oliver Milman, "US Zoos Secretly Fly 18 Elephants out of Swaziland Ahead of Court Challenge," *The Guardian* (Milman 2016). The purported

justification for the airlift was a local drought, but evidence of this was scant and financial motives clearly played a part.

7. See Sue Donaldson and Will Kymlicka, *Zoopolis: A Political Theory of Animal Rights* (Donaldson and Kymlicka 2011, ch. 6), arguing that we must turn from an exclusive focus on ending cruel practices to a focus on habitat and on the morality of various allegedly "positive interventions" in the lives of wild animals.

8. Thomas I. White, *In Defense of Dolphins: The New Moral Frontier* (White 2007, 4–5).

9. *Ibid.*, 11.

10. *Ibid.*, 13.

11. *Ibid.*, 195.

12. *Ibid.*, 200–1.

13. *Ibid.*, 205.

14. Tasneem Raja, "SeaWorld Says it Has to Keep Orcas in Captivity to Save Them," *Mother Jones* (Raja 2014).

15. *Ibid.*

16. David Kirby, "SeaWorld's Worst Nightmare: Calif. Lawmaker to Propose Ban on Orcas in Captivity," *TakePart* (Kirby 2014).

17. *Ibid.*

18. *Ibid.*

19. *Ibid.*

20. *Blackfish.*

21. Tim Zimmermann, "The Killer in the Pool," *Outside Online* (Zimmermann 2010).

22. *Ibid.*

23. *Ibid.*

24. *Ibid.*

25. *Ibid.*

26. *Ibid.*

27. *Blackfish.*

28. *Ibid.*

29. *Ibid.* See also David Kirby, *Death at SeaWorld: Shamu and the Dark Side of Killer Whales in Captivity* (Kirby 2012, 95).

30. Quoted in Kirby (2012, 350).

31. *Ibid.*

32. OSHA, "OSHA Wins SeaWorld Case" (OSHA 2014).

33. *Ibid.*

34. *Tilikum ex rel. People for the Ethical Treatment of Animals, Inc. v. Sea World Parks and Entertainment, Inc.*, 842 F. Supp.2d 1259 (SD Ca. 2012).

35. *Ibid.* at 1261.

36. *Ibid.*
37. *Ibid.* at 1262.
38. *Ibid.* at 1263.
39. *Ibid.*
40. *Ibid.* at 1264.
41. *Cetacean Community* v. *Bush*, 386 F. 3d 1169 (9th Cir. 2004).
42. *Ibid.* at. 1171.
43. *Ibid.* at 1172.
44. *Ibid.* at 1173.
45. *Ibid.*
46. *Palila* v. *Hawaii Department of Land and Natural Resources*, 852 F. 2d 1106, 1107 (9th Cir. 1988).
47. *Cetacean Community* v. *Bush* at 1174.
48. *Ibid.* at 1175.
49. *Ibid.*
50. *Ibid.*
51. *Ibid.* at 1179, citing *Friends of the Earth, Inc.* v. *Laidlaw Envtl. Servs. (TOC), Inc.*, 528 US 167 (2000).
52. Jeremy Bentham, *An Introduction to the Principles of Morals and Legislation* (Bentham [1789] 2007, 310).
53. *Ibid.*
54. *Ibid.*, 311, fn. 1. For a full examination of all known texts of Bentham relating to animals, see Jadran Lee, *Bentham on the Moral and Legal Status of Animals* (Lee 2003).
55. *Ibid.*
56. Peter Singer, *Animal Liberation* (Singer 2002).
57. Jeremy Bentham, *Not Paul, but Jesus, Vol. III: Doctrine* (Bentham [1817] 2013).
58. A valuable anthology giving extracts from centuries of thought about this question is *Animal Rights and Human Obligations*, edited by Tom Regan and Peter Singer (Regan and Singer 1989).
59. For the sources of these and other anecdotes, see Lea Campus Boralevi, *Bentham and the Oppressed* (Boralevi 1984, 166).
60. See Bentham ([1789] 2007, 311).
61. Gary L. Francione, "Animals: Property or Persons?" in Cass R. Sunstein and Martha C. Nussbaum, *Animal Rights: Current Debates and New Directions* (Francione 2004, 113). Francione's "never before" is incorrect; it omits the much higher valuation of animal capacities and their ethical worth in most ancient Greek and Roman philosophical schools, particularly Neo-Platonism. See Richard Sorabji, *Animal Minds and Human Morals: The Origins of the Western Debate* (Sorabji 1993).

62. *Ibid.*
63. *Ibid.*, 116.
64. *Ibid.*, 117.
65. *Ibid.*, 126.
66. *Ibid.*
67. Cass Sunstein, "Standing for Animals (with Notes on Animal Rights)," *UCLA Law Review* (Sunstein 2000, 1365). See also Sunstein, "Can Animals Sue?" in Sunstein and Nussbaum (Sunstein 2004, 251–62).
68. *Ibid.*
69. Elizabeth L. DeCoux, "In the Valley of the Dry Bones: Reuniting the Word 'Standing': With Its Meaning in Animal Cases," *William & Mary Environmental Law and Policy Review* (DeCoux 2005).
70. *Ibid.*
71. *Ibid.*, 685.
72. *Ibid.*, 697.
73. *Ibid.*, 732.
74. Mill, *Utilitarianism*, in John Stuart Mill and Jeremy Bentham, *Utilitarianism and Other Essays*, ed. Alan Ryan (Mill [1861] 1987, 279).
75. See *ibid.*, 228–71.
76. See for example Richard Kraut, "What is Intrinsic Goodness?" *Classical Philology* (Kraut 2010, 450–62).
77. Such is the approach of Whitehead and Rendell with marine mammals (above); similar conclusions are reached by Joshua Horwitz in *War of the Whales* (Horwitz 2015). A magisterial account of what we currently know about animal intelligence is Frans de Waal, *Are We Smart Enough to Know How Smart Animals Are?* (De Waal (2016). See also Jennifer Ackerman, *The Genius of Birds* (Ackerman 2016).
78. See his treatise *On the Motion of Animals*, which offers a "common explanation" for the goal-directed movements of human and non-human animals. See Martha Nussbaum *Aristotle's De Motu Animalium* (Nussbaum 1978), an edition and commentary.
79. See Sorabji (1993). Such insights were present continuously in Indian traditions, both Buddhist and Hindu, although Buddhist traditions are more consistent in showing concern for all animals, not just a few favored species.
80. In addition to the sources mentioned in n. 77, see David DeGrazia, *Taking Animals Seriously: Mental Life and Moral Status* (DeGrazia 1996). For some experiments developing these insights further, see Martha Nussbaum, "The Capabilities Approach and Animal Entitlements," in *Oxford Handbook of Animal Ethics*, ed. Tom

Beauchamp (Nussbaum 2011b). On social cognition, see the important collection *Animal Social Complexity: Intelligence, Culture, and Individualized Societies*, edited by de Waal and Tyack (De Waal and Tyack 2000).

81. Christine Korsgaard, "Fellow Creatures: Kantian Ethics and Our Duties to Animals," *Tanner Lectures on Human Values* (Korsgaard 2004).

82. Stephen Wise, *Rattling the Cage: Toward Legal Rights for Animals* (Wise 2000). See also Wise, "Animal Rights One Step at a Time," in Sunstein and Nussbaum (Wise 2004).

83. DeCoux (2005, 740).

84. *Nair* v. *Union of India*, Kerala High Court, no. 15/1999, June 2000.

85. The mirror test is a test to ascertain whether an animal recognizes its own image in a mirror. Typically, a black mark is applied to the back of the animal's head, visible in the mirror and not to the animal without the mirror. Then, to make sure that the tactile sensation of applying the mark is not driving the result, a sham invisible mark is applied to the other side of the head. The animal looks in the mirror. If he or she scrubs the mark off of his or her own head, after seeing the mark in the mirror, the animal is understood to have recognized that the image is an image of itself.

86. See Whitehead and Rendell (2015).

87. See the research of Paul Rozin, discussed in chapter 3 of Martha Nussbaum, *Hiding from Humanity: Disgust, Shame, and the Law* (Nussbaum 2006).

88. For Mill's appeal to dignity, see *Utilitarianism* (Mill [1861] 1987).

89. For the immense importance of agency to development ethics, see David A. Crocker, *Ethics of Global Development: Agency, Capability, and Deliberative Democracy* (Crocker (2008), especially chapter 5; also, David A. Crocker and Ingrid Robeyns, "Capability and Agency," in *Amartya Sen*, ed. Christopher W. Morris (Crocker and Robeyns 2010).

90. See particularly Donaldson and Kymlicka (2011).

91. See Tom Regan, *The Case for Animal Rights*, updated edition (Regan 2004).

92. Crocker argues for Sen's comprehensive notion of agency, basically a notion of autonomy, as preferable to Nussbaum's thinner concept of practical reason, but he should recognize that Nussbaum's reason for preferring the thinner notion is its suitability for a society in which many reasonable citizens reject autonomy and prefer authoritarian religion. Nonetheless, Nussbaum claims, a political "overlapping consensus," though it should avoid the thicker notion of autonomy,

can still include the thinner notion in its political principles. Nussbaum's reasons for rejecting a comprehensive doctrine of autonomy such as that of Joseph Raz are given in her "Perfectionist Liberalism and Political Liberalism," *Philosophy and Public Affairs* (Nussbaum 2011a), reprinted in *Capabilities, Gender, Equality*, ed. Flavio Comim and Martha C. Nussbaum (Comim and Nussbaum 2014, 19–56). Crocker's book precedes this statement, so he does not state whether he accepts these arguments of Nussbaum's. In any case, we believe that where non-human animals are concerned he could accept the flexible and multispecies notion of agency that we propose.

93. We do not have space here to expand on the relevant notions of dignity and wonder, but we agree with Jeremy Bendik-Keymer, in "From Human to All of Life: Nussbaum's Transformation of Dignity," in Comim and Nussbaum (Bendik-Keymer 2014, 175–92).

94. White (2007, 199–200).

95. We are also sympathetic to the term "wildlife sovereignty," as used by Donaldson and Kymlicka (2011).

96. White (2007, 211).

97. See Vicki Croke, *Elephant Company: The Inspiring Story of an Unlikely Hero and the Animals who Helped Him Save Lives in World War II* (Croke 2015). Croke narrates the story of Billy Williams, who worked for a British teak company in Burma, training elephants for that industry, but then joined with them to form a fighting brigade in the war. He was so respectful of elephant agency and intelligence that he used only positive reinforcement to train them.

98. See Whitehead and Rendell (2015), 110–13.

99. See the documentary film *The Whale* (Parfit and Chisholm 2011), a fascinating study of the dilemma created by the behavior of Luna, an unusually friendly young orca in Puget Sound.

100. *Natural Resources Defense Council et al. v. Pritzker et al.*, no. 14–16375 (9th Cir. 2016), available at: https://cdn.ca9.uscourts .gov/datastore/opinions/2016/07/15/14–16375.pdf. The sonar program is described in detail in Horwitz (2015).

101. *Ibid.* at 10.

References

Ackerman, Jennifer. 2016. *The Genius of Birds*, New York: Penguin.

Bendik-Keymer, Jeremy. 2014. "From Human to All of Life: Nussbaum's Transformation of Dignity." In *Capabilities, Gender, Equality.*

Comim, Flavio, and Nussbaum, Martha C. (eds.), Cambridge University Press.

Bentham, Jeremy. [1789] 2007. *An Introduction to the Principles of Morals and Legislation*, New York: Hafner Press.

[1817] 2013. *Not Paul, but Jesus, Vol. III: Doctrine*, London: The Bentham Project, University College London. www.ucl.ac.uk/Bentham-Project/publications/npbj/npbj.html.

Boralevi, Lea Campus. 1984. *Bentham and the Oppressed*, New York: Walter de Gruyter.

Comim, Flavio, and Nussbaum, Martha C. (eds.). 2014. *Capabilities, Gender, Equality*, Cambridge University Press.

Cowperthwaite, Gabriela. 2013. *Blackfish* [DVD], New York: Magnolia Home Entertainment.

Crocker, David A. 2008. *Ethics of Global Development: Agency, Capability, and Deliberative Democracy*, Cambridge University Press.

Crocker, David A., and Robeyns, Ingrid. 2010. "Capability and Agency." In *Amartya Sen*. Morris, Christopher W. (ed.), Cambridge University Press, 60–90.

Croke, Vicki. 2015. *Elephant Company: The Inspiring Story of an Unlikely Hero and the Animals who Helped Him Save Lives in World War II*, New York: Random House.

De Waal, Frans. 2016. *Are We Smart Enough to Know How Smart Animals Are?*, New York: W. W. Norton.

De Waal, Frans, and Tyack, Peter L. (eds.). 2000. *Animal Social Complexity: Intelligence, Culture, and Individualized Societies*, Cambridge, MA: Harvard University Press.

DeCoux, Elizabeth L. 2005. "In the Valley of the Dry Bones: Reuniting the Word 'Standing': With its Meaning in Animal Cases." *William & Mary Environmental Law and Policy Review*, 29(3): 681–765.

DeGrazia, David. 1996. *Taking Animals Seriously: Mental Life and Moral Status*, Cambridge University Press.

Donaldson, Sue, and Kymlicka, Will. 2011. *Zoopolis: A Political Theory of Animal Rights*, Oxford University Press.

Francione, Gary L. 2004. "Animals: Property or Persons?" In *Animal Rights: Current Debates and New Directions*. Sunstein, Cass, and Nussbaum, Martha C. (eds.), Oxford University Press.

Horwitz, Joshua. 2015. *War of the Whales*, New York: Simon & Schuster.

Kirby, David. 2012. *Death at SeaWorld: Shamu and the Dark Side of Killer Whales in Captivity*, New York: St. Martin's Press.

2014. "SeaWorld's Worst Nightmare: Calif. Lawmaker to Propose Ban on Orcas in Captivity," *TakePart*, March 6. www.takepart.com/article/2

014/03/06/seaworlds-worst-nightmare-calif-lawmaker-propose-ban-
orcas-captivity.

Korsgaard, Christine. 2004. "Fellow Creatures: Kantian Ethics and Our
Duty to Animals," *Tanner Lectures on Human Values*, 25(6): 79–110.

Kraut, Richard. 2010. "What Is Intrinsic Goodness?" *Classical Philology*,
105: 450–62.

Lee, Jadran. 2003. Bentham on the Moral and Legal Status of Animals.
Dissertation, University of Chicago.

Mill, John Stuart. 1987 [1861]. "Utilitarianism." In *Utilitarianism and
Other Essays*, Ryan, Alan (ed.), London: Penguin.

Milman, Oliver. 2016. "US Zoos Secretly Fly 18 Elephants out of Swaziland
Ahead of Court Challenge," *The Guardian*, March 9. www
.theguardian.com/world/2016/mar/09/us-zoos-secretly-fly-elephants-
swaziland-dallas-kansas-nebraska.

Nussbaum, Martha C. 1978. *Aristotle's De Motu Animalium*, Princeton
University Press.

  2006. *Hiding from Humanity: Disgust, Shame, and the Law*, Princeton
University Press.

  2011. "Perfectionist Liberalism and Political Liberalism." *Philosophy and
Public Affairs*, 39: 3–45.

  2011. "The Capabilities Approach and Animal Entitlements." In *Oxford
Handbook of Animal Ethics*. Beauchamp, Tom (ed.), Oxford University
Press, 228–51.

OSHA. 2014. "OSHA Wins SeaWorld Case," Occupational Health &
Safety, April 11. http://ohsonline.com/articles/2014/04/11/osha-wins-
seaworld-case.aspx.

Parfit, Michael, and Chisholm, Suzanne. 2011. *The Whale* [DVD], Canada:
Mountainside Films.

Raja, Tasneem. 2014. "SeaWorld Says it Has to Keep Orcas in Captivity to
Save Them," *Mother Jones*, November/December. www.motherjones
.com/environment/2014/12/seaworld-killer-whale-orca-science-
blackfish/.

Regan, Tom. 2004. *The Case for Animal Rights*, Berkeley: University of
California Press.

Regan, Tom, and Singer, Peter (eds.). 1989. *Animal Rights and Human
Obligations*, Englewood Cliffs, NJ: Prentice-Hall.

Singer, Peter. 2002. *Animal Liberation*, New York: HarperCollins.

Sorabji, Richard. 1993. *Animal Minds and Human Morals: The Origins of
the Western Debate*, Ithaca, NY: Cornell University Press.

Sunstein, Cass. 2000. "Standing for Animals (with Notes on Animal
Rights)." *UCLA Law Review*, 47(5): 1333–68.

2004. "Can Animals Sue?" In *Animal Rights: Current Debates and New Directions*. Sunstein, Cass, and Nussbaum, Martha C. (eds.), Oxford University Press.

White, Thomas I. 2007. *In Defense of Dolphins: The New Moral Frontier*, Malden, MA: Blackwell Publishing.

Whitehead, Hal, and Rendell, Luke. 2015. *The Cultural Lives of Whales and Dolphins*, University of Chicago Press.

Wichert, Rachel Nussbaum, and Nussbaum, Martha C. 2017. "Legal Protection for Whales: Capabilities, Entitlements, and Culture." In *Animals, Race and Multiculturalism: Contemporary Moral and Political Debates*. Cordeiro Rodrigues, Luis (ed.), Basingstoke: Palgrave Macmillan.

Wise, Stephen. 2000. *Rattling the Cage: Toward Legal Rights for Animals*, Cambridge, MA: Perseus Books.

2004. "Animal Rights One Step at a Time." In *Animal Rights: Current Debates and New Directions*. Sunstein, Cass, and Nussbaum, Martha C. (eds.), Oxford University Press, 19–50.

Zimmermann, Tim. 2010. "The Killer in the Pool," *Outside Online*, July 30. www.outsideonline.com/1924946/killer-pool.

Cases Cited

Cetacean Community *v.* Bush, 386 F. 3d 1169 (9th Cir. 2004).

Friends of the Earth, Inc. *v.* Laidlaw Envtl. Servs. (TOC), Inc., 528 US 167 (2000).

Nair *v.* Union of India, Kerala High Court, no.15/1999, June 2000.

Natural Resources Defense Council et al. *v.* Pritzker et al., no.14–16375 (9th Cir. 2016).

Palila *v.* Hawaii Department of Land and Natural Resources, 852 F. 2d 1106 (9th Cir. 1988).

Tilikum ex rel. People for the Ethical Treatment of Animals, Inc. *v.* Sea World Parks and Entertainment, Inc. 842 F. Supp.2d 1259 (SD Ca. 2012).

PART III

Democracy

11 | *On Some Limits and Conflicts in Deliberative and Participatory Democracy*

LUIS CAMACHO

One should be very careful when placing adjectives next to the noun "democracy." Qualifications like "representative," "participatory," and so on, may introduce ways to weaken its core. Even the deliberative participation proposed by David A. Crocker in *Ethics of Global Development: Agency, Capability, and Deliberative Democracy* (2008) as a way to apply the agency and capability approach to the improvement of democratic institutions may be hijacked by authoritarian leaders as just another way to restrict or altogether eliminate representative democracy and thereby exclude those segments of the population that oppose their policies and their continuation in power. My aim here is to show how the analysis of conflicts and limits in deliberative participation may be useful to distinguish between democratic involvement in decisions and the undemocratic use of participation for the rejection of representation. My basic premise is that there is no substitute for representative democracy as long as we live in states where government officials are chosen by free and fair elections, rather than those where we suffer under their oppression or are forced to remove them by extraordinary means because they refuse to give up power.[1] Can representative democracy, then, not be improved upon with further modifications (or modifiers), such as enhanced citizen participation or deliberation? In theory, participatory democracy is an improvement on representation by elected public officials. In practice, however, there are limits to deliberation and participation by all. This chapter explores these relationships and limits.

This chapter proceeds in two parts. First, I will compare participatory and representative democracy, and their respective strengths and weaknesses. Second, I will take a closer look at participatory democracy and offer two circumstances in which ethical conflicts might arise in its practice, namely, when participation of some person (or group) limits the freedom of another, and when another important human right conflicts with the right to participation. I will conclude by reaffirming the indispensable role for ethical theory in democracy and development.

Democracy with Adjectives

The expression "democracy with adjectives" is not new. Coined by David Collier and Steven Levitsky, "Democracy with Adjectives: Conceptual Innovation in Comparative Research" (1997) aims to differentiate kinds of political regimes resulting from changes in recent history. Part of the purpose of this chapter is to defend representative democracy in the face of recent attacks in Latin America. But, as in Collier and Levitsky's paper, I argue that some "democracies" with adjectives are not democracies at all. First, let us explore "representative" democracy. Any attempt to improve democracy should take into consideration the importance of representation, since the alternative to representative democracy in the world as we know it today is either the tyranny of authoritarian regimes or the anarchy of failed states.

The justification for this concern is to be found in recent Latin American experiences with several political leaders who – after being elected in the polls, often by only a slim margin of a relative majority – imposed their particular agenda in the name of "the people" (their followers) on the rest of society by means of appeals to "true" kinds of democracy ("street democracy," "radical democracy") as opposed to the "false" kind, by which – of course – they mean the elections or referenda whereby they could lose their grip on power.[2] By the expediency of adding an adjective to "democracy," they find a very convenient way to delegitimize dissent.[3] The end result is that the so-called "true" kind of democracy is practiced by the followers of the leader (the only ones worthy of the name "the people"), representative democracy is denied to the rest, and the possibility to change governments in a peaceful manner becomes endangered.

What several strategies to reject representative democracy – frequently labeled "elitist" and "bourgeois" – have in common is the accusation that it is a tool of those who have economic power, who are able to manipulate the press, television, and social media, and consequently influence public opinion in favor of some candidates. In Jean-Paul Sartre's famous and often repeated words, elections are "a trap for fools" (de Beauvoir 1984, 39). That these accusations only take place when election returns are not favorable is a logical inconsistency that does not seem to bother the accusers. The basic reality of democracy – the possibility for the governed to choose the government they want and be elected as public officials – is so recent in history and took so much suffering to achieve that every time it takes place in a particular country the accomplishment should be nourished with great care.

So, it is with caution that I talk here about deliberative and participatory democracy. By such, I understand the social arrangement whereby all citizens of a country enjoy the opportunity to make contributions to decision-making processes in issues affecting them. We hope that the contributions are meaningful and that the decisions are right, but there seems to be no guarantee that such is the outcome in every case. There is wisdom in crowds, but also folly. Crowds may gather to do good, but history teaches us that human beings sometimes take the side of the greater number in the cause of wrong-doing.

Although the probability of success in solving social problems seems higher with larger participation, the basic reason in favor of participatory democracy is not empirical but moral: the recognition of freedom and rights shared by all human beings. So, even if the experience of participation may turn out to be sometimes disappointing, such a fact is not a refutation of the need for participation and deliberation, since these are good in themselves and not only in their consequences. In his *Politics*, Aristotle notes that participation in public discussion enhances the feelings of courage and confidence in the participants (1975, 1313b, 1–5). He also points out that since tyrants need to impede such a feeling because it is a threat to their power, they prohibit all gatherings and meetings for study and discussion. Confidence is a sign of security and self-esteem, and accordingly Aristotle's reasoning shows the connection between discussion, deliberation, citizens' self-assurance, and rejection of oppression. We are all familiar with the hostility of authoritarian regimes toward organizations of the civil society not under their direct control.[4] And, when we read in *Politics* that the excesses of the worst forms of democracy are also found in tyrannies (1313b, 33), we may be excused if these words remind us of recent events in countries where politicians democratically elected have used their power to transform the state in non-democratic ways. Unfortunately, there is no guarantee to prevent undemocratic uses of democratic institutions and the transition from undemocratic regimes and practices to democratic institutions is often the result of struggle and suffering.

When paired with the idea of socioeconomic improvement, many consider high levels of participation and deliberation essential for advanced stages of development. A modicum of participation by large numbers of people is already present in representative democracy, as may be seen when we consider that in fair elections citizens can elect and be elected, whereas one of the ways in which an election may be unfair is by restricting such a possibility. The dictionary definition of the term "democracy" usually includes the reference to electing representatives, so that "the people" have a voice in the exercise of power, although most of the time only in an indirect way. But, we are all familiar with the fact that not all elections are democratic: There are countries where only one party is allowed to sponsor candidates in elections, and many where the opposition is harassed and their sympathizers intimidated. In both cases participation is denied to many citizens. So, the first step toward a democratic society is fair and free elections, which implies participation in electing and being elected. But, even if elections are free and fair, a state's democratic credentials include many other aspects of the political system. It is easy to agree on the notion that elections are a means to some positive outcome and not an end in themselves. Hence, the debate as to what elements should be included in a full definition of democracy.

Robert A. Dahl's five criteria for democracy are well known: effective participation, voting equality, enlightened understanding, control, and inclusiveness (1989). In this view, democracy requires freedom of organization and expression, access to sources of information with the possibility to check their reliability, and the existence of institutions able to ensure that government policies follow the preferences of citizens. Thus, democracy is not only majority rule, but also a system that protects political freedoms so that there can be public debate without censorship and independent decision-making without imposition from above. The list does not stop here. Among the commonly acknowledged necessary conditions for democracy we also find multi-party electoral competition, freedom of association and of movement, independent media, and the rule of law. In particular, an independent institution with the purpose of providing citizens the conditions to vote and making sure that their secret vote is counted seems especially important, though many countries still lack it. Given the institutional complexity, it seems obvious that the process toward democracy may include several stages.

It is because of such complexity that some listings of all the aspects included in a full definition of democracy look very much like the description of the conditions in countries ranked in the first positions of the Human Development Index (United Nations Development Programme 2017). The connection works likewise in the opposite direction (conditions present where full-fledged democracy is lacking look an awful lot like those present where we find low levels of socioeconomic development), although just as we are all familiar with the ills of underdevelopment even if we cannot imagine a perfectly developed society, we also find it easier to describe the lack of the lowest degrees of democracy than its full implementation. To the obvious objection that we can find examples of countries with high rates of economic growth and very low degrees of democracy, the equally obvious answer is that economic growth and human development are not the same. And yet, no matter how advanced a country, it seems that there always is room for improvement.

If we assume that deliberative participation is an improvement on representative democracy and that the basic form of democracy-as-representation is majority rule, then the next step is to ask in what ways deliberative participation is an improvement on representative democracy, and the answer points in the direction of a fuller notion of democracy, which reflects a social condition based on justice and peace. Quoting Amartya Sen (1999), Crocker offers a "demanding" notion of full democracy, the ideal of which includes: voting, respect for election results, protection of liberties and freedoms, respect for legal entitlements, guarantees of free discussion, uncensored distribution of information, fair comment, opportunities to present one's views, and the freedom to obtain news and the views of candidates for public office (2008, 298–9). We may wonder if all the above-mentioned necessary conditions, when found together, are sufficient for the "demanding ideal" of democracy proposed by Sen and endorsed by Crocker. If the answer is negative, it is hard to imagine what is missing. On the other hand, it is easy to see that the more aspects we include the less adequate seems the word "democracy" to encompass all of them; many of the aspects in the previous list would also appear in a declaration of universal human rights and in a description of a highly developed country, yet we don't automatically give these the "democracy" label. Sensibly, Crocker tells us that democracy is a matter of more or less, not either/or (2008, 299). The same is true of socioeconomic development.

When the issue of participatory democracy as an improvement on representative democracy is thus introduced, several questions may be raised: why we should prefer it to the opposite (its absence), how it can be implemented, and who may engage in deliberation and participation. The usual answer to the last question is a simple one: All human beings affected by decisions should have a voice in the discussion and a participation in the decision-making processes where issues relevant for them are settled. Otherwise, decisions are imposed from above without the agency of those affected, although the decision-makers may have been elected by the beneficiaries or perhaps victims of their decisions. Participation begets legitimacy.

Ethical Conflicts in the Practice of Participatory Democracy

In theory, participatory democracy is an improvement on representation by elected officials not only in the public sector – in government and public agencies – but also in institutions of the civil society.[5] Instead of limiting themselves to the occasional election of presidents, congressmen, senators, county officials, and other positions, citizens in participatory democracies are expected to engage in deliberation previous to decisions, by which the commitment of all involved has more probability of success. The limitations of democracy as mere election of representatives are thus brought into focus, since representation could be seen as a means to relinquish citizen power into the hands of a few elected individuals over whose actions the voters lose control, thereby becoming alienated. But, if the argument is pushed to its most radical conclusion, participation and deliberation previous to any decision would almost take the place of representation. In countries with high degrees of connectivity, where technology makes it possible for all people to be in touch all the time, the temptation is to substitute electronic consultation for periodic visits to the polling stations. However, although each particular means of consultation may have its drawbacks, in general it is true that instead of demanding "no taxation without representation" the citizens of many countries today find themselves in a situation where they can aim at "no decision without consultation," which implies participation and perhaps also deliberation.

Nevertheless, to demand participation in all decisions affecting individual lives will have counterintuitive consequences, not only because the number of decisions made by representatives is very large and their importance unequal, but also and especially because many matters affecting the lives of citizens cannot or should not be submitted to a referendum. Public consultation cannot decide scientific matters; human rights should not be submitted to the vagaries of public opinion. However, even though exceptions to the general principle behind participatory democracy are easy to find, as we shall see shortly, it is my contention that such exceptions – when carefully analyzed in theory and justly implemented in practice – do not contradict the general theory that justifies participatory democracy, but in fact strengthen the need for participation and deliberation of most people, although not in all actions. As a consequence of this analysis, I emphasize the need to distinguish between legitimate forms of democracy and illegitimate attempts at denying the rights of some of the citizens to satisfy the interest of others. This is another case of the general tenet according to which the right to differences should not become the excuse for different rights, i.e., for the introduction of privileges.

To analyze the limitations and conflicts in participation and deliberation it is important to place the discussion within the context of the four dimensions of democracy distinguished by Crocker: breadth, depth, range, and control (2008, 299). At first glance we may think that in an ideal situation democracy is practiced by all people (breadth), with ample participation in several levels of activities and commitment (depth), where all kinds of issues are the subject of debate and decision (range) and in such a way that the impact on events can be clearly measured and assessed (control). But, without constraints, in particular on range, increases in breadth, depth, and control may lead to undemocratic results. Moreover, as Crocker has argued, since democracy is a scalar vector, these limitations show conflicts in a continuous increase along the four axes. The first limits I propose are to the *range* of democracy, because of their implications for its *breadth*. Second, I use the example of the particular position of citizens in emergency and disaster situations in order to illustrate the tension between *depth* and the other three aspects of democracy. Given the complexity of human interactions, it seems natural that conflicts may arise in particular circumstances. Faced with conflicts between the four dimensions of democracy, there seems to be two ways to deal with them. One approach is to emphasize the notion of accepted solutions to common problems, as Crocker does from the very beginning of his book (2008, 49). People find acceptable those solutions they perceive as fair, whereas the perpetuation of injustice leads to conflict and violence. Deliberative participation helps to identify, and increase the perception of, fairness and justice in the system, if only because political situations where it is not allowed deny the freedom and agency of human beings. Since standards for successful deliberation are stricter than those for participation more generally, training for deliberation is needed and should be a priority in both formal and informal education. Of problems there is no dearth, but solutions are not accepted with conviction and commitment unless deliberation is practiced with equal respect for all legitimate participants. Both the freedom of the participants and the consequences of their free actions should be taken into consideration.

Another way to solve the problem of conflicts is to let human rights set the limit: Unless we are profoundly misguided, we do not want to consider "democratic" a regime where individual choices on private matters are taken over by communal decisions (an extreme increase in the range of participatory decision-making). To call "democratic" a regime where personal relations like friendship or marriage are decided by the community, even after deliberation and participation by all the members, seems like an abuse of language. Usual regulations about age of consent and some other aspects of personal relations are not an objection to the contrary, since they are meant to protect the vulnerable who are not in a position to make an independent decision. For those who are, communal decisions on private matters would amount to the denial of the freedom of human beings. Unless we confuse solidarity with slavery, democracy presupposes freedom of the individual; a negation of such freedom as a consequence of an unlimited range of issues submitted to public scrutiny and decision is a real but paradoxical possibility. In summary, the four dimensions of democracy as listed by Crocker cannot increase indefinitely without conflicts among them, but there are criteria to establish the limits and solve the problems.

In other words, limits on the general principle – participation is based on the right to influence decisions affecting the participant – are explained by other norms that complement the basic idea, since restrictions do not exclude categories of people as such (breadth) but make exempt from participatory processes some kinds of *actions* that can be found at the intersection of breadth and range. Some of these exemptions are well known to all of us: alleged criminals (a question of breadth) do not vote with the jury on whether they are guilty or not (a question of range); those justly affected by punishment of crimes and misdemeanors (a question of breadth) cannot invoke a right to be consulted on the outcome in the process whereby they are judged and sentenced (a question of range). Friends and lovers cannot invoke equal participation in decisions affecting them, since one's decision on having a friend or a lover cannot be imposed by the other party, no matter how profound the consequence of rejecting or breaking up a relation. Members of the board in public institutions cannot or should not take part in decisions whereby business contracts are assigned when the outcome may favor themselves or a close relative.

In all these examples, those precluded from participation are deeply affected by the decisions in which they cannot participate, and yet they are not in the position to invoke any right to be part of the decision. Plainly put, there are certain situations in which one should not expect to participate in deliberation. These situations are not demarcated by issues to which *no one ever* should participate, which would be a total limit on range (the jury participates in the judgment; the accused does not). Nor are these situations demarcated by certain categories of people who can *never on any issue* participate, which would be a total limit on breadth (public officials can participate in deliberation on many issues, just not ones where there is a conflict of interest). Rather, these situations where we make exceptions are found at certain intersections of breadth and range, and can be identified by a risk of violating the basic human rights of others. (To this last characterization I will return below.) Since we must place a limit somewhere, though, I argue that in these situations the limit should be on the range of decisions that certain people (or categories of people) are eligible to participate in, since the alternative – restricting certain categories of people from any form of participation in order to protect the range of decisions on the table – is morally far more troubling. Another situation in which limits on participatory democracy might be necessary is at the intersection of breadth and depth. A particular case where this limit might be invoked is in emergency situations, where deliberation by all at every level is not possible or is severely limited, and urgent solutions by elected representatives in charge of government agencies are needed in such a way that deep participation of people affected by the situation looks more like a problem than part of a solution. In emergency situations the demand for aid on the part of victims and the obligation of others to provide help is neither the result of deliberation nor the effect of negotiation between parties. The lack of satisfaction of basic needs (food, shelter, health care) in these conditions demands urgent action under the risk of loss of life; victims cannot extricate themselves from the situation by their own devices and those called to help and able to do so cannot ignore the plight of survivors and pretend that their indifference is morally right. But, this does not mean that the whole category of persons affected by disaster should be excluded from any form of participation (breadth). Instead, human claims to satisfaction of the most basic needs necessary for life justify limits on the *depth* of participation in decision-making on related matters.

But, we can take the example of decision-making in emergencies a step further, and recognize it as metaphor. We can recognize that for millions of people, their everyday conditions resemble emergency situations. Before they can engage in deliberation on other issues, their urgent need for food, shelter, and health care – conditions for their very existence – must be met. It is important to point out, however, that although the list of urgently needed items – usually short and precise – is not the result of deliberation but the imposition of circumstances, there may be a place for deliberative participation both in the distribution of aid and in the prevention of future calamities. Again, we do not limit breadth, but rather impose limits on range or depth when doing so is necessary to protect the human right to life and the satisfaction of basic needs.

At first sight these exceptions to the universal principle according to which people affected by decisions should have a chance to influence the outcome seem to amount to a negation of the universality of the norm. But, there is another way of looking at it: Limitations point in the direction of a more refined understanding of the relationship between participation and individual rights and reveal the focus of conflict between them. This explains why restrictions are limited to some categories of *situations* because of conflicts between personal rights of individuals involved in the process, not to categories of *people* thereby excluded from participation. What I have in mind is the situation where as many people as possible participate in decision-making processes, but within the limits set by the kinds of situations in which certain issues are submitted to participatory decision-making. That is, I argue that we can protect the breadth of a participatory process by limiting its range or depth, where failing to do so would infringe on the human rights of participants or others affected by the process.

Several examples seem to suggest two kinds of human rights that stand to come into conflict with appeals to unlimited participation. First, there is no appeal to a supposed right of participation when the decision affects someone if participating would entail the denial of the freedom of the other person. In this sense, we do not ask the school bully if he wants to stop tormenting classmates; we do whatever we can to stop him. He is affected by our decision and yet he has no claim to influence it because we are dealing with actions harmful to others. But, aside from whatever actions we might decide to take to stop his aggressive behavior, we think that he is entitled to express his opinions on other matters. If one of the parties to a friendship does not accept the decision made by the other to terminate the relationship, his or her action is a denial of the freedom of the other person, something to which he or she is not entitled no matter how deeply he or she is affected by the decision. Similarly, criminals (think, for example, of serial killers) cannot be given the chance to participate in decisions about their incarceration because if they do so the rights of citizens to live free of fear are denied. What these examples have in common is that the limitations on the range of participation derive from conflicts with the freedom of one of the parties involved. If the bully participates in the decision to stop his own actions we give him a right he should not enjoy, i.e., the possibility of denying the freedom of his classmates. In these cases, we place a limit on *range*.

But, there is another case where the grounds for limits on participation are different. A second type of conflict can arise between participation and the right to life. For example, when disasters and emergencies strike, one of the defining characteristics of the situation is that the possibility of deliberation and participation is greatly reduced for the survivors. We don't necessarily want to say that there are whole categories of decisions that are off-limits in emergencies, but time-consuming, deep deliberation during an emergency in which decisions must be made quickly can literally kill people. It is easy to understand that in these conditions the right to life of victims of tragedies comes first. So, in this case, we recognize a conflict between two important rights (participation and life), prioritize them, and then place a limit on the *depth* of participation in order to preserve the more important of the two rights.

In the light of the preceding considerations a difference between tyrannies and democracies begins to emerge: in tyrannies a single individual, the dictator or tyrant, has the power to make decisions of all kinds without consideration for the rights of others; in democracies all citizens have the power to make decisions of some kinds within the limits of respect for others. A special sort of dictatorial regime is the one that comes into being by means of an election but becomes a government for the benefit of those loyal to the leader, with the exclusion of the opposition. There is another important difference between democracies and tyrannies: authorities in democratic countries work for the benefit of all the people, although not elected with the votes of all the voters. In authoritarian regimes, on the contrary, any opposition to the leader of "the people" often becomes a sentence of exclusion from many of the everyday benefits of the state. In extreme cases, followers of this kind of leader benefit from the services of the state (social security, public education, and so on) whereas members of the opposition – frequently defined as such by the ruler or the ruling party – do not have access to what is a right of all.

This brings us to a distinction of two different environments in which participatory and deliberative democracy may take place: within democracies and within certain spheres of life in non-democracies. Usually, we assume that participatory and deliberative democracy implies the existence of a representative democracy in the country as a whole. But, when this is not the case, then participatory democracy may be implemented within any group or institution in any political system as long as the regime is not so strong as to impede even the minimal kind of organization outside their direct control. In this sense, participatory democracy could be introduced in many different settings, even when there is no representative democracy at the national level: neighborhood and county groups, universities, corporations, and all kinds of local, national, and international organizations. Participation at this level may help to strengthen opposition to undemocratic governments. When confronted with large participation in organized opposition, authoritarian regimes face a dilemma: Either they gain legitimacy but lose control if they accept the demands of the citizens – and then there is a chance for a peaceful transition to democracy, as when Pinochet lost the referendum in Chile in 1988 – or they gain control by force but lose legitimacy if citizens' demands are not met (and unrest follows, as is the case today in Venezuela because of the refusal by president Nicolás Maduro and his followers to accept the call for a recall referendum in spite of the millions of signatures asking for the application of this constitutional provision).

The preceding considerations bring us to a brief reference to the notion, often repeated by Crocker, that the solution for the problems of democracy is not less democracy, but more (and better) democracy. If one looks for examples of open disagreement with this idea it is necessary to go back in history, either to the "dictatorship of the proletariat" in the left or to "national salvation" regimes in the right, like Franco's in Spain (1936–1975) and the military dictatorships in Brazil (1964–1985), Chile (1973–1990), and Argentina (1976–1983). At that time there was no pretense by the actors that their regimes were democratic; strong authoritarian governments imposed by the military or with their help were supposed to be the cure for the chaos brought about by democratically elected officials or the end of the exploitation of the poor in capitalist countries. The solution to the problems of democracy, for these politicians, was less democracy.

Public rejection of democracy does not seem acceptable today, but this does not mean that authoritarian and undemocratic regimes have gone away in some parts of the world. They have limited themselves to a simple change of tactics by pretending that their political systems are the real democracies ("people's" democracies, a great example of which is the Democratic People's Republic of North Korea). However, here again history seems to be a good guide. Authoritarian regimes do not seem to be sustainable in the long run and usually end with a return to democracy. This, on the contrary, does not need a justification for its existence: Since human beings are free, it is the limitations on freedom that need justification, not its exercise.

Three immediate conclusions follow from the preceding considerations. First, the limits in deliberative participation are the result of exceptions to the general principle according to which people should be able to influence the decisions affecting them. Second, if these limits are not taken into consideration, conflicts arise when the different aspects of participation increase at the same time and also when participation is viewed as a substitute for representation or as an excuse to restrict representative democracy and thereby neutralize any opposition.

Third, the limits of deliberative participation are not excuses to forget the need to improve democratic regimes by an extensive and intensive involvement of all citizens. They merely show the ways to engage in participation for better public choices and policies without negatively affecting the rights of participants. In particular, the consideration of limits and conflicts in the practice of democracy should help in the denunciation of regimes that limit the right to elect and be elected by appeals to new kinds of democracy that in fact deny what is more typical of this political arrangement. On the other hand, since neither participation nor deliberation guarantee that a decision is morally right, there always is an important and irreplaceable role for ethics as the analysis of the difference between good and bad. The moral obligation to look for good belongs to all human beings engaged in deliberation.

Notes

1. On page 23 of his book, Crocker mentions several general objections to deliberative democracy. His whole book is an answer to them. See also Drydyk (2005).
2. But, good news also comes from Latin America, where the organizing of public participation in democratic countries has often been successful. See, for example, J. Ricardo Tranjan's book *Participatory Democracy in Brazil: Socioeconomic and Political Origins* (2015).
3. After losing the mid-term elections to the unified opposition by a wide margin on December 6, 2015, Venezuela's president Nicolás Maduro installed a new legislative organ loyal to the regime called "Communal Parliament," considered an organ of the "legislative body of the people from its base" and a step toward a "communal state." Whereas the National Assembly now dominated by the opposition is considered an illegitimate expression of foreign intervention, the Communal Parliament is hailed as the authentic and legitimate power of the "people." See Pardo (2015).
4. See for example Alvarez (2015).
5. It is hard to imagine drug cartels and organized crime – also a part of the civil society – embracing participation and deliberation.

References

Alvarez, L. (2015) "Al gobierno no le gusta que la gente se organice," *La Prensa* (Nicaragua), January 6, "Nacionales" section, 2.

Aristotle. (1975) *Politics*, in Encyclopedia Britannica, Inc., *Great Books of the Western World, The Works of Aristotle*, vol. II. The University of Chicago Press.

Collier, David and Levitsky, Steven. (1997) "Democracy with Adjectives: Conceptual Innovation in Comparative Research," *World Politics*, 49, 3: 430–51.

Crocker, David A. (2008) *Ethics of Global Development: Agency, Capability, and Deliberative Democracy*. Cambridge University Press.

Dahl, Richard A. (1989) *Democracy and Its Critics*. New Haven, CT: Yale University Press.

De Beauvoir, Simone. (1984) *Adieu, A Farewell to Sartre*. New York: Pantheon Books.

Drydyk, Jay. (2005) "When Is Development More Democratic?" *Journal of Human Development*, 6, 2: 247–67.

Pardo, D. (2015) "Venezuela: ¿qué es el Parlamento Comunal que instaló el chavismo luego de perder la mayoría legislativa?" BBC Mundo, Caracas, December 15. www.bbc.com/mundo/noticias/2015/12/151216_venezuela_parlamento_comunal_claves_dp.

Sen, A. (1999) "Democracy as a Universal Value," *Journal of Democracy*, 10, 3: 3–17. Tranjan, R. (2015) *Participatory Democracy in Brazil: Socioeconomic and Political Origins*. Indiana: University of Notre Dame Press.

United Nations Development Programme. (2017) *Human Development Reports*. http://hdr.undp.org/en.

12 | An Agency-Focused Version of Capability Ethics and the Ethics of Cordial Reason*

The Search for a Philosophical Foundation for Deliberative Democracy

ADELA CORTINA

1 Applied Ethics Have Attained Global Scope

As I have argued elsewhere, applied ethics, originating in the 1960s and 1970s, has gradually developed from its early stages to reach a worldwide scale (Cortina 2014). The challenge of globalisation, which came to the fore in the 1990s, made the three pioneering forms of applied ethics – development ethics, economic and business ethics, and bioethics – take on a global perspective and work together to fulfil their respective aims in a globalised world (Potter 1988; Enderle 1999; Ruggie 2013). Development ethics indeed originally arose with an international approach, because valuing peoples' development necessitates international indices and the search for solutions requires going beyond nation-states and even supranational communities. In recent times, nevertheless, the approach has become global because the challenges are global and not only international or transnational (Goulet 2006, 157–224; Crocker 2008). The Millennium Development Goals, the Post-2015 Agenda, and the Sustainable Development Goals vouch for this global reach. That does not mean that local challenges should be ignored, but that a response is required for both the local and the global; 'glocalisation' is a matter of necessity.

This is the setting in which Crocker's proposal lies, as a concept that has been gradually germinating, and in my opinion is best expressed in

* This study is included in the Scientific Research and Technological Development Projects FFI2013-47136-C2-1-P, financed by the Ministry of Economy and Competitiveness and in the activities of the research group of excellence, PROMETEO, of the Generalidad Valenciana.

his 2008 book *Ethics of Global Development*. In his own words, 'Throughout its history, development ethics has emphasized ethical assessment of the goals, institutions, and strategies of national and subnational development and constructively proposed better alternatives. In a globalizing world, development ethics takes on the additional task of offering an ethical appraisal of the global order and suggesting more just ways of managing new and evolving global interconnectedness' (Crocker 2008, 380). As Karl-Otto Apel had already proclaimed in the 1970s, there needs to be a planetary ethics (Apel 1973, 361), which now becomes a global ethics, an approach benefitting from confronting problems linked to human and international development.

We are well aware that Crocker's writings are of an unquestionably international reference in development ethics and public policies. Since his early works, his contributions in the form of articles, books, and conference papers have made him one of today's most relevant figures (perhaps *the* most relevant figure) in development ethics. His work with the International Development Ethics Association (IDEA), which he co-founded in 1984 and served as its president until 2002, must also be considered (Crocker 2008, 11–19). Crocker has in-depth knowledge of the subject and, on top of that, an outstanding *ethos*. Convinced of the cause for which he works, generous, supportive, true to his friends, and with an extremely refined sense of humour, he is the very image of what we would expect of someone working in development ethics. Having met him is fortunate, being a friend of his is a gift, and taking part in this most deserved tribute is an honour and pleasure. Here I cannot fail to recall that I met David Crocker and his wife Eddie, through another outstanding specialist in development ethics and a very great man indeed, Denis Goulet, who is unfortunately no longer with us, but still remains in our memory.

The best way to take part in a homage to an intellectual and practitioner might well be to engage in dialogue with his proposal at a key point, stressing its virtues, pointing out its possible limits, and proposing a possible way to overcome these. That is what I now intend to do, in three steps:

1. I will examine whether Crocker's *agency-focused version of capability ethics* is right to highlight the role of agency in Sen's capability approach and to connect this with ideal of agency with the

importance of democracy for development and specifically with the importance of deliberative democracy.

2. I will tackle one of the challenges faced by Crocker, that of finding a normative foundation for a global ethics that seeks to globalise deliberative democracy in a multicultural world. I do so by asking whether Crocker's proposal is capable of providing that foundation, or if this foundation requires theories to take into account the intersubjective recognition of dignity as a concept separate from agency?

3. Descending from theory to practice, I will ask if it is enough to socially guarantee individual agency for democracy to work, or if it is also necessary to cultivate agency and moral autonomy through education.

As I see it, the Sen/Crocker concept of agency needs to be complemented with that of autonomy, which is defended by Kant and essential to the concept of dialogue in the discourse ethics of Apel and Habermas, as well as my own *ethica cordis*, which sets out a warmer version of the ethics of dialogue (Cortina 2007).

2 An *Agency-Focused Version of Capability Ethics*: Agency and Deliberative Democracy

Crocker has developed an *agency-focused version of capability ethics* and applied this to the problems of over-consumption, famine, governance, globalisation, sustainable development, global justice, safety, corruption, and transitional justice. He claims that development ethics has until now concentrated on the problem of 'understanding and fighting human poverty and promoting well-being throughout the world' (Crocker 2008, 51), but that it increasingly has expanded to embrace issues such as the inequality of power, corruption and transitional justice in an ethics of global development (Crocker 2014).

His proposal is closely linked to Amartya Sen's capability approach, but has at least three traits that distinguish him from Sen:

1. Crocker's version of the capability approach emphasises agency more than Sen's.
2. As one of the factors that ethics has to take into account to assess development, Crocker places special emphasis on establishing and

consolidating democracy. He considers the 'democratic turn' taken by Sen in development ethics (Sen 1999a, 1999b, 2005a) to be highly apposite in this respect, but is surprised that Sen should not have linked the value of democracy with that of agency and proposes to do this himself by taking agency as the keystone of his proposal. This emphasis on the democratic significance of agency enables Crocker to clarify and reinforce Sen's shift towards the ideals of public discussion and democratic participation as a comprehensive development for underpinning freedom (Crocker 2008, 2).

3. Deliberative democracy is the model which best exercises and fortifies people's agency and equality. For some time now, Crocker has subscribed to the 'deliberative turn' of democracy, which started above all in the 1990s. This is the reason why the aforementioned book (Crocker 2008) has the subtitle 'Agency, Capability, and Deliberative Democracy'.

Crocker asserts that the capability approach should be more closely linked with deliberative democracy for at least three reasons:

1. Sen's normative assumptions (agency, capability, functionings) enable him to persuasively defend the importance of democracy.
2. The capability approach for social ethics and international development requires a democracy conceived as public discussion and free and *fair* elections.
3. Sen's conception of democracy and of a democratically guided development will be enhanced by deliberative democracy, in both the local and global spheres.

Sen should, however, also link democracy with agency if we take into account the reasons Sen gives for considering that democracy is valuable:

1. Democracy is *intrinsically good* because it enables citizens to participate politically and this freedom is something that people have reasons to value intrinsically. Living in a society which does not entitle one to participate is a bad thing.
2. Democracy is *instrumentally good*, because democracies do not fight with each other and are more responsive than non-democracies in the protection of human agency and well-being.

3. Democracy is *constructively good*, because it has institutions enabling citizens to learn from each other and together forge and improve a society's values and priorities (Crocker 2008, 299–304).

Taking into account above all the *intrinsic* and *constructive* reasons, the capability approach should, Crocker argues, clearly and explicitly resort or appeal to agency in its argument in favour of democracy. If people value the right to participate *in its own right* this is because they value their own agency and its exercise, wanting to be an agent-subject of their lives and not a mere patient-subject. To recall Tocqueville, 'the man who asks of freedom anything other than itself is born to be a slave' (1955, 169), but it is furthermore impossible to *construct* the values and priorities of a society without agent-subjects deliberating and deciding.

All this leads, according to Crocker, to the fact that 'Sen can and should say that democracy is intrinsically valuable because democracy provides each citizen with agency freedom and, often, agency achievement insofar as democracy provides its citizens with opportunities to shape public policies and select their leaders' (2008, 300). Sen has material to build an argument of the following type: 'democracy embodies or expresses individual and collective agency; agency is intrinsically valuable (because it is one basis for human dignity); so, democracy is intrinsically valuable' (2008, 302).

Leaving aside the matter of whether agency is a basis for human dignity for the time being, I feel that it is true that deliberative democracy has taken on new strength since the 1990s, and with it the consideration that the best political expression for citizens is as agent-subjects of their lives and not patient-objects to be acted upon. Some reasons of this type would be, for example (Cortina 2011):

1. The need to provide content for the term 'people's government' in democratic communities which have already accepted the representative system and are nevertheless aware that electing representatives alone is not sufficient for genuine democracy.
2. It is the best way to combine individual autonomy and popular sovereignty (Habermas 1998, 84–104).
3. It is the most appropriate way to reply to criticism of the rule of the majority as a mechanism for making decisions in democratic societies (Dewey 1927, 207).

4. It enables overcoming the shortcomings of a 'weak democracy' and reinforces a *strong democracy* in the tradition of Rousseau (Barber 1984).

5. The experience of popular practices of deliberation has often been positive because the active role of citizens has increased, social inequalities have been reduced, and new solutions have been provided. This is true in notable cases such as Porto Alegre and Kerala, but also in a large number of councils which opt for participatory budgeting (Ganuza and Francés 2012).

6. The deliberative model stems from the classical model of Pericles's Athens, but also from Kantian civic republicanism, which only considers legitimate those laws that the people could have wanted and which can be submitted and promulgated according to the public use of reason. According to Kant in the *Critique of Pure Reason*:

Reason depends on this freedom for its very existence, for reason has no dictatorial authority. Its verdict is always the simple agreement of free citizens, of whom each one must be permitted to express without let or hindrance, his objections or even his veto. (A 847, B 766; Bohman 1996, 35)

In actual fact, deliberative democracy should be linked with agency and the capabilities approach should take this into account.

Crocker nevertheless goes one step further and considers his *agency-focused version of capability ethics* to be the most promising ethical proposal for offering a normative standpoint that enables the consequences of globalisation to be appraised, 'The long-term goal of good and just development – whether national or global – must be to secure an adequate level of agency and morally basic capabilities for everyone in the world' (Crocker 2008, 390). From this it follows that 'Good globalization also includes the global dispersion of democratic norms, and the ideal of global citizenship' (390).

However, the inevitable question then comes up, one that Crocker himself puts forward: Can and should democracy be 'globalised'? That is, should it be imposed in authoritarian countries, resuscitated in countries in which it is under attack, and installed or deepened in global institutions? Can democracy be 'imposed' or 'installed' without undermining its moral foundations? (375). The answer to this question depends on my opinion on what the philosophical foundation of deliberative democracy is, and on how this foundation is put into practice.

3 The Philosophical Foundation of Deliberative Democracy

The starting point for any democratic system is social disagreement. Disagreements may arise in relation with preferences (what members want to do), beliefs (what members believe about the world), common goals and the policies through which that can be achieved, what the basic capabilities and human rights are, or the rules and norms for structuring social life, because these express the conduct that we expect from each other. There are great differences among the possible forms of settling these disagreements.

As I see it, disagreements about *beliefs* have to do with what Rawls calls 'comprehensive' (Rawls 2001, 19, 28–9) doctrines of the good. These doctrines can of course be discussed in the public arena, but do not have to be settled through public deliberation, because citizens are entitled to go on maintaining their comprehensive doctrine of the good. There naturally have to be debates about these fundamental outlooks in civil society, but reaching agreement on these matters is not a political matter, because the diversity of points of view is an asset of reasonable pluralism.

In contrast, as Richardson and Crocker so rightly point out, attempts may be made to solve disagreements on goals and policies through a deliberative process (Richardson 2002, 165–9; Crocker 2008, 321–9). Citizens nonetheless have to decide, either directly or through their representatives, on what levels the deliberative process will be applied and what institutions will be legitimated for and by this process.

As regards deliberating on what the *basic capabilities* will be and what we are going to recognise as *human rights*, this is a task that Sen leaves open and can only be carried out with a large number of assumptions (Sen 2005b; Cortina 2010, 106–12). In the case of *preferences*, deliberation is vital to attempt to go from the 'I prefer' to the 'we want a world like this' (Barber 1984). A democratic 'tempering' of individual choices is necessary, but in order for the results of deliberation to have any social impact, they must ultimately be enshrined in norms of action.

That is why I consider deliberation on the *norms* that govern different levels of society a key matter. A deliberative democracy is a form of political organisation, which should first of all deal with disagreements about the rules that govern social structure. There must be deliberation on different levels on the content of the rules that govern society's operation and whether they are fair and correct. These rules can be conceived in the same vein as Habermas's action norms, which he envisions as 'temporally, socially, and substantively generalized behavioural expectations' (1998, 107) that form the skeleton of a society because they express what we expect of each other, as mutual expectations of behaviour.

Today a large number of theories consider deliberation to be essential in order to talk of fair, objectively valid, or rationally legitimate norms, and give different reasons for this (Nino 1997, 160–6). I have on certain occasions talked of three types of these theories (Cortina 2010, 2011), but I now believe that it is more appropriate to talk of four theory types, precisely because I think that the Sen/Crocker approach (D2) is methodologically different from that of Rawls (D1) as well as the other two types: D3 and D4.

D1 submits the premise that *to be legitimate, democracies require deliberative processes through which citizens, who should be the ultimate authors of laws, use public reasoning to come to decisions.* The norms of a democratic society must be reasonably *acceptable* by its citizens, not just factually accepted. A normative theory of democracy, in contrast to an empirical one, requires rational acceptability of action norms. That is why Gutmann and Thompson propose three principles as expressing the willingness to seek mutually justifiable reasons: reciprocity, publicity, and accountability (1986). Crocker calls these principles *deliberative ideals* (2008, 312–14).

D1 covers a wide range of thinkers, including Rawls, Gutmann, Thompson, and Richardson. They understand deliberative democracy as being 'the conception of democratic politics in which decisions and policies are justified in a process of discussion among free and equal citizens or their accountable representatives' (Gutmann and Thompson 2004, 161). To some extent they assume the stance taken by the so-called 'later Rawls', which stresses the role of public reason linked with respect to 'constitutional fundamentals' in a deliberative democracy (Rawls 1999, 579 and 580).

I myself consider that D1 expresses a model proper to *political liberalism*, which does not seek to plunge into the depths of human reason, because it wishes to be engaged in 'politics, not metaphysics'. That is why it is content to discover by 'reflective equilibrium' the elements enabling a moral-political conception of justice to be formed.

This model expresses the moral-political point of view of Western democracies and cannot therefore understand deliberative democracy as a factor of all peoples' development, one which has to be promoted or installed in some way in other countries. When Rawls attempted to extend a *thin* moral-political concept of justice to non-liberal societies (well-ordered hierarchical and consultative societies) in *The Law of Peoples*, this application came in for a lot of criticism. How can we ever consider deliberative democracy as a requirement of justice forming part of the concept of peoples' development, which also has to be installed worldwide in a multicultural world? This therefore means that one has to go beyond political liberalism.

D2 also understands that *to be legitimate, democracies require deliberative processes through which citizens, who should be the ultimate authors of laws, use public reasoning to come to decisions.* It nevertheless goes beyond politics, though without plunging into metaphysics. Deliberative practice is thus an expression of the agency of citizens, who should be able to exercise their agency on an equal basis.

This alternative would be Crocker's proposal of the *agency-focused version of capability ethics*, with roots in a tradition claiming to be Marxist, Smithian, Kantian, and Aristotelian (Conill 2013). Sen and Crocker propose replacing 'the domination of circumstances and chance over individuals by the domination of individuals over chance and circumstances' (Sen 1984, 504; Crocker 2008, 17). To do so they develop an anthropology which does not wish to be metaphysical, but does indeed emphasize capabilities, which have to be empowered up to a threshold which identifies an appropriate level of agency and well-being. This anthropology echoes the words of Marx (1994, 64) in the *Economic and Philosophical Manuscripts*: 'in the doctrine that man is the supreme being for man; thus it ends with the categorical imperative to overthrow all conditions in which man is a debased, enslaved, neglected and contemptible being'. Sen owes a great deal to Smith and his concept of freedom, but also to the Marxist tradition of human existence and well-being. That is why Crocker considers that the idea of human agency is as appealing as the one that he found in the Yugoslav group *Praxis*.

D2 claims *universality*, unlike the proposal of political liberalism. From this standpoint deliberative democracy can and should be 'globalised', installed or deepened in global institutions, but without undermining its moral foundations. It remains unclear, however, why societies are obliged to cultivate individuals' agency? What reasons can be given to make people cultivate their own agency, not to mention that of others? Is a *quasi-metaphysical anthropology* enough? In my opinion the commitment to work for all to be able to exercise their agency equally requires the involvement of theories of *reciprocal recognition*.

D3 would agree that *to be legitimate, democracies require deliberative processes through which citizens, who should be the ultimate authors of laws, use public reasoning to come to decisions*. In doing so, however, it goes further in its claims than D1 and D2. D3 submits that human rationality requires dialogue to discover the validity of norms or other subjects of public reasoning, because *human rationality is dialogical*. This is not just a question of a Western political tradition that seeks to spread itself for pragmatic reasons, nor even of an anthropology of agency and capabilities, but of a *human need to elucidate what rules are rationally valid*. This is something that a person alone cannot do, not even a group of people: there has to be a recognition that all those affected by norms are entitled to get involved in a dialogue which attempts to defend universalisable interests. Democracy must be *inclusive*, because 'I include among "those affected (or involved)" anyone whose interests are touched by the foreseeable consequences of a general practice regulated by the norms at issue' (Habermas 1998, 107).

This is why the best model of democracy is the deliberative one and why the democratic training of will or will formation is essential to discover valid norms. As Apel puts it so well: 'Democracy, as an approximation to this ideal demand, is thus rather more than an assemblage of neutral procedures, which we decide to abide by for pragmatic reasons; it has its *ethical-normative foundation* in the *ethics of the ideal communication community*, which we have already always accepted by arguing' (1980, 272). D3 expresses the position of discourse ethics and the theory of discourse, which could include Apel and Habermas, but also all of us who work in this line, though with some major internal differences (Benhabib, Bohman, Conill, Cortina,

Dryzek, Forst, García-Marzá, Hoyos, Kettner, Maliandi, Rehg, and Ulrich).

The starting point is not the individual, but the intersubjectivity that already exists in the networks of language, which has to be strengthened. We subjects *are* in a relationship of reciprocal recognition: we are what we are thanks to our relationship with others. The moral-political demands of rational dialogue, which refer to matters of justice, are the basis of a democracy that is valid in its own right because it is the political form of expressing human practical rationality. We have a rational foundation for a normative theory of democracy, a foundation which rests on a pragmatic and counterfactual assumption of speech: the ideal speech situation, which is presupposed on the pragmatic level by anyone performing a communicative action (Apel 1973; Habermas 1983).

At one point Crocker praises Sen because 'rather than offering one theory designed to best the others or to yield a definitive blueprint of the "just society", Sen takes the ball away from philosophical theory and kicks it to an agency-oriented conception of democratic decision-making' (2008, 307). Sen nevertheless requires no more than that. Discourse ethics does indeed require more, as it places deliberation in the power of the persons affected in each case, who should attempt to satisfy universalisable interests.

In the case of democracy, the application of the 'Principle of Discourse' to the political community requires getting a dialogue between citizens under way. The Democratic Principle 'explains the performative meaning of the practice of self-determination on the part of legal consociates who recognize one another as free and equal members of an association they have joined voluntarily' (Habermas 1998, 110). In a global world it would nevertheless be necessary to take into account all those affected, even the interests of future generations, i.e. to create a cosmopolitan democracy. This would be a regulative idea in the Kantian sense, used for guidance for action and as a criterion for rational criticism.

D3 nonetheless involves a set of limits which have to be overcome:

1. It should be acknowledged that civil society is not only the place for discovering and forming judgement, but also where ideas are justified and decisions are made on several levels, because there is an institutionalised domain of civil society in which rationally justified

decisions are made, although that institutionalisation is not implemented by legal channels (García-Marzá 2008, 2016).

2. D3 forgets the transcendence of communicative power for economic life.
3. D3 considers the Principle of Discourse as an expression of a notion of abstract autonomy, which can be modulated as something moral or legal, when, in my opinion, this is already an ethical principle.
4. D3 forgets the need to build moral subjects for democracy to work.
5. D3 silences or neglects the role of emotions in building democracy.

D4 attempts to overcome these shortcomings, as I have tried to show elsewhere (Cortina 2003, 2007, 2010, 2011), but only the last three will be dealt with here. D4 understands the Principle of Discourse as an expression of the reciprocal recognition of the interlocutors' autonomy, which is an ethical category to the extent that it reveals the reality of an 'us' that has not been constructed by any agreement. The reconstruction of the assumptions of speech takes us to a 'we argue', which stems from the reciprocal recognition of those who know themselves to be valid interlocutors, obliged to joint self-legislation, and empowered to independently accept or reject, in this case, the claim of the validity of justice.

The point of reciprocal recognition, which is the point where intersubjectivity is discovered, is already an ethical point. There is no abstract autonomy, which is modulated as moral or legal, but instead the mutual recognition of autonomy, which demands to be developed in a communicative democracy. What we could call 'pragmatic socialism' surpasses political liberalism and quasi-metaphysical anthropology because the starting point is an ethical recognition that obliges the interlocutors to mutually respect their autonomy. To go one step further, such recognition, as has also been stressed by Axel Honneth and Paul Ricoeur, is not restricted to that of logical-argumentative capacity. Instead of insisting on the aspect of necessary social recognition, a logical-*cordial* recognition, which includes the other in their personal integrity, needs to be appreciated (Honneth 1992; Ricoeur 2004; Cortina 2007).

Lastly, if we want democracy to work, it is vital to construct moral subjects and democratic citizens, through formal and informal education. Political power must be communicatively legitimated and this requires citizens to form part of free associations, defending universalisable interests which put pressure on institutional political power from a 'reasoning public'. But why should it interest citizens to cultivate their own and others' agency? Why should it interest them to *seriously* deliberate in an attempt to meet common needs?

It is vital to form subjects who appreciate their own and others' agency, but also subjects with a will for justice, willing to seriously engage in dialogue, to detect what interests are universalisable, and to decide on these. These subjects must be endowed with the capacity to argue and appropriate political emotions (Krause 2008; Nussbaum 2013), but also with the capability to want what is fair, which is the driving force behind any democratic society (Cortina 2007).

4 'Making Democracy Work': Educating Citizens to Become Agents and Autonomous Subjects

In a global world, as Crocker puts so well, 'it is not enough to inquire *if*, *how*, or *why* globalization affects human choice and institutional distribution. One must have a reasoned normative view of what counts as beneficial and deleterious consequences, and how the concept of justice should be understood or decided' (2008, 389). The answer, from his perspective, is that the most promising approach is 'the "agent-oriented" capability perspective' (389). From this standpoint the relevant categories for distributive justice will be agency or autonomy, capabilities and functionings (38).

From my own standpoint and the ethics of what I call 'cordial reason': I agree with Crocker that it is a duty of justice to empower people to be agents of their lives, in both their search for happiness and in the decisions of the political community. I feel, however, that there are three difficulties in Crocker's proposal which ought to be cleared up:

1. The general category of agency as relevant for distributive justice is not the same as the type of agency that is required for democracy to work.
2. It is not possible to identify agency, in Sen and Crocker's sense, and autonomy in the Kantian or neo-Kantian sense.
3. For democracy to work there has to be a *genuine exercise of agency* and a *genuine exercise of autonomy*. This is because people may believe that they are acting as agents of their lives while they are

actually being manipulated, thus in fact making them patients or passive recipients; people may believe that they are autonomous yet actually be heteronomous. Without a proper exercise of agency *and* autonomy the person loses human quality, because agency and autonomy are valuable for their own sake, but also because democracy does not work without them.

It is true that on certain occasions Crocker addresses the questions of the kinds of persons who would make competent and virtuous deliberators and the way these skills and virtues might be brought about (2006, 190). According to him, 'without participants with the "right stuff", the deliberative approach to democracy might not manifest respect for persons, result in mutually acceptable decisions, or promote justice. As Drèze and Sen remark, democracy requires, in addition to the democratic ideals and institutions of (deliberative) democracy, citizens who "make democracy work"' (Crocker 2008, 329).

Other authors have also written about this 'right stuff'. Bohman considers that for citizens to have a minimum 'political functioning', it is necessary for them not to suffer political poverty (1996, 123–32), because 'only equality of political capacities makes deliberation fully democratic' (109). Political capacities would according to him be the capacity to get a public dialogue under way or to make proposals (110), the capacity to argue and counter-argue, the capacity to harmonise proposals, the ability for persuasive and not manipulative rhetoric (90), and to participate in deliberative movements (learning by doing) in formal and informal education. This does not mean waiting for interlocutors to have these skills in order to be able to start to deliberate, but instead involves laying the social foundations required to be able to have these and learn to deliberate by deliberating. '*Political poverty* consists of the inability of groups of citizens to participate effectively in the democratic process and their consequent vulnerability to the intended and unintended consequences of decisions' (125).

Gutmann and Thompson propose three civic virtues to enable deliberation: mutual respect, civic integrity, and civic magnanimity (1996, 79–85). Crocker adds tolerance to this (2006, 187–90). As I see it, nonetheless, these opportunities, skills, and civic virtues are not enough to be able to have agent-subjects and autonomous people – something more is needed. As regards *agency*, I agree that 'one is an agent when one deliberates and decides for oneself, acts to realize one's aims, and, thereby, makes some intentional difference in the world' (Crocker 2008, 298). Deliberative democracy is characterised by making decisions by means of deliberation, and not only by adding votes (Dewey 1927, 207–8). But it may occur that democracy appears to be deliberative, but is actually emotive, i.e. that political agents, the media, and social networks manipulate the emotions of citizens, who are not mature enough to be aware of the manipulation (Sartori 1997). That is why it is necessary to educate for citizens to be agents of their lives, i.e. for them to be *mature*, able to discern between manipulation and grounded argument (Cortina 2013). Participation is not enough. As Barber so rightly says, citizens take a very active part in strong, unitary democracy, but fail really to be agents (1984, 221 and 222). For them to be agents we need mature citizens who do not let themselves be manipulated but pursue their goals, exercise their rationality, in Rawls's sense, and have the appropriate political emotions (Krause 2008; Nussbaum 2013).

Etymologically, the term autonomy means *self-legislation*. A person is autonomous when he furnishes himself with his own laws and can be governed by these. This person is not only an agent-subject, the protagonist of his own life, but above all, a self-legislator, free to do but also to self-govern. This etymological definition of autonomy is not the one that tends to be used in daily life or in specialists' language. In both cases autonomy tends to be understood as *self-determination*: the ability to determine oneself to act one way or another. This is the case of the Principal of Autonomy in bioethics. In clinical action one has to have the patient's consent, if they are able to determine themselves, that is, if they have some psychological maturity and are not determined by external pressures or by internal events, such as very acute pain or addictions. It is necessary to find out whether patients are mature or able enough to assume that they are deciding for themselves based on reasons that appear to them to be such. It is not reasons that are judged, but the ability to determine oneself. This *capacity* is identified with agency, in my opinion.

This capacity for self-determination is actually what I was referring to in *Por una ética del consumo* when I talked about 'autonomous consumption' and I would now like to define my position further, because Crocker rightly criticised my concept of autonomy (Cortina 2002, 234–41). In dialogue with me in *Ethics of Global Development*, he claims the following:

[Cortina's ethics of consumption] seems to be assuming that human beings are more or less conditioned but not completely determined by both external and internal forces. Our consumption choices are not or do not have to be the mere effects of external causes and internal drives, passions, habits, and inclinations. Persons as agents can prevent impulses. Is this a defense of the Kantian transcendental ego that operates 'from above', against, or instead of our 'empirical' motivations? Or is there a way of understanding inner control without falling into a *metaphysical* dualism? (Crocker 2008, 244–5)

Crocker suggests investigating other theories of the self, such as those of Frankfurt and Sen, in which agents have more or less freedom to prioritize and coordinate their inclinations, affiliations, and roles. Indeed, when talking of autonomy in *Por una ética del consumo*, I understood this as being *self-determination*: as the capacity to govern oneself, from a self-reflection which enables arranging wishes and interests in order of importance, with no need to fall into metaphysical dualisms. I should have talked of 'self-determined consumption', which would be proper to agent-subjects. In fact *autonomous consumption* would be connected with what I called *consumo justo* or 'fair consumption' in my book, because it is linked to the subject's capacity to want the universal, in Kant's sense (Cortina 2002, 241–8).

A subject is autonomous, in Kant's sense, when he or she gives themselves their own laws. The point is that they do not formulate these laws based on their own *idiosyncrasy*, but take into account the laws that they could want in a world in which the goals of all autonomous beings will be respected. People have the capacity to govern their conduct by the laws extending beyond their own selfish interest, laws which they could want as citizens of a world in which everyone could accomplish their goals, on condition that they did not prevent others from doing so. This is the meaning of a Kingdom of Ends (Kant 1968, 436). As regards consumption, the person who self-determines to consume some products or others, that is, who acts as agent-subject of their consumption, must take into account, in order to be autonomous, whether it is possible to universalise their lifestyle of consumption without harming other human beings or nature (Cortina 2002, 247–8).

It follows from all this that *agency* is the freedom to lead one's own life, while *autonomy* consists of the capacity to give oneself universalisable laws and to govern oneself by these. Agent-subjects, in Sen's sense, may therefore not be autonomous, in Kant's sense, if they lack the capacity to include laws in their life plans enabling the implementation of plans that others have reasons to value to be implemented, beyond selfish interest. Democracy cannot work properly without autonomous subjects. But why should a citizen be interested in concern for universalisable interests and not only for egoistic or group interests?

As Sen has acknowledged, human rationality does not only move by *self-interest*, but always takes into account other motives: *sympathy* and *commitment* (Sen 2002, 35–7). Sympathy, which Smith already alluded to, 'refers to one person's welfare being affected by the state of others', while commitment 'is concerned with breaking the tight link between individual welfare (with or without sympathy) and the choice of action (for example, being committed to help remove some misery of others even though one personally does not suffer from it' (Sen 1977; 2002, 35). Commitment stems from a deontological tradition with Kantian roots. The recognition of the dignity of a being who is autonomous, able to give himself his own laws, goes along with the commitment to work to be able to implement life plans that he has grounds to value, on condition that this does not prevent others from realising their own aims for life (Cortina 2002, 2007). From a Kantian perspective, opting for commitment – acting in accordance with one's own autonomy – is not one more possibility amongst others, but a moral demand stemming from the recognition of absolutely valuable beings, who do not have a price, but do have dignity. In order for democracy to work, people have to cultivate their feeling of sympathy and their sense of commitment. It will then be useful to reinterpret the *agency-focused version of capability ethics* from the perspective of the cordial reason version of reciprocal recognition (Cortina 2007). Educating autonomous subjects for a democratic citizenry is thus a central pillar of the building.

References

Apel, Karl-Otto. 1973. *Transformation der Philosophie*. Frankfurt: Suhrkamp.
    1980. 'Notwendigkeit, Schwierigkeit und Möglichkeit einer philosophischen Begründung der Ethik im Zeitalter der Wissenschaft' in *Festschrift für K. Tsatsos*. P. Kanellopulos (ed.). Athens: Nomikai Ekoloseis Ant., 215–75.

Barber, Benjamin. 1984. *Strong Democracy: Participatory Politics for a New Age*. Berkeley: University of California Press.

Bohman, James. 1996. *Public Deliberation: Pluralism, Complexity and Democracy*. Cambridge, MA: The MIT Press.

Conill, Jesús. 2013. 'The Philosophical Foundations of the Capabilities Approach' in *Handbook of the Philosophical Foundations of Business Ethics*. Vol. II. Christoph Lütge (ed.). Munich: Springer, 661–74.

Cortina, Adela. 2002. *Por una ética del consumo. La ciudadanía del consumidor en un mundo global*. Madrid: Taurus.

    2003. *Covenant and Contract: Politics, Ethics and Religion*. Leuven: Peeters.

    2007. *Ética de la razón cordial*. Oviedo: Nobel.

    2010. 'Communicative Democracy: A Version of Deliberative Democracy'. *Archiv für Rechts- und Sozialphilosophie* 96(2): 133–50.

    2011. 'Ciudadanía democrática: ética, política y religión'. *Isegoría* 44.

    2013. *¿Para qué sirve realmente la ética?* Barcelona: Paidós.

    2014. 'Four Tasks for Forward-Looking Global Ethics'. *Journal of Global Ethics* 10(1): 30–7.

Crocker, David A. 2006. 'Sen and Deliberative Democracy' in *Capabilities Equality: Basic Issues and Problems*. Alexander Kaufman (ed.). New York: Routledge, 155–97.

    2008. *Ethics of Global Development: Agency, Capability and Deliberative Democracy*. Cambridge University Press.

    2014. 'Development and Global Ethics: Five Foci for the Future'. *Journal of Global Ethics* 10(3): 245–53.

Dewey, John. 1927. *The Public and Its Problems*. New York: Holt.

Enderle, Georges (ed.). 1999. *International Business Ethics: Challenges and Approaches*. University of Notre Dame Press.

Ganuza, Ernesto and Francisco Francés. 2012. *El círculo virtuoso de la democracia: los presupuestos participativos a debate*. Madrid: CIS.

García-Marzá, Domingo. 2008. 'Sociedad civil: una concepción radical'. *Recerca* 8: 27–46.

    2016. 'Enfoques mesodeliberativos: sobre la articulación institucional en las democracias deliberativas'. Unpublished manuscript.

Goulet, Denis. 2006. *Development Ethics at Work: Explorations 1960–2002*. New York: Routledge.

Gutmann, Amy and Dennis Thompson. 1996. *Democracy and Disagreement*. Cambridge, MA: The Belknap Press of Harvard University Press.

    2004. Why Deliberative Democracy? Princeton University Press.

Habermas, Jürgen. 1983. *Moralbewusstsein und kommunikatives Handeln*. Frankfurt: Suhrkamp.

1998. *Between Facts and Norms*. Cambridge, MA: The MIT Press.

Honneth, Axel. 1992. *Kampf um Anerkennung*. Frankfurt: Suhrkamp.

Kant, Immanuel. 1968. *Grundlegung zur Metaphysik der Sitten*. Kants Werke. Akademie Textausgabe. Vol. IV. Berlin: Walter de Gruyter, 385–464.

Krause, Sharon R. 2008. *Civil Passions: Moral Sentiment and Democratic Deliberation*. Princeton University Press.

Martínez, Emilio. *Ética del desarrollo de los pueblos*. Madrid: Trotta.

Marx, Karl. 1994. 'Critique of Hegel's Philosophy of Right' in *Marx: Early Political Writings*. Joseph J. O'Malley (ed.). Cambridge University Press.

Nino, Carlos S. 1997. *La constitución de la democracia deliberativa*. Barcelona: Gedisa.

Nussbaum, Martha C. 2013. *Political Emotions: Why Love Matters for Justice*. Cambridge, MA: The Belknap Press of Harvard University Press.

Potter, Van Rensselaer. 1988. *Global Bioethics: Building on the Leopold Legacy*. Michigan State University Press.

Rawls, John. 1999. *Collected Papers*. Samuel Freeman (ed.). Cambridge, MA: Harvard University Press.

2001. *Justice as Fairness: A Restatement*. Erin Kelly (ed.). Cambridge, MA: The Belknap Press of Harvard University Press.

Richardson, Henry S. 2002. *Democratic Autonomy: Public Reasoning about the Ends of Policy*. Oxford University Press.

Ricoeur, Paul. 2004. *Parcours de la reconnaissance. Trois études*. Paris: Éditions Stock.

Ruggie, John Gerard. 2013. *Just Business: Multinational Corporations and Human Rights*. New York: W. W. Norton & Company.

Sartori, Giovanni. 1997. *Homo Videns*. Rome: Gius. Laterza & Figli Spa.

Sen, Amartya. 1977. 'Rational Fools: A Critique of the Behavioural Foundations of Economic Theory'. *Philosophy and Public Affairs* 6: 317–44.

1984. 'Development: Which Way Now?' in *Resources, Values and Development*. Oxford: Blackwell.

1999a. *Development as Freedom*. New York: Anchor Books.

1999b. 'Democracy as a Universal Value'. *Journal of Democracy* 10(3): 3–17.

2002. *Rationality and Freedom*. Cambridge, MA: The Belknap Press of Harvard University Press.

2005a. *The Argumentative Indian*. London: Allen Lane.

2005b. 'Human Rights and Capabilities'. *Journal of Human Development* 6(2): 151–66.

Tocqueville, Alexis de. 1955. *The Old Regime and the French Revolution*. Translated by Stuart Gilbert. New York: Anchor Books.

13 | The Double Democratic Deficit*

Global Governance and Future Generations

FRANCES STEWART

Introduction

David Crocker has spent much of his distinguished career investigating the ethics of global development, drawing on Sen's capability approach. In particular, he has been concerned with how democracy fits into the capability approach, and the role that might be played by deliberative democracy (Crocker 2008). This chapter is in the same spirit, exploring deficiencies that arise in advancing capabilities as a result of deficiencies in the reach of democracy. The normative frame underlying the capability approach critically includes individual agency as intrinsic to advancing development.[1] Development should not just be about the achievement of particular material (and other) goals, but is also defined by *how* any state of affairs (or set of functionings) is brought about (Sen 1985). A particular set of achievements which respects individual agency is thus assumed to advance development more than the same set attained by some form of central planning or market functioning in which individual freedoms are limited. The latter may advance individual well-being, but not necessarily capabilities since agency is absent. Moreover, it is not only a matter of valuing the process, but outcomes also depend on who is included in decision-making; structures which exclude not only limit agency but may also generally lead to worse sets of capabilities.[2]

This chapter explores two types of democratic deficit. First, the deficiency of mechanisms of global governance, which implies a lack of agency over global (as against national) problems, and in turn

* I am very grateful to the editors and anonymous referees for very helpful comments on an earlier draft.

leads to a distortion of decisions and consequently lowers overall well-being, as well as seriously limiting agency. Second, the absence of future generations in current deliberations, even though they are greatly affected by many of them, which represents a major democratic deficit. The first type of deficit is in principle straightforward to solve through new or reformed global institutions, although there are severe political obstacles to the realization of such reforms. The second type of deficit raises much more challenging issues, since we are considering people who are not alive today and who cannot therefore be themselves included in the deliberations which affect them.

This chapter first briefly reviews the concepts of agency, autonomy and deliberative democracy, and their relation to the capability approach, so as to clarify the normative framework adopted, which is used to define what would count as a democratic deficit. It then discusses the two types of democratic deficit. In highlighting these two aspects, I do not claim that democratic structures are satisfactory in other ways. Indeed, there are many problems with current political decision-making, including a virtually total lack of democratic structures in a number of countries, as well as the power of special interests and limited and biased information, which constrain democracy in many so-called democratic states. Finally, the chapter considers possible ways of remedying the two deficits.

A Normative Framework

The idea that expansion of freedoms constitutes the goal of development provides the basis of the capability approach (Sen 1999b). The focus on freedoms explains why development is seen as the expansion of capabilities (what people may be or do) rather than of functionings (what they actually be or do) since advancing capabilities implies that individuals have choice over which capabilities they wish to realize. Valuing agency as well as realized capabilities also follows from the centrality of freedoms. Agency is defined by Sen as 'what a person is free to do and achieve in pursuit of whatever goals or values he or she regards as important' (Sen 1985, 206); 'The people have to be seen . . . as being actively involved . . . in shaping their own destiny, and not just as passive recipients of the fruits of cunning development programmes' (Sen 1999b, 53), or, as Crocker states, people and nations should have the opportunity to be 'authors of their own lives and development path' (Crocker 2008).

Having agency therefore means that individuals have control over, or at least significantly influence, factors affecting their lives. Within the family, it implies that each individual has freedom to make her own choice on work, consumption and so on. In relation to both markets and states, it implies that people can choose which capabilities they wish to realize and how. Nonetheless, everyone is subject to constraints – complete control over one's own life is not a realizable ideal. In practice there are degrees of agency.

When it comes to determining priorities at a larger level – such as those of governments, including deciding levels of taxation and expenditure, allocations of expenditure among sectors, regulations of market activities and the manifold other influences governments have on patterns of development and societal workings – individual agency is relevant but not sufficient since a single individual is generally powerless to bring about change at a national (or even sub-national) level. Here collective action is needed. Crocker makes the useful distinction between *direct* agency – where individuals themselves make the decisions which affect the relevant outcomes – and *indirect* agency when people contribute indirectly to the realization of their goals, for example through representative democracy (Crocker 2008, 154). Sen refers to the need for reasoned and informed public discussions, in a democratic setting, to make these choices. Crocker suggests that here the concept of 'deliberative democracy' is a useful addition to the capability approach, a means of securing agency at these levels of decision-making (Crocker 2006). Both agree that democratic structures are essential and that this is not just a matter of majoritarian voting. As Sen states, 'We must not identify democracy with majority rules. Democracy has complex demands, which certainly include voting and respect for election results, but it also requires the protection of liberties and freedoms, respect for legal entitlements, and the guaranteeing of free discussion and uncensored distribution of news and fair comment' (Sen 1999a, 5). Moreover, majoritarian democracy can overrule the preferences of minorities, who may be treated little differently from populations subject to non-democratic rule. Hence there is a need for particular structures to protect minorities, including human rights laws, and mechanisms to allow for inclusive democracy (such as power-sharing and proportional representation).

At the national level, deliberative democracy involves decision-making on the basis of reasoned and informed discussions about national priorities. In a deliberative democracy, people (or their representatives) make decisions on the basis of such reasoned discussion, and not in response to private interests (Crocker 2006). According to Fishkin and Luskin (2005), deliberative democracy should be informed, balanced, conscientious, substantive and comprehensive. A democratic deficit may then be said to occur where people do not have direct or indirect agency over important decisions that affect their lives, and where conditions for deliberative democracy are absent.

In practice, the ideal of deliberative democracy is rarely realized even in countries with democratic structures. As Crouch has argued, 'free market democracy' is increasingly being replaced by 'corporate authoritarianism', as companies dominate political finance and control the media and many think tanks (Crouch 2014). Others have noted particular deficiencies of democracy in the newly 'democratic' countries (see Roberts 2016). From this perspective, while countries are located on a spectrum in terms of democratic freedoms, it can be argued that there is a democratic deficit in most national decision-making. In increasing numbers of countries, however, at least some structures are in place which permit a degree of national autonomy[3] and indirect agency at the national level and below.

However, this chapter is not concerned with this type of constraint on agency at the national level (or below), but in two other areas in which agency is severely limited. The first is at the global level which increasingly affects individual lives. Here I argue the deficit is far greater than at lower levels of decision-making since democratic structures are not even in place despite many fora for discussions, often in, or organized by, the United Nations. Indeed, it could be argued that the conditions for 'deliberation' (or reasoned discussion) are in a way in place. But in the absence of democratic structures, and the presence of many powerful actors, such reasoned discussion means very little in terms of actual decision-making. While the Security Council does act as a decision-making body, its structure is not democratic and its remit is limited to matters of security. The second area where democratic participation is absent is that concerning decisions affecting future generations. Our actions today have huge implications for the lives of future generations, yet, by definition, they are not 'at the table', just as the present generation was not at the table for the many historic decisions which affect us. Consequently, there appears to be a double democratic deficit – in addition to democratic deficiencies at the national level and below – which results from the almost total absence of any sort of democratic governance structures responsible for decisions in which global interactions are important; and equally, the complete absence of future generations from discussions and decisions which are made today but substantially affect these unrepresented future generations.

The aim of this chapter is to consider the nature of this double democratic deficit, and to sketch some mechanisms which might help to reduce the two deficits. The next section will discuss the nature of both the global deficit and the generational one, pointing to the huge influence of global developments over individual lives, and the limited power people have to influence relevant decisions, as well as the importance of decisions today on the lives of future generations. The third section discusses possible avenues for overcoming the double deficits.

The Democratic Deficits

The Global Deficit

Globalization of world trade, capital movements, migration and communication means that an increasing number of events which influence people's lives in an important way have a global origin, coming from outside the country in which people affected by the decisions live. Examples are macro-economic policies, capital flows, the activities of multinational corporations (MNCs), conflict and migration patterns, health and disease, and most importantly the environment which also relates to the generational deficit. Below I focus primarily on the areas of macro-economic policy, capital flows and MNCs. Environmental considerations are discussed later.

Global Macro-Economic Influences

Economies are continuously affected by macro-economic events and decisions occurring outside their borders. Expansionary fiscal policies have effects beyond the country where they take place, as do austerity policies, particularly when these policies emanate from large economies. For primary goods-producing developing countries, the terms of

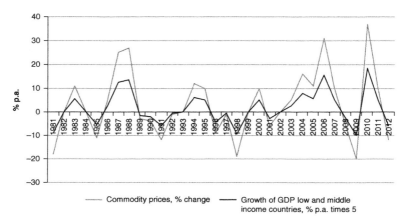

Figure 13.1. Emerging and developing GDP growth rate and commodity prices growth.

trade largely determine their development trajectories, yet are decided by events outside their control. Poor international terms of trade in the 1980s, for example, due to recession in the developed countries in the early 1980s, led to a decade of negative growth and indebtedness in developing countries. The terms of trade only improved significantly in the 2000s, largely due to output growth in China, leading to sustained growth of African and Latin American economies. But the subsequent slow-down in the Chinese economy has led to a renewed decline in commodity prices and mounting problems for primary goods-producing economies which are consequently experiencing rising debt and lower growth in the 2010s. The growth in output of developing and emerging economies mirrors the changes in commodity terms of trade, over which they have no control (Figure 13.1).

The terms of trade problem was recognized decades ago and a commodity price stabilization scheme was proposed by developing countries. Indeed, the Integrated Programme for Commodities (IPC) was agreed by the United Nations Conference on Trade and Development (UNCTAD) in 1976, covering eighteen commodities (accounting for 87 per cent of least developed country exports), to be supported by a Common Fund (CF), with the intention of stabilizing commodity prices. However, the IPC made very little progress, partly due to delay and downsizing of the CF. When eventually, the CF was agreed in 1989 it was devoted to supporting productivity in commodity production, not to stabilizing prices. Limited compensatory finance is available from the International Monetary Fund (IMF) and the European Union (EU) and primary-product-producing countries remain victims to the oscillations in commodity prices over which they have no control. This is not a purely developing country issue. Fluctuations in the oil price, due to the activities of the Organization of the Petroleum Exporting Countries (OPEC), and, in particular, decisions of Saudi Arabia, affect the balance of payments and standard of living of developed countries too, while their markets expand (or contract) in response to changes in the largest economies, notably the United States, China and the EU.

International flows of private capital – especially financial capital – can also destabilize economies, both when the capital flows in and when it flows out. When capital flows in it tends to raise the national exchange rate, making it more difficult for countries to export; and when it flows out it can lead to spiralling devaluation. Major financial crises result, usually followed by prolonged recession – examples include the African debt crisis of the 1980s, Mexico in 1994, the East Asian financial crisis of the late 1990s. The resulting recessions and adjustment are typically associated with rising poverty (Cornia, Jolly and Stewart 1986; Fitzgerald 1998; Ranis and Stewart 1998; Springer and Molina 1995). Yet there is no global governance of these flows.

The imbalances which result from these global events – and sometimes from domestic policy – push countries into the hands of the International Financial Institutions (IFIs), notably the IMF and the World Bank. Countries then face 'conditionality' – a set of typically harsh macro-economic conditions, requiring cutbacks in government expenditure, privatization, tariff and quota reductions, often with highly negative effects on poverty and development (Garuda 2000; Ortiz et al. 2010; Stiglitz 2004; Vreeland 2003). Again, these are programmes over which recipient countries have little or no control.

In each of these cases, decisions taken elsewhere in the world, sometimes by government, sometime by private agents, sometimes by international agencies, affect countries' macro-economies, as well as the distribution of income and levels of poverty, while the people affected have no control over the decisions. There is clearly a lack of agency, which could only be countered by global institutions in which all countries were represented.

There are some participatory global institutions, but they are generally non-democratic, with poorer countries systematically un- or under-represented and limited in their powers, being mainly advisory. These include some ad hoc groupings of selected countries, which meet from time to time; and some international institutions with economic responsibilities. The ad hoc groupings, such as the G20, are not mandatory, are selective in membership and in issues covered and lack power to enforce any decisions they may make. They are neither democratic nor generally effective in influencing decisions.

The international economic institutions seem more promising: they include the IFIs; the World Trade Organization (WTO); the Economic and Social Council (ECOSOC) of the United Nations; and some economic activities of specialized agencies, such as the United Nations Development Programme (UNDP), the Food and Agriculture Organization (FAO), the United Nations Industrial Development Organization (UNIDO), and UNCTAD. The IFIs, however, have three deep flaws from the perspective of advancing agency of those populations they affect. First, the advanced countries control the great majority of votes in their governing bodies. Second, they deal with countries on a country-by-country basis and do not consider the aggregate global effects of their policies. Third, they do not have any power over non-borrowing countries – including most developed countries as well as China and other significant developing countries. Since it is these countries that have the biggest impact on global economic conditions, this means the Institutions cannot contribute to effective global governance. In principle, UN bodies are more promising, as all countries are represented in their governing bodies. Moreover, ECOSOC's remit is a broad one. However, ECOSOC lacks power and money, which is also true of the specialized agencies such as the UNDP, UNCTAD, UNIDO and FAO. The WTO is narrowly trade-oriented and concerned only with trade liberalization and not with the terms of trade. Before Trump it had succeeded in ruling out 'beggar-my-neighbour' trade policies, although at the expense of the import protection countries may need to develop. With the exception of the WTO, these UN organizations do contribute to relevant discussion of global conditions, but not to global economic governance.

The Power of Multinational Corporations

The growth of MNCs, i.e. companies which have headquarters in one country and activities in others, is another important aspect of globalization. These companies are able to escape national taxation and regulation as a result of their international location and transactions. As Keohane states, 'Globalisation means that it is more difficult for national governments to hold corporations accountable' (Keohane 2003, 130). MNCs account for a very large proportion of world trade. For 2000, it was estimated that MNC sales of the largest 500 companies were $13.7 trillion or almost half of world sales of goods and services. About one-third of world trade occurs between subsidiaries of MNCs. The value of the sales of the top 30 companies in 2015, according to Forbes, exceeded the national income of 141 countries. Size is important in two respects. First, it means that MNCs' influence is pervasive. Second, national governments, particularly of poor countries, are virtually powerless, given the imbalance in the ratio of the size of companies to that of their economies. Countries' position vis-à-vis MNCs is further weakened because they wish to attract investments from them to promote output and employment, and therefore enter into competitive bidding with other countries in a race to the bottom that benefits the company greatly, but does little for the country.

In the 1970s, there was some attempt to limit the power of MNCs and to introduce some global governance over them. First there was a spate of nationalization and efforts to improve the terms of technology transfer but these policies were reversed with deregulation and privatization in the 1980s and after. The result is that MNCs notoriously pay very little tax. Total tax avoidance by the companies greatly exceeds the total flow of aid. For the mid-2000s, for example, revenue lost through tax evasion and avoidance was estimated at $385 billion, about three times net aid flows in 2005 (Cobham 2005). Some MNCs pay little attention to national regulations, resulting in periodic disasters, a notorious example being Union Carbide in Bhopal in India; and they can cause massive environmental damage, through oil spillages and dumping of poisonous waste. For example, UNDP estimates that there were over 7,000 spillages in the Niger Delta between 1970 and 2001 (UNDP 2006); a mining company, OK Tedi, poisoned a river in Papua New Guinea by dumping waste, while Trafigura, a Dutch company, deposited its waste in the Ivory Coast. Lobbying and corrupt practices enable the companies to influence the regulatory framework (or its absence) and to persuade officials to turn a blind eye to contraventions. Discussing tax evasion, Otusanya notes that 'Accountants and tax experts whom the Nigerian government has entrusted with the responsibility of assessing, collecting, detecting and reporting cases of anti-revenue activities, have been key players in these practices' (Otusanya 2011). The Panama Papers, leaked in 2016, give some indication of the lack of accountability of global corporations.

Even large developed countries find it difficult to regulate and tax the largest global companies: for example, Google, Apple and Starbucks notoriously pay very little tax in European countries, while Google provides information about its users to governments.[4] Developing country governments are mostly powerless on their own in relation to these companies. The result is a clear case where there is lack of autonomy and agency. There is no 'coherent international regime' (Koenig-Archibugi 2004). There were some attempts to introduce a Code of Conduct for MNCs in the 1970s, but this was abandoned with the deregulations of the 1980s. Most agreements since then have been towards liberalizing conditions and providing investor protection. The proposed Transatlantic Trade and Investment Partnership (TTIP) under negotiation, for example, will *reduce* regulatory requirements towards food safety, the environment and banking and companies will acquire the right to sue governments for damage to their profits from government policies. This right has already been incorporated in a number of trade agreements, and hundreds of companies have initiated cases against governments. For example, a Swedish company, Vattenfall, is suing the German government for its decision to phase out nuclear plants following the Fukushima disaster.

Moving away from strictly economic activities, other areas where there are important global interactions in which people's lives are affected by action outside national orders include conflict and migration; health; and the environment. Military interventions by one country in another obviously involve a loss of autonomy – a violation of territorial integrity and state sovereignty – for the country where the conflict occurs, unless a democratic government has invited such intervention. In principle, Security Council endorsement increases the democratic legitimacy of such actions, yet most of the fierce wars involving international action have not received Security Council approval: for example, in Vietnam in the 1960s and 1970s,

Afghanistan in the 1980s and 2000s and Iraq and Syria in the 2000s. International migration (both forced and unforced) is growing and opens up choices for many individuals; through remittances, it contributes both to sending countries' economies at a macro level, and to household incomes. But there is almost no global governance of such migration and migrants are dependent on the rules of individual countries to which they (wish to) migrate (Alonso 2015). Health is another area where global interactions are important. Infections do not recognize national boundaries, and a disease that starts in one country can rapidly spread to others. This is now well recognized and, in principle, the World Health Organization (WHO) provides guidance and initiates action as needed. Yet, the WHO lacks funding and decision-making powers, so that in practice an ad hoc approach is adopted to successive global health scares. Finally, the environment involves many externalities requiring global action. Since this is also at the heart of the future generations deficit, it will be dealt with in the next section.

The global democratic deficit is clear from these examples. As a result of a lack of global economic governance, people's jobs, their incomes, the prices they receive for their output and pay for their consumption, even their survival are affected by decisions taken outside the country in which they live. Governments' ability to tax (and therefore spend) and to regulate is similarly constrained by global actors. Moving away from economics, even more devastating, in some cases, people's dwellings are bombed, their hospitals destroyed, their livelihoods and lives taken away by external aggressors. They have no agency with respect to these decisions. Global democratic deliberation is absent.

The Generational Deficit

Many actions taken today affect future generations. These include the areas just discussed. But while they clearly have implications for future generations, the contemporary interactions are the source of the most glaring democratic deficit. Decisions affecting the environment determine the potential capabilities of future generations most critically. The clearest example is climate change. Current levels and patterns of energy use contribute to CO_2 emissions and thus affect likely climate change, which in turn will condition the lives of those unborn. The present concentration of carbon emissions in the atmosphere is around 400 ppm, which already exceeds the estimated safe level of

350 ppm according to some climate scientists (Hansen et al. 2008; Röckstrom 2009). A somewhat higher level (450 ppm) is thought to be safe by some others (Stern 2006). The latter level will be reached in 2030 on present trends, unless substantial action is taken. Yet decisions concerning emissions are made by the current generation of decision-makers with *no representation* of future generations. Moreover, the situation is compounded by the absence of effective global governance arrangements, since, as in a classic prisoner's dilemma game, each country can 'free ride' on the efforts of other countries, and hence every country is motivated *not* to take action to limit emissions. The result is likely to be a situation with much less emission limitation than citizens of most countries would want, and much less than is in the interests of future generations.

The climate change question – and other environment issues, such as preservation of species – is subject to both types of democratic deficit. Citizens of poor countries, in particular, are likely to be worst affected by climate change, yet they make least contribution to the total emissions which cause it. In 2010, rich countries' emissions per head were 11,579 kilotons and low-income countries' were 0.3 kilotons, while the UNDP estimated that high-income countries had just 1.5 per cent of the risk of being affected by natural disasters of that faced by poor countries, during 2000–4 (UNDP 2007). More generally, poor countries are worse affected because of heavy reliance on agricultural production, which is the worst affected sector, and they include more low-lying and tropical countries, therefore suffering disproportionately from rising sea levels and increasing temperatures. Governments of poor countries are also less able to protect people from adverse climatic events and poor people are in the weakest position to protect themselves. In the light of this, it seems likely that citizens of poor countries would have a stronger preference for reduced emissions than citizens of rich countries. Yet there is limited action they can take, and they have no voice in decisions that are made in rich countries.

The way that investment decisions are taken exemplifies the limited attention given to future generations. In investment evaluations, future costs and benefits are discounted in both public and private decision-making. For public investments, assessments of the value of future costs or benefits are made on the basis of an assumed interest rate, or social discount rate, which reduces the value of future incomes and costs; a dollar received in a year's time is thus valued less than a dollar

Table 13.1 *Present value of future income*

Present $ value	Discount rate		
of $100 in	1%	5%	10%
25 years	78	29.50	9.20
100 years	37	0.76	0.01

received today. The further into the future that costs or benefits arise, the more they are discounted compared with costs or benefits incurred today. Much of the discussion among economists of how much present action to take with respect to climate change is indeed about what the appropriate discount rate should be.[5] Clearly, action which will yield benefits in 100 years' time is much more likely to be taken if the 'interest rate' is lower, such that the future value is discounted less.

With respect to private decision-making, profit-making enterprises have to adopt high discount rates because of the high cost of borrowing. A review of commercial bank lending rates shows that commercial interest rates are high, even when the 'official' rates are low. For example, Lloyds loans start at 5.4 per cent APR, but the typical rate is 13.8 per cent.[6] The small business lender, IWOCA, charges more than 20 per cent *per annum*.[7]

Because of the law of compound interest, discount rates have a very large effect. With a discount rate of 5.0 per cent, $100 twenty-five years from now is worth just $29.50 today, and $100 in one hundred years would be worth just $0.76. Table 13.1 illustrates how our valuation of the future varies with the interest rate adopted. In other words, adopting a discount rate involves valuing income streams received by future generations much less than current income.

It has been argued that discounting the future represents an economist's perspective, in contrast to philosophers who see no reason for discounting because they see no reason to value the well-being of future generations less than that of people alive today (Broome 1994; Caney 2014). Perhaps, unfortunately, however, it is economists, not philosophers, who advise on investment decisions. Economists have put forward several reasons for applying a discount rate when making public decisions. One is that future generations, it is assumed, will be richer than us, stemming from a belief that the long-run growth in output per head will continue – yet this is threatened by environmental issues and cannot any longer simply be assumed. The possibility of catastrophic effects resulting from climate change would suggest that we should make special efforts to avoid climatic disaster if we are risk averse, and hence would justify *more* investment to safeguard the future, yet many use fear of risk as a reason for using a higher discount rate. A further reason suggested for discounting the future is not so much a reason as an explanation: we have a 'defective telescope' when it comes to the future, as Pigou (1920) put it. Doubtless, this is the real reason: we care less about the far future, in particular, a future in which we do not feature, than the present and near future. That precisely is why the generational democratic deficit is so important; the well-being of future generations will only be cared for properly if they are somehow brought into decision-making. In their absence they lose not only agency but also well-being.

Philosophers have considered the question of the just treatment of future generations extensively, often using a rights-based approach. Much of the discussion has been stimulated by, and is intended to apply to environmental issues, Rawls (1971), Barry (1977), Baier (1981), Beckerman and Pasek (2001) and Caney (2010). Mostly such discussion is about how much we should value the lives of future generations rather than about their (lack of) agency. In contrast, while the fundamental assumption of this chapter shares the view of many philosophers that future generations have equal claims (or rights) as current generations, and this is the reason we should give weight to their well-being and agency, the chapter's prime concern is with the lack of agency. The reason for this concern is partly that agency is an important component of the freedoms of future generations, but to a greater extent it derives from a more political and pragmatic argument. Where people are not represented in decision-making, their interests tend to be overlooked, irrespective of the rights issue. Or, in other words, realization of rights generally requires participation in decision-making.

To overcome the double democratic deficit which applies to climate change decisions, there is a need for global decision-making in which *all* citizens alive today and future generations are represented, if their agency is to be respected. With respect to the former, the need for global decision-making and institutions is now widely recognized. There have been a series of global meetings to secure agreement on containing emissions as well as other environmental issues – starting in Kyoto (1997). The Kyoto protocol, with 192

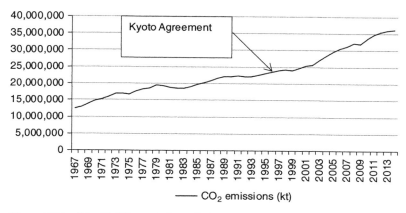

Figure 13.2. World CO_2 emissions (kt).

country signatories, agreed emission targets, but lacked an enforcement mechanism. The protocol was updated by a Doha amendment in 2012. By November 2015, there were just 59 signatories to the Doha amendment – 144 are needed to bring it into operation. Japan, New Zealand and Russia did not sign up to Doha, Canada withdrew from Kyoto and the USA never ratified the original Kyoto protocol. A Paris agreement for post-2020 was reached in 2015, in which every country would determine its own emission targets and report achievements on a five-yearly basis to the secretariat of the United Nations Framework Convention on Climate Change (UNFCC). Again there are no enforcement mechanisms. The threshold for the coming into force of the convention has been reached, with 165 signatories. However, the US withdrew in 2018. Yet, as can be seen from Figure 13.2, to date these global protocols have had no apparent impact on CO_2 emissions. The negative effect of this failure is likely to affect future generations much more than present ones, and their lack of presence in global deliberations could be an important element explaining why action has been so weak and delayed.

While I have focused on CO_2 emissions as probably the most threatening environmental issue, there are many other areas where similar arguments apply, such as the destruction of species and water shortages.[8] Again, the majority of the likely victims of failures to deal with these environmental issues are future generations. There are also many other ways in which our actions today may bring future harms;

overuse of antibiotics is an example (Wise 1998). Yet those who will be most affected are clearly not represented in current negotiations. Some do talk of 'our grandchildren' but do not see beyond them to their grandchildren. Others argue that technology will have come to the rescue by the time they are born. But this is only likely if we (those alive today) introduce the required incentives for technological development.

This section of the chapter has argued that the world faces two serious democratic deficits: the global democratic deficit and the generational democratic deficit. I have illustrated them with reference to macro-economic policy, international trade and decisions that impact the environment, although the list of arenas in which these deficits exist is lengthy. Both types of deficit seriously restrict agency since they mean that there are many decisions which affect people over which they have neither direct nor indirect control, nor even influence. In brief they result in 'agency vulnerability' or 'the risk of being limited in one's ability to control the social and economic forces that propel one into change' (Kosko 2013, 293). The next section of the chapter will discuss whether and how these deficits might be corrected.

Correcting the Democratic Deficits

If people are to realize their democratic freedoms, and their agency including the capability of participating in decisions which affect them, these democratic deficits need to be corrected. Before discussing how, it is helpful to return to the question of the criteria we might use to determine whether democratic freedoms prevail. We can't present a full and deep discussion of democracy in this short chapter, but a brief discussion is needed, in order to throw light on what is needed to counter the democratic deficits. There are many different types of democracy and participation. At one extreme is direct democracy, ancient Greece style, in which people participate directly in all major decisions. Beyond a very limited scale, a village for example, this is difficult to achieve. Consequently, indirect participation, by electing representatives or delegates, is commonly adopted for democratic institutions in larger groups. As noted earlier, Crocker has argued that agency can be exercised indirectly in this form. However, electronic means might relax this constraint and make it possible for more, if not total, direct participation. Deliberative democracy, discussed earlier, also implies that relatively small numbers are involved, so that reasoned discussion can take place with full participation by all; again, this points to indirect rather than direct democratic institutions. While global electronic discussions are increasingly enabling a much wider range of participation in discussions, these have important limitations, for example in not being representative. Crocker would characterize many of these features as forms of participation falling along a continuum from 'thinnest' to 'thickest', with passive and consultative forms of participation at one end and full deliberative participation at the other. 'The further we go down the list, the "thicker" is the participatory mode in the sense of more fully expressing individual or collective agency.' Moreover, 'different kinds of participation are likely to differ with respect to their consequences' (Crocker 2008, 344).

Beyond indirect representation, institutions are needed to guard against majoritarian authoritarian democracies which can neglect or abuse minorities and human rights more generally (Rodrik 2015). Hence both national and global democratic institutions require safeguards, including legal protection of human rights (freedom of speech, freedom to form political parties, the rule of law and so on) and protections for minorities (i.e. 'thick' democracy).[9] Indeed, at a global and intergenerational level these protections become especially important as the potential for abuse is so large. Strong global constitutional guarantees are needed to protect the human rights of future generations, as a necessary if clearly not sufficient condition. Habeas corpus, for example, introduced in England in the twelfth century, still provides protection for British citizens in the twenty-first century.

Given these general requirements for democratic decision-making, in particular, comprehensive representation in reasoned discussions, we now consider global and intergenerational issues separately.

Global Democracy

There are several approaches to extending (indirect) democracy at the global level, all of which have been extensively discussed.[10] One way to extend democracy to the global level would be to allow (elected) governments to represent their citizens in global organizations, giving these organizations real powers over global issues, such as those discussed above. In some ways this would represent a continuation of current practice, in which national governments 'speak' for their people. However, several changes are needed. First, we should change the governance of some existing institutions, notably the IFIs, so that the balance of power reflects population size and not wealth. Second, we could give power over decisions to such existing institutions as are broadly democratic, such as ECOSOC. Note, however, that in ECOSOC there is one country one vote, which is an improvement on one dollar one vote, but is not equivalent to one person one vote because of the very different population sizes across countries. Having two sets of votes in ECOSOC, one by country, as at present, and one by country weighted by population, would be one way of overcoming this problem.[11] Third, an alternative approach would be to extend the powers of the Security Council to economic, social and environmental matters, or to institute an Economic, Social and Environmental Security Council, while reforming membership to be globally representative. But it would also be necessary to alter the voting rules, removing the veto, and requiring a significant majority for decisions. The construction of country representation and voting rules need to be designed to ensure that smaller and poorer countries have sufficient representation (see Daws and Stewart 1998). A fourth approach would be to review and reform the governance of each global agreement or convention which could improve their democratic basis.

In general, these are incremental changes which could be introduced step-by-step. A much more radical approach would be to initiate a world government, with a constitution, resources, a bureaucracy, a legal system, a police and an army, with its own directly elected parliament. This is the vision of many who considered world peace would only come about through world government, such as Franciscio de Vitoria in the sixteenth century (advocating a 'republic of the whole world' – *res publica totius orbis*), Karl Krause in the nineteenth century (a world republic consisting of the five federations, governing each region) or Wendell Wilkie, Emery Reeves and Bertrand Russell, among many others, in the twentieth century. Bertrand Russell thought world government was essential to prevent the extinction of mankind (Russell 1952). The establishment of world government is the most straightforward way of extending our capabilities to the global level. Yet it might also imperil political and cultural freedoms (Beitz 1999; Waltz 1979; Walzer 2004). Moreover, it does not seem likely to be politically acceptable in the near future, so incremental progress, as sketched above, is more feasible.

It is not difficult to imagine ways of improving agency with respect to global issues, thereby reducing the global democratic deficit, as outlined above, even though each of the solutions raises difficult issues. In particular, the more centralized decision-making, the more remote it is from most people, and people's agency could become so indirect that it might hardly qualify as agency. Yet the problems of lack of global governance are severe, which is why it is worth investigating and promoting democratic institutions for global governance despite the problems. However, fierce political opposition to moves towards forms of democratic global governance is likely from governments and corporations which would lose power. Such opposition is the chief obstacle to progress, rather than a lack of ideas of how to overcome the global democratic deficit. In contrast, to overcome the generational democratic deficit poses much more challenging problems: how can one represent the agency of people who are not yet born? I turn to this question now.

Generational Democracy

To overcome the generational democratic deficit would be to achieve what seems to be a logical impossibility: to involve people who are not yet born in current decisions. What is required is to introduce some institutional mechanism whereby the interests of future generations can be represented. Kamijo et al. (2016) do this in an experimental game, whereby half the participants are told they represent the future generations and half the present. The (unsurprising) result is that a substantially higher proportion of participants selected 'sustainable' options (62 per cent) compared with 28 per cent when future generations were not represented. Something like this game needs to be incorporated into actual global (and non-global) decision-making.

Next I present a series of suggestions of institutional change that might contribute to bringing future generations into global and national decision-making. First, the creation of a special UN agency whose task would be to represent future generations in all fora (UNIFGEN). This agency would analyse how current decisions would affect future generations; identify desirable policies and investments; and act as an advocate for future generations. Such an agency would be similar to UNICEF, which aims to represent a constituency – children – who cannot represent themselves. Second, several constitutional changes would help overcome the deficit at national levels. These include the institution of Ombudsmen, for future generations, whose task would be similar to that of the special agency – i.e. to ensure that current law and other policies are just with respect to future generations. Third, the appointment (or election) of people to represent future generations in every major decision-making body would contribute to including future generations in global, national and local decision-making. At the global level, representatives of future generations could be drawn from or recommended by UNIFGEN. Fourth, a general commitment to do justice to and, in particular, not to harm future generations, should be incorporated in national constitutions, and the objectives and norms of global bodies.

These proposals are consistent with some made by others to deal with the problem at a national level, including, among others, having future generations represented in legislatures (Ekeli 2005), and instituting an Independent Council for the Future and a parliamentary committee to scrutinize legislation from this perspective (Caney 2016). None of these suggestions can truly overcome the deficit, but they may contribute to reducing its import. More generally, there is a need to build the idea of justice across generations into accepted norms so that it becomes an important consideration in deliberations and decisions, even without the sort of special representation suggested above. Such a change would parallel the ways in which children's and animal rights are increasingly integrated into our moral perspectives.[12]

Conclusion

This chapter has explored the question of how agency and democratic freedoms can truly be realized in a context where global interactions take power away from national decision-makers; and where intergenerational interactions take power away from future generations. It suggests that there are two democratic deficits which are harming the advance of agency and in so doing distorting decisions. The ideal of deliberative democracy cannot be realized if important actors are excluded from the deliberations. The chapter makes some suggestions about how each of the deficits might be overcome, at least partially. Strong political obstacles to such change are likely. But recognizing the problem is a necessary beginning.

Notes

1. See the chapters by Drydyk *et al.* (Chapter 8) and Koggel (Chapter 6) in this volume for detailed discussions of agency in the capability approach.
2. Sen has defined this as the instrumental aspect of democracy (Sen 1999b).
3. National autonomy is here defined as a situation where national governments are largely in control of elements that affect the nation, and are not subordinate to other actors.
4. World-wide, Google agreed to 64 per cent of government requests (79 per cent of those of the US government), www.google.com/transparen cyreport/userdatarequests/countries/?t=table, accessed 26 August 2018.
5. See Stern (2006).
6. http://loansexpertonline.co.uk/Lloyds-tsb-loan.php, accessed 21 October 2016.
7. www.iwoca.co.uk/, accessed 21 October 2016.
8. There have been some successes in global agreements: there was a successful global environmental agreement on phasing out chlorofluorocarbons (1987) and hydrofluorocarbons (October 2016) and a number of agreements to restrict overfishing have allowed the recovery of some species (herring in the North Sea, for example).
9. See Crocker (2008), especially chapter 10.
10. For example, for a discussion of reforms to economic governance see Stiglitz (2006); for reform of the Security Council see Daws and Stewart (1998), Fassbender (2004) and von Einsiedel, Malone and Ugarte (2004); for proposals for the reform of ECOSOC see Martens (2006); for discussions for and against world government see Beitz (1999), Cabrera (2004), Held (1995), Rawls (1999), Tan (2004).
11. I owe this idea to Lori Keleher.
12. See Wichert and Nussbaum in this volume for a novel discussion of the importance of agency in understanding the rights of animals; in their case focusing on cetaceans.

References

Alonso, J. A. 2015. 'Managing Labour Mobility: A Missing Pillar of Global Governance'. Committee for Development Policy Background Paper 26 ST/ESA/2015/CDP/26. DESA, United Nations.

Baier, A. 1981. 'The Rights of Past and Future Persons'. In *Responsibilities to Future Generations: Environmental Ethics*, E. Partridge (ed.). New York: Prometheus Books, 171–83.

Barry, B.. 1977. 'Justice between Generations'. In *Law, Morality and Society: Essays in Honor of H. L. A. Hart*, P. M. S. Hacker and Joseph Raz (eds.). Oxford: Clarendon Press, 268–84.

Beckerman, W., and J. Pasek. 2001. *Justice, Posterity and the Environment*. Oxford University Press.

Beitz, C. 1999. 'International Liberalism and Distributive Justice: A Survey of Recent Thought'. *World Politics* 51(2): 269–96.

Broome, J. 1994. 'Discounting the Future'. *Philosophy and Public Affairs* 23 (2): 128–56.

Cabrera, L. 2004. *Political Theory of Global Justice: A Cosmopolitan Case for the World State*. New York: Routledge.

Caney, S. 2010. 'Climate Change, Human Rights and Moral Thresholds'. In *Human Rights and Climate Change*, S. Humphreys (ed.). Cambridge University Press, 69–90.

Caney, S. 2014. 'Climate Change, Intergenerational Equity, and the Social Discount Rate'. *Politics, Philosophy & Economics* 13(4): 320–42.

Caney, S. 2016. 'Political Institutions for the Future: Five-Fold Package'. In *Institutions for Future Generations*, A. Gosseries and I. G. Ricoy (eds.). Oxford University Press.

Cobham, A. 2005. 'Tax Evasion, Tax Avoidance, and Development Finance'. Queen Elizabeth House Working Paper 129. Oxford Department of International Development.

Cornia, G. A., R. Jolly and F. Stewart. 1986. *Adjustment with a Human Face*. Oxford University Press.

Crocker, D.. 2006. 'Sen and Deliberative Democracy'. In *Capabilities Equality*, A. Kaufman (ed.). London: Routledge.

Crocker, D. A. 2008. *Ethics of Global Development: Agency, Capability, and Deliberative Democracy*. Cambridge University Press.

Crouch, C.. 2014. *Post-Democracy*. Cambridge: Polity.

Daws, S., and F. Stewart. 1998. 'An Economic and Social Security Council'. In *Development Economics and Policy: The Conference Volume to Celebrate the 85th Birthday of Professor Sir Hans Singer*, D. Sapsford and J-R. Chen (eds.). Basingstoke: Macmillan, 389–417.

Ekeli, K. S. 2005. 'Giving a Voice to Posterity: Deliberative Democracy and Representation of Future People'. *Journal of Agricultural and Environmental Ethics* 18(5): 429–50.

Fassbender, B. 2004. 'Pressure for Security Council Reform'. In *The UN Security Council: From the Cold War to the 21st Century*, D. M. Malone (ed.). Boulder, CO: Lynne Rienner, 341–56.

Fishkin, J. S., and R. C. Luskin. 2005. 'Experimenting with a Democratic Ideal: Deliberative Polling and Public Opinion'. *Acta Politica* 40(3): 284–98.

Fitzgerald, E. V. K. 1998. 'Global Capital Market Volatility and the Developing Countries: Lessons from the East Asian Crisis'. Centro Studi Luca d'Agliano Development Studies Working Papers 124. Torino, Oxford.

Garuda, G. 2000. 'The Distributional Effects of IMF Programs: A Cross-Country Analysis'. *World Development* 28(6): 1031–51.

Hansen, J., M. Sato, P. Kharecha, D. Beerling, R. Berner, V. Masson-Delmotte, M. Pagani, M. Raymo, D. L. Royer and J. C. Zachos. 2008. 'Target Atmospheric CO_2: Where Should Humanity Aim?' *Open Atmosphere Science Journal* 2: 217–31.

Held, D. 1995. *Democracy and the Global Order: From the Modern State to Cosmopolitan Governance*. Stanford University Press.

Kamijo, Y., A. Komiya, N. Mifune and T. Saij. 2016. 'Negotiating with the Future: Incorporating Imaginary Future Generations into Negotiations'. SDES-2016–7. Kochi University of Technology.

Keohane, R. O. 2003. 'Global Governance and Democratic Accountability'. In *Taming Globalization: Frontiers of Governance*, D. Held and M. Koenig-Archibugi (eds.). Cambridge: Polity, 130–57.

Koenig-Archibugi, M. 2004. 'Transnational Corporations and Public Accountability'. *Government and Opposition* 39(2): 234–59. doi: 10.1111/j.1477–7053.2004.00122.x.

Kosko, S. J. 2013. 'Agency Vulnerability, Participation, and the Self-Determination of Indigenous Peoples'. *Journal of Global Ethics* 9 (3): 293–310. doi: 10.1080/17449626.2013.818385.

Martens, J. 2006. 'The Reform of the UN Economic and Social Council (ECOSOC): A Never-Ending Story?', www.globalpolicy.org/social -and-economic-policy/social-and-economic-policy-at-the-un/reform -of-ecosoc-and-the-social-and-economic-policy-process-at-the-un/ 47509.html, accessed 19 October 2016.

Ortiz, I., J. Chai, M. Cummins and G. Vergara. 2010. 'Prioritizing Expenditures for a Recovery for All: A Rapid Review of Public Expenditures in 126 Developing Countries'. Social and Economic Working Paper. New York: UNICEF.

Otusanya, O. J. 2011. 'The Role of Multinational Companies in Tax Evasion and Tax Avoidance: The Case of Nigeria'. *Critical Perspectives on Accounting* 22(3): 316–32. doi:http://dx.doi.org/10.1016/j.cpa.2010.1 0.005.

Pigou, A. C. 1920. *The Economics of Welfare.* 4th edn. London: Macmillan.

Ranis, G., and F. Stewart. 1998. 'The Asian Crisis: Social Consequences and Policies'. *IDS Bulletin* 30(1): 40.

Rawls, J. 1971. *A Theory of Justice.* Cambridge, MA: Belknap Press of Harvard University Press.

Rawls, J. 1999. *The Law of Peoples: With, 'The Idea of Public Reason Revisited'.* Cambridge, MA: Harvard University Press.

Roberts, K. M. 2016. 'Democracy in the Developing World: Challenges of Survival and Significance'. *Studies in Comparative International Development* 51(1): 32–49.

Röckstrom, J., W. Steffen, K. Noone et al. 2009. 'A Safe Operating Space for Humanity'. *Nature* 461(24 September): 472–5.

Rodrik, D. 2015. 'Is Liberal Democracy Feasible in Developing Countries?' 50th Anniversary Conference of Studies in Comparative International Development, Brown University, 30 October 2015.

Russell, B. 1952. *The Impact of Science on Society.* London: Allen & Unwin.

Sen, A. 1985. 'Well-Being, Agency and Freedom'. *The Journal of Philosophy* 82: 169–221.

Sen, A. 1999a. 'Democracy as a Universal Value'. *Journal of Democracy* 10 (3): 3–17.

Sen, A. 1999b. *Development as Freedom.* Oxford University Press.

Springer, G. L., and J. L. Molina. 1995. 'The Mexican Financial Crisis: Genesis, Impact, and Implications'. *Journal of Interamerican Studies and World Affairs* 37(2): 57–81. doi: 10.2307/166271.

Stern, N. 2006. *The Economics of Climate Change: The Stern Review.* Cambridge University Press.

Stiglitz, J. E. 2004. 'Capital-Market Liberalization, Globalization, and the IMF'. *Oxford Review of Economic Policy* 20(1): 57–71.

Stiglitz, J. E. 2006. 'Global Public Goods and Global Finance: Does Global Governance Ensure That the Global Public Interest Is Served?' In *Advancing Public Goods*, J.-P. Touffut (ed.). London: Edward Elgar, 149–64.

Tan, K. C. 2004. *Justice without Borders: Cosmopolitanism, Nationalism and Patriotism.* Cambridge University Press.

UNDP. 2006. *Niger Delta Human Development Report 2006.* Abuja, Nigeria: UNDP.

UNDP. 2007. *Human Development Report: Fighting Climate Change. Human Solidarity in a Divided World.* London: Palgrave Macmillan.

von Einsiedel, S., D. M. Malone and B. S. Ugarte (eds.) 2004. *The UN Security Council in the 21st Century.* Boulder, CO: Lynne Rienner.

Vreeland, J. 2003. *The IMF and Economic Development.* Cambridge University Press.

Waltz, K. N. 1979. *Theory of International Politics*. Toronto: McGraw-Hill Publishing Company.

Walzer, M. 2004. *Arguing about War*. New Haven, CT: Yale University Press.

Wise, R. 1998. 'Antimicrobial Resistance Is a Major Threat to Public Health'. *British Medical Journal* 317(7159): 609–10.

14 | Deliberative Democracy and Agency

Linking Transitional Justice and Development

COLLEEN MURPHY

Introduction

David Crocker is one of the first philosophers to take up questions of both development ethics and of transitional justice. He conceptualizes development from a capability perspective, linking the process of development with the expansion of the freedom of individuals. He conceptualizes transitional justice as a set of normative goals associated with the process of dealing with past wrongdoing in the context of a transition from conflict or repression to democracy. In his analysis of both topics, deliberative democracy and agency are central.

In this chapter, I explain why normative analyses should, as Crocker does, focus jointly on development ethics and transitional justice. The two areas overlap empirically and share a deep similarity of normative orientation. In the first section, I provide an overview of Crocker's definition of development. In the second, I discuss transitional justice. After looking at the range of normative goals that Crocker lays out, I explain the deeper connections among what may seem at first glance to be separate and distinct normative ideals. The third section examines the overlap of development and transitional justice empirically and theoretically. The fourth highlights differences and possible tensions in their joint pursuit.

1 Development

In the *Ethics of Global Development*, David Crocker (2008) advances a theory of global development that reflects and builds on thirty years of thinking in this area. Drawing extensively on the capability approach of Amartya Sen, Crocker defines and assesses development in terms of the promotion of capability, functioning, and agency.

Capabilities are constitutive dimensions of well-being (Crocker 1999a; Nussbaum 1999; Sen 1999). They reflect genuine opportunities to do and become things of value, including being mobile, being educated, being respected, and being healthy. The genuine opportunities an individual enjoys are in turn a function of two general factors: what an individual has and what an individual can do with what she has. What an individual has is defined broadly, including mental and physical capacities, income, and family support. What an individual can do with what she has is also broad, encompassing the rules and norms defining legal, political, social, educational, and economic institutions, as well as the natural and built environment. Thus, when considering whether an individual enjoys educational opportunities, it is necessary to consider not only that individual's mental capacities but also whether the income needed to pay for education (if required) exists, whether gender norms support education for an individual of a given gender, the relative location of a school from one's home and modes of transportation available to get to that location, and the quality of instructors that are available.

At the core of Crocker's view is a commitment to deliberative democracy; through deliberative democratic practices and institutions individuals and communities can exercise the agency on which Crocker places fundamental importance. Agency is a broader notion than well-being, encompassing goals and aims that an individual may adopt that are not necessarily tied to their own well-being. I may exercise my agency in supporting an institution or social justice cause to which I am committed. In addition to articulating a compelling vision of global development, Crocker's seminal book on development ethics, *Ethics of Global Development: Agency, Capability and Deliberative Democracy*, is important for the clear, detailed, and comprehensive overviews that it provides of debates and frameworks within development ethics, the capability approach of Amartya Sen, the capabilities approach of Martha Nussbaum, and contemporary understandings of deliberative democracy.

According to Crocker's reconstruction of Nussbaum's arguments, Nussbaum provides a list of central capabilities that, she argues, individuals have reason to value. Examples of items included in her list are capabilities to engage in social interaction with others and to formulate a conception of the good. In Nussbaum's view, these capabilities comprise a partial conception of human flourishing. The list of capabilities is political in the sense that it "identifies those capabilities and opportunities people should have *regardless* of their conception of the good" (Crocker 2008, 192). Thus, it reflects a rather freestanding conception of human flourishing. Moreover, the list of capabilities captures part of the requirements of social justice and reflects claims that governments should enshrine and protect in their constitution. Constitutionally protecting these capabilities means that governments are constrained by the commitment to protecting capabilities. Although communities are constrained by justice to constitutionally guarantee threshold levels of central capabilities, communities are free to identify precisely where the threshold lies for each capability protected and to specify very general descriptions of central capabilities.

To defend her list, Nussbaum (1999) appeals to a Kantian conception of human dignity. Nussbaum argues that her list of central capabilities reflects the demands of dignity, or more specifically the claims that we can make on others and our government in virtue of our dignity. Second, Nussbaum justifies her list via a process of cross-cultural dialogue. Her list, she claims, reflects an overlapping consensus among philosophers and others on the basic dimensions of human flourishing. Furthermore, because her list is not grounded in an appeal to a particular comprehensive conception of the good, people with vastly different conceptions of the good can endorse her list for political purposes, namely, as providing the basis for constitutional guarantees.

Crocker (2008) is skeptical of Nussbaum's justifications of her list of central capabilities. He claims that the ideal of human dignity does not seem to be grounding the list of capabilities Nussbaum advances. More deeply, he disagrees with the privileging of philosophical analysis and philosophically structured dialogue and consensus as the grounds for deciding what should be constitutionally protected and which specific central capabilities are to be valued. In Crocker's view, any list of capabilities devised by philosophers should be simply a stimulus for public debate and deliberation about constitutional principles and public policies. But, the question of which capabilities are valuable and which should be constitutionally protected should never be outside the scope of public deliberation. In Crocker's words,

Lists of capabilities or human rights that citizens have reason to value ... rather than functioning beyond the reach of deliberative and popular bodies, these lists should be viewed as generic topics or menus for discussion or specific proposals for democratic bodies and citizens to discuss ... If the list is subject to additions and corrections as well as a tool for stimulating, elevating, deepening, or broadening public discussion, well and good. If the list is determined prior to public deliberation and dogmatically shuts off debate, such a list ...

is not appropriate for self-governing people (2008, 204).

Crocker's hesitancy to endorse Nussbaum's list stems in part from his deep commitment to agency. Crocker places central importance upon recognizing, respecting, and cultivating the ability of individuals to shape their own destinies and choose which courses of action they will pursue. In the context of well-being, it matters that individuals and communities be in a position where they can determine individually and/or collectively which genuine opportunities will be prioritized and pursued in the course of an individual life or as a matter of public policy.

The exercise of agency on the part of a group links directly to deliberative democracy. For it is through deliberation that communities can come to decide which dimensions of well-being, defined in terms of capabilities, will be a priority to foster and protect. For Crocker, not every kind of deliberation is the right kind of deliberation, or the deliberation that should ground and justify the selection of valuable capabilities. Crocker suggests that deliberative democratic theories offer important resources for understanding the "agency-manifesting processes" of deliberation that should guide social choice. Deliberative democracy "is the theory and practice of a model of democracy that emphasizes the exchange of reasons in the making of democratic decisions" (2008, 309). Deliberative democratic theory articulates the processes and conditions required for inclusive and public deliberation that is premised on a fair resolution of policy questions among free and equal individuals.

Regulating such deliberation, in Crocker's view, are three general principles (reciprocity, publicity, and accountability), which are designed to promote the fairness of deliberation, and certain background conditions that preserve the justice of deliberation and the equality of all deliberators. What is of particular interest for my purposes is the explanation that Crocker offers for these background conditions, which were first articulated by Henry Richardson. The first background condition is equal political liberty, protecting liberties like freedom of speech. For Crocker, "These liberties or civil and political rights *must be protected and not merely be part of the legal code* (2008, 318, emphasis added)." Crocker writes that one way of understanding this condition is the idea that "each citizen is able to be at or above a threshold of minimally adequate political functioning" (317). The second enabling condition is equality before the law, which ensures that each citizen be guaranteed the same constitutional rights. The third condition is economic justice, whereby "people have the real opportunity to advance to or at least a level of minimally adequate well-being" (318). With such conditions in place, Crocker writes, societies are well situated to deliberate and decide whether to prioritize functionings or capabilities in public policies, which capabilities to choose, and how varying capabilities should be weighted.

I am not entirely convinced by Crocker's objections to Nussbaum, and want to note two primary concerns I have with his analysis. The first is whether Crocker can justify the constraints on democratic deliberation he supports without falling vulnerable to the objections he raises against Nussbaum. The second centers on whether democratic deliberation should always be prioritized in the manner Crocker advocates.

How are we to understand the status of the conditions being articulated above by Crocker? One interpretation, suggested by the claim that certain liberties *must* be protected, is that these conditions constrain public deliberation, but are themselves beyond the scope or purview of democratic deliberation. That is, it should not be a subject of deliberative discussion whether or not all citizens should be guaranteed the same constitutional rights or whether indeed all citizens should be guaranteed particular freedoms like freedom of speech. To do so would deny the moral equality of all citizens. The problem with this interpretation is that it is vulnerable to precisely the objection Crocker levels against Nussbaum. Philosophers, in this case deliberative democratic theorists, are making substantive determinations of the freedoms that citizens should enjoy and that it is important for the state to protect. However, Crocker argued against Nussbaum that questions of valuation should be made through a process of social choice.

Moreover, using this interpretation, the substantive difference between the constraints of public deliberation and the constraints defended by Nussbaum diminish. That is, there is significant overlap between the rights that must be guaranteed as background conditions for democratic deliberation and the rights that Nussbaum grounds as constitutional guarantees based on her list of central capabilities. For example, the political and material dimensions of the capability of control over one's environment encompass rights of political participation, rights of free speech and association, and rights to property, which are a condition for economic justice.

A different interpretation of these background conditions would be that they have the status Crocker urges for Nussbaum's list of capabilities. The background conditions are not beyond the scope of public deliberation but should themselves be a subject for public discussion and critique. To explain this in Crocker's own words: the conditions articulated by Richardson "should be viewed as generic topics or menus for discussion or specific proposals" (2008, 204). In this case, it is entirely open to a community to reject the idea that all should be given the same fundamental rights or to reject the salience of conditions of economic justice as desiderata for ideal public deliberation. One virtue of this interpretation is consistency. Crocker would not be vulnerable to the same criticism he leveled against Nussbaum and I articulated above. But, this consistency comes at a price. For on this interpretation, it is not clear why deliberative decision-making should be the justificatory grounds for claims about the rights, functionings, and capabilities people have reason to value. Some, but not all, may exercise agency in political deliberation. But, perhaps more, especially if there are marginalized groups within a community, instead of reflecting considered analysis of the reasons for and against certain positions on the rights to constitutionally guarantee and capabilities of value, decisions may instead reflect the preferences of the most powerful and most popular. We also have reason to be skeptical that the outcomes of deliberation will be better than the outcome of philosophical analysis and reflect what actually is the case concerning which capabilities matter and what capabilities constitutions should protect.

The tension between specifying to some degree a normative ideal for a particular subject (e.g., development or, as we consider below, transitional justice) and respecting the agency of members of a community to determine the normative priorities that will guide their policy-making and the processes and programs through which such priorities will be pursued is present whenever democratic procedures are adopted. It is a tension present in discussions of transitional justice as well, as theorists disagree about whether to articulate substantive conceptions of the normative goals taken to be constitutive parts of transitional justice, such as reconciliation.[1] Navigating the tension, in my view, requires careful consideration of the questions that will be put to democratic deliberation, and the process by which questions that will be taken up will be determined.

2 Transitional Justice

Transitional justice can be broadly defined as the process of dealing with past wrongs as a society is transitioning from an extended period of conflict or repression to democracy. David Crocker was one of the first philosophers to focus attention on transitional justice. Writing seminal pieces in the context of the South African Truth and Reconciliation Commission's (TRC) process to deal with apartheid-era abduction, torture, killing, and severe ill-treatment during its transition from apartheid to democracy, Crocker specifically focused on articulating the wide-ranging and diverse normative goals toward which processes like the TRC aim. Transitional justice processes include a broad range of measures, including amnesty, criminal trials, reparations, truth commissions, memorials, and programs of lustration in which individuals are barred from serving in specific official positions. The aims of processes are, according to Crocker, "truth, public platforms for victims, accountability and punishment, rule of law, compensatory justice, institutional and long-term development, public deliberation, and reconciliation" (quote from Crocker 2018, 4; see also Crocker 1999b, 2002).

In my own work (Murphy 2017), I have tried to articulate the underlying connections among the diverse moral imperatives that Crocker identifies as imperatives of transitional justice. My main claim is that transitional justice is a distinctive kind of justice; it is not retributive, corrective, and distributive justice or a combination of these kinds. To make this argument, I draw upon a central insight of philosopher David Hume (1978, 1998). Principles of justice are problem-responsive, offering normative guidance to societies facing a specific question of justice. Questions of justice, in turn, arise in the context of specific circumstances of justice. To illustrate, the problem of how to stabilize property, the specific question of justice Hume himself took up, arises in the context of limited scarcity of goods. Where goods are abundant, rules specifying property claims are not necessary; it is not necessary to stabilize property claims if individuals can simply and easily find what another may take. Where goods are absolutely scarce, rules for specifying property claims are futile. Individuals will not restrain their behavior in the face of such rules if living in a context of extreme need.

Four key features, I argue, characterize the circumstances of transitional justice (Murphy 2017, ch. 1). First, transitional societies are pervasively structurally unequal; that is, the institutionally defined terms for interaction among citizens and between citizens and officials are such that there exist fundamentally different degrees of freedom open to citizens to pursue their goals and shape the terms of interaction. This inequality passes a threshold that renders the institutional structure itself illegitimate; there exists a right to rebel on the part of citizens. For a paradigm example of pervasive structural inequality, consider apartheid South Africa. The apartheid order was predicated on differential freedoms and opportunities available to citizens as a function of their race. Segregated education, housing, and public services were not, and were not intended to be, equal. Moreover, black South Africans were stripped of any opportunity to participate in the political process or select representatives and legal avenues to express opposition to apartheid more or less did not exist. The second circumstance of transitional justice is what I call normalized collective and political wrongdoing. Groups targeting other groups for the sake of furthering political objectives commit wrongdoing, consisting in the violation of human rights done. Such wrongdoing is normalized in the sense that it becomes a basic fact of life around which citizens must orient their conduct. The third circumstance of transitional justice is what I call serious existential uncertainty, or a deep lack of clarity surrounding the political trajectory of a community. Whether or not conflict will resume or democracy will be consolidated remain genuinely open questions. Finally, there is fundamental uncertainty about authority; the standing of the state to deal with past wrongs is doubtful because the state is frequently implicated in the wrongs being addressed.

In these four circumstances, the core question of justice I claim is: how should a society justly pursue societal transformation? Societal transformation requires relational transformation, or reconciliation, one of the normative goals Crocker cites. Reconciliation requires that the relationships among citizens and between citizens and officials need to be fundamentally overhauled such that they become what they were not before: relationships among equals. Such transformation is necessary because of the pervasively unequal character of interaction prior to a transition. Moreover, pervasive structural inequality is characteristically used to both justify targeted wrongdoing and depends on normalized collective and political wrongdoing to be maintained. Repression is a tactic that is characteristically used to entrench and maintain structural inequality. Its links with human rights violations is another reason pervasively unequal relationships must be transformed.

Political reconciliation is the process of repairing damaged political relationships such that they are predicated on reciprocal respect for agency (Murphy 2010). For political relationships to reciprocally respect agency, three sets of requirements must to a threshold level be satisfied. The first set of requirements stems from the rule of law, another normative goal of transitional justice in Crocker's view. Law is the governance of conduct on the basis of legal rules. For laws to govern conduct in practice they must be such that they can figure in the practical reasoning of citizens. This in turn requires publicity, prospectivity, clarity, consistency, and constancy in the rules themselves and requires the behavior of officials to be congruent with what declared rules demand. Second, the way in which citizens view one another and officials must be trustful in a minimal sense; when minimal, citizens presume of officials and fellow citizens lack of ill will and threshold levels of competence to discharge duties they have qua citizen or a specific official role. It must be the case that presuming this default is reasonable. Finally, threshold levels of relational capabilities must obtain, as well as a threshold capability to avoid poverty. As is the case with the capabilities in terms of which development is defined, the genuine opportunities to be recognized as a member of a political community and participate in institutions depend on what an individual has and what an individual can do with what he or she has. Thus, fostering relational capabilities and the capability to avoid poverty will depend on the institutional development of the kind Crocker mentions as a normative aim of transitional justice.

The *just pursuit* of transformation denotes the moral importance of tending to the intrinsic moral demands to which being a victim or a perpetrator of wrongdoing gives rise (Murphy 2017, ch. 4). These include, in the case of victims, acknowledgment of wrongdoing, recognition of the standing of the victim as a rights holder and member of a political community, and reparations. For perpetrators, the demands include condemnation of wrongdoing and holding to account those responsible for such wrongs. The relationship between these two sets of demands (e.g., the requirements of transformation and the demands of transformation's just pursuit) can, I believe, be usefully conceptualized as structurally analogous to a standard picture of just war theory. We recognize that war may be unjust in two different ways: by failing to satisfy the criteria regulating just decisions to go to war (such as right cause, legitimate authority, proportionality, and last resort) and/ or by failing to satisfy the criteria regulating conduct in war (such as the principle of discrimination between combatants and noncombatants and proportionality). Similarly, processes of transitional justice may fail to be just in two ways, by failing to promote reconciliation/relational transformation or by failing to promote reconciliation in a just manner.

The place of democracy and the role of individual agency within transitional justice are subjects of ongoing debate. The "transition" of transitional justice has classically been defined as a transition from repression or conflict to democracy. However, the necessity of including democracy (as well as the necessity of being in transition) has been challenged. As I argue in my book, democracy is a constitutive element of the transformation toward which processes of transitional justice aim (Murphy 2017). This is for both intrinsic and instrumental reasons. Democracy is a form of governance predicated on a form of collective decision-making in which citizens are equal at an important stage of such decision-making (Christiano 2011, 2015). A minimally egalitarian form of democracy is predicated on a formally equal voting process, the aggregate outcome of which determines who holds political power coupled with rights to influence deliberation and shape the agenda for deliberation and the rule of law. Intrinsically, democracy is a necessary component of transitional justice because it is necessary for relationships to be relationships among equals. To be an equal, all citizens have an equal say in who will be holding political power to determine the shape of the terms for political interaction and an ability to influence on what issues political power is exercised. To lack such rights would be for some to lack an important aspect of the process dimension of freedom. Instrumentally, minimally egalitarian democracy has been shown empirically to reliably protect fundamental human rights, such as rights against torture, arbitrary imprisonment, or disappearing. Nondemocratic forms of government reliably fail to protect these rights. For these reasons, democracy is an essential part of transitional justice; the justice of transitional justice is achieved in part through democracy (Christiano 2011).

Democracy is not only essential as a part of the end-goal or over-arching objective of transitional justice processes; it is also an essential part of the process itself. There is no unique way to deal with past wrongs such that societal transformation is promoted in a just manner. There are a number of reasons for this. In terms of transformation itself, the character of damaged relationships varies across communities. What precisely needs to be transformed will thus differ as well. For example, the extent to which the rule of law eroded and how it was undermined, the depth of distrust and to whom such distrust is targeted, and the prevalence of poverty are a few areas where we might find such variation. Furthermore, there is no unique process for satisfying the intrinsic moral demands associated with dealing with perpetrators and victims of past wrongs (Murphy 2017, ch. 4). Just responses to wrongdoing are such that they treat perpetrators and victims in a manner that is fitting and appropriate. A number of factors influence whether a particular response to wrongdoing is fitting. The nature of the wrong done is the first factor; in particular, fitting responses must factor in the extent and kind of harm done to victims as well as whether the wrong was committed by or against a group. The relationship between respondent and subject of a response also matters. Certain reactive attitudes, like resentment, are appropriate responses by victims toward perpetrators; a third party feeling resentment toward a perpetrator would not be appropriate. Punishment is generally recognized to be appropriate for a state with authority to inflict, but not appropriate for an ordinary civilian to mete out. Finally, there will be cultural variation to some extent in what responses further the moral objectives involved in responding to victims and perpetrators. Such variation arises because of the expressive nature of many objectives of responses to wrongdoing, such as acknowledgment of the status of victims as rights bearers and condemnation of wrongdoing. What is required to acknowledge a victim is a member of a political community or to express condemnation of wrongdoing successfully may be to some extent culturally determined. In this context, deliberative democratic practices may play a key role in accurately identifying what processes will be just in the sense of responding in a fitting and appropriate manner to victims and perpetrators of wrongdoing. Through deliberative democratic discussions, a community can collectively come to decisions about what exactly is in need of transformation and what processes for pursuing transformation should be pursued. Similarly, debate about what form of acknowledgment and condemnation will be apt can contribute to ensuring that processes of transitional justice are just in the manner through which transformation is pursued. For such deliberative processes to have these contributions, it is critical that all segments of a society, especially those previously marginalized and victimized, have a voice. In these ways, the process of determining how past wrongs will be addressed requires precisely the deliberation and public platform for victims that Crocker lists.

3 Affinities

What is the relationship between development and transitional justice? In this section, I want to outline two different sources of deep affinity between the two: one empirical and one theoretical.

Empirically, countries pursuing development and countries pursuing transitional justice often overlap. Many countries in the Global South face the challenge of dealing with legacies of wrongdoing stemming from conflict and repression. The International Center for Transitional Justice, a leading nongovernmental organization on transitional justice working with countries around the world, concentrates its work in countries throughout the African continent, Middle East, Latin America, and Asia, areas where the demands of development are especially pressing. Countries in the Global South are also countries facing especially acute challenges of development. Thus, many of the countries where international nongovernmental organizations are offering advice and assistance with the pursuit of transitional justice are also countries in which other international nongovernmental organizations are offering advice and assistance with the pursuit of development. It is not surprising given the damage that war and repression leave in their wake. War destroys the built infrastructure of communities, including hospitals, schools, homes, and roads for transportation. Such destruction impedes the ability of individuals to be mobile, healthy, educated, and sheltered. Moreover, the strength of economies suffers, as businesses find an environment that lacks the stability that would make investment attractive and businesses flourish.

The overlap between transitional justice and development is not strictly empirical. There are deep affinities in the goals of development and the goals of relational transformation, when each is conceptualized as defined above. Most fundamentally, a genuine opportunity to avoid poverty is a constitutive component of transformation. When defined from a capability perspective, poverty entails

the absence of acceptable choices across a broad range of important life decisions – a severe lack of freedom to be or to do what one wants. The inevitable outcome of poverty is insufficiency and deprivation across many of the facets of a fulfilling life: inadequate resources to buy the basic necessities of life; frequent bouts of illness and an early death; living conditions that imperil physical and mental health. (Foster et al. 2013)

Focusing on the reduction or mitigation of poverty, in particular poverty arising from being a victim of wrongdoing, in transitional justice processes can at the same time promote central goals of development. The mitigation of poverty, defined from a capability perspective, is at the same time the promotion of the aspect of development concerned with well-being.

Poverty mitigation or reduction also fosters agency, for poverty compromises and erodes the ability of individuals to interact in a manner reciprocally respectful of the agency of citizens and officials. Poverty can impede the ability of individuals to participate in educational, political, and economic institutions. Hunger can make concentration at school more difficult. Illness can make sustained employment impossible. It can impede the recognition of individuals who are poor as full members of the political community. And poverty can make acting within the constraints of law more difficult (Wolff and de-Shalit 2013). A genuine opportunity to avoid poverty thus impacts the other capabilities of interest in the relational transformation of transitional justice. Poverty can also erode conditions for being respected and recognized as a member of one's community.

Unsurprisingly given the affinity of their overarching objectives, processes of transitional justice can contribute to development in complementary ways. Reparations, for example, characteristically offer compensation to individuals who have been wronged. The compensation aims to repair the damage caused and harm suffered through wrongdoing. Such reparation can also make a small contribution toward the alleviation of poverty, thereby advancing the well-being of its recipients. The symbolic and communicative function of reparations, moreover, can be equally significant. Reparations express the standing of those who are its recipients as rights bearers and as members of the political community, contributing the expansion of recognition of a victim as a member of the political community, which is especially important when wrongdoing was aimed at denying precisely this fact. Such recognition in turn can facilitate the ability of an individual to pursue other functionings that he or she values.

4 Areas of Divergence

In addition to the areas of complementarity, however, the overlap is not complete and there are conditions under which transitional justice and development may pull in different directions.

First, though transformation and development have overlapping priorities, the demands of development may go beyond those of societal transformation. Relational transformation or reconciliation at the core of transitional justice concentrates fundamentally on the conditions that need to be in place for certain relational capabilities to be possible. However, there are dimensions of well-being and priorities of development processes that will not be of central concern to transitional justice. For example, there is increasing recognition that sustainable development requires attention to natural hazard mitigation. Standing only to increase in their severity and frequency, hurricanes, cyclones, droughts, and earthquakes can erase progress from development projects and processes. But, tending to the vulnerability of a society to these natural hazards is not a direct concern to transitional justice, but rather is an independent concern for the promotion of sustainable development within communities.

Second, the repair of political relationships at the core of transitional justice is pursued through processes dealing with past wrongs and their ongoing impact. Thus, there will be projects that may promote development and even relational capabilities of interest, but will not be properly considered projects of transitional justice because they are not projects that foster such capabilities in a manner predicated on dealing with past wrongs. The work of agricultural extension in bringing knowledge, training, and expertise to rural farmers, for example, can have a significant impact on increasing the yield of a given crop and the market literacy of those who are poor. However, such extension work does not in the typical case serve as a form of reparation for those who were subjected to violations of economic rights, nor is such work framed as a way of transforming relationships among members of a particular society.

Finally and relatedly, there are constraints on the pursuit of transitional justice that are not present in the same way in the pursuit of development. Poverty may make one more vulnerable to being a victim of wrongdoing and victims may be among the poorest within a community, but not all victims are poor. Thus, the individuals who receive reparations or other forms of compensation for having been wronged may not overlap with the individuals who should be a priority from a development perspective. A core priority and concern with the treatment of particular victims and particular perpetrators who are the focus of transitional justice processes may require resources to be devoted to a group that may not have a similar priority when considering development and who is poorest from a capability perspective. Furthermore, the most efficient pursuit of agency and well-being may be foreclosed by the constraints that the just pursuit of societal transformation imposes.

5 Conclusion

In concentrating on both development ethics and transitional justice in his work, David Crocker was one of the first philosophers to correctly identify normative connections and affinities between these ideals. In this chapter I have concentrated on these connections and affinities, underscoring the importance of considering both normative goals in the broader pursuit of the expansion of individual freedom or capability. Development from a capability perspective focuses directly on the expansion of the range of doings and beings of values individuals have a genuine opportunity to achieve. Transitional justice focuses on relational freedom and relational capabilities, and the importance of repairing relationships when the freedom enjoyed is pervasively unequal. Not only theoretically but also practically, the pursuit of development projects and the pursuit of transitional justice processes overlap, as many societies emerging from extended periods of conflict and/or repression face the dual tasks of redressing past wrongs and fostering broader development. By following Crocker's lead and conceptualizing the normative goals of both development and transitional justice with a distinct emphasis on capabilities, we are better positioned to understand how we might foster both and what should be prioritized should conflict arise.

Note

1. For an account of reconciliation that rejects the appropriateness of articulating a substantive view, see Schaap (2009). For an overview of substantive accounts of reconciliation, including my own substantive view, see Murphy (2010).

References

Christiano, Thomas. 2011. "An Instrumental Argument for a Human Right to Democracy." *Philosophy & Public Affairs*, 39(2): 142–176.

Christiano, Thomas. 2015. "Democracy." In *Stanford Encyclopedia of Philosophy*, Edward N. Zalta (ed.). http://plato.stanford.edu/archives/spr2015/entries/democracy/.

Crocker, David A. 1999a. "Functioning and Capability: The Foundations of Sen's and Nussbaum's Development Ethic." *Political Theory*, 20(4): 584–612.

1999b. "Reckoning with Past Wrongs: A Normative Framework." *Ethics & International Affairs*, 13: 43–64.

2002. "Punishment, Reconciliation, and Democratic Deliberation." *Buffalo Criminal Law Review*, 5: 509–549.

2008. *Ethics of Global Development: Agency, Capability and Deliberative Democracy*. Cambridge University Press.

2018. "Obstacles to Reconciliation in Peru: An Ethical Analysis." Unpublished manuscript.

Foster, James, Suman Seth, Michael Lokshin, and Zurab Sajaia. 2013. *A Unified Approach to Measuring Poverty and Inequality*. Washington, DC: World Bank.

Hume, David. 1978 [1739]. *A Treatise of Human Nature*, 2nd edition. L. A. Selby-Bigge (ed.). Oxford University Press.

1998 [1751]. *An Enquiry Concerning the Principles of Morals*. Tom L. Beauchamp (ed.). Oxford University Press.

Murphy, Colleen. 2010. *A Moral Theory of Political Reconciliation*. Cambridge University Press.

2017. *The Conceptual Foundations of Transitional Justice*. Cambridge University Press.

Nussbaum, Martha. 1999. *Women and Human Development*. Cambridge University Press.

Schaap, Andrew. 2009. *Political Reconciliation*. New York: Routledge.

Sen, Amartya. 1999. *Development as Freedom*. New York: Anchor Books.

Wolff, Jonathan, and Avner de-Shalit. 2013. *Disadvantage*. Oxford University Press.

15 Consensus-Building and Its Impact on Policy*
The National Agreement Forum in Peru

JAVIER M. IGUÍÑIZ ECHEVERRÍA

1 Introduction

The enormous importance of democratic institutions and practice is clear. David A. Crocker writes that "our greatest national and global challenge" consists of "developing deeper, more inclusive, and more resilient democratic institutions and ways of life" (2008, 329). In the "capabilities approach," designed and promoted by Amartya Sen (1980; 1992; 1999) and Martha Nussbaum (2000; 2011), much importance is given to public deliberation and democratic institutions (Sen 1999, chapter 6). It can be said that there is a consensus about it within the community of researchers who are dedicated to deepening the capabilities approach. In the analysis of one of the debate points with Amartya Sen concerning the convenience of drafting defined lists of capabilities, Martha Nussbaum considers that her vision of the capabilities approach "also recognizes that, in a working democracy, deliberation takes place at several levels and in many concrete contexts" (2011, 74). Within those levels she distinguishes those that correspond to discussion on "fundamental political principles," the strengthening of certain concrete rights, constitutional amendment, and legislation.

These two tools – public deliberation and democratic institutions – are not only valuable in and of themselves, but also as important aspects of human development and tools to achieve such development, more specifically, to fight the multiple expressions of poverty. In a recent study concerning India, Jean Drèze and Amartya Sen

* With the collaboration of María Luisa Valdez, Paula Arriaga, Gustavo Mendoza, and Anuntxi Monsalve. Various anonymous reviewers have also helped to improve the original version.

(2013) have shown that deliberation and well-established democratic institutions, in a context of prolonged and substantial economic growth, have had a limited positive effect on the resolution of the basic (and too often tragic) privations faced by most of the Indian population. Hence, the importance of developing the field of study concerning the efficacy of democratic institutions and the practice of public deliberation on public policies, as well as the importance of such deliberations and policies for human development.[1] This chapter deals with some aspects of that research field by examining the composition of Peru's National Agreement Forum (NAF) and the characteristics of its workings, and evaluating its impact on Peruvian public policies from 2002 to 2012.[2]

The generalized recognition of the forum's usefulness in establishing personal bonds and mutual respect among representatives of competitive institutions from the political and social arenas has always come with a lack of awareness and understanding of the way it operates and an enduring question concerning the efficacy of its contribution, especially when it comes to putting substantial matters on the agenda and influencing public policy. This chapter will attempt to (1) briefly describe the unusual democratic institution known as the National Agreement Forum in Peru; (2) argue that specific characteristics of the NAF – especially the broad participation of its members, the consensus-based form of democratic decision-making through which it operates, and the values expressed in the agreements themselves – give moral force to the agreements it produces; and (3) offer an evidence-based assessment of the NAF's ability to influence state policy. We conclude that one reason for the effectiveness of the NAF in influencing public policy is precisely the moral force it generates through the three aforementioned characteristics, allowing it to collaborate in legitimizing state actions, while also making it hard for policymakers to completely disregard the "soft" directives contained in its agreements.

2 National Agreement Forum

The NAF, which began its work in 2002, discusses various matters of national importance, and generates so-called "State Policies," which are approved by consensus. In these roughly two-page policy briefs, published in Spanish, Quechua, Aymara, Ashanika, and English, valuable objectives are presented together with the adequate guidelines and criteria to achieve them. During the last fourteen years, the forum has approved thirty-four State Policies, as well as other medium- and long-term commitments. These policies are framed into four grand objectives: I. Democracy and Rule of Law, II. Equality and Social Justice, III. Country Competitiveness, and IV. Efficient, Transparent, and Decentralized State. The objectives expressed in these State Policies should remain as such in the long run, that is, at least for a number of future governments.[3] The NAF has the year 2021, the bicentennial of Peru's independence, as its horizon. At this point, all State Policies and achievements are meant to be revaluated.

The forum is composed of three types of members. First, representatives of the executive at the three levels of government (national, regional, and local); second, representatives of the political parties present in Congress; and third, representatives of a wide range of institutions of civil society that have national leading presence. The president of the Republic presides over the National Agreement and usually delegates the presidency of the forum's plenary sessions, which have been 111 so far, to the president of the Council of Ministers, who attends these sessions with other ministers (depending on the matters to be addressed). In special circumstances – such as the commemoration of the NAF's tenth anniversary and the approval of Policy 33, on water resources – the session was directly presided over by the president of the Republic. In the case of regional and local governments, both the president of the National Assembly of Regional Governments (ANGR) and the president of the Peruvian Association of Municipalities (AMPE) are regularly present in these plenary sessions. As of today, there are fifteen political parties, all of which change after every electoral process. As far as civil society is concerned, ten organizations are part of the forum, including most of the more important national-level ones.

The NAF employs what can be considered as one of the "thicker" modes of participation in the spectrum elaborated by Crocker, which starts with "nominal participation" (the thinnest one) and ends with "deliberative participation" at the thickest. We cannot say that the NAF is a combined elite/non-elite type of institution, despite the evident asymmetry of the power held by its members in the society in which they interact. This asymmetry is quite often reflected through conflict (e.g., strikes, road and street blockades). It may be true that, as Crocker (2008) reminds us by summarizing Goulet's view of deliberative participation, "the mere fact of consensus does not justify the consensus, since the 'agreement' may be the result of elite manipulation" (345). However, that is not the case here. The lists show that the NAF is not, as in the case of many deliberative institutions around the world, "at the neighborhood and city level" (363). All the members of the NAF represent some of the most important national organizations, many of which are capable, by their own nature, of prioritizing their own interests in predictable ways. Oftentimes this may disrupt the normal workings of the economy and the political scene. Amazonian people, often too divided, are not present, and for similar reasons neither are youth organizations, just to mention a few potential participants. This can be done through mobilizations, lobbies, or other means. It should be noted that the poorest in Peru are not as nationally unified and strongly organized as the "comparatively privileged but not most privileged" can be (Drèze and Sen 2013, 287).

3 Consensus, Moral Basis, and Its Impact on Public Policy

As Drèze and Sen (2013, 243) point out, seeking and achieving consensus can be seen as a democratic method: "Various democratic methods, such as decisions by consensus, have been used in limited settings around the globe over the centuries." In the case being presented here, the stage is limited to a particular political context and a specific institution.[4] I argue that the broad participation of the members of the NAF and the consensual character of what is approved contribute moral force to the NAF's agreements.

In practice, such agreements are not binding on the government. Disagreements are never registered, much less published, which is why no examples of them are presented here. In fact, the majority of the many recommendations elaborated through NAF dialogue have not been applied in practice, despite the fact that laws in Congress are required to indicate the NAF State Policy to which they correspond. Many governmental policy decisions cannot be attributed to the NAF, even though the State Policies frequently end up collecting and reaffirming, through precise statements, proposals that are part of the emerging consensus in society. This chapter is, in part, a reaction to those that easily discard efforts to build institutions that operate through non-binding rules, and to those that do not recognize any benefit from consensual agreements. In other words, we deal with long-term policy proposals that have a "chance of working," as Crocker insists,[5] and as we will demonstrate in the last part of this chapter. Obviously, the democratic process, and deliberative methods as a whole, amply transcend the "limited settings" of the NAF.

In this chapter, the term "impact" is relatively loose but, as we will see below, not without some recognizable significance. The convenience of agreements not being binding is a matter of continuous discussion – for some it is a defect, while for others it is adequate or even preferable, as the very fact that these are not binding frees up the participants to more easily discuss and come to an agreement on otherwise politically difficult topics, deferring the actual law-making to Congress. Here we can once more come back to Crocker – in this case, to his insistence on the importance of "the dynamic of the process leading to a normatively compelling consensus" (2008, 345). Part of the moral force of the NAF comes from the intensive and broad participation of the forum's members, be it in working groups that discuss successive drafts of medium- and long-term commitment projects, or in the plenary sessions, in which each member has the same status. Each member has the same status because a rejection by any of the members, dismissing the possibility of agreement on that specific matter, would impede the agreement. The consensus has to be understood as one in which the intensity of the support is diverse but clear, given the existing power of veto. Some participants simply consent to the discussed text being approved because the authors have succeeded in making it as compatible as possible with the participants' values and interests.[6]

Obviously, consensus does not imply total agreement on the meaning of principles and values that are expressed in the State Policy. Regarding agreements in general, Sunstein successfully expresses the process of arriving at consensus on policy issues at the level of the NAF forum when he detects the importance of "incompletely theorized agreements." As Alkire points out, "Policy makers do not need to agree precisely on what justice is; they need only to rule out clearly undesirable options" (Alkire 2010, 24).[7] That intensity depends in part on the matter being discussed and the specific interests of the different representatives. What could be considered as a mere consensus should not be dismissed, for it reveals that at the center of the NAF there exists a will to not "torpedo" the agreements, although in other political scenarios the political or trade union rivalry can be, and is, very aggressive.

Finnis argues that consensus can be a "mark of truth" only under ideal conditions, in which parties are knowledgeable, of good will, and disposed to be frank (and only in regard to matters for which consensus is appropriate). And even in these conditions consensus is not a criterion of truth, but a mark of truth – that is, a welcome consequence of discussants' willingness to engage in practical reflection (Alkire 2002, 41).

Our hypothesis is that an important factor of the impact of State Policies, albeit not the only one, is the moral force that comes with the procedure of consensus and from the values that are publicly expressed in the agreements. As Sen points out, they are an expression of "values [which are] relevant in the making of public policy" (1999, 274). Sen explains that those who elaborate policies take into account the values of social justice for two reasons. The first fits well with the work of the NAF, for "justice is a central concept in identifying the aims and objectives of public policy and also in deciding on the instruments that are appropriate in pursuing the chosen ends" (1999, 274). This statement should not be understood as normative, but as a reality that truly steers deliberations. Both aspirations and instruments are related to an eminent political end, also highlighted by Sen, which is the capability of politics of persuading citizens and widening its own drawing power. This persuasion also depends on the capacity to "understand the values of the public at large, including their sense of justice" (1999, 274). I point this out to show that we also believe that the deliberative exercise of politics has, among others, these two complementary objectives (i.e., expressing aspirations and constituting instruments), both of which give functionality to values in the political exercise. To the extent to which the State Policies, once collectively approved, are made public, they produce a public image that is strategically sought after by governments, parties, and civil society organizations that are members of the NAF. They then end up embracing and basing themselves on an idea of justice that is respected and desired by the citizenry and the voters.

We shall not dwell any further on the effect of the moral force of the procedures and ideas in society, but rather in highlighting that the impact of the NAF on state policy formation is one that, in my judgment, comes – at least in part – from that moral force. In any case, and on firmer ground, the impact that we shall present does not come from the mandatory character of the agreed policies as, once again, these policies are not binding.

4 Methodology

On the occasion of the NAF's ten-year anniversary, it seemed appropriate to address anxieties about the impact of its State Policies by consulting 177 public and private individuals with a direct relationship to or public responsibilities in the fields toward which these policies are directed. A combined question, which we present here in part, was sent to them, with instructions to write

two paragraphs with your testimony, that add to a maximum of 250 words, and which point out with the greatest precision how State Policies were a sustenance in making decisions in the executive branch, designing laws, drafting government plans, issuing trade union pronouncements, among other things. Likewise, what consensuses were achieved at the forum that facilitated the promotion and support of specific initiatives.

A total of 164 responses were received from national, regional, and local political leaders (current and former), among them 3 presidents and 15 prime ministers, as well as other ministers and public officials; political, trade union, and social leaders; and public opinion leaders and other professionals.[8]

Obviously, this survey cannot and does not have any pretension of being statistically representative, much less a statistically significant test of "impact." Moreover, I am using the term itself somewhat loosely. While a formal analysis of "impact" might attempt to classify the effects according to criteria such as strength and character, this analysis instead classifies it by the aspects of public policy (what Crocker would call the "range" in democratic decision-making) that have been influenced by the NAF's State Policies. The brief answers are also not an expression of a complete evaluation of the NAF by those who responded. The survey has been carried out with people who (1) know enough about the experience and the nature of the NAF to hold a valid opinion and (2) have participated in the government decision-making process (at all levels) or have been active in the political or trade union world during the past decade.

5 Results

The answers to the survey were diverse, as was the degree of explicitness about the impact of specific State Policies about which many of those surveyed were asked. What follows is a selection of excerpts from these responses.

5.1 Institution-Building

Survey responses suggest that one important impact of the NAF has been in promoting the creation of new governmental institutions, and in the institutionalization of particular policy priorities. That is, the NAF has contributed in diverse ways to the country's institutionalization. As a former president of the planning agency (Centro Nacional de Planeamiento Estrategico, or CEPLAN) recalls, State Policy 5 has two achievements: "the creation by law of the National System of Strategic Planning and the National Centre of Strategic Planning" (Paz Soldán Franco 2014). The first president of the Council of Ministers of the current government has expressed the intention of "promoting various State Policies, among them, the tenth Policy, Poverty Reduction, through the creation of the Ministry of Development and Social Inclusion – MIDIS" (Lerner Ghitis 2014). A president of the Council of Ministers of a former government points out that "we created the Ministry of the Environment and CEPLAN inspired by the State Policies of the NAF" (Del Castillo Gálvez 2014). The president of the Congress of the Republic requested that the NAF, among other institutions, elaborate a list of priorities to be included in the legislative agenda. In his words, collaborating with the multi-party dialogue translated into "the presiding boards becoming plural and surprise laws being finished with the creation of a concerted legislative agenda that made legislative work foreseeable" (Isla Rojas 2014). Policy 32 (Risk Disaster Management) "has allowed to elevate the matter to the highest level of decision making and, at the same time, to have an articulating framework of existing initiatives" (Quijandría Acosta 2014).

5.2 State Plans and Strategies

Many voices affirm that another important effect of the NAF has been its influence on state policies and strategies on national priorities such as poverty, drug trafficking, rural development, and national security. For example, "For the Anti-Corruption High Level Commission, the 26th State Policy has constituted the starting point for the work defining the National Plan for the Fight against Corruption in the 2012–2016 period" (Silva Hasembank 2014). In the field of education, "During my time as Education Minister, the 2021 National Education Project (PEN) was recognized" (Chang 2014). A former regional president pointed out that "one example of the adequate application of the NAF in relation to policy number 10, Poverty Reduction, is the case of the Ayacucho region" (Molina Chávez 2014). For the family, "it is important to highlight the actions that, motivated by that State Policy, have been put into effect: the National Plan for the Support of the Family 2004–2011; the Action Plan for Infancy and Adolescence 2012–2021; and the National Plan for Support of the Families 2012–2017, which will be approved soon" (Arroyo Cuyubamba 2014). In the field of the Armed Forces, a prominent member of these has pointed out that "the ninth Policy, which corresponds to national security, was very much on my mind . . . during the formulation of the White Book of National Defense in 2005" (Chiabra León 2014). Concerning agrarian development, Policy 23 "has provided the generation, during the last decade, with important normative instruments, such the National Strategy for Rural Development, the National Strategy for Food Safety, the National Plan for Overcoming Poverty, and the Green Map or National Agrarian Agreement" (Rheineck Piccardo 2014). As for drugs, Policy 27 "facilitates the consensus between the involved entities that will later translate into the National Strategy for the Fight against Drugs, which is approved by the Council of Ministers" (Masías Claux 2014).

5.3 Law-Making

State Policy 2 has had some impact in the law-making process. For example, "the 2nd State Policy . . . was the starting point for the making of the Law of Political Parties" (Andrade Carmona 2014). In the field of health, "one of the main developments achieved, taking as a basis the 13th State Policy, has been the passing and implementation of the Framework Law of Universal Health Insurance" (de Habich Rospigliosi 2014). As far as science and technology are concerned, a congressman declared that he has "found in the purposes of the

20th State Policy of the National Agreement, the fundamental framework for directing my legislative efforts towards improving access to the benefits of science and its technological applications" (Guevara Amasifuén 2014). Referring to Policy 25 (Care for the Institutionality of the Armed Forces and Their Service to Democracy), it is expressed that "it promoted the granting of the right to vote to its members" (Mora Zevallos 2014). The NAF also empowers those who demand the implementation of State Policies. For example, it expressed that "as far as the trade union movement is concerned, these policies have been useful in permanently demanding their application and as grounds for basing our demands" (Gorriti 2014).

5.4 Government Policies

Some declarations on the impact of State Policies point toward measures we may consider as government policies. In the case of Policy 24 (on the efficiency of the state), it has been expressed that, in the framework of such policy, the coming together of the state and the citizen has been promoted. Among other measures, "we managed to improve or simplify more than 54,000 processes at the national level, and we established the Single Text of Administrative Procedures in the Municipalities" (Velásquez Quesquén 2014). In the fiscal field, on the other hand, "the National Agreement has inspired important changes in fiscal policy" (Arias Minaya 2014). State Policy 29 (Access to Information, Freedom of Expression, and Freedom of the Press) "has served as support for many of the reforms in the field of the modernization of public administration, through the implementation of diverse mechanisms that assure citizens' access to information" (Delgado Zegarra 2014). A couple of specific examples mentioned in that statement have been the creation of transparency portals and complaint books. The aspiration to contribute to the articulation of policies is evident. For example, referring above all to Policy 20 (Science and Technology), "The NAF is also a privileged space for policies on economics, education, competitiveness, labor market, tax regime, etc., to be aligned with the policies for the development of Research, Development and Innovation" (Léon-Velarde Servetto 2014). In the field of Policy 21 (Infrastructure and Housing), "the government, fulfilling what this policy states, has retransferred to the private sector the responsibility of designing, building and promoting infrastructure and housing in the country, reserving for itself the role of facilitator and regulator of these activities" (Scheelje Martin 2014).

5.5 Contribution to a Plural Dialogue

The NAF has also done much to contribute to a plural dialogue with multiple stakeholders. Policy 14 (Access to Full, Dignified, and Productive Employment) "served as a reference point for the participants" in the National Labor Council (Checa Ledesma 2014). The Round Table for the Fight against Poverty (MCLCP) "has counted on the forum in an unconditional manner, for putting issues on the national agenda and involving diverse segments of society" (Garatea Yori 2014). More generally, the contribution of the NAF itself is recognized when pointing out that its silent labor helps in "achieving consensus between the different actors of the national life: academy and civil society, communities and companies, trade unions and business associations, State and political parties" (Fujimori Higushi 2014). In a similar vein, some have pointed out that the NAF "has demonstrated that deliberation and disagreement are vital to democracy, because they are expressions of pluralism, but do not preclude a consensus" (Flores Nano 2014).

5.6 Supporting State Initiatives

The NAF also supports state initiatives. In the framework of the State Policy 6 (Foreign Policy for Peace, Democracy, Development, and Integration), "the National Agreement has given important support to the decision of the Peruvian Government of taking its controversy of maritime delimitation (with Chile) to the International Court of Justice" (Wagner Tizón 2014). The NAF has contributed with a greater plural dialogue. "It was for this reason that the tax reform that we proposed was achieved" (Merino Lucero 2014). In the field of Justice, the NAF "actively participated through three representatives in the Commission in charge of elaborating the National Plan for Integral Reform of the Administration of Justice, CERIAJUS" (Alvarado Dodero 2014).

As we have pointed out above, the range of terms that allude to impact that are freely used by those who responded to the open questions suggests the possibility of a gradation by the degree of closeness to what we most clearly could consider impact. The pretension of precision cannot be too high for the matters and the agreed policies, and the measures adopted by the decision-makers have a diverse relation among themselves.

6 Discussion

After presenting the composition and characteristics of the National Agreement Forum in Peru and the State Policies agreements reached, we have picked up some theoretical elements of Sen's connection between values and political activity, and reflections on deliberative democracy from Crocker and Alkire in support of an explanation of the potential impact on government policies that a national agreement approved by consensus could have.

This chapter has thus shown some of the impact that the National Agreement has had on public policies in the twelve years following 2002 – that is, during almost three full governmental periods, the first three consecutive democratically elected governments in the history of Peruvian Republic. The declarations gathered from public and private decision-makers, among them many high-level officials, indicate that State Policies have been, in diverse ways, taken into account – they have not necessarily been applied, but they have at least been consulted.

In this text, we have suggested that such influence could come from a moral power, which results from the representativeness of the members of the NAF, from the characteristics of that which is agreed to, and from the fact that it has been achieved by consensus. Such power over political agents is surely less effective than the one that would come from a binding relationship that obligates some part of the state to implement the agreed policies, but what I have tried to show here points toward a certain degree of influence that should not be disdained. Indeed, to some, the main impact of the forum is that it manages to gather various leaders for a broad cross-section of civil society – government officials and representatives of political parties (both in alliance with and opposition to the government), unions, business associations, religious groups, and so on – and engage them in dialogue.

The method used to obtain the relevant information does not pretend to be sufficient or appropriate to determine the magnitude of the impact. After all, here it is true, as Crocker reminds us, that "much more research is needed about what sorts of impact these institutions have had on people's lives and the surrounding society" (2008, 363). For one, the characteristic opacity of the functionaries that design measures in the state makes clear that a broader study (i.e., one that is more complete, methodologically speaking) concerning range would find impacts that have not been detected here. For example, a question that had a greater proportion of answers coming from the same officials and leaders that design policies, laws, etc., would allow the addition of many other sources to those used in this study, and would also add more precision in noting impact.

7 Conclusion

The results shown indicate both a positive perception in the highest spheres of different government bodies and some of the effects that the NAF has had in the political decision to implement measures of different sorts. More than opening new roads for the country's politics, the NAF seems to express in an explicit manner those courses of public action that seem desirable for broad sectors of society, represented by the diverse members of the NAF. The relationship between values and politics that we have briefly gathered in this text suggest the existence of a connection between those participants, the feelings of the citizenry, and the political convenience of taking State Policies into account.

Even so, it should be evident that, despite its broad representation, the achieved consensus in the NAF does not exactly express or guarantee an identical consensus in society, where more contextual elements, rules of the game, and actors come into the picture. The lack of representation by indigenous peoples and youth are two glaring examples. It is also not guaranteed that the implementation of the policies is the best possible answer to the issues in question. The freedom of the political leader or policy maker to choose the specific manner of implementing a public policy is significant, and the programmatic differences between parties can be large when it comes to achieving ends and implementing criteria that are established in the State Policies of the NAF.

As we pointed out at the beginning of this study, it becomes necessary – from a perspective of the capabilities approach – to complete this query on the impact of the NAF not only by implementing other methodological approaches, but also by taking an additional step that establishes the impact of the measures of the policies adopted by governments toward reducing the lack of adequate job opportunities, preventing and recuperating from sickness, being educated, and social participation in general – all of which, if not addressed, prevent the citizenry (and especially the poor) from fully taking the reins of their future.

Notes

1. A detailed and balanced discussion of several of the issues involved is presented by David A. Crocker (2008, Part IV).
2. Even though it is true that "[h]uman development anticipates the likely impacts of policy choices on poor and marginalized communities and future generations" (Alkire 2010, 24), this research does not aim to evaluate the incidence of state policies in human development. This should be part of another research agenda.
3. See www.acuerdonacional.pe for the text of the approved policies in all five languages.
4. The discussion around the general importance and consequences of consensus in democracy exceeds the scope of this chapter.
5. See Crocker (2008, 364) asking democrats not to be foolish when using deliberative methods.
6. Not everyone embraces the approved text with the same enthusiasm. Somebody close to the NAF, De la Puente (2016), for instance, classifies the types of critical consensual agreements into "acceptance with reserve," "silent disagreement," and "adherence to the central, but not to the secondary" (2016, 5). It has been repeated several times in the forum that "a good agreement is that which leaves everybody somewhat unhappy."
7. According to the experience of the NAF, it is right to say that, as in the words of Alkire, Sen has suggested "the space for consensus might be widened if the capabilities and functionings are conceived at a sufficient level of generality" (Alkire 2002, 31). Obtaining and sharing information is also very important (Alkire 2002, 31). See also (Alkire 2010, 24).
8. The full set of complete answers is published in Acuerdo Nacional (2014).

References

Acuerdo Nacional. 2013. *Politicas de Estado*. Lima, November. www .acuerdonacional.pe.
Acuerdo Nacional. 2014. *Acuerdo Nacional. Consensos para enrumbar el Perú*. Lima: Acuerdo Nacional.

Alkire, Sabina. 2002. *Valuing Freedoms*. Oxford University Press.

Alkire, Sabina. 2010. "Human Development: Definitions, Critiques, and Related Issues." OPHI Working Paper No. 36, OPHI: 1–54.

Alvarado Dodero, Fausto. 2014. "Minister of Justice 2002–2004." Extract from *Acuerdo Nacional*.

Andrade Carmona, Fernando. 2014. "President of Somos Perú." Extract from *Acuerdo Nacional*.

Arias Minaya, Luis Alberto. 2014. "National Superintendent of Tax Administration 2000–2001." Extract from *Acuerdo Nacional*.

Arroyo Cuyubamba, Víctor. 2014. "National Evangelic Council of Peru." Extract from *Acuerdo Nacional*.

Chang, José Antonio. 2014. "President of the Council of Ministers 2010–2011." Extract from *Acuerdo Nacional*.

Checa Ledesma, Pablo. 2014. "Representative of the General Confederation of Peruvian Workers (CGTP), Viceminister of Labor 2011–2012." Extract from *Acuerdo Nacional*.

Chiabra León, Roberto. 2014. "Minister of Defense 2003–2005." Extract from *Acuerdo Nacional*.

Crocker, David A. 2008. *Ethics of Global Development: Agency, Capability, and Deliberative Democracy*. Cambridge University Press.

de Habich Rospigliosi, Midori. 2014. "Minister of Health." Extract from *Acuerdo Nacional*.

de la Puente, Juan. 2016. "Hey tú, vota y cállate." *La república*, Lima, May 27.

Del Castillo Gálvez, Jorge. 2014. "President of Council of Ministers 2006–2008." Extract from *Acuerdo Nacional*.

Delgado Zegarra, Jaime. 2014. "Congressman." Extract from *Acuerdo Nacional*.

Drèze, Jean, and Amartya Sen. 2013. *The Uncertain Glory: India and Its Contradictions*. Princeton University Press.

Flores Nano, Lourdes. 2014. "Representative of Partido Popular Cristiano at NA." Extract from *Acuerdo Nacional*.

Fujimori Higushi, Keiko. 2014. "President of Fuerza Popular." Extract from *Acuerdo Nacional*.

Garatea Yori, Gastón. 2014. "President of the Round Table for the Fight against Poverty (MCLCP) 2001–2007." Extract from *Acuerdo Nacional*.

Gorriti, Juan José. 2014. "Vicepresident of the General Confederation of Peruvian Workers (CGTP)." Extract from *Acuerdo Nacional*.

Guevara Amasifuén, Masías. 2014. "Congressman." Extract from *Acuerdo Nacional*.

Isla Rojas, Víctor. 2014. "President of Congress of the Republic 2012–2013." Extract from *Acuerdo Nacional*.

Léon-Velarde Servetto, Fabiola. 2014. "Rector of Universidad Peruana Cayetano Heredia." Extract from *Acuerdo Nacional*.

Lerner Ghitis, Salomón. 2014. "President of Council of Ministers 2011." Extract from *Acuerdo Nacional*.

Masías Claux, Carmen. 2014. "Executive President of the National Commission for Development and Life without Drugs." Extract from *Acuerdo Nacional*.

Merino Lucero, Beatriz. 2014. "President of the Council of Ministers 2003." Extract from *Acuerdo Nacional*.

Molina Chávez, Ernesto. 2014. "President of the Regional Government of Ayacucho 2007–2010." Extract from *Acuerdo Nacional*.

Mora Zevallos, Daniel. 2014. "Minister of Defense 2011." Extract from *Acuerdo Nacional*.

Nussbaum, Martha. 2000. *Women and Human Development: The Capabilities Approach*. Cambridge University Press.

    2011. *Creating Capabilities: The Human Development Approach*. Cambridge, MA: The Belknap Press of Harvard University Press.

Paz Soldán Franco, Mariano. 2014. "President of CEPLAN's Directive Council 2012–2013." Extract from *Acuerdo Nacional*.

Quijandría Acosta, Gabriel. 2014. "Viceminister of Strategic Development of Natural Resources of the MINAM." Extract from *Acuerdo Nacional*.

Rheineck Piccardo, Juan. 2014. "Viceminister of Agriculture 2011–2013." Extract from *Acuerdo Nacional*.

Scheelje Martin, Leopoldo. 2014. "Representative of CONFIEP in NA." Extract from *Acuerdo Nacional*.

Sen, Amartya. 1980. "Equality of What?" In *Tanner Lectures on Human Values*, S. McMurrin (ed.). Salt Lake City: University of Utah Press.

    1992. *Inequality Reexamined*. New York: Russell Sage Foundation.

    1999. *Development as Freedom*. Oxford University Press.

Silva Hasembank, Susana. 2014. "General Coordinator of the Anti-Corruption High-level Commission." Extract from *Acuerdo Nacional*.

Velásquez Quesquén, Javier. 2014. "President of Council of Ministers 2009–2010." Extract from *Acuerdo Nacional*.

Wagner Tizón, Allan. 2014. "Minister of Foreign Affairs 1985–1988 and 2002–2003." Extract from *Acuerdo Nacional*.

PART IV

Development Ethics, Agency, and Democracy

New Challenges and New Directions

16 | *From Agency to Perfectionist Liberalism*

DAVID A. CROCKER

It would be ideal if I could reply in detail to each and every one of these stimulating and challenging pieces. That, however, would require more time and space than I have available. Instead, I have elected to address three related themes that more than one of my fellow development ethicists have found problematic in my work. This chapter has two parts. First, it analyzes different concepts of agency and argues that the Senian notion of critical and ethically responsible agency is an indispensable but insufficient "perfectionist" good. Second, the chapter addresses the question of how we should interpret Sen's phrase "reason to value." I am convinced by Serene J. Khader and Stacy J. Kosko's argument in this volume (Chapter 7) that we should interpret the phrase as a kind of perfectionism, and I argue for critical and responsible agency as one of the goods to be promoted in good development. In the next chapter, the volume's concluding chapter, I first argue that an agency-focused capability approach (CA) is best understood as a perfectionist liberalism in contrast to Rawls's and Nussbaum's versions of political liberalism. Then, second, I reply to criticisms by Koggel, Murphy, and Camacho, and argue for liberal, deliberative, and representative democracy as both a universal value and essential development goal. In and through my engagement anew with these issues, I hope to improve the agency-focused capability approach to development and chart some promising directions for the current and next generation of development ethicists.

The concept of agency – its nature, value, limits, and relation to democracy – is central to my work in development ethics (DE), as the title of this volume (*Agency and Democracy in Development Ethics*) reflects, and is featured in many of the volume's chapters. In this chapter I ask: How should we understand agency as both an empirical and normative concept? What are the types of agency? What role can and should agency play in the capability orientation to development theory-practice? What are the advantages (and limitations) of an

agency-oriented or agency-focused version of the capability orientation? In the concluding chapter I ask whether the ideal of agency is
a universal good or ideal, one that is or should be part of every reasonable comprehensive ethical outlook. Alternatively, is agency (at best)
part of a Rawlsian overlapping political consensus in democratic societies? How might the ideal of agency be justified or defended? In the
present chapter I argue that agency is a necessary but not sufficient part
of a "perfectionist" ideal, and in the next chapter I argue that
Nussbaum is mistaken in her rejection of perfectionist liberalism in
favor of political liberalism.

Sen's Concept of Agency and the Agency-Focused Capability Approach

Let us provisionally accept that values are an essential part of development and that one task of DE is to clarify, defend, and apply ethical
principles to development theory and practice in such a way that the
global scourges I sketched in the introduction to this volume might be
more effectively identified and combatted. The question arises immediately, of course, "what values?" (as well as "who should decide?"
and "how?").

In his 1985 essay, Sen made a distinction between agency and well-
being. Although sometimes this distinction is less prominent in his
writing, it continues (pace Nussbaum) to the present day in one form
or another (Sen 2009, 19–20, 227–229, 249–250, 252, 271, 286–290,
296). It is a distinction, however, that Nussbaum has rejected; she
claims, at least until recently, that her concepts of capability and
practical reason are sufficient for her capabilities ethic and her effort
to defend an inclusive theory of justice (2011, 197–201).[1]

What does Sen mean by agency, and how have I interpreted and
defended his concept? The best way to answer these questions is in
relation to the concept of an agent. In earlier writings, I have reconstructed Sen's scattered remarks about the concept of an agent in the
following way: A person (or group) is an agent with respect to action X,
to the extent that the person (i) decides for themself (rather than someone or something else causing the decision) to do X, (ii) forms an
intention to do X on the basis of deliberated reasons, (iii) is guided by
and performs the intended action (or contributes to its performance),
and (iv) the action brings about the intended change (and perhaps

Table 16.1 *Matrix*

	Well-being	Agency
Achievements	Well-being Achievements(Functionings)	Agency Achievements
Freedoms	Well-being Freedoms(Capabilities)	Agency Freedoms

unintended changes) in the world (Crocker 2008, 156–157; Crocker and Robeyns 2009, 80–82). The more all four conditions are fulfilled, the more is the person an agent in that context and, thereby, exercising his or her agency freedom. Here, agency freedom refers to both effective opportunities for agency as well as an internal capacity for exercising agency.

Agency contrasts with passivity. A person is a nonagent to the extent that he or she (i) makes no decision at all but is the passive "recipient" of someone else's decision, is manipulated by another agent, or is victimized by the forces of circumstances; (ii) fails to deliberate, scrutinize emotions or intuitions, or base his or her decision on reasons; (iii) fails to act; or (iv) the action has no impact on the natural or social world. Hence, Sen's concept of action, as I have reconstructed it, is multidimensional, and, as I will show, is importantly similar to recent feminist conceptions of relational autonomy and agency.

Before comparing and evaluating my conception of agency in relation to other conceptions, it is important to set Sen's ideas about agency in relation to his concept of well-being. First, Sen's concept of agency is a normative (and empirical) commitment that is in tandem with his evaluative (and empirical) concept of well-being. For Sen we should understand and evaluate human actions and institutions in relation to whether and to what extent (i) people's agency is exercised and respected, and (ii) people's well-being is promoted. These two fundamental human aspects can interact in various ways, and each can take the form of an achievement or a freedom to be achieved (Crocker 2008, 151; Sen 2009, 61–64), as shown in Table 16.1.

For Sen, a person's well-being consists of "doings" (activities) and "beings" (ways or states of being) that the person has good reason to value if his or her life is to go well. This concept, then, is one of personal "advantage" (or self-interest in a sufficiently broad sense not to be identified with selfishness). Part of our human well-being is being well nourished, being in good health, having self-respect, and taking part in the life of the community. Sen, as is well known, calls these well-being achievements "functionings," and he contrasts them with another dimension of value, namely, capabilities. Of objective value is not only healthy functioning, but also being able to be healthy in the sense of having the external opportunities or freedoms to so function and the internal capacities to continue to so function. A slave may be well nourished but does not have the freedom to continue in this state of being should the slave owner decide to punish him by withholding food and water or sell him to another slave owner with a reputation for maintaining malnourished slaves.

Where does agency fit in with this concept of well-being? If one has the capability to be well nourished then one has the freedom to eat well or not to eat well, to maintain one's nutritional well-being and the advantage this brings or to choose a way of life that reduces the agent's well-being but advances some other goal that she has chosen, such as going on a hunger strike to protest discrimination or tyranny. Agency comes on the scene in two ways. First, we often have to exercise our agency to decide between two aspects of our well-being when these two goods contingently exclude each other. Sen remarks that "there may be, for example, a trade-off between a person's capability to be well nourished and her capability to be well sheltered (poverty may make such difficult choices inescapable)" (2009, 233, n.*).

Second, agency comes into play because human beings are more or less able either to choose to promote their own well-being or to risk or sacrifice their personal advantage for some other goal, such as a life of austere asceticism or the self-denial of a hunger striker. In relation to the hunger striker in contrast to the person suffering from famine, Sen makes the telling point that there is a difference between the two cases with respect to capability. Both the famine sufferer and the hunger striker lack nutritional well-being but only the latter has the effective freedom to avoid malnourishment. An agent, for Sen, has the freedom to choose not only whether and how to advantage himself but also what else is important in his life, for example, whether he should feed – to his own possible detriment – his starving neighbor or organize politically to aid famine relief.

At this point I should make it clear that Sen's distinction between agency and capability is related to his view of well-being as personal advantage (self-interest) and agency as that aspect of a person that can responsibly choose either for or against his own well-being, narrowly construed. Nussbaum fails to grasp that it is precisely Sen's concept of agency that enables him to distinguish his pretty narrow notion of well-being, addressing only achievements and functioning related to one's own advantage, one's life going well, from freedom to choose and achieve goals whether altruistic or nonaltruistic. Among the fundamental choices that are exercises of agency freedom are choices to sacrifice or risk one's well-being for a cause (or one's conception of the good). An important exercise of agency freedom is an individual or group's decision to "select, weigh, trade off, and sequence capabilities as well prioritize them in relation to other normative considerations, such as agency, efficiency, and stability" (Crocker and Robeyns 2009, 72; see also 61–64, and Crocker 2008, 150–163). In that sense agency is a "capability of capabilities, a super-capability or a meta-capability," in contrast to well-being freedoms or capabilities (Crocker 2008, 223). Because Nussbaum does not permit trade-offs among her ten capabilities, she has no use for Sen's thicker or more robust ideal of agency (see Crocker 2008, 205–206).

Like well-being, agency has both a freedom and an achievement dimension. As agents, persons individually and collectively decide and sometimes achieve their goals – whether these goals are altruistic, intended to benefit themselves, or both. Moreover, as agents, persons have more or less opportunities and power to exercise their agency. For Sen, "agency freedom is freedom to achieve whatever the person, as a responsible agent, decides he or she should achieve" (Sen 1985, 204; 2009, 19, 22–24, 206–206, 208–220, 238). This is not to say that people can achieve anything they decide, for agency "is inescapably qualified and constrained by the social, political and economic opportunities available to us" (Sen 1999, xi–xii). These conditions, what Rawls calls the "basic structure" of a society, certainly more or less constrain and limit agency (as do physical conditions independent of society). Sen's concept of agency is an empirical notion in the sense that it points to Sen's belief that humans, in spite of internal and external causal factors, are more or less capable of determining their own lives. One reason is that the antecedent conditions and social forces not only limit and constrain but also open up possibilities for what humans can do and be individually and collectively. The causal past and present can enable and extend the reach of agency freedom and agency achievement. A second reason why human beings can forge their own lives is that as human agents, individually and especially collectively, they can act to change the very conditions that condition and constrain them:

Overcoming these problems [deprivation, destitution and oppression] is a central part of the exercise of development. We have to recognize, it is argued here [in *Development as Freedom*], the role of freedom of different kinds in countering these afflictions. Indeed, individual agency is, ultimately, central to addressing these deprivations. On the other hand, the freedom of agency that we individually have is inescapably qualified and constrained by the social, political and economic opportunities that are available to us. There is a deep complementarity between individual agency and social arrangements. It is important to give simultaneous recognition to the centrality of individual freedom *and* to the force of social influences on the extent and reach of individual freedom ... Development consists of the removal of various types of unfreedoms that leave people with little choice and little opportunity of exercising their reasoned agency. The removal of substantial unfreedoms, it is argued here, is *constitutive* of development. (Sen 1999, xi–xii; see also 31)

Sen's capability approach not only argues that agency freedoms exist but that responsible agents *should* exercise their freedom – through various kinds of action, including public participation – in such a way that it promotes the agency and well-being of others: Individual freedom is quintessentially a social product, and there is a two-way relation between (i) social arrangements to expand individual freedoms and (ii) the use of individual freedoms not only to improve the respective lives but also to make the social arrangements more appropriate and effective (Sen 1999, 31):

In terms of the medieval distinction between "the patient" and "the agent," this freedom-centered understanding of economics and the process of development is very much an agent-oriented view. With adequate social opportunities, individuals can effectively shape their own destiny and help each other. They need not be seen primarily as passive recipients of the benefits of cunning development programs. There is indeed a strong rationale for recognizing the positive role of free and sustainable agency – and even of constructive impatience. (11)

In his second book with Jean Drèze on India, Sen joins Drèze in affirming the fundamentality of agency in assessing the ends and means of development and public discussion:

There are, we have argued, rich lessons here [in the "developmental challenges faced in India"], which cannot be seized without taking interest in the ends and means of development in general and in the intrinsic value, constructive role and instrumental importance of public participation in particular. The basic approach involves an overarching interest in the role of human beings – in running their own lives and in using and expanding their freedoms. (Drèze and Sen 2002b, 33)

Given this understanding of agency and its relation to well-being (capability and functioning), to fix ideas let us compare this Senian concept of agency with alternative concepts of this contested term, provisionally assess each concept, and, finally, further develop the Senian notion.

A Broad Definition of (Metaphysical, Commonsense) Agency

Philosopher Markus Schlosser offers a "very broad" metaphysical definition of agency: "Whenever entities enter into causal relationships they can be said to act on each other and interact with each other, bringing about changes in each other. In this very broad sense, it is possible to identify agents and agency, patients and patiency, virtually everywhere" (2015). Schlosser employs the agent/patient distinction when he distinguishes actors causally affecting other entities and in turn being affected by them. For Sen, because running your own life and shaping your own destiny is intrinsically good, in good development outside agents should avoid treating persons, even vulnerable and deprived persons, as passive objects of cunning development plans. Rather, those who would benefit from development assistance should be treated as self-determining agents and helped to help themselves.

Minimal Agency

The standard philosophical view is that an agent is one who consciously – with some "representational mental states" (Schlosser 2015) – performs *intentional* actions. Some cognitive science scholars, however, have expanded the notion of agency "downward" and have defended a notion of "minimal agency," which they intend to apply – across the board – to robots, simple organisms, intentional individual agents, and collective agents: "agency involves, at least, *a system doing something by itself according to certain goals or norms within a specific environment*" (Barandiaran, Di Paolo, and Rohde 2009, 369).

The authors intend this statement to be a description that does justice to both scientific and everyday ideas about agency. They go on to offer what they call a "generative definition," which they propose as a precise candidate to capture all (and only) cases of agency: "we define agency as an autonomous organization that adaptively regulates [according to a certain goal or norm] its coupling with its environment and contributes to sustaining itself as a consequence" (Barandiaran, Di Paolo, and Rohde 2009, 367). The authors hope that this definition will generate a more specific definition that will be the basis for attribution of either agency or nonagency with respect to such cases as a robot moving around an arena, "a bird gliding on wind currents," and "tremors affecting a Parkinson disease patient" (368). Even bacteria regulate themselves as they cope with the environment and "can be said to have the intrinsic goal *to be*: to bring about the continuation of their existence" (Schlosser 2015). This notion of minimal agency is relevant for our understanding of intentional human agency, for not only does it provide a basis for the continuity of humans with the nonhuman living and robotic worlds, it also enables us to grasp those "many instances of human agency that can and should be explained without the ascription of representational mental states" (Schlosser 2015). An example, would be the "skilled coping" (Schlosser 2015) of habitual actions such as driving a car or juggling a soccer ball.

Nonhuman Animal Agency

In their contribution to this volume, Wichert and Nussbaum defend a capabilities ethic for the treatment of cetaceans (whales and dolphins). In a long but important passage, Wichert and Nussbaum make clear that this ethic is based on a normative notion or, better, several notions of animal agency. Here is Wichert and Nussbaum's formulation of the generic concept of animal agency and its surprising relation to public policy and democracy:

[The idea of animal agency is] that animals are not merely passive recipients of experience but shapers of lives. To be adequate to the complexity and variety of animal lives, the notion of agency must be developed in a flexible and species-specific way, and this will require intimate and detailed knowledge of each animal species. But for all, there is something that it is to be a maker of a life. And in political terms, although animals will not be democratic citizens, along the familiar human models of democracy, there is something that it is to respect animals as democratic agents, participants in shaping the world we share with them [footnote omitted]. Respect for agency is lacking in Utilitarian approaches and underdeveloped in approaches focused on intelligence. Rights-based approaches do better [footnote omitted]. And the Capabilities Approach is one species of a rights-based approach, in that it argues for fundamental entitlements grounded in justice. But the challenge for such an approach is to develop a notion, or notions of agency in terms of an Aristotelian notion of a form of life actively striving for its characteristic end. (Chapter 10, p. xxx)

Three points are relevant about this passage. First, it is striking that Nussbaum conceives of nonhuman animal agents as "democratic agents" (in some presumably nonstandard sense of democracy) in that they actively shape the world that they share with citizens. This point seems little more than a rhetorical flourish to say that both nonhuman and human animals strive for ends and have an impact on a shared world. However, merely having an actual impact on the world is not sufficient for being a democratic citizen, for autos have an impact on the world and they are neither legal nor responsible citizens. It is the case, however, that there are some structural similarities between Nussbaum's agency-based approach and my own efforts to defend democracy by appealing, among other things, to human agency (as one fundamental human good). One important difference, however, which I will address in the next chapter, is that Nussbaum's concept of animal agency is part of her *political* liberalism[2] and my concept of agency is part of a fallibilist, *perfectionist* liberalism.

Second, Nussbaum has been developing her CA's relevance for the treatment of animals for a decade, most notably in "Beyond 'Compassion and Humanity': Justice for Nonhuman Animals" (2004), *Frontiers of Justice: Disability, Nationality, Species Membership* (2006), and *Creating Capabilities: The Human Development Approach* (2011). In the 2004 and 2006 writings, she employs the normative concept of animal species-specific *striving* for survival and flourishing. But, to my knowledge, she uses the term "agency" to designate this species-specific animal activity only in the 2011 volume.

Prior to 2006, Nussbaum occasionally employed a robust concept of agency (2000, 58, 69, 72–73), and positive references to human agency are sprinkled throughout *Creating Capabilities* (2011, 30, 56, 88). However, in both *Women and Human Development* (2000, 14) and in "Appendix B, Sen on Well-Being and Agency," in *Creating Capabilities* (2011, 197–201), she rejects Sen's categorical distinction between agency and well-being for two reasons. She fears that Sen empties well-being of activity and in contrast exalts agency to an otherworldly status of Kantian autonomy. Moreover, Nussbaum believes that her own capability/functioning distinction, and her thin view of agency as practical reason, gives her all she needs for an adequate view of human freedom (without the excesses of a Kantian view of human autonomy).

In *Frontiers of Justice*, Nussbaum explicitly compares human agency to animal agency with respect to "striving" in her efforts to capture species-specific animal striving. Rather than understanding agency as the Senian notion of the power to choose and prioritize well-being capabilities or to choose to risk one's well-being for some altruistic goal, Nussbaum sees nonhuman animals "not as receptacles of pleasure or pain," but similar to human agents in striving by means of practical reason to fulfill their *teloi*:

> In the *Frontiers of Justice* . . . I argue that the idea of social justice is inherently bound up with the least minimal sentience (the capacity to experience pain, especially) and with the accompanying capacity for striving and some type of agency. Intuitively, it seems to me that the idea of doing injustice to an animal makes sense in much the way that the idea of doing injustice to a human being makes sense: both can experience pain and harm and both are attempting to live and act, projects that can be wrongly thwarted. (2011, 158)

The Capability Approach sees animals as agents, not as receptacles of pleasure or pain. This deep conceptual difference [with utilitarianism] can help the approach develop a more pertinent sort of respect for animal striving and animal activity. (160)

Why is Nussbaum willing to attribute some form of agency to both humans and nonhumans but explicitly reject Sen's agency/well-being distinction? One conjecture is that she believes her notion of capabilities, especially practical reason, does all the work needed for freedom, that Sen's notion of agency is too Kantian and perfectionistic, and that her notion of flourishing should include altruistic dimensions and not just Sen's notion of personal advantage. One reason for Nussbaum's current willingness to use the term "agency" may be that generic agency, as species-specific striving for an end (*telos*), will cover not only most humans, but also higher animals, such as the dolphins, and even nonconscious and nonsentient animal life. To do so, of course, Nussbaum must elide human intentionality, autonomy, and moral responsibility from the *generic* notion.[3]

Uncritical Agency

For Nussbaum, nonhuman animal agency, at least in all species except the most intelligent species, involves an animal's striving to realize its animal-specific nature or telos. Creatures do not choose to be dogs rather than cats (although sometimes nonhuman animals at early ages are "imprinted" with the behavior of other species by their "adopted" parents). Some humans exercise a very minimal kind of agency. They act and make a difference in the world, but they only minimally, if at all, scrutinize options, deliberate about the options, become informed, or freely choose their action. They do more or less unthinkingly what their culture expects and prescribes. Here agency is uncritical, unscrutinized, uninformed, and nonautonomous. It is the opposite of "critical agency" (Drèze and Sen 2002b, 258), "informed agency" (Drèze and Sen 2002a, 14; 2002b, 91, 200), "reasoned agency" (Drèze and Sen 2002b, 79; Sen 1999, xii), or "responsible" agency (Sen 1985, 204).

Sen provides a telling example, one that has stayed with me for many years but one that I have delayed (until now) to analyze. In his 2002 book on India with Drèze, Sen discusses what I am calling "uncritical agency" in relation to the natality practice that "many" Indian mothers "seem to have" (2002b, 258). These mothers prefer sons to daughters and upon finding out, through amniocentesis, the gender of their expected baby more often abort female than male fetuses. Although these women could be said to have the "freedom and power to act" and they certainly decide, act, and make a difference in the world, they lack an important feature of "critical agency," namely "the freedom and power to question and reassess the prevailing norms and values" (258). Without such scrutiny and assessment, women's agency is uncritical with respect to natality. And Drèze and Sen conjecture that other aspects of women's agency in India, such as women-led efforts to eliminate or reduce sex differentials in mortality and fertility rates, "cannot be expected, *on its own*, to produce a similar elimination of sex differentials in birth rates and abortion and correspondingly in the population of children" (2002b, 258). A dimension of a robust idea of autonomous agency is that of becoming aware of, critically evaluating, and either rejecting, modifying, or accepting regnant traditions, practices, and values.

Our low evaluation of "uncritical agency" and high evaluation of "critical agency" stand in sharp contrast to recent views of *New York Times* pundit David Brooks: "Attachment theory nicely distinguishes between the attachments that form you and the things you then do for yourself. The relationships that form you are mostly things you didn't choose: your family, hometown, ethnic group, religion, nation and genes. The things you do with your life are mostly chosen: your job, spouse, and hobbies" (Brooks 2017, A25). Although the term "mostly" qualifies his claim a bit, notice that the "things that form you" are mostly what you do not choose, such as your family, hometown, ethnic group, religion, nation, and genes. And, Brooks should add to this list, if you are an Indian woman in at least some Indian subcultures, your preference for sons. Brooks proceeds then to denigrate rootless liberals and freedom fans who renounce the "security" that comes from being rooted in and embracing the "given." But, does not his disjunction assume that we can choose and does not that assumption also imply that it is up to us if and when we should try to reinterpret, modify, or even renounce our upbringing, family, ethnicity, religion, nation, and even genes (gene therapy). In the service of the promised secure base of our original "attachments," Brooks is promoting a traditionalism and uncritical communitarianism that blesses, endorses, and encourages acceptance of early attachments without recognizing that some of those very traditions (the Enlightenment, critical tradition) are committed to scrutinizing other traditions and altering them (and themselves) when they are unjust or oppressive. Moreover, it is not clear why your spouse, job, and hobbies can and should be chosen in contrast to those "attachments" that, according to Brooks, should be uncritically embraced.

A caveat, and one that Brooks might admit if pushed, is in order. Rather than uncritically exercising her agency and thereby unthinkingly acting on her "son preference," an Indian woman in actuality may examine her options for and against abortion and – in order to appease an abusive husband or one that she believes has properly ordered her to abort – decide to abort.[4] Although the ethical quality of her decision might be questioned, we should see her as making a decision following her exercise of critical agency. This suggests that something more than questioning and even reassessment is called for, namely, autonomous and ethical agency. We exercise critical agency when we reinterpret or assess or reassess prevailing norms and values. But, if we decide to adopt or forge a norm at odds with convention we are moving from critical agency to something more – ethical or responsible agency. We deeply admire those who not only questioned and assessed prevailing Nazi norms and values, but exercised their agency, at their peril, to resist Nazism and act on a vision of Germany based on equal agency and well-being. An inspiring example of both critical and ethical agency is the White Rose group in Nazi Germany. The Third Reich executed these university students for protesting Hitler's tyranny and the Reich's persecution of the Jews. Annette Dumbach and Jud Newborn close their study, *Sophie Scholl and the White Rose* (2006), with these words: "if people like those who formed the White Rose can exist, believe as they believed, as they acted, maybe it means that this weary, corrupted, extremely endangered species we belong to has the right to survive and to keep trying" (185).[5]

One way in which uncritical agency can be weakened and eventually overcome is through a liberating education, one that is both formal and informal (experiential). This sort of education promotes a kind of ethical agency, which I will discuss later when I take up Koggel's agency ethic of caring and, subsequently, when I agree with Adela Cortina's argument for the importance of civic education at all levels. Liberating education informs its beneficiaries – or, better, enables them to inform themselves about the world, its important facts and universal values.

Sen and I are deeply committed to the view that critical agency is both possible and extremely valuable. And I have followed Sen in arguing that the "constructive value" of democracy – in addition to its intrinsic and instrumental value – provides the social relations and procedures by which individuals and groups can exercise both critical agency, with respect to traditional and "prevailing norms and values" and ethical agency in extending the reach of norms we have good reason to value.

Ethical Agency: Autonomous Relational Agency

In her probing and challenging contribution to this volume, Christine Koggel (Chapter 6) skillfully analyzes the multidimensional concept of agency that I have reconstructed from the writings of Amartya Sen and sought to develop in an explicitly democratic direction in my own agency-focused version of the capability approach to development. She also argues that there are good reasons to extend this Senian concept of agency so as to accommodate some insights from feminist relational theory. In this section, I analyze Koggel's arguments, accept some of Koggel's criticisms, and offer a revised and expanded concept of multidimensional agency as relational autonomy. This extension and enrichment of my Senian concept of agency is indebted not only to Koggel, but also to such feminist thinkers as Mark Piper, Andrea Veltman, Andrea C. Westlund, and especially, Catriona Mackenzie (Veltman and Piper 2014) and Marina Oshana.

Although there have been feminist rejections of the concept of autonomy, most recent feminists not only embrace some concept of autonomy but explicitly connect it to some version of the empirical notion and normative ideal of agency. Marina Oshana, for example, gives the following account of autonomy:

A person is autonomous when she has (1) the ability to superintend those of her decisions, activities, and personal associations that are central to human agency; (2) the warrant to do so, and (3) the power to act on that ability ... Most feminists do not advocate just a commitment to a legal or moral right to self-governance but also a commitment to self-governance as an actual state of life ... the practical control autonomy demands draws both from sources internal to the agent and from external authority of a variety that mandates the absence of domination. (Oshana 2014, 152)

It is not clear whether Koggel shares Oshana's project to link a feminist conception of autonomy to a notion of agency, one that stresses that human agents freely form intentions, not only act intentionally, but also – when not dominated by others – *own* that action and the difference it makes in the world. In Koggel's chapter the terms "autonomy" or "autonomous" occur only three times. In two of those times, she is quoting or paraphrasing Des Gasper and Irene van Staveren's criticism that Sen assumes that humans, modeled on males, are independent, individualist, and autonomous apart from social conditioning and at odds with caring. Koggel, however, does not endorse this criticism of Sen and in fact urges Gasper and van Staveren to consider ways in which agency and caring can be compatible. Koggel's third mention of "autonomy" or "autonomous" is when she endorses Sarah Clark

Miller's multidimensional concept of agency in which autonomous as well as rational, emotional, and relational abilities are claimed to be important and harmfully "squandered" when a person cannot act as an agent (Miller 2012, 26, quoted by Koggel in Chapter 6 on p. xxx). Why does autonomy not play a more prominent role in Koggel's chapter?[6] My hunch is that she has an incomplete conception of what Sen means by agency freedom and agency achievement. For Sen, one has agency freedom not only, negatively, when one is not coerced by others or by circumstances, but also, positively, when one shapes her identity and decides on her responsibilities. Hence, for those feminists who endorse and reconstruct autonomy (and link it to agency), synonyms for autonomy are often "self-determination" and "self-governance."

Koggel endorses Sen's views that (i) human agency should be among the ends and means of good development, (ii) women's agency has an important role to play in progressive social change, and (iii) gender equality – and more generally human moral equality – is a good thing and gender inequalities should be overcome. Koggel, however, argues that to achieve a society in which unfreedom and gender inequality are overcome, the Senian idea of human agency should be expanded in several ways.

With respect to each of Koggel's proposals for expansion, I first clarify each proposal, then evaluate whether or not it identifies a deficiency in the Senian view, and if it does, what might be done to remedy the problem. First, Koggel finds in Sen too much of the economist's view of the agent as an independent rational (self-interested) chooser, one who fails to draw on the emotional aspects of human agency. She advocates that Senians expand his notion of human agency to include emotional dimensions. It is not clear just what she finds missing in Sen's account, but I would guess that Koggel believes Sen's account lacks sympathy for others and compassion for their plights. For Koggel, a human agent does not only run her own life but has compassionate responsibility for the agency and well-being of other people. Caring for others can and should enhance the agency and well-being of others.

How can and should Sen and Senians reply to Koggel's first criticism and proposal? First, I, for one, agree with Koggel in the sense that a responsible agent should not only be responsible for (and care for) herself, but also should be responsible for the well-being (valuable functionings and capabilities) and agency freedom and achievements of others. Exercising that responsibility would indeed benefit from feelings of sympathy and compassion, but a scrooge-like person may have the responsibility to aid even when lacking sympathy. And a sentimentalist might be overly sympathetic for those with minor deprivations and upon scrutiny see that she was carried away by her feelings and has no responsibility to act and help. More generally, emotions are a mixed blessing, and Sen and Senians believe that both negative and positive feelings should be scrutinized with respect to their appropriateness in a particular context and whether or not they should be acted on (Sen 2009, xvii, 36, 39, 50). Whether we should feel sympathy or a responsibility to drop a dollar into the street beggar's cup might or might not pass the scrutiny involved in Sen's use of Adam Smith's test of the Ideal Spectator.

A second defect that Koggel finds in Sen is that he does not take sufficiently seriously the relational aspects of human agency. He fails, she argues, to recognize negative relationality when he neglects the way in which deeply entrenched gender norms reduce women's agency, even when women are gainfully employed outside a patriarchal home. He fails to affirm the positive relationality involved when women exercise their own agency in caring for children, the elderly, and the disabled. For Koggel, Sen is content to make caring and an ethic of caring one option among many for an agent to choose. In contrast, Koggel argues, Sen should argue that men as well as women have a responsibility to care and not merely a right to care. Let us consider each of Koggel's relationality criticisms and her proposal that Sen's concept of agency be made relational.

Koggel contends that Sen has a seriously defective approach to enhancing women's agency. Given his overly male-centric conception of agents as economic and political choosers, his basic solution for gender inequality is for social structures that enable women to be employed outside the home (a zone of patriarchy) and to engage in politics. Women, like men, should find remunerative employment and political engagement in public discussion outside the home as the venues for exercising their agency. The defect in this solution, says Koggel, is that it fails to recognize that women in the marketplace and in deliberative political venues are deeply affected by male dominance. Sen is much too optimistic that the gender inequities at home will be escaped by women participating in the market and public discussion:

Sen's failure to fully account for the detrimental effects of oppressive norms is reflected in the agency-enhancing policies that he ends up endorsing. These policies already reveal norms that escape the scrutiny and challenge required for the kind of public discussion that can lead to real change. We need to attend to broader framework issues that reflect and manifest social and political structures and conditions of oppression. (Chapter 6, p. xxx)

Although she could be clearer as to these structures and conditions of oppression, among them are surely traditional and still current gender stereotypes. To be a real man is to be self-sufficient, self-possessed, dominant, entitled, active, and resourceful. To be a good woman is to be needy, vulnerable, subservient, passive, dependent on and concerned for others.[7] This two-track gender ideology more or less invisibly shapes what happens in the workplace and public sphere with the result that equal gender agency in these venues is an illusion. Koggel argues that this social conditioning must become visible, be scrutinized, and be replaced by a struggle for gender equality at home as well as at work and in politics.

There is much to recommend in Koggel's critique and proposal. Two late 2017 studies of two Ford Motor company facilities and many other US blue collar jobs expose the multiple ways that men dominate women in the workplace. Among the most egregious forms of domination are sexual harassment and abuse, which management and union leadership often condones and falsely denies (Chira and Einhorn 2017). As the #MeToo movement has spread from entertainment and sports to politics, business, and education, male predatory behavior and abuses of power have been made painfully public (Chira 2017). One hopes that these articles will help make harassment and domination visible and promote public discussion that includes the deep causes of sexism.[8] Moreover, nothing in Sen's account commits him to deny that such largely invisible oppressive conditions in many times and places in fact limit women's agency, and certainly their critical agency.

Recall our earlier analysis of the way that son preference in India conditions and limits women's agency. Just as natality inequality in India "cannot be removed, at least in the short run, by the enhancement of women's empowerment and agency, since that agency is itself an integral part of the cause of natality inequality" (Drèze and Sen 2002b, 258), so merely getting women out of the house and into employment and public discussion is insufficient to expand their agency from uncritical to critical and responsible agency. Sen could and should apply what he said in relation to "critical agency" in the son-preference case to "critical agency" in the case of women's employment and political participation cases: "What is needed is not merely freedom and the power to act, but also freedom and power to question and reassess the prevailing norms and values. The pivotal issue is critical agency" (Drèze and Sen 2002b, 258), and, I will add presently, "ethical agency."[9]

Just as Sen can and should modify his optimism with respect to gender progress in both the workplace and public discussion, so Koggel's criticism of my proposal to deal with gender inequality and other problems through deliberative democracy needs to be revised. She is right that I underestimated the way that background conditions of gender injustice would compromise the progressive results of deliberative democracy. Moreover, prescribing antecedent institutions of liberal constitutionalism to "regulate and enable public participation" of women only relocates the problem to a higher or antecedent level, as well as limits the solution to advanced democratic countries. It is the case that deliberative democracy gradually brings about as well as benefits from such liberal institutions as equal political liberty, rule of law, economic justice, and procedural fairness. But, it is also sadly true that these "enabling conditions" for deliberative democracy as well as the practice of deliberative democracy may in fact perpetuate gender inequality unless traditional gender norms can be made visible, scrutinized, and rejected in favor of women's voices and power. Furthermore, one way to do that is to encourage the mobilization of both men and women to exercise their agency to confront, resist, and overcome entrenched economic and political power. In the next chapter, I return to Koggel and reply more fully to her critique of my view of the progressive potential of deliberative democracy.

There is a second way in which Koggel criticizes Sen's account of agency and seeks to enrich it with a view of *relational* agency. While the first relational criticisms concerned the empirical point that agency is inhibited by prior oppressive structures, including traditional gender norms, the second criticism is normative: Sen and Senians pay insufficient attention to the relationality of caring, both in and outside of the home, as a responsible way of exercising agency. Sen and Senians should expand their ideal of agency by adding the ethics of caring.

It is true that in his concept of *well-being*, Sen emphasizes that agents desire what they take to be their personal advantage – their own lives going well with respect to valuable functionings and freedoms to so function. (Many, however, use their agency freedom to define their well-being such that it includes various affiliations and relationships, from family, to profession, to ethnicity and beyond). And it is true with respect to agency, Sen emphasizes that although groups and societies may have an important role in enhancing individual agency or providing opportunities for joint or shared agency, "there is no substitute for individual responsibility" (Sen 1999, 283). For Sen, there is a strong affirmation of "ethical individualism" in the sense that the ultimate commitment is not to group well-being or agency but to individual well-being and agency, although well-being and agency can and sometimes should be shared or converge.

More basically, while we want to make sense of the notion of ethical agency, we should resist the idea that all exercises of agency are ethically defensible. Agents can (but ought not to) do bad things as well as good things.[10] Moreover, the features of agency – action done for a reason, following deliberation, with a guiding intention, and having an intended impact on the world – not only do not justify the action but make it even worse than it would have been if the action had been unintentional or coerced by others.[11] The most we can say is that the agential features of the action are both good-making and bad-making. It is good that the agent exercised her agency but bad that the act chosen and performed or its consequences are unethical or unjust. I agree with Koggel that, although getting the relative weights or proportions right is usually a challenge, agents should not only care for their own well-being and agency, but also care for the well-being and agency of others. However, one cannot *deductively derive* the general principle of responsibility for others from the norm of agency. The ideal of agency is that persons have the freedom to run or control their own lives and that agency freedom and achievement, whatever they might be, are among the ultimate goods.

How do Sen and Senians justify responsibility for others and a just society? It is, I believe, no more and no less than what Sen calls a "social commitment."[12] One is free to exercise one's agency solely to benefit oneself (or one's family or tribe), and in that case one chooses no more than to promote one's narrower or broader personal advantage. However, a *responsible* or *ethical* agent, can and should *choose* agency goals or ultimate goods beyond or in addition to her personal advantage, for example, the well-being and agency of others and the ideal of moral equality of persons. And these ideals can and should be realized by building institutions that provide the freedoms for individuals to exercise their own agency and achieve basic levels of well-being for others as well as themselves. Sen himself appreciates "the force of the claim that people themselves must have responsibility for the development and change of the world in which they live" (Sen 1999, 282). Both religious and nonreligious people can and should accept that "as people who live – in a broad sense – together, we cannot escape the thought that the terrible occurrences that we see around us are quintessentially our problems. They are our responsibility – whether or not they are also anyone else's" (1999, 282):

As competent human beings, we cannot shirk the task of judging how things are and what needs to be done. As reflective creatures, we have the ability to contemplate the lives of others. Our sense of responsibility need not relate only to the afflictions that our own behaviour may have caused (though that can be very important as well), but can also relate more generally to the miseries that we see around us and that lie within our power to help remedy. That responsibility is not, of course the only consideration that can claim our attention, but to deny the relevance of that general claim would be to miss something central about our social existence. It is not so much a matter of having exact rules about how precisely we ought to behave, as of recognizing the relevance of our shared humanity in making the choices we face. (Sen 1999, 283)

Agency is a necessary component of this ethical outlook but by no means sufficient. For a commitment to one's own agency (and well-being) should be constrained by and balanced with, on the one hand, our responsibility for the agency and well-being of others, and, on the other hand, our commitment to shared humanity and human equality. I leave open that an agency ethic should also include a subordinate principle, one defended by Wichert and Nussbaum, requiring respect for nonhuman animal agency.

One implication of my view of ethical agency is that the ethical agent can and sometimes should exercise his agential responsibility in such a way that he cares for others, such as the young, the elderly, or the disabled at the expense of his own well-being and agency. In extreme cases one can exercise one's agency in such a way as to severely limit if not extinguish one's own ability to be in control of one's life. Examples would be when the freeman sells himself into slavery, the wife freely submits to her imperious husband, or the religious devotee vows obedience to a religious superior. In this sense, while we want to reserve a place for ethical agency as a free and responsible choice to do good or do what is right, we agree with those, such as Mackenzie (2014) and Oshana (2014), who defend the view that agency is ethically neutral in the sense that agents can (but should not) decide to submit themselves to authority. Agency, however, is not neutral. Fans of agency view self-determination and self-governance as one of the ultimate and universally valid goods in addition to and constrained by the ultimate goods of (human) well-being and human equality.

Agency and "Reason to Value"

We turn to the question of how we should understand the status within development and liberal theory-practice – of the results of our analysis and interpretation of different kinds and views of agency. I do so through the lens of what I have learned from Serene J. Khader and Stacy J. Kosko's chapter in the current volume (Chapter 7). Their penetrating analysis of Sen's ambiguous phrase "reason to value" has prompted me to develop and label my normative views about agency as a kind of "perfectionism."

The concept of agency that has dialectically emerged from our analysis and evaluation of other notions of agency makes progress, I believe, over my earlier work on the concept of agency. Not only are persons (or groups) agents to the extent that they freely make decisions on the basis of reasons and deliberation, intentionally act, and make a difference in the world. To the extent that they are informed about, question, and scrutinize "prevailing norms and values," they are *informed* and *critical* agents. To the extent they imaginatively supplement current practical and normative options with options "from near and far," they are *enlightened* agents. To the extent that they respect and care for the well-being (freedoms and achievements) and agency (freedoms and achievements) of others, whom they judge to be moral equals, our agents are *responsible* and *ethical* agents.

Khader and Kosko begin their piece with an epigraph in which Sen uses the phrase *reason to value*: "In pursuing the view of development as freedom, we have to examine . . . the extent to which people have the opportunity to achieve outcomes that they value and have reason to value" (Sen 1999, 291). Abbreviating *reason to value* as R2V, Khader and Kosko argue that the phrase is ambiguous, and perhaps reveals some tensions in Sen's originating version of the CA. R2V, however, has generally served to assure development scholars and practitioners that Sen's CA is not a paternalistic prescription from outside and above. Rather, the phrase has often been uncritically taken to mean that although development is something that people must do for themselves, development efforts can and should provide people with opportunities that they *already* value.

R2V, however, has been construed in at least three ways, and Khader and Kosko not only analyze these ways but evaluate them in relation to Sen's, Senians', and their own ethical commitments. What are these three ways of interpreting "Y values and has reason to value X"?

First, in the *procedural autonomy* gloss of R2V, Y has in fact reasoned that X is valuable. Although this interpretation fits with Sen's refusal to provide a canonical or universal list of valued or valuable functionings/capabilities and is clearly anti-paternalistic and favorable to a kind of value pluralism, it is inconsistent with repeated claims (i) by Sen and others that a person can have R2V things she does not actually value, and (ii) by CA proponents that some functionings/capabilities are unreasonable or morally objectionable. Although the stance of "uncritical agency" would illustrate this interpretation of R2V, neither Sen nor I would accept the obvious moral relativism in which development efforts would endorse and promote uncritically more effective realization of "prevailing norms and values" (Drèze and Sen 2002b, 258), such as son preference in parts of India and sexism and racism in the USA and other countries.

A second interpretation of R2V is that of *structured process*, the result of which is such that Y has reasoned or would reason that X is valuable. Khader and Kosko discuss two variants. In a deliberative democratic process (which they shorthand as "deliberative process"), participants in the process are assured that *whatever* issues from the process – say, "son preference" in natality – is rationally valuable. In what Khader and Kosko term an "opportunity process," the process is looser and only requires that the agent is exposed, perhaps by a development worker or an enlightened peer, to a wider opportunity set than the "customary" one for that culture or group, for example, information concerning birth control or a husband's new willingness to put up with a female baby. In any case, what follows from either process is the participant's warrant or reason to value or disvalue something.

How should we evaluate this second interpretation? Khader and Kosko are correct when they say "this is the interpretation that Crocker seems most committed to, both in his writing and in public lectures and discussion" (Chapter 7, p. xxx). Indeed, with respect to deliberative process, I argued in *Ethics of Global Development: Agency, Capability, and Deliberative Democracy* (*EGD*) that the deliberative process is superior to and a check on the philosopher's ideal vision and the Supreme Court's infallibility. But I stopped short of endowing democratic decisions, even deliberatively democratic decisions, with giving participants conclusive reasons, let alone hard justification, for valuation. And, at least once, I rejected the idea that the deficiencies of democracy can and *always* should be remedied by more rather than less democracy (2008, 321). Moreover, I identified an important role that the individual thinker or social critic can and should play in challenging unjust – let alone tyrannical – decisions made by a simple or even super majority (2008, 203). But I should have gone further in conceding that even the best democracies can and do make mistakes in choosing policies and leaders.

Likewise, I have modified my views with respect to the agential process of expanding options, including the options of democratizing a nondemocratic group or government. In *EGD*, I endorsed only the process of opportunity expansion with respect to convincing an "uncritical" – perhaps brainwashed or manipulated – nondemocrat to accept or work for democracy: "Part of an individual's having the freedom to decide for or against the democratic way of life would be having information about alternatives and being able, if she chose, to exercise critical scrutiny of claims and counter-claims" (2008, 360). Moreover, I noted that having this democratic option already presupposed some features of democracy. I wanted – and still want – to avoid any suggestion that democracy should be *imposed coercively* on a reluctant people.[13]

Similarly, when I examined the approach of a development worker promoting democratic decision-making, I refused to move beyond expanding the nondemocrat's options and being reasonably sure she was not being coerced or manipulated to reject democracy and the robust agency on which it is based:

> What about those who decided to stay [in a nondemocratic group] and continued to oppose democratic and deliberative modes? I think the only consistent answer for the defender of agency is to accept this decision (as long as it was not imposed). There might be some suspicion that conditions for a free choice really did not exist – that people were still being forced or conditioned to accept non-freedom. But, at some point, reasonable doubt should be satisfied. Then the proponent of autonomy regretfully respects the group members' autonomous choice no longer to exercise their agency. The leaders, presumably, accept the will of the people and agree to stay in charge. (Crocker 2008, 361)

I now would go substantially further than I did in *EGD* because I have come to see that my commitment to agency (and the exercise of agency as one argument for democracy) is an ethical commitment to relational and ethical agency as a universal good. Confronted with the apparently free rejection (democratic or personal rejection) of agential democracy, the democracy promoter should do more than experience regret and respect the "rejecter" (for having made a free, if mistaken, decision). What else should she do? Not impose, coerce, or manipulate, for that would violate the "rejecter's" agency and the democracy promoter's commitment to agency.

The development agent and democracy advocate has several non-coercive strategies, agency-respecting ways of bringing, perhaps slowly, the antidemocrat to the point of embracing democratic ideals and practices. One way would be through the give-and-take of reasonable dialogue in which the arguments against democracy are scrutinized and, where possible, rebutted and arguments for democracy are advanced. A second way would be to invite the critic to be an observer, if not a participant observer, in some democratic form of life and governance. Perhaps the antidemocratic would find in practice she is making or acquiring some "democratic" intuitions or beliefs that she cannot now give up and that are at odds with her theoretical antidemocratic theory. Perhaps, such observations played a role in Alexis de Tocqueville (2004) changing his identity from privileged aristocrat to (partial) democrat. A third way to win over the democratic skeptic, if not opponent, would be democratic mobilization against creeping or entrenched authoritarianism. As the evils of autocracy become existentially clear, the merits of democracy may become more compelling.

Increasing dissatisfaction with the second Khader and Kosko interpretation of R2V leads them and now me to see that the *practice* of the second interpretation dialectically leads to what they call "the perfectionist interpretation" of R2V. In contemporary political philosophy and political theory, a perfectionist political theory is one in which its proponents hold that there is an objective (human) good and one that a justified political arrangement should promote (see Wall 2009, 2012). Using the perfectionist idea to interpret R2V, the CA should be construed as saying that when people have reason to value some X, whether a functioning or a freedom, "X *is* valuable." Another way to make the point is to say that people have a reason to value X is to say that people have a good or justified reason for valuing X – whether or not people presently value X or would value X following a democratic process or an expanded menu of options.

Khader and Kosko argue for the third interpretation of R2V on the basis that the actual practice of either of the second interpretation's two processes presupposes ethical judgments about one or more objective goods and that the third interpretation is most consistent with Senian claims that some functionings and freedoms are unreasonable or unethical to value because of their content: "If part of the appeal of the CA is that it does not take people's preferences at face value and that it allows criticism of oppression and deprivation, it is difficult to see how it can do without at least some commitments about which functionings are valuable" (see Khader 2011 and Chapter 7 in this book, p. xxx). Moreover, Khader and Kosko convincingly argue that the CA cannot "license more than local-level judgments about deprivation, such as those embodied in the Human Development Report," unless the CA has a "general view" (p. xxx) of which functionings and capabilities are *really* valuable.

I now concede that the processes of democratic decision-making, as well as the struggle for a better democracy, presuppose objective values, and I propose that these values should be understood as agency, well-being, and equality. And the development practitioner's choice of what options to include in an expanded menu presupposes that the agent's choice is an objective good and that some of the options are objectively better than others. Moreover, on the third interpretation of R2V, I agree that the "deliberative process" or expanded-menu ("opportunity") process are really "vehicles for helping the agent recognize the (objective) value of certain capabilities" (Khader and Kosko, Chapter 7, p. xxx) and, I would argue, ethical responsibilities. Moreover, the three ultimate values (agency, well-being, and equality) that I argue undergird the democratic and expanded-menu processes are compatible with a commitment (within limits) that different groups – exercising their agency – can and should realize these values in different ways in different contexts.

Khader and Kosko conclude their chapter by arguing that those working in the CA tradition, which includes me, should either (i) drop the R2V phrase altogether and the idea that development ethicists exclusively work to provide people with more and better access to what they *already* value, or (ii) keep the phrase R2V and interpret it in a perfectionist manner ("*good* reason to value") but one that understands democratic and menu-expanding processes as good but fallible ways to gain insight into which functionings are objectively (most) valuable.

"Reason to Value," the Agency-Focused CA, and Liberal Perfectionism

Khader and Kosko's discussion has convinced me to characterize my position as a form of perfectionism as it has come to be defined in contemporary moral and political philosophy. Although I deplore the moralistic and excessively utopian ring of the term "perfectionism," I follow Steven Wall in interpreting perfectionism in moral theory as a theory that defends a conception of human flourishing or the objectively good life. Relatedly, perfectionism in political theory is the view that "the state can legitimately promote the good, even when what is good is subject to reasonable disagreement" (2009, 100). Finally, perfectionism in development ethics would be the view that agents and agencies, whether local, national, or international, can and should promote the good in development, that is, good development. Although there may be other perfectionist goods, such as a healthy environment and nonhuman animal agency, the perfectionist account of the good human life that I hold is that of the triad of (i) critical, autonomous, and ethical agency; (ii) well-being (deliberated functionings and capabilities); and (iii) moral equality.

Khader and Kosko are quite right in drawing out some important implications and complexities about their perfectionist rendering of R2V. On the one hand, Sen and Senians are right to be insist that the recipients of development interventions not be treated as passive beneficiaries, let alone victims of harmful interventions. Rather these recipients should be helped to help themselves – to "wield agency in deciding what kinds of lives they want to lead, and whether and how to value the ways of being and doing that will allow them to lead such lives" (Drèze and Sen 2013, 232. On the other hand, Khader and Kosko rightly insist that local development recipients also should exercise – and be enabled to exercise – what I have called critical, informed, and ethical agency. A good government and good development agents (whether local, national, or global) not only should question and assess but also try to transform – noncoercively – recipients' existing values and desires. How might this be done in such a way as to avoid paternalism? For as Gerald Dworkin's useful definition emphasizes, coercion is essential to paternalism: "Paternalism is the interference of a state or an individual with another person, against their will, and defended or motivated by a claim that the person interfered with will be better off or protected from harm" (Dworkin 2017). Among the noncoercive ways to promote commitment to and implementation of the goods of equal agency and well-being are the liberating "force" of good arguments, moral encouragement, civic education, and the informal education of civic engagement. In situations of uncritical conventionality, dogmatic tribalism, severe oppression, or individual preferences well adapted to a harsh reality, an individual's judgments are likely to be problematic if not deeply flawed. For the perfectionist, a good political arrangement or development approach should not be neutral but should be one that promotes the objective good.

The most serious rival to a perfectionism in politics is the view that the state cannot legitimately promote the good – at least when the good that is to be promoted is subject to reasonable disagreement. The most prominent recent example would be later writings of John Rawls (Rawls, 1996, 1999, 2001). The most serious rival to my perfectionist agency-focused version of the CA is the political liberalism of Martha Nussbaum, to which I turn in the next chapter.

Notes

1. For an alternative interpretation of Nussbaum's position on Sen's agency and well-being distinction see: Keleher (2007a) chs. 4 and 5; and (2014).
2. However, we might question to what extent, if any, the notion of animal agency is a metaphysical concept, part of a comprehensive doctrine, rather than a concept within a political conception.
3. For an attempt to emphasize the continuity of human and nonhuman animal agency with respect to intentionality, rationality, agency (as self-direction), and moral agency (traits that come in degrees in individuals and across species), see "Animals as Agents" in Thomas (2016).
4. Rather than being a thoughtless perpetuation of conventionality, son preference can be a rational and critical decision. To complicate the choice situation even further, given broader gender, marriage, and aging norms in India, the grim reality is that daughters will typically leave the family home and live out their lives caring for their husband's parents, whereas sons will bring in another caregiver (his wife) to care for his aging parents. The calculation to prefer security in one's twilight years can be very rational and critical. Women (and men) might recognize that they cannot – on their own – change social norms, whatever their own preferences and attitudes about the inherent value of girl children or even their desire to have a girl, and thus decide to use sex-selective abortion to guard against dying alone. I owe this point to Stacy J. Kosko.
5. See Hurowitz (2018) for a celebration – on the 75th anniversary of the Reich's execution of three members of the White Rose – of the White Rose's courageous contestatory acts.
6. It is striking that, when Koggel summarizes Miller's view, autonomy is missing from the "triad of relationality, emotionality, and rationality" (Chapter 6, p. xxx).
7. See Crocker (1983, 238–245); Keleher (2007b).
8. "In many blue-collar environments, women say, they are just told to go along with the culture, to accept that 'boys would be boys, we're pigs and we know it,' as Ms. Hurst [a miner who quit her job] said she was told" (Chira 2017).
9. Contrary to Koggel's narrow view of Sen's development strategy, Drèze and Sen recognize the importance of cultivating nonsexist values in and through egalitarian politics, feminist activism, and women's organizations: "In so far as cultural and political factors appear to be at work, some acknowledgement must also be given to the case of cultivating non-sexist values and egalitarian politics (and the role of feminist activism and of women's organizations)" (2002b, 262).

10. Here I disagree with Joseph Raz: "Autonomous life is valuable only if it is spent in the pursuit of acceptable and valuable projects and relationships. The autonomy principle permits and even requires governments to create morally valuable opportunities and to eliminate repugnant ones" (Raz 1986, 173). Raz, however, is correct when he says that "the autonomous murderer is, if anything, worse than the nonautonomous murderer" (1986, 380).

11. Cf. Crocker (2014, 247).

12. In future work I intend to evaluate Cortina's project, based on a kind of Kantian universalizability, to provide a rational foundation for other-directed responsibility and social justice. Also important will be coming to grips with Forst (2007).

13. However, it was arguably justified for the USA to "install" democracy in Germany and Japan following World War II. Moreover, it might be acceptable for a democracy to fine eligible voters for not voting.

References

Barandiaran, X. E., E. Di Paolo, and M. Rohde. 2009. "Defining Agency: Individuality, Normativity, Asymmetry, and Spatio-Temporality in Action," *Adaptive Behavior*, 17(5): 367–386.

Brooks, David. 2017. "Our Elites Still Don't Get it." *New York Times*, January 16, A25.

Chira, Susan. 2017. "Dead Mice, Stolen Tools, and Lewd Remarks: Coping with Harassment in Blue-Collar Jobs." *New York Times*, December 31, A12.

Chira, Susan, and Catrin Einhorn. 2017. "Decades after the Company Tried to Tackle Sexual Misconduct at Two Chicago Plants, Continued Abuse Raises Questions about the Possibility of Change." *New York Times*, December 19. www.nytimes.com/interactive/2017/12/19/us/ford-chicago-sexual-harassment.html.

Crocker, David A. 2003. *Praxis and Democratic Socialism: The Critical Social Theory of Markovic and Stojanovic*. Atlantic Highlands, NJ: Humanities Press Brighton, Sussex, UK: Harvester Press.

Crocker, David A. 2008. *Ethics of Global Development: Agency, Capability, and Deliberative Democracy*. Cambridge University Press.

Crocker, David A. 2014. "Development and Global Ethics: Five Foci for the Future," *Journal of Global Ethics*, 10(3): 1–8.

Crocker, David A., and Ingrid Robeyns. 2009. "Capability and Agency." In *The Philosophy of Amartya Sen*. Edited by Christopher Morris. Cambridge University Press.

Drèze, Jean, and Amartya Sen. 2002a. "Democratic Practice and Social Inequality in India," *Journal of Asian and African Studies*, 37(2): 6–37.

Drèze, Jean, and Amartya Sen. 2002b. *India: Development and Participation*. Oxford University Press.

Drèze, Jean, and Amartya Sen. 2013. *An Uncertain Glory: India and Its Contradictions*. Princeton University Press.

Dumbach, Annette, and Jud Newborn. 2006. *Sophie Scholl and the White Rose*. Oxford: One World.

Dworkin, Gerald. 2017. "Paternalism," *The Stanford Encyclopedia of Philosophy* (Winter 2017 Edition). Edited by Edward N. Zalta. https://plato.stanford.edu/archives/win2017/entries/paternalism/.

Forst, Rainer. 2007. *The Right to Justification: Elements of a Constructivist Theory of Justice*. New York: Columbia University Press.

Hurowitz, Richard. 2018. "Remembering the White Rose." *New York Times*, February 22, A23.

Keleher, Loretta. 2007a. *Empowerment and Development*. Proquest. http://drum.lib.umd.edu/handle/1903/7584.

Keleher, Lori. 2007b. "Perspectives on Empowerment," Ph.D. dissertation, Department of Philosophy, University of Maryland.

Keleher, Lori. 2014. "Sen and Nussbaum: Agency and Capability-Expansion," *Ethics and Economics*, 11(2): 54–70.

Khader, Serene J. 2011. *Adaptive Preferences and Women's Empowerment* (Studies in Feminist Philosophy). Oxford University Press.

Mackenzie, Catriona. 2014. "Three Dimensions of Autonomy: A Relational Analysis." In *Autonomy, Oppression, and Gender*. Edited by Andrea Veltman and Mark Piper. Oxford University Press.

Miller, Sarah Clark. 2012. *The Ethics of Need: Agency, Dignity, and Obligation*. New York: Routledge.

Nussbaum, Martha C. 2000. *Women and Human Development: The Capabilities Approach*. Cambridge University Press.

Nussbaum, Martha C. 2004. "Beyond 'Compassion and Humanity': Justice for Nonhuman Animals." In *Animal Rights: Current Debates and New Directions*. Edited by Cass R. Sunstein and Martha C. Nussbaum. Oxford University Press.

Nussbaum, Martha C. 2006. *Frontiers of Justice: Disability, Nationality, Species Membership*. Cambridge, MA: Harvard University Press.

Nussbaum, Martha C. 2011. *Creating Capabilities: The Human Development Approach*. Cambridge, MA: Belknap Press, Harvard University Press.

Oshana, Marina. 2014. "A Commitment to Autonomy Is a Commitment to Feminism." In *Autonomy, Oppression, and Gender*. Edited by Andrea Veltman and Mark Piper. Oxford University Press.

Raz, Joseph. 1986. *The Morality of Freedom.* Oxford University Press.

Rawls, John. 1996. *Political Liberalism,* expanded paperback edition. New York: Columbia University Press.

Rawls, John. 1999. *The Law of Peoples with "The Idea of Public Reason Revisited."* Cambridge, MA: Harvard University Press.

Rawls, John. 2001. *Justice as Fairness: A Restatement.* Cambridge, MA: Harvard University Press.

Schlosser, Markus. 2015. "Agency," *The Stanford Encyclopedia of Philosophy* (Fall 2015 Edition). Edited by Edward N. Zalta. https://plato.stanford.edu/archives/fall2015/entries/agency/.

Sen, Amartya. 1985. "Well-being, Agency and Freedom: The Dewey Lectures 1984." *Journal of Philosophy,* 82: 169–221.

Sen, Amartya. 1999. *Development as Freedom.* New York: Knopf.

Sen, Amartya. 2009. *The Idea of Justice.* Cambridge, MA: Belknap Press, Harvard University Press.

Thomas, Natalie. 2016. *Animal Ethics and the Autonomous Animal Self.* London: Palgrave Macmillan.

Tocqueville, Alexis de. 2004. *Democracy in America.* Translated by Arthur Goldhammer. New York: Library of America.

Veltman, Andrea, and Mark Piper. 2014. "Introduction." In *Autonomy, Oppression, and Gender.* Edited by Andrea Veltman and Mark Piper. Oxford University Press.

Wall, Steven. 2009. "Perfectionism in Politics: A Defense." In *Contemporary Debates in Political Philosophy.* Edited by Thomas Christiano and John Christman. Malden, MA and Oxford, UK: Wiley-Blackwell.

Wall, Steven. 2012. "Perfectionism." In *Routledge Companion to Political and Social Philosophy.* Edited by Fred D'Agostino and Gerald F. Gaus. New York: Routledge.

17 | *Perfectionist Liberalism and Democracy*

DAVID A. CROCKER

Political Liberalism and Perfectionist Liberalism

Political Liberalism

In an important footnote in their contribution to this volume, Wichert and Nussbaum note that in my 2008 book *Ethics of Global Development (EGD)*, I "argue for Sen's comprehensive notion of agency, basically a notion of autonomy, as preferable to Nussbaum's thinner concept of practical reason" (Chapter 10, p. xxx, n. 92). Wichert and Nussbaum go on to state that I had not been able to take into account Nussbaum's central argument, set forth, among other places, in *Creating Capabilities* (2011a, 89–93) and in much greater detail in "Perfectionist Liberalism and Political Liberalism" (2011b) in opposition to Sen's more robust notion of agency and in favor of Nussbaum's thinner concept of agency as a key component of her "political liberalism." Her main argument turns on her claim that political liberalism and its concept of practical reason is more appropriate "for a society in which many responsible citizens reject autonomy and prefer authoritarian religion" (p. xxx, n. 92). For a state to promote Senian agency in a society in which some believers are committed to religious authority is to disrespect those believers. In contrast, the ideal of practical reason or "political autonomy" can be a part of *political* principles that citizens of any reasonable "comprehensive" moral outlook, according to Nussbaum, can and should accept.

Nussbaum increasingly argues that her version of political liberalism, which owes much to Rawls (1996) and Charles Larmore (1996), is both superior to perfectionist liberalism and is absolutely essential to her present version of the capability approach.[1] In the same footnote, Wichert and Nussbaum challenge me to say whether or not I accept

Nussbaum's arguments in her 2011b essay. I accept the challenge, but not her arguments, to which I now turn.

This topic is relevant for a volume on development ethics. Although Rawls offers his notion of political liberalism as relevant for the United States and democratic European countries, Nussbaum correctly remarks that Rawls offers no "compelling reasons" that his notion is not relevant for other democracies (Nussbaum 2014, 6). Indeed, Nussbaum contends further that "the same issues that make political liberalism a normatively good position for a Western domestic society are reasons present in every existing democratic state" (2014, 6), namely, "a plurality of reasonable comprehensive doctrines which has not converged on agreement under the conditions of freedom" (12). In this regard, Nussbaum briefly analyzes cases of India and South Africa, and we might add in Latin America the states of Chile, Costa Rica, Uruguay, and in Africa the countries of Morocco and Liberia. Finally, although Nussbaum concedes that dictatorships have a long way to go before political liberalism is an option for a political arrangement, she makes the bold claim that political liberalism is "for every nation" as well as for the "transnational" or global order of nations and international structures. Given that development ethics is concerned with overcoming the unfreedoms of poverty and domination not only in developing and transitional countries but also within developed countries and the global order, the issue of political versus perfectionist liberalism should be a key issue for development ethics as it moves forward. The debate, as Nussbaum remarks, "is a deep one, and it ought to continue until we understand all the options and issues as well as we can" (Nussbaum 2011b, 41). My aim is to enter that debate, clarify and defend a capability approach (CA) version of perfectionist liberalism, and offer this alternative to political philosophy as well as to the theory and practice of development ethics.

Due to limitations in space, I can only provide the briefest sketch and evaluation of Nussbaum's political liberalism and my alternative, which I will argue is a modest form of perfectionist liberalism. More extensive treatment must await another occasion. What does Nussbaum mean by "political liberalism"? What are her arguments supporting it over perfectionist liberalism, and how sound are her arguments? How should we understand perfectionist liberalism in general and my version of the CA as an exemplar? What is my first cut as to the merits of and challenges for this theory-practice of development?

Political liberalism contrasts with what has become its chief rival, perfectionist liberalism. Perfectionists, in general, argue "the state can legitimately promote the good, even when what is good is subject to reasonable disagreement" (Wall 2009, 100). Antiperfectionism, of which the political liberalisms of Rawls, Larmore, and Nussbaum are leading examples, hold "that the state cannot legitimately promote the good – at least when the good that is to be promoted is subject to reasonable disagreement" (Wall 2009, 100). Similarly, many development ethicists, although they eschew the term perfectionist, argue that a good political arrangement, including its policy with respect to other countries, can and should use the state to promote the human (individual and communal) good (and, perhaps, nonhuman goods as well).

There are four components in Nussbaum's concept of political liberalism. First, she, like Rawls, starts from the "fact" of reasonable pluralism – the recognition that democracies, like that of the United States, are characterized by citizens who hold reasonable but "incompatible comprehensive views of human life and its goals" (Nussbaum 2003, 26). By a "comprehensive view," Nussbaum, following Rawls, means an ultimate metaphysical, epistemological, ethical view – whether religious or secular – concerning the meaning and purpose life in all aspects, and not just the political sphere. The disagreements among people in such (democratic) societies are deep and tenacious; not only are these disagreements not likely to disappear but they appear and thrive in the ethos of democratic freedoms.

Second, political liberalism is a "freestanding" but partial moral conception, a "substantive moral consensus," whose purpose is to inform and orient citizens in the political sphere – regardless of their comprehensive doctrines. This network of moral ideas is not itself a comprehensive doctrine but, Rawls and Nussbaum claim, can be supported by adherents of any, liberal or nonliberal, comprehensive doctrine that is also reasonable. Rawls put it like this in the 1996 paperback edition of *Political Liberalism*:

Political liberalism is not a form of Enlightenment liberalism, that is a comprehensive liberal and often secular doctrine founded on reason and viewed as suitable for the modern age now that the religious authority of Christian ages is said to be no longer dominant. Political liberalism has no such aims. It takes for granted the fact of reasonable pluralism of comprehensive doctrines, where some of those doctrines are taken to be non-liberal and religious. The problem of political liberalism is to work out a political conception of political justice for a constitutional democratic regime that a plurality of reasonable doctrines, both religious and nonreligious, liberal and non-liberal, may freely endorse, and so freely live by and come to understand its virtues. (Rawls 1996, xl)

An analogy that both Rawls and Nussbaum employ is that the political conception is like a "module," that is, an independent unit that can be combined in various ways with other structures, namely the reasonable comprehensive doctrines. In the case at hand, the unit is a complex of concepts that together is the object of an "overlapping consensus" in the sense that all reasonable comprehensive perspectives support the module (although Nussbaum admits that some comprehensive doctrines may have a more or less "strained" relation with the module). The "module" is not itself a comprehensive doctrine nor does it "aim to replace comprehensive doctrines, religious or nonreligious, but intends to be equally distinct from both and, it hopes, acceptable to both" (Rawls 1996, xl).

Third, the module – for example, Rawls's "political conception of political justice" and Nussbaum's CA – includes a political, not metaphysical or philosophical, concept of the person as someone who cooperates on fair terms with others as long as they reciprocate and do not violate anyone's human rights. In the political sphere (and not in private or religious life), the political concept of the person is not that of autonomy as self-direction and self-governance, in the sense of running one's life in *all* matters and spheres of life.[2] To avoid confusion with a robust or thick idea of autonomy, one that features critical and ethically responsible agency, Nussbaum employs instead the idea of "practical reason" and sometimes, following Rawls, "political autonomy," which she dubs a (thin) "cousin of autonomy" (2011b, 36).

In her most recent "lists" of politically liberal capabilities, Nussbaum defines "practical reason" as "being able to form a conception of the good and to engage in critical reflection about the planning of one's life" (Nussbaum 2003, 39; 2006, 76–78). "Critical reflection about planning one's life" certainly seems to be at odds with some traditions of authoritarian religion and politics. Nevertheless, Nussbaum believes this notion of what in the previous chapter I called "critical agency" ("not merely freedom and the power to act, but also freedom and power to question and reassess the prevailing norms and values" [Drèze and Sen 2002, 258]) is a proper but strictly limited part of her political liberalism because it is a capability but not a functioning:

> First of all, one must emphasize the all-important distinction between capability and functioning. Raz and Mill think that unless people are actually doing this forming, reflecting, and planning, their lives are *ipso facto* less worthwhile. I say only that (according to the political conception) a life that does not have the *capability* to do this sort of criticizing and planning is not a life in accordance with human dignity. (Nussbaum 2003, 39)

That is, the devotee of an authoritarian comprehensive doctrine would not be able to support critical agency if the state endorsed and promoted the *practice* or *functioning* of critical agency in contrast to merely having the *opportunity* or *freedom* for the activity. Just as the Amish – whose religion mandates no political participation, such as voting – can support the Amish having the freedom to vote, so a nonliberal religion can support having real opportunity for critical reflection and planning but not the related activity. But, I ask, does the "political realm" – at least in a democracy – make sense without the critical activity, and not just the opportunities, of citizens both in and out of government? For Sen and Senians the answer is clear:

> While democratic institutions provide opportunities for achieving democratic ideals, how these opportunities are realized is a matter of democratic practice. The latter depends inter alia on the extent of political participation, the awareness of the public, the vigour of the opposition, the nature of political parties and popular organizations, and various determinants of the distribution of power. Both democratic institutions and democratic practices are important in achieving democracy in the fuller sense, but the presence of the former do not guarantee the latter. (Drèze and Sen 2002, 347)

The same is true of the practice, and not merely the freedom, of argument. Nussbaum concedes that political life does (or should have?) "respect for argument" (2003, 38), a public exchange of reasons and citizens open to evidence. Such skills, even if limited to the political sphere, seem to be clear cases not just of capabilities but of activities or functionings. These exercises of agency both should be promoted and, as Cortina argues in this volume, cultivated by a democracy and part of a citizen's responsibility to make democracy work.

Now suppose, as US citizen and political writer James Mann argues in fact has been occurring in the United States since January 2017, the president of a mature democracy imperils its democratic norms by "abandoning the very notion of civil discourse by refusing to accord his political opponents even a minimum of respect," and by scorning as alien "the usual practice of ordinary democratic give and take" (2018, 6). Citizens – both inside and outside government – should vigorously affirm that essential to the *practice* of democratic government are citizens' critical deliberations with respect to reason, evidence, and truth.

Nussbaum (and Rawls) might object that this enlarging of the "political" to include these components of democratic citizenship would amount to making the "module" unacceptable to those comprehensive doctrines that feature uncritical obedience to authority. It would elevate the "political realm" to become at least a partial comprehensive doctrine, which illiberal comprehensive doctrines could not support. Yet, such elevation, even if it would put a "strain" on nonliberal comprehensive doctrine, is democratically responsible. To rule out such democratic activities would leave merely an institutional shell of democracy. Mann criticizes the Trump administration's lack of respect for "an independent press as a restraint and watchdog on government" and, "beyond the press," for "the concepts of objective truth, rational discourse, and scientific expertise, the Enlightenment ideals on which the country was founded" (2018, 6). The price that political liberalism pays is the contraction of the political sphere to democratic institutions devoid of the exercise of critical and responsible democratic agency.

Nussbaum does concede that people, especially children, cannot acquire the capability for practical reason without being initiated into the activities of critical agency, exchange or reasons, and rational argument. Acquiring the capability of practical reason, admits Nussbaum, requires[3] some "learning by doing" if citizens are to have the capability to think and argue critically, to decide and act responsibly. Even if such active citizenship were designed to be merely the means to the end of acquiring the citizen capabilities, it would be difficult to separate ends and means let alone to prohibit youth from finding such activity as intrinsically valuable. Such a valuation of citizen activity would put an enormous "strain" on those whose comprehensive doctrine required an unquestioning obedience to authority and a rejection of rational argument. The perfectionist liberal, as well as the engaged citizen, would welcome that occasion of "strain" as an opportunity to give reasons for liberalizing an illiberal comprehensive doctrine. It is not enough for Nussbaum to say that the strain between "module" and authoritarian obedience is the authoritarian's "business" (2003, 38) and not a problem instead for the narrow if not nondemocratic character of her political liberalism.

In contrast, on my version of the CA and perfectionist liberalism, public or even (accredited) private education should be committed to nurturing in youth both the capability for and responsible functioning of democratic citizenship. Even though it more or less burdens those parents (and children) of nonliberal comprehensive doctrines, Nussbaum comes close to the truth when she asserts: "even if there were a substantial burden, it could be surmounted because the state has a compelling interest in teaching students how to formulate and defend their own ideas and to engage in debate about a variety of positions" (2003, 42). Going one step further, I contend that public education is responsible for encouraging and challenging students to think for themselves and act responsibly.

A fourth component of Nussbaum's political liberalism is that she designs her political conception of justice (her capabilities approach) to be equally acceptable to both liberal and illiberal comprehensive doctrines, whether religious or secular. But she adds a big qualification: the political conception should be so shaped so as to respect adherents of comprehensive doctrines as persons, as dignified ends in themselves. What does Nussbaum mean by respect for persons? What does she mean by reasonable? What comprehensive doctrines does this criterion make respect-worthy and which does it exclude?

For Nussbaum, the political notion of respect, in contrast to the emotion of admiring someone, is that of treating a fellow citizen as a political equal, as a being with dignity, who is searching for and perhaps has found for himself meaning in life: "It is because we respect persons that we think their comprehensive doctrines" – if reasonable – "deserve space to unfold themselves, and deserve respectful, nonderogatory treatment from government (whatever treatment they receive from citizens in the 'background culture')" (Nussbaum 2011b, 33). Religious persons in the just society should respect comprehensive atheists, and atheists should respect religious authoritarians. Neither should merely forbear, put up with, or be indifferent to the other. And in neither case should the politically liberal democratic state enshrine a comprehensive view in its constitution or issue derogatory comments about any reasonable comprehensive doctrines. For a state even to promote thick autonomy in public or accredited educational institutions would be for it to send a message of "expressive subordination," which the adherent of a contrary comprehensive doctrine would and should find disrespectful and even insulting. Instead of being treated with respect as a being with dignity, the adherent would be treated as an inferior citizen.

How far should this respect go? Should a government or its officials respect all comprehensive doctrines? Nussbaum, like Rawls and Larmore, answers "no." Respect should be shown only to those comprehensive doctrines that are reasonable. But at this point Nussbaum finds serious problems in the views of both Rawls and Larmore, for these two theorists, from which she has learned so much, define reasonable in relation not only to *ethical* criteria, which Nussbaum endorses, but also to *theoretical* or *epistemic* criteria, which Nussbaum rejects.

Given that a liberal political conception includes the moral notion that citizens are in some sense free and equal, the ethical component of reasonableness excludes slavery; racist or ethnic supremacy, embodied for example by the Ku Klux Klan; sexist supremacy (misogyny, patriarchy); and nationalist/religious supremacy, such as that of some Burmese Buddhists like the firebrand monk Wirathu. For Rawls, unreasonable comprehensive doctrines also include those with theoretical or epistemic deficiencies such as "piecemeal-ism," inconsistency, incoherence, or isolation from a body of thought.[4] An example, which Nussbaum mentions, would be New Ageism.[5] I would add creationism and those forms of alternative medicine, such as homeopathy, elevated to a philosophy of life.

Why does Nussbaum reject employing theoretical criteria? Because she contends that mainstream comprehensive religious doctrines, such as many forms of Christianity and Islam, as well as some forms of Judaism, have one or more of these theoretical deficiencies and yet, Nussbaum argues, we should respect their adherents. Nussbaum gives as an example the, for many, incoherent Christian doctrine of the Trinity. Rather than relegate orthodox Christianity to unreasonableness, Nussbaum rejects the principles of coherence as well as other epistemic standards of reasonability.

Nussbaum's rejection of theoretical criteria for reasonability leaves her only with what she calls the "ethical definition of 'reasonable'"

(2011b, 33). The focus of this definition is not on the content or grounds of the doctrine. Rather a "reasonable comprehensive doctrine has to do with the *person* who endorses it: A reasonable doctrine is one endorsed by a reasonable citizen. And what is a reasonable citizen? One who among other things is seriously committed to the political value of "equal respect for persons." It doesn't matter the way a doctrine is grounded: "Whether it be tradition-based, authority-based, argument-based, faith-based, or based in nothing but its allure, a religious doctrine deserves to be called 'reasonable' if and only if it is the sort of doctrine that can be endorsed by a reasonable citizen" (2011b, 33). With respect to content, Nussbaum's ethical definition implies that it doesn't matter whether a comprehensive doctrine is silly, crazy, or flaky just in case it can be endorsed by a reasonable person defined in Nussbaum's ethical terms.

How should we evaluate Nussbaum's proposal for deciding on which comprehensive doctrines are reasonable and hence should be respected and not insulted by the political principles? There are three problems. First, if Nussbaum is correct in emphasizing that citizens can and do respect persons and not, directly at least, their doctrines, then they can respect a person's free choice or exercise of her agency and still reject the content or grounds of her comprehensive doctrine (see Wall 2014, 483). Second, as we saw above, making the content of political liberalism dependent on the support of illiberal religious or secular comprehensive doctrines pays the price of emptying democracy of critical and responsible citizen agency. Finally, with no epistemic restrictions on reasonability, Nussbaum's political liberalism is saddled with accepting the silly, irrational, and flaky as respect-worthy. Fourth, just as Nussbaum did not feel obliged to respect racist or sexist doctrine because the citizens in a democratic society are to be free and equal, so she should endorse (critical and responsible) agency in democratic citizens and not feel constrained to respect those comprehensive doctrines that feature uncritical obedience to religious or political authority.

Perfectionist Liberalism

How should we understand the agency-oriented CA as an attractive form of perfectionist liberalism and one that might answer objections from the political liberal and other perspectives? Steven Wall gives a clear analysis of perfectionism as "an account of the good human life, an account of human well-being, a moral theory, and an approach to politics" (Wall 2017). With respect to politics, perfectionists argue against political liberals, such as Nussbaum, that the state, or more generally any "political arrangement" – "political institutions, constitutions, laws, policies, directives, etc." (Wall 2009, 114, n. 2) – can legitimately promote the good, even "when the good is subject to disagreement, reasonable or otherwise" (Wall 2009, 99).

Wall argues that all perfectionists "advance an objective account of the good and then develop an account of ethics and/or politics informed by this account of the good" (Wall 2017). Wall's account is general and basic. It will enable us to see the agency-oriented CA as a type of perfectionism that illustrates each of the four categories above. Focusing on perfectionism's basic or core claims enables us to follow Wall and sidestep some of the common objections that have been pressed against perfectionism and might be pressed against my version of the CA (or the merit of bringing it into the perfectionist camp). I will leave for another occasion any attempt to show that my version of perfectionist political theory is superior to other such versions, such as those of Joseph Raz (1986), Thomas Hurka (1993), or George Sher (1997). My main aim is to show that my perfectionist liberalism is on balance superior to Nussbaum's political liberalism and provides the CA and development ethics a better way to move forward than does Nussbaum's alternative.

Without providing justification, beyond "wide reflective equilibrium," for any of the three components of the perfectionist liberalism that I have assumed in the previous chapter, earlier in this chapter, and in past work, and now explicitly propose, I will list and briefly discuss these components in rapid-fire succession. The agency-based CA's human goods include (1) (critical and responsible) agency freedom and achievement, (2) well-being freedom and achievement, and (3) moral and political equality. Each is intrinsically good as well as instrumentally good. This view is an "internal" value pluralism in which individual and communal agents can and should exercise their agency and prioritize the three goods in relation to each other in different ways in different contexts. An agent can and sometimes should sacrifice agency freedom for achievement (or vice versa), sacrifice well-being for some agency goal (or vice versa), or sacrifice either agency or well-being to equality (or vice versa). It is up to the person as agent in the sense that she has the right to decide (not that she cannot err in deciding), and in that sense agency is the first value among equals.

In dialogue with Adela Cortina and Jesus Conill, in *EGD* (222–224), I view agency as sometimes (but not always) having causal priority over well-being, but not having normative priority. I now want to be clear that agency, well-being, and equality are equally important perfectionist goods. I am perfectionist with respect to these three goods, but I agree with Cortina and affirm that humans should be self-determining with respect to a "model of the good life" (Cortina 2002, 213) and whether "religion, art, science, business, sports, or leisure is at the top of one's hierarchy of valued activities" (Crocker 2008, 226). Hence, this perfectionism is a *liberal* perfectionism in which all three goods – agency, well-being, and equality – are to be promoted but not necessarily "maximized." Threshold realization, to be determined by personal and democratic choice in dialogue with theoretical reflection, suffices. This perfectionism is *liberal* because liberty or freedom runs through all three goods: both agency and well-being have freedom, as well as achievement aspects. The answer to Sen's 1979 question in the Tanner Lectures, "Equality of What?" (Sen 1980) is equality of (positive and negative) basic liberty.

These three perfectionist goods are objective in two senses. First, the value of these goods does not refer to mental states such as "pleasurable experience or informed desire" (Wall 2009, 101). Second, these goods are objective in the sense that they are most likely to be identified, as I suggested in the previous chapter in my reply to Koggel, by rational scrutiny of both reasons and emotional reactions. As Sen puts it, "the case for reasoned scrutiny lies not in any sure-fire way of getting things exactly right (no such way may exist), but on being as objective as we reasonably can" (2009, 40).

In sharp contrast to Nussbaum's rejection of any epistemic criteria for reasonability, Sen argues for "a particular discipline of reasoning" or "objective reasoning" in "thinking about issues of justice and injustice." As Sen says, "one of the main points in favour of reason is that it helps us to scrutinize ideology and blind belief" (2009, 35):

It is, of course, true that many crude beliefs originate in some kinds of reason – possibly of rather primitive kinds (for example, racist and sexist prejudices survive often enough on the basis of the perceived "reason" that non-whites or women are biologically or intellectually inferior. The case for reliance on reason does not involve any denial of the easily recognized fact that people do give reasons of some kind or other in defence of their beliefs (no matter how crude). The point of *reasoning* as a discipline is to subject the prevailing beliefs and alleged reasons to critical examination. (Sen 2009, 35–36, n. *)

The meta-ethic here is one of fallibilism: the goal is to pursue ethical objectivity and arrive at or near to the truth, which requires that one keeps open to the possibility that one has reasoned poorly, got things wrong, and could do better in getting things right (Bernstein 2006; Sen 2009, 48–49). Sen rightly echoes his one-liner about democracy: "The remedy for bad reasoning lies in better reasoning, and it is indeed the job of reasoned scrutiny to move from the former to the latter" (Sen 2009, 49). Finally, following both Sen (2009, ch. 1) and Hilary Putnam (2002, 2004), I assume that this pursuit of moral truth is not "the search for some ethical *objects*" (Sen 2009, 41) like Platonic forms or natural laws.

An essential component of a perfectionist political theory, Steven Wall compellingly argues, is what he calls the *"rejection of state neutrality"* (Wall 2009, 102). On Sen's and my CA, the state should not be neutral (with respect to either content or grounds) for it should be promoting in various ways the goods of (critical and responsible) agency, well-being (valuable capabilities and functionings), and (moral and political) equality. The state, as well as other institutions, such as the market, nongovernmental institutions, and social movements, should expand freedoms and remove the "major sources of unfreedom: poverty as well as tyranny, poor economic opportunities as well as systematic social deprivation, neglect of public facilities as well as intolerance or overactivity of repressive states" (Sen 1999b, 3). Good and just states promote the human goods of agency, well-being, and equality while bad and unjust states should be developed so as to be able and likely to do so:

The constitutive role of freedom relates to the importance of substantive freedom in enriching human life. The substantive freedoms include elementary capabilities like being able to avoid such deprivations as starvation, undernourishment, escapable morbidity and premature mortality, as well as freedoms [that is, agency freedoms] that are associated with being literate and numerate, enjoying political participation and uncensored speech and so on. In this constitutive perspective, development involves expansion of these and other basic freedoms. Development, in this view, is the process of expanding human freedoms, and the assessment of development is to be informed by this consideration. (Sen 1999b, 36)

Governments should not be normatively neutral, and Sen identifies five interconnected institutional "facilities" or "instrumental freedoms" by which states – often supplemented, aided, or even replaced by nonstate agents – can and should promote (protect, nurture, restore) basic freedoms: political freedoms, economic facilities, social opportunities, transparency guarantees, and protective security (1999b, 38–40).

A major worry of antiperfectionists, such as Cortina in this volume (Chapter 12), is that a perfectionist state would exclusively use coercion to "impose" or "install" the theory's conception of the good. It is true that in our agency-oriented CA the state can and should coercively prevent and punish actions in which agents exercise their agency to violate the agency and well-being rights of others. However, there also are many noncoercive ways in which the state and other institutions can and should promote the human (and nonhuman) good, especially when one of the three principles is that of critical and responsible agency. Democratic political organizations and movements can noncoercively encourage agency skills and ethical commitments. Democratic constitutions can endorse citizen participation as well as citizen rights and freedoms (Crocker 2008, 202–203). Public and accredited education can and should nurture and freely strengthen critical and responsible agency, especially commitments to help others help themselves. Polities on all levels can bestow global, national, and local awards and honors on exemplary individuals and groups who have used their agency to overcome the unfreedoms of poverty, tyranny, and inequality. National and international development agencies can and should encourage local, national, regional, and global groups to make their own decisions and to make them through democratic procedures that they freely forge.

What, however, of those in the community who disagree fundamentally with this threefold normative vision, which in various ways is to be both coercively and noncoercively implemented? Here we must discuss different ways that a perfectionist state would accommodate different kinds of dissenting groups and individuals.

- Racist and sexist practices should be prohibited by a liberal constitution in which all citizens are free and equal. But adherents of these types of inherently inegalitarian ideologies would have the civil and political rights of free speech and assembly to defend their views publicly. Nussbaum would not permit these groups to propose their principles for a democratic vote (Nussbaum 2011b). I would consider constitutional amendments decided by a supermajority, but does even a supermajority have a democratic right to bind future generations?[6]

- Religious and other groups committed to gender and other hierarchies and that reject critical reflection and inculcate obedience to authority have the rights of free speech, including professing their faith and trying to win others noncoercively to their faith or worldview.[7] Adult members have the right to exit from the group or to try to liberalize and democratize the group from within (but may be expelled for their efforts). Although it might require coercion of the parents, children should be exposed to perfectionist and liberal democratic values and be given reasons to accept them in public or accredited education.

- Adherents of epistemically unreasonable comprehensive doctrines, such as astrology, creationism, or New Ageism are free to defend (not inculcate or brainwash) their doctrines in intellectual and political debates, deliberations, and academic exchanges with liberal and democratic perspectives. Different comprehensive doctrines – liberal and illiberal, democratic and autocratic – will be in competition to convince and influence elected and appointed officials as well as citizens, who elect their representatives. Nussbaum permits rational argument in private relationships and debates but not in the public sphere (2011b, 39).[8] I doubt that it is possible or desirable to split citizens into private and public beings. At stake are not political principles, meant to offend no one, but the best (truest) comprehensive doctrine and its implications for policies and laws. Although *Washington Post* pundit E. J. Dionne plausibly claims that leaders (I would add "and citizens") of a democratic society have an obligation to solve current problems, forge a national purpose, and maintain a commitment to democratic freedoms (2018), this does not mean that they should forge what Rawls and Nussbaum call "political principles," ones that every "reasonable" comprehensive doctrine is able to support.

Rather than search for an overlapping consensus on political values, which would more than likely approach the lowest common or bland denominator, citizens and their elected leaders should argue over which existing, modified, or new comprehensive doctrine or doctrines is/are most rationally justifiable at this time and should be the moral compass for the nation's ideals, institutions, and practices. E. J. Dionne puts it well: "Within this context [of core obligations], citizens exercise their right to argue about how to define the public interest, how to identify the central problems, and how to choose among competing values" (2018).

Often, the executive, judicial, and legislative process will involve advocates of one comprehensive doctrine putting up with or forbearing compromise with adherents of a rival doctrine. Often, differences will be temporarily and provisionally "resolved" by a democratic vote. Sometimes one side may learn from an opposing side and modify its comprehensive doctrine. Sometimes, previous rivals may forge a new comprehensive perspective by creatively integrating two or more opposing perspectives. Sometimes, adherents to radically different doctrines can agree for different reasons on a concrete policy. In any case, in my version of perfectionist liberalism, the political sphere is not a stage for creating the object (module) of an overlapping consensus; rather it is a playing field for contending, interacting, and evolving comprehensive doctrines. The result would be that at any given time the state or political arrangement would be promoting – directly or indirectly – one (or more) conception(s) of the good. In the case of the agency-oriented CA, the result would be promoting our normative triad as fundamental principles and Sen's five freedoms (as both instrumentally and intrinsically good).

In future work I will take up Adela Cortina's argument, influenced by Jürgen Habermas, Karl-Otto Apel, Axel Honneth, and Rainer Forst, that deliberative interaction of citizens involves "reciprocal recognition" and "cordial," sympathetic reasoning. In addition to agency as self-determination and self-governance, Cortina stresses Kantian autonomy as "self-legislation" and finds in the deliberative interaction of "we argue" the foundation for arriving at the truth about justice and responsibility for all humans: "The reconstruction of the assumptions of speech takes us to a 'we argue,' which stems from the reciprocal recognition of those who know themselves to be valid interlocutors, obliged to joint self-legislation, and empowered to independently accept or reject, in this case, the validity claim of justice" (Chapter 12, p. xxx). For Cortina, this "ethics of cordial reason" not only draws on emotional resources but also is advanced in and through civic education: "educating autonomous subjects for a democratic citizenry" (Chapter 12, p. xxx). I look forward to exploring in detail the way in which the agency-focused version of the CA may learn from and perhaps contribute to the cordial reason version of reciprocal recognition.

Democracy

In *EGD*, I argued that good development should include a democratic component, that Sen's CA would be strengthened and advanced by recent theory and practice of deliberative democracy, that globalization should be democratized, and that democracy should be globalized. Since the book's publication, I have benefitted greatly from Sen's recent work on the ideas of justice and democracy as well as from some searching criticisms of my views by Christine Koggel, Colleen Murphy, Luis Camacho, and other scholars and practitioners. The second part of this final chapter provides me with a welcome opportunity to engage Sen's new work and my critics. It also enables me to develop some political and institutional aspects of my perfectionist liberalism in which good governance – democracy – assumes and promotes critical and ethical agency, capabilities that people have good reason to value, and moral and political equality.

I proceed in four steps. First, I summarize my analysis of democracy and its dimensions and argue that the CA should continue to view democracy as a "universal value" and as a kind of ideal for which to strive. Understood in the right way, and in spite of Sen's (2009) and others' (for example, Watene and Drydyk 2016) recent criticisms of ideals and "ideal theory," democracy can and should function as a kind of ideal for both "developed" and "developing" countries. Second, I address Christine Koggel's objections to my "model" of deliberative democracy and Colleen Murphy's related criticism that I am guilty of the same sin I find in Nussbaum's work, namely, I subordinate democratic practice to philosophical theory. Finally, I evaluate Luis Camacho's assessments of my view of participatory democracy.

Democracy as an Ideal

For Sen, democracy is public reasoning that occurs in the context of political assessment and governance. It occurs in political bodies as well as nongovernmental bodies on the local, regional, national, and global level. It is helpful to distinguish between public reason involved in public *dialogue*, on the one hand, and public reason involved in policy decisions and actions on the other. The former aims at the objective – albeit partial or incomplete – moral truth. The latter is practical reason, which is hopefully informed by moral truth and answers the question of "what is to be done?" Democracy aims, among other things, at giving a group's members the opportunity to exercise their agency in reducing injustice and advancing justice:

> The central issues in a broader understanding of democracy are political participation, dialogue and public interaction. The crucial role of public reasoning in the practice of democracy makes the entire subject of democracy related closely with the topic that is central to this work [*The Idea of Justice*], namely justice. If the demands of justice can be assessed only with the help of public reasoning and if public reasoning is constitutively related to the idea of democracy, then there is an intimate connection between justice and democracy, with shared discursive features. (Sen 2009, 326)

To see more clearly the sort of public reasoning involved in democracy, let us first examine and amplify Sen's conceptions in the *Idea of Justice* and elsewhere on the nature and values of democracy. If we start with the generic idea of democracy as "rule by the people," how does Sen conceive democracy? As we saw earlier, in *India: Development and Participation*, Sen and Drèze contend that democracy is a set of demanding ideals, institutional arrangements, and human actions or practice to make democracy "work":

> Democratic ideals represent various aspects of the broad idea of "government of the people, by the people and for the people." They include political characteristics that can be seen to be intrinsically important in terms of the objective of democratic social living, such as freedom of expression, participation of the people in deciding on the factors governing their lives, public accountability of leaders, and an equitable distribution of power. (Drèze and Sen 2002, 347)

Just as with respect to the matters of justice, the point is not to imagine let alone realize true or perfect democracy but to enhance "the range and vitality" (Sen 2009, 408, n. ‡). of existing democracies.

Although Sen shuns the idea of "an imagined perfect democracy" (2009, 408, n. ‡), he does in effect compare better and worse democracies, as well as nondemocracies, along at least five dimensions. This "comparative method" is analogous to the one he employs to judge some countries as more just or unjust than others or one country improving or regressing with respect to justice. This comparative method contrasts with the method he rejects, namely, the "transcendental method" or "transcendental institutionalism." The comparative method asks "How would justice be advanced?" while the transcendental method asks "What would be perfectly just [or democratic] institutions?" (2009, 9). Sen identifies two problems with transcendental institutionalism. First, which we will take up subsequently, there may be no way to get reasoned agreement on what counts as "the just society." Second, even if feasible, a concept of a perfectly just or perfectly democratic institution is neither sufficient nor necessary for what is required, namely comparing two or more concrete approaches that focus on how to avoid more injustice or advance to more justice.

With respect to distributive justice, Sen does not follow Hobbes, Kant, Rawls, and many others to offer a *theory* of *the* perfectly just society. Rather, he provides "an exercise of practical reason that involves" the actual choice of a framework, a network of concepts, for choosing among feasible societal alternatives. For me, and implicitly for Sen, these concepts or "metrics" for comparing and advancing justice include agency (freedom and achievement), well-being (capabilities and functionings), and equality.[9] These concepts capture what Sen calls "realizations" – ways of human "being and doing" in contrast to institutions and rules. And these concepts can be called "ideals." They are not principles of institutional perfection but function rather as foci of action, a moral compass that helps orient people as to how to assess, what to reject, and what to pursue.[10]

With respect to democracy, Sen also puts forward not some model of perfect or true democracy but rather some dimensions that characterize the different axes along which people "rule" in a democracy. I have interpreted Sen's remarks about the five democratic dimensions and labeled them as dimensions of breadth, range, depth, separation of power, and control or impact (Crocker 2008, 299; 2012, 50–53; 2013,

107–109). Together, I argue, these dimensions help us understand the universal but complex and contextually sensitive ideal of democracy. Democracy is scalar: it is always more or less with respect to each of the five dimensions and at some point a polity is so democratically deficient in the dimensions that it is a nondemocracy or antidemocracy.

First, democracies aspire to be ruled by the many (people) and not by one or a few, but democracies differ with respect to *breadth* – the proportion of citizens and variety of people who rule. Athenian democracy, in which only 35,000 male members of the assembly ruled over about 300,000 (Rawls 1999, 29, n. 27, 52) excluded slaves, women, and *metics*, the latter being noncitizen resident aliens in Athens. Democracy in the United States gradually expanded the franchise, but current voting restrictions, such as age or citizenship, as well as gerrymandering and other discriminatory practices, have excluded many from political participation. In its last (2015) national election, Ethiopia had more than 92 percent turnout of eligible voters, but the Ethiopian People's Revolutionary Democratic Front (EPRDF) won 500 of 547 seats in Parliament. With only 6 percent of the nation's 100 million people, the Tigraway ethnic group dominates EPRDF while the Oromo and Amhara ethnic groups, with 60 percent of the populations, have no Parliamentary seats. Among Sen's concern with breadth is that all adult citizens participate in "ruling," but even noncitizens and nonresidents should have some "voice," that is, opportunities to express their interests and beliefs about what should be done. A national leader must listen and learn not only from leaders of other countries but from unsuccessful parties as well as citizens and residents of other countries.

Just as rational scrutiny about truth claims benefits from the criticisms and ideas of others both "near and far," so, contends Sen, (almost) no one should be completely left out of democratic participation. The more inclusive is popular rule, the more likely that bias, parochialism, and blind tradition – especially with respect to racial, ethnic, and religious minorities – will be mitigated and that justice will be promoted. To be decided by democratic decision-making is how much breadth is enough and how much is too much. At what age should youngsters vote and when, if ever, should convicted or punished felons have the right to vote?

Second, democratic societies differ with respect to the *range* of democratic institutions and the scope of the issues they take up. Some societies restrict democracy to political institutions. Some theorists, like John Dewey, expand democratic institutions not only to all social institutions, such as the family, economic enterprises, and religious organizations, but emphasize that democracy is "a way of life" that should permeate all conduct and all associations (Dewey 1927, 143). Sen clearly contends that democracy is more than *political* institutions and gives important democratic roles to the United Nations, citizen organizations, nongovernmental organizations (NGOs), and groups of activists. It is not clear, however, to what extent Sen believes these groups should be internally democratic and to what extent and when he believes they should have the cultural liberty to practice nondemocratic governance.

Democracies also differ with respect to the *scope* of the issues that are decided democratically. Democratic decisions (elections), are made to decide on at least some leaders, and legislatures may decide on matters ranging from war and peace, to regulation of the economy, to matters of personal privacy. What are essential matters for "democratic will" and which matters should be off-limits? To some extent, at least, that itself is a question for democratic choice.

Third, when we compare democratic bodies and theories, it is clear that there are many different ways in which citizens may "rule" or *participate* in governing. Citizens can participate directly or through elected representatives. Democracies can be shallow, with minimal or perfunctory voting, or deep, with robust criticism, protest, petitioning, deliberation, and other forms of civic engagement. In *The Idea of Justice*, Sen continues his earlier emphasis that citizens do and should participate not just by balloting, as important as that can be, but also by public reasoning, protesting, agitating, deliberating, deciding, and concerted action.

Democracy, for Sen, is not only instrumentally valuable in that it gives people voice and is a tool for overcoming their deprivations and resisting tyranny (Crocker 2008, 302–303). Democracy is also *intrinsically* valuable in that it enables individuals and groups to exercise and express their own (critical, reasoned, and responsible) agency – to decide for themselves how to act and together what to do rather than being the pawns of others or the victims of circumstance (Crocker 2008, 299). Sen also calls this the "process" aspect of choice or freedom. Democracy, as we saw above, is also constructively valuable in that individuals and groups can and should critically reflect on their values, modifying old ones and forging new ones in and through public discussion in the public sphere (Crocker 2008, 303–307).

Fourth, in addition to differing in breadth, range, and depth, democracies also differ with respect to the *distribution, separation, and balance of power*. In *The Idea of Justice*, Sen happily embraces John Kenneth Galbraith's notion of "countervailing power" (2009, 81–82). Not only is institutional balance instrumentally important but domination by one institution, party, or leader violates peoples' agency or autonomy, which is intrinsically bad. Moreover, without checks and balances, corruption raises its ugly and wasteful head. Most basically, Sen rightly connects his view of countervailing power to his deep commitment to impartiality and a plurality of interacting perspectives as an effective means of achieving improved governance.

Fifth and finally, Sen's ideal of democracy includes *effectiveness or control*. Direct or indirect rule by the people must make, like agency itself, more or less difference in the world. Many so-called democracies are such in name only, for effective control of policy and governmental action occurs without direct or even indirect popular control. And some democracies are comparatively better than others, for their citizens not only have more voice but more impact.

If these five dimensions are components of Sen's ideal of democracy, they do not individually or together exemplify the "transcendental approach" that Sen rejects. One might think that a full realization of each dimension would result in the perfect democracy, to which all societies and groups should aspire and in relation to which all of them should be judged. This is not the case and for two reasons. First, it would be possible to expand any of the dimensions so far that the result would be morally problematic if not worse. As Camacho sees in his chapter, to be discussed in more detail presently, rule by literally everyone would include rule by babies, the comatose, and madmen. Popular rule on every question would put others in charge of selecting our friends and lovers. Requiring every group to be internally democratic would violate collective liberty. State powers could be so separate as to be in constant and destabilizing conflict.

Moreover, depending on the context, realizing more of one dimension – say, breadth – may result in realizing less of another – say, depth. That result may be, on balance, good or bad depending on the context.

Unlimited breadth would guarantee shallowness. Robust depth might imperil needed breadth. However, in certain contexts, comprehensive breadth, coupled with a unanimity rule and "Chatham House rule," can have a valuable role to play. In his chapter in this volume, Javier Iguíñiz Echeverría argues that the *Acuerdo Nacional* (National Accord) for a decade has enabled Peruvians across the political spectrum to identify and try to deal consensually with the country's most pressing long-term issues. Breadth, which Iguíñiz Echeverría admits should be expanded even more to include more women and indigenous groups, is impressive and contributes to the nation's stability and social peace, but the price – probably worth paying – is a lack of resolution of divisive and immediate issues. Moreover, the group's discussions are not transparent and their short- and medium-term impact is modest. Just getting a sharing of views and some long-range planning is perhaps all that can be expected given the deep polarization of Peruvian society since the days of *Sendero Luminoso* (the Shining Path) and the Fujimori government's *autogolpe* (self-coup), repression, and corruption. At least temporarily, an emphasis on one of democracy's five dimensions – breadth – requires a de-emphasis on one of the other dimensions – some aspects of depth.

The larger point is that one responsibility of a democratic polity is to deliberate and decide – given its history and current challenges – what *sort* of democracy it can and should be. In its particular historical "conjuncture," how should its particular democratic institutions determine, balance, and limit the five dimensions of democracy? These five dimensions are not an ideal of perfect institutional democracy. But they are still a focus for decision and action as each evolving democracy is responsible to exercise its agency and decide on its breadth, range, depth, balance of powers, and control. Just as Sen eschewed – in *Development as Freedom* – "a unique blueprint" for "the just society," so in *The Idea of Justice* he remarks that "for democracy too the central question is not so much the characterization of an imagined perfect democracy (even if there could be agreement on what it would be like) but how the reach and vigour of democracy can be enhanced" (2009, 408, n. ‡). A concrete blueprint or recipe would be insufficiently sensitive to societal differences, put too much power in the hands of theorists, and take too much power away from democratic group members.

Replies to Koggel and Murphy

Prior to her chapter in the present volume, Christine Koggel did
a review in the *Journal of Human Development and Capabilities*
entitled "The Practical and the Theoretical: Comparing *Displacement
by Development* and *Ethics of Global Development*" (2015,
144–153). In this important and challenging essay, Koggel compares
Penz, Drydyk, and Bose's *Displacement by Development* (henceforth
DD) with my *EGD*. *DD* is a response to a particular moral challenge –
displacement of people in and through development projects – by
providing a menu of values that the authors assert has been found
relevant by development ethicists for dealing with moral challenges.
These seven values "do not," say the authors, "make up an ethical
doctrine or normative political theory" (Penz, Drydyk, and Bose 2011,
150; Koggel 2015, 144). Nor do they amount to a prescription: an
algorithm, recipe, or off-the-shelf solution to the displacement challenges. Rather, the seven are a menu of values intended "to frame
debate within development ethics rather than settling it, leaving debate
open, for instance, on the meaning and measure of well-being, on the
nature of equity and the demands of justice, and so on" (Penz, Drydyk,
and Bose 2011, 157; Koggel, 2015, 144). The framework enables the
authors to clarify commonalities as well as differences and confusions
among the two main approaches to displacement by development,
namely, the "managerialists," who see human and communal displacement as a necessary and unfortunate side-effect of development progress; and the "movementists," who unfailingly see as an unmitigated
disaster the development that causes displacement. What is exciting
about the *DD* approach is the way it challenges both groups and more
especially "developers," "resisters," and communities affected (for
good and ill) to enter into dialogue and deliberation to recognize and
mitigate the human costs involved and come up with and choose more
ethical solutions. From my perspective, this sort of approach could be
interpreted as illustrating, if not aiming to realize, ideals of agency,
well-being, and equality.

However, when Koggel compares *DD* and *EDG*, she interprets
EDG as an example of the transcendental institutionalism that Sen
criticizes and rejects. I think Koggel is mistaken in this interpretation
and that, while there are differences between *DD* and *EGD*, they are
not as great or important as she claims.

Koggel's mistake was to take my view of deliberative democracy as *the* required or optimal democratic institution to be installed by the agency-focused CA rather than one "resource" for CA democratization. Most basically, Koggel failed to consider my (and Sen's) agency-focused approach to democracy's dimensions, and the way that this theory of democracy amounts to a democratic ideal but of a very different sort than the transcendental institutionalism that Sen now rejects. My aim in the last subsection was to show that Sen continues (in Sen 2009) to embrace, employ, and advocate the kind of democratic ideal he and Drèze did in 2002 and elsewhere. What Koggel does address and trenchantly reject is what she calls my "model" of deliberative democracy. However, this view of deliberative democracy is best understood not as a model to be slavishly installed but as one way in which a community can exercise its agency and institutionalize the complex ideal of democracy.

Sen himself considers several past efforts, both institutional arrangements and citizen activity, to realize the democratic promise in people's lives. To his inventory of democratic institutions from sixth-century BCE Buddhist councils through Akbar's seventeenth century CE protection of religious (and nonreligious) liberty, to Mandela's fond remembrance of village-level deliberative democracy, Sen adds democratic institutions such as constitutional rights, effective courts, responsive electoral systems, functioning parliaments and assemblies, open and free media, and participatory institutions of local governance (such as India's *panchayats* and *gram sabhas*). Threading through these historical cases is the theme of public reasoning and "government by discussion," which is a central focus of *The Idea of Justice*:

In this work, democracy is assessed in terms of public reasoning (Chapters 15–17), which leads to an understanding of democracy as "government by discussion" (an idea that John Stuart Mill did much to advance). But democracy must also be seen more generally in terms of the capacity to enrich reasoned engagement through enhancing informational availability and the feasibility of interactive discussions. Democracy has to be judged not just by the institutions that formally exist but by the extent to which different voices from diverse sections of the people can actually be heard. (Sen 2009, xii–xiii, see also 3, 324, 326)

What I did in *EGD* was to examine recent democratic experiments, such as participatory budgeting and other deliberative practices, taking place throughout the world, and "distill" from them ways that citizens were moving away from clientelism and other forms of autocracy and trying to enhance "the reach and vigour of democracy." The result was not intended *pace* Koggel as *a* – let alone, *the* – model of deliberative democracy if by "model" is meant a "rigid, autonomy-threatening," prescriptive recipe or blueprint. Instead, I offered my discussion of deliberative democracy as a *resource* – "an important resource for the capability approach in its efforts to deepen democracy, design participatory institutions, and make democracy central to development challenges of our times" (Crocker 2008, 297). In particular, my discussion of the theory and practice of deliberative democracy – of its aims, internal ideals, participant virtues, enabling conditions, processes, and limits – was offered as one way concretely to realize Sen's "ideal of public reasoning" (2003, 31). He explicitly linked this ideal to the "social practices" of "tolerance of different points of view (along with the acceptability of agreeing to disagree) and the encouragement of public discussion (along with endorsing the value of learning from others)" (31).

Moreover, contrary to Koggel's judgment that my argument for deliberative democracy is at odds with the spirit of Sen's work and that he should reject my project, it should be noted that Sen at several points cites approvingly the key works in deliberative democracy, such as those of Seyla Benhabib, James Bohman and William Rehg, Joshua Cohen, Jon Elster, Amy Gutmann and Dennis Thompson, and Jürgen Habermas (Sen 2009, 42, n. 44, 324, 325, n. *; cf. 1999b, 329, n. 9).

Koggel also faults me for not showing in detail what such deliberative democracy would look like in practice. This is surprising because I did exemplify deliberative democracy with several concrete innovations, especially those analyzed in *Empowered Participatory Governance: Institutional Innovations in Empowered Participatory Governance* (Fung and Wright 2003; see Crocker 2008, 22–23, 310–312, 320–321, 354, 362–363). However, I could have done much more to show that deliberative democracy was not a utopian dream but was realized in various and creative ways in different places. I could and should have given examples – with respect to innovations in deliberative democracy – of the point I made in relation to creative modifications and innovations with the tradition of the blues: "The blues composer, guitarist, or vocalist can creatively modify and supplement the blues format. Likewise, deliberative democrats offer their model not as something to impose on groups but as something they have putative reason freely to accept and modify as they see fit" (Crocker 2008, 362).

Perhaps the best volume that provides a richly nuanced account of such democratic innovations is *Bootstrapping Democracy: Transforming Local Governance and Civil Society in Brazil* (Baiocchi, Heller, and Silva 2011). The authors analyze and evaluate eight municipal governments in medium-sized nonuniversity cities in Brazil. Four of the cities have participatory budgeting (PB) and four do not. Not only do the four with PB do a better job than the non-PB cities in promoting citizen well-being but they do so in different (as well as better and worse) ways. What impresses the authors is the way in which at least three out of the four PB cities did not slavishly duplicate Porto Alegre, the PB poster child, but showed creativity and originality in forging their own versions of PB: "Of all our findings [with respect to the concrete possibilities and challenges of building local institutions of participatory democracy], most striking, but in retrospect one that should have been anything but surprising, was the degree to which local actors proved to be extremely inventive, indeed ingenious, in designing local variants of PB" (Baiocchi, Heller, and Silva 2011, xi).

I conclude my reply to Koggel by responding to a criticism that Colleen Murphy first made of *EGD* in 2010 (Murphy 2010) and repeats in her chapter in the current volume and that Koggel has taken up and supplemented in her 2015 review of *DD* and *EGD* (Koggel 2015). In *EGD*, I had argued that a nation's constitution should not be beyond the reach of democratic decision-making, that rightly understood democracy and constitutionalism are not at odds with each other, and that Sen's emphasis on public deliberation and inclusive, deep democracy is more defensible than Nussbaum's view that her list of ten valuable capabilities should be *beyond* the reach of democratic decision-making. I understood myself to be siding with Sen in giving priority to democratic processes over constitutions rather than with Nussbaum in giving priority to constitutions, which would entrench her list of capabilities and constrain democratic bodies and processes. I cited Sen's following remark:

My skepticism is about fixing a cemented list of capabilities that is seen as being absolutely complete (nothing could be added to it) and totally fixed (it could not respond to public reasoning and to the formation of social values).

I am a great believer in theory, and certainly accept that a good theory of evaluation and assessment has to bring out the relevance of what we are free to do and free to be (the capabilities in general), as opposed to the material goods we have and the commodities we can command. But I must also argue that pure theory cannot "freeze" a list of capabilities for all societies for all time to come, irrespective of what the citizens come to understand and value. That would be not only a denial of the reach of democracy, but also a misunderstanding of what pure theory can do, completely divorced from the particular social reality that a particular society faces. (Sen 2005, 158)

The two positions are more nuanced than the list (constitution) versus democracy dichotomy because Nussbaum makes *some* room for theoretical dialogue and political deliberation, and Sen finds a democratic role for "lists." Moreover, as I and others such as Cass Sunstein (2002) and Supreme Court Justice Stephen Breyer (2005) argue, good democratic constitutions and good democracies are not at odds, for a constitution should protect democracy's internal morality of inclusive equality and active liberty. And a democracy should be able to amend and improve its constitution.

Now, however, I want to reply to the dilemma the horns on which Murphy and Koggel seek to impale me. Here is the impaling (if not appalling) argument:

1. Crocker either constrains democratic deliberation with prior enabling conditions or he does not.
2. If he does so constrain democratic deliberation, (a) he is guilty of the "sin" with which he charged Nussbaum: "Philosophers ... making substantive determinations of the freedoms that citizens should enjoy" (Murphy, Chapter 14 in this volume, p. xxx; Koggel 2015, 149–150) and (b)his "model" "would exclude virtually the whole of the Third World and many other disadvantaged people in the First World" (Koggel 2015, 150).
3. If Crocker does not so constrain democratic deliberation, then minorities and other vulnerable people are not protected from the "preferences of the most powerful" (Murphy, Chapter 14 in this volume, p. xxx).
4. Therefore, either Crocker is guilty of the same sin he finds in Nussbaum and makes his model irrelevant to the Third and much of the First World or his "model" does not sufficiently protect the marginalized and vulnerable from elite domination.

The argument's first premise is excessively vague because the constraint could be the result of a democratic body democratically constraining itself or constraining itself in such a way that its democratic features are maintained. Following Richardson, the conditions that I discussed – equal political liberty, equality before the law, economic justice, procedural fairness[11] – were not introduced as constraints but rather as "institutions needed to preserve the background justice of democratic deliberation." "Needed" here, however, does imply the conditions were necessary for democratic deliberation as does my opening claim that the background conditions are "presupposed" by democratic deliberation (Crocker 2008, 317). However, I do not and did not intend that meaning. When I labeled the conditions as "enabling" or described the conditions as "conducive" to democratic deliberation I was backing away from seeing these conditions as necessary (or sufficient) for democratic deliberation and haltingly moving toward viewing them instead as *helpful*. That was immediately clear when I said what Koggel missed – that democratic deliberation could exist without these conditions. For, as I made clear, deliberating groups often exist – sometimes underground – in "dictatorships, racist and anti-poor oligopolies, or in failed states beset by civil war." I conceded that these democratic groups would be more vulnerable than, say, a parliament in a stable democracy, and to survive they might have to employ some nondeliberative means, but the group – as occurs in many countries mobilizing for a democratic transition – could still be practicing internal deliberative democracy and striving to democratize the larger society.

Equally important is that I insisted on a point that both Murphy and Koggel miss. It is not that first a country must obtain the enabling conditions for democratic deliberation and then practice deliberative democracy. Rather, in and through an increasingly, sometimes incremental, deliberative democracy a country may gradually achieve and consolidate equal political liberty, rule of law, economic justice, and procedural fairness. Although the topic of Sen's one-liner is democracy and not deliberative democracy, I have interpolated "deliberative" in brackets to make my point: "A country does not have to be deemed fit *for* [deliberative] democracy; rather, it has to become fit *through* [deliberative] democracy" (Sen 1999a, 4).

Like Nussbaum, Murphy and Koggel have a legitimate worry about the way that a completely unconstrained democracy risks dominance by a tyrannical majority or elite capture by a powerful minority. I share their worry but believe there are more democratic ways of protecting the vulnerable than Nussbaum's list and kind of constitutionalism (see Crocker 2008, 356–360). First, engaged citizens and their movements not only exercise individual and collective agency by challenging injustice, but they often make progress – incremental or dramatic – in advancing democracy on one or more of the five democratic dimensions and making democracy "work" better. Especially important is building a more inclusive democracy – with respect to vote, voice, and representation of the marginalized and vulnerable. In the process of political struggle, democratic citizens learn by doing (Crocker 2008, 320), and there is some evidence that more inclusive and deeper democracies reduce inequalities and domination. And such reduction of inequality is part of the virtuous circle that nurtures and is nurtured by deliberative democracy (Crocker 2008, 321).

In *EGD* I did admit, but only at one point, that it was too glib to say in the face of criticisms of democracy as such and deliberative democracy in particular that all we need is more and better (deliberative) democracy (Crocker 2008, 321). For even with good will (and especially with bad will and parochial, racist, or tribal values) democracies and even deliberative democracies can make unjust and undemocratic decisions. Then it is time for citizens to stand up and be counted in relation to their deepest commitments. As critical and ethical agents they are responsible to call out and resist injustice and tyranny and find ways to advance justice and democracy. A reasoned defense and applications of their commitments may play a role in convincing their fellow citizens to share and implement the commitments. For perfectionist liberalism, those commitments prioritize the values of critical and ethical agency, well-being, and equality. Sen, in *The Idea of Justice*, cites and endorses (2009, 380) my long-term goal: "the long-term goal of good and just development – either national or global – must be to secure an adequate level of agency and morally basic capabilities for everyone in the world – regardless of nationality, ethnicity, religion, age, gender, or sexual preference" (2009, 389–390). Sen goes on to add that that my proposal becomes possible only when and because agency and valuable capabilities are the basis for human rights, social justice, and individual and collective responsibilities. I accept this point as a friendly amendment.

It is also important to insist, as Sen does throughout his career, that "the practice of democracy," a practice in which citizens are politically engaged and make democracy work, is in some sense the end to which the democratic ideals and democratic institutions are oriented. And it is this democratic activism that is the best hope for enhancing social justice – equality of agency and basic well-being both within and between countries – on all levels.

For Sen, in his recent work, and for many who have learned from him, what is *most* important is not a theoretical vision of either a perfectly just or a perfectly democratic society or even of the principles that should inform such a society but a practical commitment – inspired by a normative vision – to making comparative progress in advancing equal agency and basic well-being rights for all. The importance of Sen is not to offer yet another view of a perfectly just society but to challenge human agents to recognize that – since they have the power to combat injustice and advance justice – they have a strong responsibility to do so.

Participatory, Deliberative, and Representative Democracy

The subtitle of *EGD* was "deliberative democracy," and much of the volume was an effort not only to carry forward Sen's defense of democracy as a universal value but also to promote – in and for development theory-practice – participatory democracy in general and deliberative democracy in particular. Although I discussed representative democracy a couple of time in *EGD* and subsequently (Crocker 2008, 155–156, 313; 2012, 52), I did so almost entirely from the standpoint of citizen agency, that is, citizens' direct agency in voting and directly influencing representatives or elected officials as well as indirect agency of intentionally influencing representatives through holding the latter accountable for acts of commission or omission. What I neglected to do in any detail was to analyze the nature and types of representation, the importance of representation (especially in a large and complex society), better and worse kinds of representation, and the actual and ideal relations between, on the one hand, representative democracy, and on the other hand, participatory and deliberative democracy. Camacho's lucid and penetrating chapter (Chapter 11)has challenged me – and I hope others – to take up these topics in future work. His chapter also evaluates and finds some limitations and risks in both participation and deliberation, some of which I failed to address throughout the book. To these problems and Camacho's attractive solutions, I briefly turn.

First, Camacho is certainly right that democratically elected presidents in Latin America and elsewhere all too frequently get elected (sometimes in rigged elections), and then replace their polity's democratic features, such as presidential term limits, a parliament, an independent judiciary, or a free press with a "democracy with adjectives," such as "street democracy" and "radical democracy," or, we add, "managed democracy" or "people's democracy." In fact, as Camacho clearly sees, political and social power becomes substantially concentrated in a unified state and the now-entrenched autocrat appeals to "democracy with adjectives" to rally his "troops," stifle dissent, and maintain his grip on power. With this antidemocratic idea of participation, participatory democracy is not democracy at all. It is neither rule by the people nor is it even minimalist electoral democracy: a political arrangement in which the governed choose their government and public officials are elected. To make this anti-autocratic point clearly, I added more recently a fifth dimension to my analysis of democracy as rule by the people (Crocker 2012, 52; 2013, 108), namely, democratic governance should include some sort of separation of powers as well as some degree of breadth, range, citizen participation, and control.

A second contribution that Camacho makes is a compelling argument against an *unqualified* notion of participation. In my 2008 book, I used "participation" in three related ways. Most comprehensively, "participation" stood for any of the four (now five) axes or dimensions of popular rule: breadth (who rules?), range (rule on what topics and in which institutions), depth (how do they rule?), separation of powers (how rule is "divided"?), and control (how effective?). More narrowly, "participation" is captured only by the depth dimension: different ways in which citizens rule, such as direct versus indirect, balloting, protesting, voice, exit, expressing preferences, deliberating, majority rule (and other modes of closure), and bargaining. In my discussion of local, face-to-face development I distinguished seven different modes of participation, ranked from thinner to thicker with deliberative democracy ranked highest due to its fullest exercise of agency. Finally, and most narrowly, by "participation" and, especially, "participatory democracy," I referred to ways in which citizens *directly* govern or influence governing in contrast to rule by those elected (or appointed by those elected). In Athenian democracy, participation was largely direct (and by lot). In modern nations, much democratic rule is done by elected representatives and other officials.

For me and, I believe, for Camacho, deliberation may occur whenever citizens, their representatives, judges, or juries, and so forth, exchange reasons and argue to reduce disagreement and decide, often by majority vote, what should be done. In all three meanings of participation, deliberation is one kind of participation (deliberative participation) but not the only kind. Sometimes, Camacho seems to use participation and deliberation interchangeably, but the context usually makes clear which one (or both) that he has in mind.

In spite of its (mis)use in the hands of autocrats, Camacho acknowledges that participation has the merit of energizing citizens, giving them self-confidence and self-esteem and providing a counterweight to tyranny. He also makes the important point, but one that I did not make strongly enough, that both participation and deliberation are intrinsically and instrumentally valuable within groups resisting and contesting a tyranny or democratic decay. Camacho's main aim, however, is to show that "to demand participation in all decisions affecting individual lives will have counterintuitive consequences, not only because the number of decisions made by representatives is very large and their importance unequal, but also and especially because many matters affecting the lives of citizens cannot or should not be submitted to a referendum" (Camacho, Chapter 11, p. xxx). Here is a more succinct formulation of this idea, which I will call the "Unlimited Participation Principle (UPP)": "X has a right to influence any decision in which the decision would affect X." What are some of the counterintuitive implications and how might they be avoided?

Camacho submits several cases to show that we do or should reject UPP. If and when a lover breaks off a relationship, the jilted partner had no right to participate in the decision.[12] Even though many people may be affected by a scientific investigation, it doesn't follow that any of them have a right to participate in research decision-making. That someone charged with a crime in a jury trial will be affected by the jury's decision, does not give the accused the right to participate in the jury's deliberations. Nor does the person found guilty in a trial have a *right*[13] to participate in the judge's sentencing decision even though that decision may lead to the person's death.[14] We might also add that a student should have no role (other than her performance in the class) in deciding what grade the professor gives her, even though she may be significantly affected by the grade. In the grading case, as well as the jilted lover and sentencing cases, the affected person arguably would have a "right of appeal" *after* the decision had been made. And in an extreme case of grading, a student in danger of being drafted and sent to Vietnam might legitimately have appealed for a higher grade.

Assuming my (now) five dimensions of democracy, Camacho nicely illustrates my general point that democracy is a scalar affair and that "scoring" higher on one dimension may result in scoring lower on another dimension. Ancient Athens's mode of governance was a kind of democracy, rather than autocracy, owing to its great depth, range, separation of powers, and control. Its minimal breath justifies our calling Athens an "incomplete democracy" but not in terming it, as does Rawls (1999, 29 n. 27, 52), an "autocracy." Although inclusiveness is an important democratic demand, it can go too far, when it includes (as voters) such demographics as children, the severely disabled, and foreign tourists, who do not have the right to vote or participate in other ways. More generally, the broader the franchise, the shallower might be a polity's democratic depth. The greater the range of topics to be democratically decided, the greater the risk that the government might violate citizen rights to privacy or artistic rights to freedom of expression. In emergency situations there is scant time for consultation with those affected and saving lives and satisfying basic needs takes obvious priority over deliberation. In a conflict of interest, a person who is likely to benefit personally from an agency decision should recuse himself from the group that makes the decision.

How should the line be drawn between justified and unjustified participation and, more generally, between conflicts between two or more of democracy's dimensions? Camacho suggests two and only two answers. His preferred answer is to appeal to human rights. Citizens (should) have a right of privacy not to have the state and its democratic voters decide on whom or what sort of (adult) person they can love or marry. Citizens should have the right, protected by law, not to have the state require (some) religious or nonreligious belief or affiliation either. This "human rights" answer is important but in need of supplementation.

A second method for limiting one democratic dimension or balancing it with another is through democratic decision-making, and

Camacho quotes my appeal to deliberative democracy that emphasizes social choice through public discussion that "aims at solutions – solutions that nearly everyone can accept – to common problems" (Crocker 2008, 49). My formulation was mistaken. "Nearly everyone" should usually be replaced by "at least a simple majority" (Crocker 2008, 344) and sometimes by a "super majority."[15] More basically, a community's legal and moral rights should be matters of broad and deep public and democratic discussion. Whether, or under what conditions, the right to vote should be extended to convicted felons, as it was at one time to women and eighteen-year-olds, should be decided by public debate and democratic decisions. Even what Rawls calls "constitutional essentials" can and should benefit from amendments following broad and deep deliberation as well as voting.

Of course, democracies can and do err, sometimes egregiously. Camacho sees that in recognition of this commonplace, I frequently fall back on Dewey's "old saying that the cure for the ills of democracy is more democracy." But Camacho did not also see that I did not fully embrace the "old saying" or Sen's repeating it (Sen 2003, 34). For I also made it clear that individuals (theorists, social critics, or citizens) and groups of engaged citizens sometimes have the responsibility to speak out against democratic blunders. With the following statement, Camacho is spot-on in concluding his chapter and providing me with a way to circle back to the importance of development ethics: "Since neither participation nor deliberation guarantee that a decision is morally right, there always is an important and irreplaceable role for ethics as the analysis of the difference between good and bad. The moral obligation to look for good solutions belongs to all human beings engaged in deliberation" (Camacho, Chapter 11, p. 304).

Notes

1. Nussbaum's earlier clarifications of and arguments for "political liberalism" occur in (Nussbaum 2000, 2003, 2006, especially 388–392). See also Nussbaum's introductory essay, "Capabilities, Challenges, and the Omnipresence of Political Liberalism" in Comim and Nussbaum's edited book *Capabilities, Gender, Equality: Toward Fundamental Entitlements* (Nussbaum 2014, 1–15), which, she says, should be read as a crucial addendum to (2011b).

2. I do not see that the perfectionist liberals must go – as Nussbaum says (2003, 41) that they must – beyond critical reflection and the planning and directing of one's life to the denial that only God justifies moral claims.

3. Catriona Mackenzie (2014) mistakenly contends that Nussbaum thinks that citizens can acquire the practical reason capability without the correlative functioning and Mackenzie finds this "implausible" (34).

4. Nussbaum views Larmore as excluding from reasonability any religion that grounds its doctrine solely on "faith" (2011b, 5).

5. Interestingly, one might think that Nussbaum would include astrology as a reasonable comprehensive doctrine, but she demurs because its fatalism leaves no room for practical reason (2011b, 5).

6. See Francis Stewart's chapter in this volume (Chapter 13) for a discussion of the democratic deficit with respect to future generations.

7. In *EGD*, I argued that in public deliberation one should only advance claims that one believes one's fellow deliberators understand and accept. I did permit, as does Rawls (2001, 90) that one could explain where one was "coming from" even though that would include one's controversial comprehensive illiberal or liberal doctrine. But I denied that one should try to *justify* one's political judgments by reference to one's comprehensive doctrine. (Rawls permits the "introduction" of one's comprehensive doctrine into public debate but only if "in due course" the adherent also, as required by "the duty of civility," seeks to make her case for public policies "in terms of public reasons" [1999, 52; 2001, 90]). I now think that my earlier and limited view of justification is mistaken and inconsistent with my current view that to respect each other each deliberator can and should be free to lay all his cards on the table in the hopes of getting at the truth and convincing others.

8. I note that Rawls affirms the importance of give and take and voting – in accordance with public reason – among those who hold different liberal and *political* conceptions of justice (see 1999, 169, 178).

9. Arguably, these three are more fundamental and inform the democratic ideals that Drèze and Sen list in the quote with which I began this subsection.

10. Philip Pettit employs the metaphor of a moral compass as a "reference point ... to guide us in a principled way through the thicket of public issues" faced by "ordinary citizens, public officials, or would-be activists" (2014, xii).

11. In addition to the inconsistency problem occasioned by the role that "enabling conditions" play in *EGD*, Murphy also submits that the democratic ideals of reciprocity, publicity, and accountability create the same problem. My reply would be the same.

12. Cf. Nozick's telling case (1974, 269):

If four men propose marriage to a woman, her decision about whom, if any of them, to marry importantly affects each of the lives of those four persons, her own life, and the lives of any other persons wishing to marry one of these four men, and so on. Would anyone propose, even limiting the group to include only the primary parties, that all five persons vote to decide whom she shall marry? She has a right to decide what to do, and there is no right the other four have to a say in the decisions which importantly affect their lives that is being ignored here.

13. However the judge's sentencing *may* weigh the defendant's contrition and, in cases of diversion to a "program," the defendant's commitment to that program. I owe this point to John Lawrence Crocker.

14. It is interesting that the role of *victims* in judicial decisions has varied. In the eighteenth century the victim of crimes had a larger role than in the last thirty years. In many jurisdictions, prosecutors can bring a case to trial regardless of the victim's preference. More recently conservatives have brought back the role of victims – "victim impact statements" – at the sentencing phase of a trial. As the Larry Nassar sexual abuse case amply shows, it is arguably justified for victims to have roles in the judges' sentencing decisions. Still, there is the worry that victim testimony tends to decrease both the number and length of sentences when the victim is, say, a white banker's wife than when the victim is a black prostitute. I owe these points to discussion with John Lawrence Crocker.

15. A question worth pursuing concerns when a submajority vote is sufficient. An obvious case is a plurality electoral process in which the winning candidate polls more votes, but less than a majority than any other candidate. A more difficult case would be where failure to legislate will mean that the rights of some are violated. Suppose the law in a community permits the dumping of industrial waste into a stream that only four households use for drinking, swimming, fishing, and so forth. Should it take a majority of the town to prohibit the dumping or is this a place for the right of citizen petition to the town council? I am indebted to John Lawrence Crocker for raising these questions.

References

Baiocchi, Gianpaolo, Patrick Heller, and Marcelo K. Silva. 2011. *Bootstrapping Democracy: Transforming Local Governance and Civil Society in Brazil.* Stanford University Press.

Bernstein, Richard. 2006. "Creative Democracy – The Task Still before Us." In *The Pragmatic Century.* Edited by Sheila Greeve Davaney and Warren G. Frisina. Albany: State University of New York Press.

Breyer, Stephen. 2005. *Active Liberty: Interpreting Our Democratic Constitution*. New York: Alfred A. Knopf.

Cortina, Adela. 2002. *Por una ética del consumo: la ciudadanía del consumidor en un mundo global*. Madrid: Taurus.

Crocker, David A. 2008. *Ethics of Global Development: Agency, Capability, and Deliberative Democracy*. Cambridge University Press.

Crocker, David A. 2012. "Democratic Leadership, Citizenship, and Social Justice." In *Leadership and Social Justice*. Edited by Thad Williamson and Douglas Hicks. New York: Palgrave Macmillan.

Crocker, David A. 2013. "Amartya Sen on Democracy and Justice." *Indigo* 8: 102–109.

Dewey, John. 1927. *The Public and Its Problems*. Athens, OH: Swallow Press.

Dionne, E. J. 2018. "We Could Be a Much Better Country. Trump Makes It Impossible." *Washington Post*, January 14, A17.

Drèze, Jean, and Amartya Sen. 2002. *India: Development and Participation*. Oxford University Press.

Fung, Archon, and Erik Olin Wright. 2003. *Deepening Democracy: Institutional Innovations in Empowered Participatory Governance*. New York: Verso.

Hurka, Thomas. 1993. Perfectionism. New York: Oxford University Press.

Koggel, Christine M. 2015. "The Practical and the Theoretical: Comparing *Displacement in Development* and *Ethics of Global Development*." *Journal of Human Development and Capabilities* 16, 1: 142–153.

Larmore, Charles. 1996. *The Morals of Modernity*. Cambridge University Press.

Mackenzie, Catriona. 2014. "Three Dimensions of Autonomy: A Relational Analysis." In *Autonomy, Oppression, and Gender*. Edited by Andrea Veltman and Mark Piper. Oxford University Press.

Mann, James. 2018. "Damage Bigly." New York Review of Books 65, 1 (January 18): 4–8.

Murphy, Colleen. 2010. "Author Meet Critic Roundtable Discussion of David Crocker, *Ethics of Global Development: Agency, Capability, and Deliberative Democracy*." Paper presented at the Association for Practical and Professional Ethics. Cincinnati, OH. March 4–7.

Nozick, Robert, 1974. *Anarchy, State, and Utopia*. New York: Basic Books.

Nussbaum, Martha C. 2003. "Political Liberalism and Respect: A Response to Linda Barclay." *SATS: A Nordic Journal of Philosophy* 4: 25–44.

Nussbaum, Martha C. 2006. *Frontiers of Justice: Disability, Nationality, Species Membership*. Cambridge, MA: Harvard University Press.

Nussbaum, Martha C. 2011a. *Creating Capabilities: The Human Development Approach*. Cambridge, MA: Belknap Press, Harvard University Press.

Nussbaum, Martha C. 2011b. "Perfectionist Liberalism and Political Liberalism." *Philosophy and Public Affairs* 39, 1: 3–45.

Nussbaum, Martha C. 2014. "Introduction: Capabilities, Challenges, and the Omnipresence of Political Liberalism." In *Capabilities, Gender, Equality: Toward Fundamental Entitlements*. Edited by Falvio Comim and Martha C. Nussbaum. Cambridge University Press.

Penz, Peter, Jay Drydyk, and Pablo S. Bose. 2011. *Displacement by Development: Ethics, Rights and Responsibilities*. Cambridge University Press.

Pettit, Philip. 2014. *Just Freedom: A Moral Compass for a Complex World*. New York and London: W. W. Norton.

Putnam, Hilary. 2002. *The Collapse of the Fact/Value Distinction and Other Essays*. Cambridge, MA: Harvard University Press.

Putnam, Hilary. 2004. *Ethics without Ontology*. Cambridge, MA: Harvard University Press.

Rawls, John. 1996. *Political Liberalism*, expanded paperback edition. New York: Columbia University Press.

Rawls, John. 1999. The Law of Peoples with *"The Idea of Public Reason Revisited."* Cambridge, MA: Harvard University Press.

Rawls, John. 2001. *Justice as Fairness: A Restatement*. Cambridge, MA: Harvard University Press.

Raz, Joseph. 1986. *The Morality of Freedom*. Oxford University Press.

Sen, Amartya. 1980. "Equality of What?" In *The Tanner Lecture on Human Values*, Vol. I, 197–220. Cambridge University Press.

Sen, Amartya. 1999a. "Democracy as a Universal Value." *Journal of Democracy* 10, 3: 3–17.

Sen, Amartya. 1999b. *Development as Freedom*. New York: Knopf.

Sen, Amartya. 2003. "Democracy and Its Global Roots: Why Democratization Is Not the Same as Westernization." *The New Republic*, 229, 4: 28–35.

Sen, Amartya. 2005. "Human Rights and Capabilities." *Journal of Human Development* 6, 2 (July): 151–166.

Sen, Amartya. 2009. *The Idea of Justice*. Cambridge, MA: Belknap Press, Harvard University Press.

Sher, George. 1997. *Beyond Neutrality: Perfectionism and Politics*. Cambridge University Press.

Sunstein, Cass. 2002. *Designing Democracy: What Constitutions Do*. Oxford University Press.

Wall, Steven. 2009. "Perfectionism in Politics: A Defense." In *Contemporary Debates in Political Philosophy*. Edited by Thomas Christiano and John Christman. Malden, MA and Oxford, UK: Wiley-Blackwell.

Wall, Steven. 2014. "Perfectionism, Reasonableness, and Respect." *Political Theory* 42, 4: 468–489.

Wall, Steven. 2017. "Perfectionism in Moral and Political Philosophy." In *The Stanford Encyclopedia of Philosophy* (Winter 2017 Edition). Edited by Edward N. Zalta. https://plato.stanford.edu/archives/win2017/entries/perfectionism-moral/.

Watene, Krushil, and Jay Drydyk. 2016. *Theorizing Justice: New Insights and Future Directions*. London: Rowman & Littlefield International.

Index